CITIZENS WITHOUT SOVEREIGNTY

CITIZENS WITHOUT SOVEREIGNTY

EQUALITY AND SOCIABILITY IN
FRENCH THOUGHT, 1670–1789

Daniel Gordon

PRINCETON UNIVERSITY PRESS

PRINCETON, NEW JERSEY

PUBLISHED BY PRINCETON UNIVERSITY PRESS, 41 WILLIAM STREET,
PRINCETON, NEW JERSEY 08540
IN THE UNITED KINGDOM: PRINCETON UNIVERSITY PRESS, CHICHESTER,
WEST SUSSEX

LIBRARY OF CONGRESS CATALOGING-IN-PUBLICATION DATA

GORDON, DANIEL, 1961–
CITIZENS WITHOUT SOVEREIGNTY : EQUALITY AND SOCIABILITY IN FRENCH
THOUGHT, 1670–1789 / DANIEL GORDON
P. CM.
INCLUDES BIBLIOGRAPHICAL REFERENCES AND INDEX.
ISBN 0-691-05699-4 (CL)
1. FRANCE—INTELLECTUAL LIFE. 2. ENLIGHTENMENT. 3. DESPOTISM—
FRANCE—SOCIAL ASPECTS. 4. FRENCH LANGUAGE—SOCIAL ASPECTS—
FRANCE. I. TITLE.

DC33.4.G62 1994 001.1′0944—DC20 94-5876

THIS BOOK HAS BEEN COMPOSED IN GALLIARD

PRINCETON UNIVERSITY PRESS BOOKS ARE PRINTED ON ACID-FREE PAPER
AND MEET THE GUIDELINES FOR PERMANENCE AND DURABILITY OF THE
COMMITTEE ON PRODUCTION GUIDELINES FOR BOOK LONGEVITY OF THE
COUNCIL ON LIBRARY RESOURCES

PRINTED IN THE UNITED STATES OF AMERICA

1 3 5 7 9 10 8 6 4 2

CONTENTS

ACKNOWLEDGMENTS

THIS BOOK IS A PRODUCT of interests that I developed in the outstanding intellectual environments of Columbia University and the University of Chicago. As an undergraduate at Columbia, I had the privilege of studying modern intellectual history with Laurence Dickey and hearing Eugene Rice lecture on "the secularization of wisdom" in early-modern Europe. Marc Raeff also kindled my interest in the early-modern police state and the relation between intellectuals and government. At the University of Chicago, where I wrote the doctoral thesis on which this book is based, I had the good fortune of being encouraged by three fine supervisors: Keith Baker, Stephen Holmes, and François Furet. I am grateful to François Furet for providing a model of theoretical sophistication and for suggesting that philosophy is important not only as the substance of a particular branch of history, the history of ideas, but as a method for posing any historical problem. While I see him as a historian with remarkable theoretical powers, I regard Stephen Holmes as a political theorist with a superb understanding of history. I am thankful for his useful criticism and assistance. Keith Baker made many valuable suggestions both when I was composing the thesis and when I was revising it for publication. In revising Chapter 2 in particular, I benefited from the conversations and exchange of sources that took place at Stanford University in 1991 when he and I began to collaborate on research into the concept of society. My debt to Keith Baker, moreover, is not simply due to the help he gave me in this particular project. His open disposition and critical mind, and his interest in classic problems and novel solutions, have shaped my attitude toward the historian's vocation. I have not been able to attain his level of objectivity and insight, but some standards are not meant to be attained in deed; they are meant to be internalized in the mind, where they provide a source of inspiration. I am grateful to Keith Baker for providing such a standard.

Two other professors at the University of Chicago deserve my thanks. Jan Goldstein's course on nineteenth-century French intellectual history was a highlight of my experience at Chicago and helped me, by way of comparison, to think about some of the distinctive aspects of French thought before the age of democracy. The regular exchange of ideas between the History Department and the Romance Languages Department is one of the strong points of the academic environment at Chicago, and it was in this context that I was able to meet Robert Morrissey, a professor of French Literature. I am grateful to him for introducing me to historical semantics and the textual database of the Project for Research on the Treasury of the French Language, of which he is the Director.

I wish to express my appreciation to Orest Ranum and Melvin Richter, who read the manuscript of this book and made many useful suggestions, and to Nathan Alexander, who assisted me in proofreading the text. I would also like to thank Istvan Hont and Hans Erich Bödeker for inviting me to the conference, entitled "Unsocial Sociability and the Eighteenth-Century Discourse of Politics and Society," which took place in Göttingen on June 26–30, 1989. I have profited from many of the unpublished papers presented at the conference, but especially from the "Preliminary Suggestions for Discussion," drawn up by Professors Hont and Bödeker themselves.

I have had many useful exchanges with other friends and scholars. They are too numerous to identify in entirety, but David Bell, Ann Blair, Jonathan Cowans, Elizabeth L. Eisenstein, James Engell, Peter France, Claudine Frank, Dena Goodman, Patrice Higonnet, James Johnson, Lawrence Klein, Catherine Kudlick, John Christian Laursen, Dorothy Medlin, Jeffrey Merrick, Benjamin Nathans, Jeremy Popkin, Bryant T. Ragan, Jeffrey Ravel, Paul Robinson, Paul Rosenberg, and Pierre Saint-Amand deserve my explicit thanks. Dena Goodman has been especially receptive to my ideas and generous in sharing her own. I have gained much from her understanding of the Enlightenment and from her friendship.

As a graduate student I received a grant from the Georges Lurcy Foundation to study in France, and I am glad to have an opportunity to thank this institution for its generous support.

CITIZENS WITHOUT SOVEREIGNTY

INTRODUCTION

HOW DO PEOPLE LIVING in an authoritarian regime maintain their sense of dignity? To revolt against the system is one possibility. To exit the system, through emigration or suicide, is another. But beyond protest or escape lies another strategy, which is to invest the seemingly insignificant areas of life that the authorities do not control with the maximum amount of meaning. From this perspective, the task facing citizens without sovereignty is to take an inventory of the disparate spaces that remain free and to order these spaces into a coherent whole, an imaginary sphere in which virtue and autonomy acquire meaning in relation to the activities that are possible.

The history of France from the reign of Louis XIV to the French Revolution provides a special opportunity to think about this process of transfiguring reality so as to preserve dignity. Because France was an absolutist system in which the kings claimed a monopoly on sovereignty, everyone else was officially powerless in the public sphere. In contrast to England, France had no national elections or political parties, and its inhabitants, including even the members of the Parlements, had no constitutional right to resist royal policies. The defining features of French citizenship were not political rights but permanent residency on French soil and obedience to the king. Citizenship did not imply membership in governmental institutions.[1]

It is common to believe that French intellectuals in this period took the initiative against absolutism and voiced the complaints of a subjugated people. The Enlightenment is known as a great backlash against absolutism, a critique of monarchical government, a breakthrough toward democracy. But very few of the *philosophes* advocated political equality. Most of them accepted not only the concept of royal sovereignty but also the concept of privilege, the juridical principle that made France a community of differentiated estates and orders rather than a community of individuals possessing the same status before the law.

Some sociologists and historians have appreciated the fact that French men of letters before 1789 were not democratic, that there was no intelligentsia as in imperial Russia—no group of thinkers who plotted to overthrow the regime. In this context, Norbert Elias's work is particularly important. Elias inverted the traditional image of the Enlightenment, treating

---

[1] Charlotte Catherine Wells, "The Language of Citizenship in Early Modern France: Implications of the *droit d'aubaine*" (Ph.D. diss., Indiana University, 1992), especially 163–64, 261–62, 269, 284.

it as part of the absolutist system rather than its enemy. He focused on the royal court as an instrument with which the monarchs pacified the nobility and exerted control over French culture. In the wake of this "civilizing process," according to Elias, not only the nobility but also the bourgeois class, including bourgeois writers, became subservient to the state. This subjection was evident in the universal tendency of French men of letters to glorify courtliness. Courtliness was the basis of life at Versailles, but more broadly, it was a set of norms that assigned supreme importance to the refinement of manners in everyday life. Elias believed that the emphasis on external refinement became the keystone of French high culture because it effectively served two purposes. It subordinated the elites to the state by getting them to see themselves as polished gentlemen instead of potent warriors and magistrates. And it sustained the elites' sense of pride by giving them an aesthetic criterion, polite manners, with which they could measure their superiority over the rest of the population.[2]

Elias wrote primarily about seventeenth-century France, but it is clear that he saw no mutations in the evolution of French culture before 1789. His brief analyses of Voltaire, Turgot, Holbach, and other Enlightenment writers highlighted the continuing fascination with manners in French thought and the direct relationship between courtly notions of "civility" and Enlightenment conceptions of "civilization."[3] It is interesting to note that the work of a distinguished specialist on the Enlightenment, Robert Darnton, is consistent with Elias's interpretation (though there appears to be no direct influence of one upon the other). Darnton suggests that the Enlightenment evolved into a part of the elitist and hierarchical establishment. During the last decades of the absolute monarchy, the *philosophes* pursued favors from above, not revolution from below. They were attached to the court and had more interest in gaining pensions in the royal academies than in criticizing inequality. "Rather than challenge the social order, they offered a prop to it," he writes.[4]

These views are intriguing, but in this book I have tried to establish how French authors created a unique ideological space that was neither democratic nor absolutist. Many French thinkers in the years 1670–1789 were profoundly egalitarian without advocating the distribution of sovereign power. They accepted the state's monopoly of the means of administration but did not bow in slavish subservience to it. The rise of an egalitarian ethos that was not democratic was possible through the invention of a new mode

[2] Norbert Elias, *The Court Society* (Oxford, 1983), and *The History of Manners* (New York, 1978). I discuss these works more fully in Chapter 3.

[3] See especially *The History of Manners*, 40–50.

[4] Robert Darnton, "The High Enlightenment and the Low-Life of Literature," in *The Literary Underground of the Old Regime* (Cambridge, Mass., 1982), 14. I consider Darnton's views more fully in Chapter 4.

of thought, one that made the concept of equality meaningful as the rule of social life without implying the elimination of hierarchy in political life. A distinction between social equality and political equality runs throughout French classical culture and the Enlightenment. This distinction may seem elementary in itself, but the social domain of existence was not a preexisting area that French writers simply construed in egalitarian terms. Indeed, the novel aspect of French social egalitarianism was not the affirmation of equality per se but the invention of the social as a distinctive field of human experience.

To understand the significance of this invention, it is necessary to understand the barriers in the absolutist system that made it difficult to articulate any concept of society as a detached field of experience. One such barrier was the very idea of absolute monarchy. Defenders of royal sovereignty did not formally recognize the existence of a social realm in the sense of a sphere of activities separate from the supervision of the monarch. In their view, no important forms of exchange could subsist without the intervention of sovereign authority. Nothing, then, was apolitical. The invention of the social field required a demonstration that some meaningful activities are self-instituting; that in some situations human beings can hang together of their own accord; that humans, in short, are sociable creatures.

Another barrier to the construction of the social field was Christian metaphysics. Christian thought located perfection in the afterlife rather than in a specific domain of worldly life. More profoundly, religion posed an obstacle to formulating ideals of social autonomy because human life as a whole was understood to be in a state of dependence upon the metaphysical beyond. As Brian Singer writes:

> Within the religious imaginary, society is without a sphere of immanence from which it can appear as given of itself. It appears instead as given from without by a divine other, as subjected to a sphere of transcendence that alone provides it with its form, finality, and meaning. As such, society cannot be perceived, known, or acted upon except insofar as such perceptions and actions are sanctioned by, draw their inspiration from, and in the last analysis, retrace the will of God.[5]

It might seem that the growth of science in the early-modern period was enough to destroy this ontology and to release "society" into the open air where it could be recognized as a thing in itself. But the rise of an empirical disposition was perhaps as inimical to "society" as religion was. French thinkers of the seventeenth and eighteenth centuries did not wish to represent "society" simply as a set of facts. They were in search of a heavenly city:

---

[5] Brian C. J. Singer, *Society, Theory, and the French Revolution: Studies in the Revolutionary Imaginary* (London, 1986), 13.

an idealized refuge from the powers that be, a locus of equality in a world otherwise dominated by arbitrary distinctions of rank.

Ernst Cassirer stated, "The strongest intellectual forces of the Enlightenment do not lie in its rejection of belief but rather in the new form of faith which it proclaims, and in the new form of religion which it embodies."[6] Far from being a simple product of secularization, "society" issued from the effort to project the ecumenical function of reason onto a worldly object. François Furet has spoken of "the appropriation of ontology by society" as well as of "a link between the emancipation of society from transcendent justification and the eventual substitution of society for transcendency as a principle of thought."[7] These are penetrating formulations, and they have guided my concerns throughout this book. But it is worth noting that Furet and Singer see the formation of a social religion as part of the evolution of democratic ideology. Their views accord with the school of interpretation that portrays prerevolutionary creativity as a movement toward the radical republicanism of 1789. Republican thought, however, originated not in prerevolutionary France but in ancient Greece and Rome. The concept of the *polis* as a self-sustaining association of active citizens did not have to be invented but only revived, and the high point of this revival in France, prior to 1789, was the Renaissance.[8] French classical culture and the French Enlightenment did not add much to the republican tradition, partly because that tradition was already well developed, but mainly because the absolutist structure of the regime made it inherently treasonous and utopian to cultivate this mode of thought.

The philosophical significance of French thought about society lies in the ways that it mediated between these other ideologies: its acceptance of absolute monarchy and its simultaneous idealization of activities that the monarchs did not care to control; its concern with worldly interaction and its simultaneous effort to imbue secular exchange with spiritual meaning; its repudiation of the republican ethos and its simultaneous articulation of a nonpolitical *polis* where citizens without sovereignty could be free.

One of the signs that a new style of thinking had emerged was the rise of a new vocabulary. The term *sociabilité* was coined in the early eighteenth century and became the slogan of moderate literati who idealized private life and saw reciprocity as the bond among humans in "society." In 1765, the *Encyclopédie*, edited by Denis Diderot and Jean d'Alembert, included an entry on the word *social* and stated that it was "a term recently introduced in [our] language." The word *société* itself was centuries old, but the frequency of its usage rose considerably in French writing in the seventeenth and eigh-

6 Ernst Cassirer, *The Philosophy of the Enlightenment* (Princeton, 1979), 135–36.

7 François Furet, *Interpreting the French Revolution* (Cambridge, 1981), 192.

8 On Renaissance legal and political thought, see Wells, "The Language of Citizenship," 20–46, 176–235.

teenth centuries. Much of this book is concerned with the meaning of these terms and the ways in which writers employed them to evoke the possibility of a free existence within the gaps and interstices of a hierarchical regime.

The fact that these words are ubiquitous in today's language, including the language of historical writing, makes it particularly interesting and problematic to analyze them. Any historian who tries to write a book without using the terms "social" and "society" will realize just how indispensable they have become in the discussion of collective life. Many of the alternatives to "society," such as "regime" and "nation," have a more political or statist resonance. Those terms seem inadequate when one wishes to talk about patterns of exchange that would form a determinate system regardless of the nature of the political constitution. Other words, such as "group" or "association," do not have the connotations of permanence and broad extension that "society" has. It is daunting to consider the possibility that historical discourse as we know it derives intimately from an earlier phase of cultural production, a period in which authors were intent on proving that individuals naturally cluster into peaceful and durable systems of interaction, that there must be an immanent meaning to activity outside the political sphere because otherwise life would simply have no meaning.

In order to avoid using a descriptive language that might be implicated in the language being described, and in order to make what Willard Quine calls the "semantic ascent" ("the shift from talking in certain terms to talking about them"),[9] I have tried to use the words "social," "society," and "sociability" only in an analytical manner in the following chapters—either to draw attention to the ways that other authors use them or to define ideal types of the forms of human interaction. I have not employed them casually to talk about such things as "French society," "social institutions," and "the social order," for to do so would dilute the significance of the language in question. This lexical consciousness and the repeated italicization of the relevant French words (*société*, *social*, *sociable*, *sociabilité*) whenever they appear in primary sources will, I hope, heighten the reader's sensitivity to the vocabulary and evoke a feeling of surprise that such a thing as social discourse ever came into existence.

While focusing on "society" as a specific way of talking about the world, I have tried not to ignore society in the conventional sense of concrete practices, for the linguistic approach is insufficient even for the analysis of language. Words have meaning not only within semantic fields but also within institutional fields. If the concept of sociability helped to transfigure absolutist reality, then it is important to stipulate what that reality was. If it was designed to lend dignity to action within the unregulated spaces of the

---

[9] Willard v. O. Quine, "Semantic Ascent," in *The Linguistic Turn, Essays on Philosophical Method*, ed. Richard Rorty (Chicago, 1992), 169.

regime, then it is useful to know what those spaces were and why the state left them alone. I have devoted Chapter 2 (The Language of Sociability) exclusively to semantic issues, but in the other chapters I have drawn upon institutional history in various ways. My approach to institutions is often schematic, partly because of my limited knowledge but also because there seems to be no alternative when one wishes to understand intellectuals in context. It is necessary to treat institutions analytically—to seize their organizing principles and to denote them in concise terms that resonate in the discourse used to interpret philosophical texts. Conversely, it is necessary to treat texts institutionally—which does not mean reducing them to the "interests" of their authors but focusing on the configurations of institutional space within the texts and how these configurations line up, so to speak, with the institutional map drawn by people in power. Without this mutual accommodation, without an institutional history condensed into ideal types and an intellectual history delineating the structure of imagined organizations, the different kinds of history cannot illuminate each other. Practitioners of the subdisciplines will remain strangers to each other, instead of cooperating in the humanistic study of how consciousness manages to discover a home in a hostile world.

1

ABSOLUTISM AND THE IDEAL TYPES OF SOCIABILITY

Where the word of a king is, there is power; and who may say
to him, What doest thou?
(Jacques-Bénigne Bossuet, *Politique tirée des propres paroles de
l'Ecriture sainte*)[1]

The Well-Policed State

ON JUNE 29, 1709, Louis XIV sent Nicolas Delamare, a commissary of the Paris police, on an important mission.[2] It was a time of severe famine. Scarcity had brought the inhabitants of the city of Troyes to the brink of revolt. Delamare's assignment was to restore peace. A difficult task—but this official was well suited for the responsibility because he had already acquired forty years of experience in maintaining order in Europe's second-largest city. He knew everything relating to public security: how to apprehend prostitutes, thieves, and murderers; how to control dangerous floods and fires; how to confiscate seditious publications at short notice; and how to quell the outbursts of a hungry populace during time of famine. Having served continuously since the critical year 1667, when Louis XIV gave the police a vast range of administrative functions that he had taken away from the corporate authorities of Paris, Delamare was now seventy years old and the dean of police officials.[3] Here is his account of what happened when he arrived in Troyes.

---

[1] Jacques-Bénigne Bossuet, *Politique tirée des propres paroles de l'Ecriture sainte* (Geneva, 1967; first published, 1709), 92.

[2] The following episode is recounted by Nicolas Delamare in his *Traité de la police où l'on trouvera l'histoire de son établissement, les fonctions et les prérogatives de ses magistrats, toutes les loix et tous les règlements qui la concernent*, 2d ed. (Amsterdam, 1729), 2:909–13. Delamare's surname is sometimes written De Lamare and, as in the *National Union Catalogue*, de la Mare.

[3] On Delamare's career, see A. de Boislisle, "Nicolas Delamare et le *Traité de la police*," *Bulletin de la Société de l'Histoire de Paris et de l'Ile de France*, vol. 3, 1876; *Correspondance administrative sous Louis XIV*, ed. G. Depping (Paris, 1851), 2:863–64; Jacques Saint-Germain, *La Vie quotidienne en France à la fin du Grand Siècle* (Paris, 1965), 110, 120, 203. On the workings of the Paris police in the seventeenth and eighteenth centuries, the most informative source is Delamare's *Traité*. A useful secondary study is Alan Williams, *The Police of Paris* (Baton Rouge, 1979).

The leading officers of the bailiwick came to me and informed me of the condition of the town and its great famine and the fact that the previous day there had been enormous popular excitement. The homes of the magistrates, the local mint, and the royal tax bureau had been attacked by the people, who had tried to force their way in. The next day, the same people gathered tumultuously in the great market square and threatened to begin their violent acts again. I went there with my officers and the two guards at my disposal. As soon as I appeared, the poor people threw themselves on their knees and cried out to me, "Monseigneur, we are dying of hunger; it is poverty that makes us assemble." I had those who seemed to be the leading persons of the assembly come close to me. I made them understand that the king had sent me specifically to the provinces to learn about their needs and to take care of them; that they would soon see abundance restored in their town and the end of their wretchedness through the orders I would give. But to make themselves worthy of the kindness of His Majesty and of my care in the execution of his orders, they must abandon this mutinous and seditious spirit and retire each to his own house and live in peace. If they persisted, however, I would punish the guilty so severely that they would serve as an example to the others. These warnings and threats were listened to very attentively and the tumultuous assembly dispersed.[4]

Delamare then issued an ordinance requiring all farmers within three leagues of Troyes to sell their grain only in the town. He placed limits on how much grain an individual could buy in one day. And he required the wealthy inhabitants to bring grain that they stored in their town houses and châteaux to the marketplace.

The effects of these orders were visible the next market day in the abundance of wheat and barley and the immediate drop in the price of grain. The price of bread fell accordingly. I had the satisfaction of walking along the streets and seeing the people in joy and hearing them applaud this happy change.[5]

Confident that he had imposed "order and discipline,"[6] Delamare left Troyes to attend to disturbances in other towns.

Like any account of an event given by someone who participated in it, Delamare's story is open to question. We may doubt that the inhabitants of Troyes obediently dispersed as soon as the imperious commissary issued a command, or that hunger disappeared immediately after he imposed economic restrictions. But Delamare's effectiveness is less important than the nature of the story he tells and what it reveals about royal authority. There is little doubt that he exercised his commission as he described—in a highly

---

[4] Delamare, *Traité*, 2:909.
[5] Ibid., 2:909–10.
[6] Ibid.

authoritarian way. For in his vision of the world, human beings constantly generated disorder through their innate "pride" and "self-love." Good laws were not enough to keep them in check. "However holy and just be the laws, the natural penchant of the human heart for liberty and independence would render them useless if a powerful authority did not continuously oversee their enforcement."[7] Delamare believed in a "well-policed state" (*un état bien policé*), and he explained this concept at great length in his mammoth three-volume work, the *Traité de la police* (Treatise on Police, first published 1705–19).

For Delamare, "police" signified above all the idea of a stark separation of responsibilities. Louis XIV, whom Delamare saw as a new Caesar Augustus, was to set policy. The loyal commissaries, of whom Delamare was one, were to enforce the policy, make decisions about how to apply it in various circumstances, and draw an elite satisfaction from their service for the public welfare. Everyone else must simply obey. "The best and most useful of all laws is the one that prohibits people from deliberating upon whether or not the laws are just and orders them to obey as if they [the laws] had been established by God himself."[8] With its emphasis on the depravity of human nature and the unlimited power of the state, Delamare's political thought appears to be an extreme view of absolute monarchy. But his severe philosophy was not an eccentric by-product of his special vocation. In fact, he only made explicit some of the important notions that informed the practice of government in early-modern France.

As seen through its venerable legal traditions, France was a vast set of groups, each of which had its own endowments or privileges. The term *privilège* literally meant "private law" (from the Latin *privus* and *legum*). A law was private not in the sense that it was kept secret, nor in the sense that it pertained to the rights of privacy (of which absolutist jurists had no conception), but in the sense that it applied only to *particular* persons rather than every citizen. Every corporation, such as the three estates (clergy, nobility, commons), the provinces, guilds, and universities, had particular liberties and regulations that distinguished it from the rest of the population. The danger threatening a regime of this kind was that the spirit of exclusion and the clash of interest groups might escalate into violent conflict. It was the purpose of the king in this order to define the privileges of his subjects and to establish harmony out of their self-regarding claims. The monarch's absolute authority was virtually a logical necessity within such a particularistic regime. For the idea of a community based on juridical differentiation implies the presence of someone who is above difference: someone whose

---

[7] Ibid., 1:246.
[8] Ibid., 1:240.

duty is to the public good; someone who can regulate and adjudicate privilege; someone whose authority is sufficiently beyond question that he can impose a final decision upon his subjects.[9]

But while the king's authority was supreme, it was traditionally limited by the very circumstances that made this supremacy desirable. As William H. Sewell writes:

> The price of the king's theoretically absolute power was his recognition of the privileges of preexisting institutions. He had the power to regulate and adjudicate privileges, and, as the head of the state and the font of honor, to create new institutions and to grant new privileges. He also had the formal power to abolish privileges as well as to create them, but this power was severely circumscribed in practice. Any wholesale abolition of privileges by the king would violate his own raison d'être and thus jeopardize his "absolute" power. The corporate ideology of the Absolute Monarchy rendered it absolute only within a system of essentially fixed privileges.[10]

The monarch was also constrained by religion, for while his authority stemmed from the needs of a community based on legal differentiation, legal differentiation itself drew its justification from Christian cosmology. The seventeenth-century jurist Charles Loyseau began his *Traité des ordres et simples dignités* (Treatise on Orders and Simple Dignities, first published in 1610) by observing that the various subdivisions or "orders" of the clergy, nobility, and commons made up a "general order," which is the kingdom of France. But this general order or collectivity was only a part of an even larger entity, the order of the universe that included "the celestial intelligences" and all inanimate and animate beings.[11] Human life drew its principles of

---

[9] For discussion of the corporate structure of early-modern France and its relation to the concept of absolute government, see Roland Mousnier, *The Institutions of France Under the Absolute Monarchy*, vol. 1: *Society and the State* (Chicago, 1979); Roland Mousnier and Fritz Hartung, "Quelques problèmes concernant la monarchie absolue," *Relazioni del X Congresso Internazionale di Scienze Storiche* (Florence, 1955), 4:1–55; Michel Antoine, *Le Conseil du Roi sous le règne de Louis XV* (Geneva, 1970); Michel Antoine, "La Monarchie absolue," in *The French Revolution and the Creation of Modern Political Culture*, vol. 1: *The Political Culture of the Old Regime*, ed. Keith Michael Baker (Oxford, 1987), 3–24; Michael P. Fitzsimmons, "Privilege and Polity in France, 1786–1791," *American Historical Review* 92, no. 2 (April 1987):269–95; William H. Sewell, Jr., "Etat, Corps and Ordre: Some Notes on the Social Vocabulary of the French Old Regime," in *Sozialgeschichte Heute, Festschrift für Hans Rosenberg zum 70. Geburtstag*, ed. Hans-Ulrich Wehler (Göttingen, 1974), 49–68; William H. Sewell, Jr., "Ideologies and Social Revolutions: Reflections on the French Case," *Journal of Modern History* 57 (1985):57–85.

[10] Sewell, "Ideologies and Social Revolutions," 64.

[11] Charles Loyseau, *Traité des ordres et simples dignités* (Paris, 1613), 5–6. See also the partial translation in *University of Chicago Readings in Western Civilization*, vol. 7: *The Old Regime and the French Revolution*, ed. Keith Michael Baker (Chicago, 1987), 13.

organization from the cosmic system in which it was embedded. What were these principles?

According to the traditions of medieval theology that influenced French juridical thinking, God invested the cosmos with two fundamental principles: diversity and hierarchy.[12] Diversity stemmed from God's omnipotence, his capacity to create whatever he wished. Out of this plenitude of creative power emerged an infinite array of forms of animate and inanimate matter. In creating a thing, God invested it with a certain amount of his own spiritual essence. The precise amount of spirituality that it contained determined its nature and distinguished it from all other things. This meant that the components of the universe made up a hierarchy or chain of being extending from God himself, the most purely spiritual of beings, down to the black earth of the field, the most "corporeal" substance. As a species, humans were located at about the middle of the chain of being because they were a combination of corporeal and spiritual tendencies. But a chain of being also existed among humans, since they were not equally endowed with spiritual capacity. Members of the clergy were superior to the laity. Nobles were superior to commoners. Men were superior to women. The precise nature of these and other distinctions could be a matter of dispute among theologians and jurists. But nearly all agreed that the universe was a great ladder of which humanity occupied not one but several rungs. The purpose of law was to endow the subgroups of humanity with the names, esteem, liberties, and responsibilities appropriate to their station in the system of cosmic precedence. Legal discrimination thus corresponded to the spiritual diversity that allegedly existed in the human population. When the king conferred a privilege, it was not, in theory, an arbitrary act. It was an act of cosmic recognition.

A variety of theories and concrete rituals in the absolute monarchy emphasized the cosmic source and limits of the king's authority. The monarch ruled by "divine right." He did not create the polity but was placed within it by God to act as His representative. In the royal coronation ceremony, the king was annointed with holy oil. Thereafter, he received communion in the manner of the priesthood, taking the consecrated wine as well as the consecrated bread.[13] These rituals made the person of the king sacred and height-

[12] On the metaphysical conceptions that informed the concepts of estates and orders, see Roland Mousnier, *Les Hiérarchies sociales de 1450 à nos jours* (Paris, 1969); William H. Sewell, Jr., "Etat, Corps and Ordre"; François Olivier-Martin, *Histoire du droit français des origines à la Révolution* (Paris, 1948), especially 22–23, 103–8, 204–6, 240–46; Arthur Lovejoy, *The Great Chain of Being* (Cambridge, Mass., 1936); Georges Duby, *The Three Orders: Feudal Society Imagined* (Chicago, 1980), especially 66–80.

[13] Sewell, "Ideologies and Social Revolutions," 63; Sewell, "Etat, Corps, and Ordre," 56, 65. G. Père, *Le Sacre et le couronnement des rois de France, dans leurs rapports avec les lois fondamentales* (Paris, 1922).

ened his authority. But they also underscored the existence of a universal order that was anterior to his authority and that was supposed to guide his rule.

Overall, the French monarchy under Louis XIV was based on a set of balanced principles, but the balance tilted more toward royal supremacy than toward limitations on royal power. A set of institutions and traditional procedures, the "constitution," served as a kind of check on royal will. The monarch, however, was "absolute" instead of constitutional, for the traditions limiting his authority never rested in the hands of a prestigious and authoritative agent of enforcement. The king himself had the final authority to interpret the meaning of the limitations upon his authority. Unlike the English monarchs after 1688, who recognized that Parliament could enforce constraints upon the royal prerogative, Louis XIV and his successors never recognized that any institution had the right to override the royal will. Procedures did exist by which judicial corps could remonstrate against royal edicts. Individuals could also beseech the monarch through petitions. But there was no constitutional right to disagree persistently, not to mention a right to revolt. The king's word was final.[14]

The rationale for circumscribing the modes in which opposition could be expressed was simple and profound: to give authority to more than one voice within the polity would lead to irresolvable disagreements, the breakdown of obedience, and, ultimately, dislocation of the state and its dismemberment by a more unified nation. To achieve any degree of stability and security, every community must contain a single will that people obey even when they disagree with it. This is the argument that Bodin made in *The Six Books of the Commonwealth* (1576), in which he affirmed that the monarch possessed an infinite "reserve of right in his own person"—an unquestionable authority that included "the right to impose laws generally on all subjects regardless of their consent."[15] Bodin, who claimed to be the first person to define the word "sovereignty" (*souveraineté*),[16] used this term to refer to the superiority of the royal will vis-à-vis the will of other humans. Sovereignty, to be sure, did not mean that a king who committed acts against religion was free from punishment by God. It did not mean that whatever the king did was necessarily in the best interest of the whole realm. It did, however, mean that the king had to be obeyed even when he seemed to be ignoring his own duties and harming the community.

Bodin was a humanist who published his *Six Books* in the wake of civil war and unprecedented atrocities committed by French Catholics and Protes-

---

[14] Roland Mousnier, *The Institutions of France Under the Absolute Monarchy*, vol. 2: *The Organs of State and Society* (Chicago, 1980), 595–97, 601–10.

[15] Jean Bodin, *The Six Books of the Commonwealth*, ed. M. J. Tooley (New York, 1955), 25, 32.

[16] Ibid., 25.

tants against each other. Like other humanists of the late sixteenth century, he sought to delineate zones of intellectual consensus, or "areas of accommodation,"[17] in a world torn by violent religious strife. In his political thought, he emphasized the secular sources of political order—the needs that every commonwealth, regardless of the religion of its inhabitants, must fulfill in order to exist and thrive. Bodin turned political theory toward secular questions not because he was antireligious but because he wished to create harmony among people of different religious persuasions; to establish truths that were neutral with respect to theology. The need of every commonwealth for a sovereign authority appeared to him to be one such neutral truth. Bodin, then, was not a lover of arbitrary rule but a lover of peace, and we should see him for what he was, not for what his idea of sovereignty would become in the hands of French rulers in the seventeenth and eighteenth centuries. But we should also not ignore the inherent tendency of the concept of absolute power to unleash aggressive governmental action. As an essentially secular principle designed to be compelling to people of all religions, the idea of sovereignty became a convenient tool for rulers who wished to ignore religious traditions instead of being limited by them. The concept of sovereignty also provided the best rationale for violating corporate privileges. For no matter how important the maintenance of privileges might seem for preserving a community's customary *identity*, royal sovereignty was (by definition) even more important for preserving the community's very *existence*. One of the purposes of sovereignty-based political thought was to shift political discussion away from the question of how to preserve the traditional identity of a particular community and toward the question of how to establish and maintain a community per se. By emphasizing this general problem of order, Bodin legitimized the power of the state in a way that could easily lend itself to the violation of time-honored norms. The concept of sovereignty provided an ideal justification for ignoring the chain of being and reorganizing the polity as a chain of command.

Several factors were important in producing a desire among the French monarchs to tap the full potential of their theoretical sovereignty. Among these were personal factors. Louis XIV, who did more than any other French king to enhance the power of the throne, was motivated in part by an intense desire to humble the nobility. He never forgot the insults he had received as a small boy during the Fronde. For him, the centralization of government was an act of revenge. But the outbreak of the Fronde (1648–

[17] On the concept of "areas of accommodation," see R.J.W. Evans, "The Wechel Presses: Humanism and Calvinism in Central Europe, 1572–1627," *Past and Present*, supplement 2 (1975):1–53. Ann M. Blair has applied this concept specifically to Bodin in *Restaging Jean Bodin: The 'Universae Naturae Theatrum' (1596) in its Cultural Context* (Ph.D. diss., Princeton University, 1990).

53), the last revolt of nobles against incursions upon their privileges, was a sign that the drift toward an absolutist administration was well under way even before Louis XIV began to rule.

The prime factor stimulating the movement away from constitutional and religious tradition was an impersonal one: the growing importance of large-scale warfare in a system of competing nation states. A series of wars, in particular the Thirty Years' War (1618–48), convinced the French monarchs of the need to invest huge sums of money in the weaponry, uniforms, supplies, and training of France's small and technologically backward army. This "military modernization"[18] created the need for a broader and more lucrative tax base, which in turn unleashed a set of constitutional conflicts in which the monarchs were forced to affirm their uncontestable sovereignty. As Roland Mousnier writes:

> Ever larger armies and fleets made imperious demands for more, better, and more costly armament. Taxes had to be raised beyond what the king's subjects deemed legitimate limits, and fairly often beyond what the taxpayers really could afford to pay. The difficulties of levying taxes, contributions, and forced loans, of one sort or another, and the opposition to such levies, frequently involving armed conflict, forced the royal government, more often than not against its will, to accomplish its ends either by turning to new institutions or by changing the way in which old institutions functioned, and to circumvent freedoms, exemptions, and privileges of many kinds, whether of corporations, provinces, fiefs, seigneuries, cities, or communities, even though these were well-established customs, consecrated by tradition.[19]

In order to extract more taxes from the population, the French monarchs had to circumvent customary checks on their authority, but they also had to make the population more taxable. The kingdom had to become more prosperous so that the citizens could transfer a larger set of resources to the state. The kingdom also required an officialdom that could maintain peace within the nation (the first prerequisite of prosperity); design policies oriented toward economic growth; and efficiently skim taxes off the created wealth. For these purposes, in the seventeenth century, a number of new royal servants were created, or older ones invested with an unprecedented degree of responsibility. The Controller General, the Intendants of Finance, the Provincial Intendants, and the Lieutenant General of Police in Paris were the most important of these. These administrators were charged with

---

[18] On the causes of "military modernization" in France, see Brian M. Downing, *The Military Revolution and Political Change* (Princeton, 1992), 113–39, and John A. Lynn, "The Growth of the French Army during the Seventeenth Century," *Armed Forces and Society* 6 (1980):568–85.

[19] Mousnier, *The Institutions of France*, 2:xv–xvi. See also Downing, *The Military Revolution*, 118–27.

duties that were previously exercised by representatives of corporate groups. The old class of officials, known as *officiers* and including the Chancellor and the members of the various Parlements, often believed that their own posts were an ancient and venerable part of the constitution and that their public function was to preserve corporate liberties. After the "paulette" edict of 1604, many *officiers* could transmit their positions to their heirs like property. This only gave them yet another reason to believe that their responsibility was to advise the king to respect corporate rights. The new class of officials were called *commissaires* because they received their post through royal commissions or appointments that could be revoked at the pleasure of the king. Bodin, who was the first to articulate the distinction between *officier* and *commissaire*, opposed the extension of the latter,[20] but the concept of sovereignty that he espoused was easily used to justify such an extension. By expanding the role of *commissaires* in government, the monarchs sought to enhance efficiency and to make themselves the principal object of loyalty among all persons exercising public functions.

With the growth of this new administrative elite, France began to exhibit some of the key features that Max Weber defined as the criteria of a bureaucratic state.[21] These features can be listed as follows:

1. The concentration of the means of administration in a single unified state apparatus free of personal or customary ties to the community over which it ruled. This centralization served to instill in the population, as Marc Raeff says, "the notion of the state as a separate, autonomous entity with its own . . . goals, interests, and needs."[22]

2. A permanent administration organized for the continuous fulfillment of duties, as distinct from periodic assemblies such as the Estates General. This governmental machinery had a steady existence that was not dependent on the rise and fall of stars in the ministry. "I change my ministers but the bureaux remain," Louis XV is reported to have said.[23]

3. The recruitment of a class of officials on the basis of merit—this professional labor force being used to displace what Weber called the "histori-

---

[20] For discussion of the distinction between *officier* and *commissaire*, including Bodin's view of the distinction, see Otto Hintze, "The Commissary and His Significance in General Administrative History," in *The Historical Essays of Otto Hintze*, ed. Felix Gilbert (Oxford, 1975), 267–301. See also Mousnier, *The Institutions of France*, 2:27–83.

[21] See the section entitled "Bureaucracy" in Max Weber, *From Max Weber: Essays in Sociology*, ed. H. H. Gerth and C. Wright Mills (New York, 1946), 196–244.

[22] Marc Raeff, "The Well-Ordered Police State and the Development of Modernity in Seventeenth- and Eighteenth-Century Europe: An Attempt at a Comparative Approach," *American Historical Review* 80 (1975):1230.

[23] John Bosher, *French Finances, 1770–1795: From Business to Bureaucracy* (Cambridge, 1970), 46. See also Michel Antoine, "L'Entourage des ministres au XVIIe et XVIIIe siècles," in Michel Antoine et al., *Origines et histoire des cabinets des ministres en France* (Geneva, 1975), 17–20.

cally inherited avocational administration by notables."[24] These function-aries had a sense of loyalty based on duty to the state rather than loyalty to particular corporate bodies.[25]

All these features represent trends in the absolute monarchy, not defini-tive accomplishments. Older constitutional structures and norms, though attenuated, remained in force so that by the late seventeenth century, the institutional order of the absolute monarchy displayed two important ten-sions. The first was a procedural tension between a mode of government based on consultation (discussion with corporate representatives) and a mode of government based on command (independent decisions by *com-missaires*). The second was a substantive tension, expressed most strikingly in the state's fiscal policies, between *justice*, in its traditional sense of preserv-ing customary distinctions, and *public welfare*, in the new sense of mobiliz-ing resources to maximize wealth and revenue.[26] The second of these could also be defined as a tension between two different views of the relationship between politics and time. The older and more passive mode of government was oriented toward the maintenance of an inherited and essentially fixed order of things. The new and more active mode of government was oriented toward transformation for the sake of practical improvement. The idea of progress, so often associated with the Enlightenment, was really an inven-tion of the absolute monarchy. And modernity, defined by Raeff as a nation's "conscious desire to maximize all its resources and to use this new potential dynamically for the enlargement and improvement of its way of life,"[27] was born in the king's administration.

At this point it is useful to return to Delamare's idea of a "well-policed" state that gave meaning to the trend toward government by *commissaires*. In the sixteenth century, political theorists had employed the word *police* as a translation of the Greek term *politeia*, meaning polity or constitution. When used to describe a monarchical regime, such as France, *la police* meant the sum of legal and religious customs that a king could tamper with only at the peril of undermining the stability of the community and his own prestige.[28]

---

[24] *From Max Weber*, 224–25.

[25] Mousnier, *The Institutions of France*, 2:74–75.

[26] Keith Michael Baker, *Inventing the French Revolution* (Cambridge, 1990), 115–16; Fran-çois Bluche and Jean-François Solnon, *La Véritable hiérarchie sociale de l'ancienne France: Le tarif de la première capitation (1695)* (Geneva, 1983).

[27] Raeff, "The Well-Ordered Police State," 1222.

[28] Henri Estienne, *Deux dialogues du nouveau langage français italianizé* (Paris, 1883), 1:95–98; Edmond Huguet, *Dictionnaire de la langue française du seizième siècle* (Paris, 1962). *Police* was a key term in the constitutional thought of Claude de Seyssel, and scholars have focused on its usage. See J. H. Hexter, *The Vision of Politics on the Eve of the Reformation* (New York, 1969), 224–26; Donald R. Kelley, *The Beginning of Ideology: Consciousness and Society in the French Renaissance* (Cambridge, 1983), 189–91; and the appendix entitled "'Police' and Its

The word *police* was also one of the most common terms used to denote the superiority of one mode of collective life over another. In this respect it was an important antecedent of the French word *civilisation*, which was coined in the middle of the eighteenth century.[29] *Policé* meant polished, refined, cultivated, and advanced. The moral overtones of the word were enhanced by its phonetic resemblance to the Greek word *polis*, or city-state, and its inevitable association with Aristotle's famous declaration that the *polis* existed not merely for the preservation of life but for the living of a moral life of friendship, communication, and political autonomy.

Henri Estienne, a sixteenth-century humanist and classical purist, affirmed that *police* had no proper meanings outside of those usages that corresponded to Greek concepts such as *politeia*. Nevertheless, he observed that others were using the term, incorrectly in his opinion, to refer to the security and prosperity of a town, as in the phrase *une ville bien policé*.[30] This popular usage appears to have had little importance in political theory prior to the late seventeenth century. But the administrative transformation described above required some kind of ideological inspiration and justification, and the semantic weight of the word *police* shifted accordingly. More precisely, urban security and prosperity became the principal meanings of *police* in both its descriptive and its normative senses. In his dictionary of 1687, Pierre Richelet defined *police* as "A word that comes from Greek and means the regulation of a town. Police consists in making various regulations for the welfare [*commodité*] of a town, and these various regulations should concern [the sale of] goods, the professions, the streets and the byways." The dictionary also defines *policé* as "Well regulated, where there is good police." As an example of correct usage it gives the phrase, "A well policed state" (*Un état bien policé*).[31] Antoine Furetière's dictionary of 1690 first defines *police* as "The order and administration to be observed for the subsistence and maintenance of states. . . . In general it is opposed to *barbarism*. The savages of America had neither laws nor police when they were discovered." The definition continues:

> Police refers more specifically to the rule given for the cleanliness and security of a town, for the taxation of commodities, and for the enforcement of the laws

---

Usage," in Claude de Seyssel, *The Monarchy of France*, trans. Donald R. Kelley and Michael Sherman, ed. J. H. Hexter (New Haven, 1981), 182.

[29] On *police* as a forerunner of *civilisation*, see Lucien Febvre, "*Civilisation*: Evolution of a Word and a Group of Ideas," in *A New Kind of History*, ed. Peter Burke (New York, 1973), 226–29; Jean Starobinski, "The Word Civilization," in *Blessings in Disguise*, trans. Arthur Goldhammer (Cambridge, Mass., 1993), 12–17; Peter France, "Polish, police, *polis*," in *Politeness and Its Discontents: Problems in French Classical Culture* (Cambridge, 1992), 53–73.

[30] Estienne, *Deux dialogues*, 1:97.

[31] Pierre Richelet, *Dictionnaire français* (Paris, 1680), 186.

pertaining to merchants and artisans. The jurisdiction and direction of the police of Paris used to belong to the Civil Lieutenant.[32] They have been stripped and belong now to an Official or Lieutenant General of Police. In Paris there are 48 Commissaries [*Commissaires*] who work for the police . . .[33]

Furetière also included the verb *policer*: "To make laws and regulations of police for maintaining public tranquillity. . . . There are still many nations that have no police, who live without laws, like animals." Instead of referring to a constitutional check upon government, *police* now meant the administrative competence of government, its practical goals and active functions. But by being opposed to "barbarism," the "savages" of America, and the life of wild animals, *police* retained its ethical connotations. Implicitly, the superiority of a collectivity no longer pertained to the traditions that limited the will of the state; it was now a matter of the efficiency of the state's public administration. The concept of centralized administration and the concept of civilization were thus amalgamated.

Furetière's reference to the Lieutenant General of Police in Paris suggests that governmental action in the field of practical urban problems stimulated transformations in the field of political semantics. The creation of an important office bearing the term *police* in its title added stature to the concept of administrative *police* as distinct from the older notion of *police* as the constitutional limits upon government. Prior to the mid-seventeenth century, the oversight of security in Paris rested in the hands of venal officers and the Parlement of Paris. To resolve jurisdictional ambiguities and to deal with the complex problems of a growing city, Louis XIV decided to create a single urban authority. In 1667, he relieved the Parlement and the older officers of their powers and vested them in the newly created *Lieutenant de Police* (later renamed *Lieutenant Général de Police*). The Crown selected the first Lieutenant of Police and all his successors not from the members of a particular corps but from the *maîtres des requêtes*, a pool of *commissaires* who owed allegiance only to the Crown. Legislation gave the Lieutenant of Police and his subordinates the power to arrest criminals, to regulate markets, to enforce sumptuary laws, to supervise charities and hospitals, to enact rules for the prevention of fires and floods, to inspect construction projects, and to organize the cleaning of streets and the disposal of rubbish.[34] This was the institution that Delamare worked for—an institution that was unique in terms of its almost limitless administrative competence.

[32] The *Lieutenant Civil* was an officer who worked under the auspices of the Parlement of Paris. He exercised various functions pertaining to security and subsistence prior to the appropriation of all police functions in Paris by the Crown in 1667.

[33] Antoine Furetière, *Dictionnaire universel, contenant généralement tous les mots français* (Paris, 1690).

[34] Henry Buisson, *La Police: Son histoire* (Vichy, 1950) contains the principal documents relating to the establishment of the *Lieutenant de Police*.

In the Dedication to his *Traité de la police*, Delamare defined police as the body of rules "which have as their aim only the service of the king and the public good." In a chapter called "The General Concept of Police," he stated that the first inhabitants of the earth united into families. Out of families villages were formed, and then towns. "Finally from the union of many towns, great states have been formed." This pseudo-Aristotelian conception[35] of a state as a collection of towns differed from the traditional French view of the polity as a collection of corporate groups. This conception allowed Delamare to discuss the kingdom of France as if it were essentially an urban entity, even though the majority of the population lived in rural areas. As the following passage shows, it also helped him to claim the legacy of classical political thought.

> It [police] sometimes means the general government of all states, under whatever form they are established, and in this sense it is divided into monarchy, aristocracy, and democracy . . . but usually it is taken to mean the public order of each town [*ville*]. . . . It seems that it is uniquely the latter [definition of police] that philosophers and jurists have had in view when they praise police so highly. . . . Plato defined the police as "the life, regulation, and law specifically suited for maintaining the city [*cité*]." . . . Aristotle also named it "the good order and government of the town [*ville*]."[36]

This passage obscures the distinction between the Greeks' philosophy of the independent city-state and the absolutist policing of a town within a larger realm. First Delamare says that the meaning of *police* as the maintenance of urban order is more common than its meanings as polity and constitution— which may well have been true of the word *police* in his own time but was not true of the words *polis* and *politeia* in Greek philosophy. And by interchanging *cité* (the independent city-state) and *ville* (a dense collection of dwellings forming part of a larger nation) in his pseudotranslations of the Greek thinkers, Delamare raised the status of practical urban administration and gave it a classical patina.[37] In other words, he defined the polity as a collec-

---

[35] Aristotle (*Politics*, bk. 1, ch. 2) explained the genesis of the *polis* by stating that human association originated in the union of male and female. From this union emerged the family and then the village, which Aristotle defined as a collection of related families, i.e., a clan. The union of several villages formed the *polis* or state. Delamare, who refers to this discussion in his notes, adds an extra stage, the formation of the town, to the evolutionary series, so that we have the following sequence: family—village—town—state.

[36] Delamare, *Traité*, 1:2.

[37] The meanings of the word *cité* in Delamare's time included a "group of free men constituting an independent political society having its own government." Synonyms were *état*, *nation*, *république*. See *Trésor de la langue française* (Paris, 1977). Various historical dictionaries show that the word *ville* meant simply a collection of dwellings, though the phrase *villes franches* signified free communes with their own magistrates. While *droit de cité* meant citizenship or the right to participate in the political forms of the town, *droit de ville* appears to have meant only

tion of *nonindependent* towns that required administrative oversight (*police*). Yet he imbued each of these towns, and the collection as a whole, with the philosophical luster attached to the Greek concept of the *independent* city (*polis*). It was this reduction of the *polis* to an object of administration that later outraged the republican Rousseau. Regarding the word *cité*, he declared, "The true meaning of this term has been almost entirely effaced. Most people take a town [*ville*] for a city [*cité*], and a burgess for a citizen. They do not appreciate that houses make a town and citizens a city."[38]

Delamare also made use of historical mythology to add prestige to *police*. He claimed that the new Paris police force was modeled on the police force that Augustus established in Rome and that his successors established in Gaul. When the Franks conquered Gaul, according to Delamare, they maintained the Roman police in all of the towns. Those who exercised police authority were known as Counts (*Comtes*). The Counts reported to the French kings and could be dismissed if they failed to fulfill their police duties. But in the tenth century, the Counts took advantage of the chaos stemming from the Norman raids to make themselves masters in the French provinces. From police *commissaires*, they became seigneurs. Delamare then recounted how, beginning in the twelfth century, the kings gradually regained their jurisdiction. Louis XIV's reforms of the Paris police in 1667 definitively restored the ancient Roman constitution.[39]

This remarkable account, which inverts the actual history of the transition from seigneurialism to bureaucratic absolutism, was designed to give *police* an aura of tradition. Delamare stated that history reveals "the origins of each establishment" and "the seeds of our rules and maxims of police." The distant past is a guide to present affairs because every institution "appears in its pure form at the time of its birth."[40] By claiming to find the roots of police in Rome and in the early history of France, Delamare suggested that administrative centralization was an original feature of the French constitution. One implication that he drew from this history was that the authority of the Paris police extended throughout France. The jurisdiction of the Lieutenant of Police, he wrote, "is universal because he is the first official of the capital of the realm; and just as in *Orbe Romano*, Rome, so in France, the town of Paris is the Mother City, *communis patria*."[41]

Delamare's obsession with establishing an ancient precedent for what was really a modern administrative revolution did not preclude him from simul-

---

the right to reside in a town. By not recognizing these distinctions, Delamare showed his lack of interest in political self-determination.

[38] Jean-Jacques Rousseau, *Du Contrat social* (Paris, 1966), 52 (Rousseau's footnote).

[39] Delamare, *Traité*, 1:27–48.

[40] Ibid., Préface. (Delamare's preface is very long, but the pages are not numbered. The quoted words occur on the last page.)

[41] Ibid., 1:99.

taneously highlighting the progressive nature of police authority. Although he claimed that the origins of police were ancient, he emphasized that the character of police authority was dynamic. Police "consists in leading man to the most perfect happiness that he can enjoy in this life."[42] In terms of the tension described above in the relation between politics and time, Delamare gave his own synthesis of the politics of the past and the politics of the future. He envisioned the nation advancing in population and happiness under the auspices of the ancient police constitution that it had recently regained under Louis XIV. Several maps in the *Traité de la police* depict Paris at various stages of its history from ancient times to the early eighteenth century. The maps portray the growth of the town and the increasingly rational way in which it was divided into territorial units for the sake of efficient administration. Concerning the most recent map of Paris, Delamare observed, "It is only necessary to throw a glance at this last map of Paris and at that which preceded it, in order to observe how much this town has grown and improved under the reign of Louis le Grand."[43]

Delamare thus sought to embed the concept of progressively achieved welfare within the concept of French constitutional tradition. The mythic constitutional tradition that he defined was not a corporate tradition. It was a statist and utilitarian one; a tradition of pursuing that which does not yet exist—more centralization, more regulation, more population, more welfare, more power for the sovereign. In the presence of this enterprise, real customs that limited royal government became meaningless. In opposing the right of judicial bodies to review police ordinances, for example, Delamare stated simply, "Since there is nothing more favorable than the public good, which is the object of police, all other privileges cede to it."[44]

Delamare is a symbol of the political culture within which French literary and philosophical culture developed. Many of the classic histories of French thought focus on the absolute monarchy as a set of "abuses" rather than a progressive mode of rulership that made the Age of Enlightenment possible. But the centralization of government and its development into a system of "police" were the primary forces working to break down tradition, including traditional modes of thought. The insistence upon complete freedom of action as the essential trait of sovereignty was one precondition of the Enlightenment. For the tendency to regard royal sovereignty as something separate from corporate privileges, rather than something embedded in them, made it possible for the *philosophes* to define political goals that aimed to transform rather than preserve the community. It made possible the idea of progress and elevated the imagined potential of human will.

[42] Ibid, Préface (second of unnumbered pages).
[43] Ibid., 1:90.
[44] Ibid., 1:164.

Promoters of the well-policed state themselves could be described as enlightened on account of their opposition to corporate tradition and their concern with the general welfare. Conversely, Enlightenment thinkers often favored the rational use of royal authority over the maintenance of constitutional tradition.[45] From absolutism to Enlightenment to the welfare state of today, there is more continuity than one usually imagines. But there were also changes occurring in France other than those that can be classified easily in terms of the growth of a paternal state.

Sociability and Democracy

While Delamare's *Traité de la police* effectively illustrates the presuppositions of absolutism as a political system, it does not provide a basis for understanding the dynamics of the regime—the unanticipated trends that absolutism unleashed in cultural and public life. The history of the absolute monarchy is complex; the institutional reconfigurations and cultural responses that emerged in the wake of the centralized absolutist state were numerous. But historians have often permitted themselves to streamline their accounts of the dynamics of the absolutist system in order to explain the system's most radical by-product: the French Revolution. Who can think of the absolute monarchy without thinking about its great downfall in 1789? And as if its downfall defines its essence, historians tend to see the absolute monarchy only in relation to its subversion. They can hardly avoid calling it the *ancien régime* (Old Regime), a term that evokes the process through which democracy superseded a corrupt and antiquated way of life. Old Regime and French Revolution—the two form a conceptual pair in which each element gives meaning to the other. The expression *ancien régime* was in fact coined in the early months of the Revolution and became a key component in revolutionary discourse about itself. As François Furet writes:

> The notion of the Ancien Régime is inextricably linked to the French Revolution. It is the Revolution's inverted image, its bad side, its negation: not only that which preceded the Revolution but that in opposition to which the Revolution defined itself as repudiation, rupture, and new beginning.[46]

Because historians today are usually democrats, it is hard for them to resist writing about the *ancien régime* as a defunct antecedent of democracy. I have deliberately not used the term *ancien régime* in my description of the pre-

---

[45] Keith Michael Baker, "Science and Politics at the End of the Old Regime," in *Inventing the French Revolution*, 153–66. See also my discussion of the physiocrats in Chapter 5.

[46] François Furet, "Ancien Régime," in *A Critical Dictionary of the French Revolution*, ed. François Furet and Mona Ozouf (Cambridge, Mass., 1989), 604.

revolutionary period because I wish to characterize the absolute monarchy, including the Enlightenment that unfolded within it, without presuming that the French Revolution was its compulsory end. One must not think of the Revolution as the fated punishment for everything hierarchical that existed before 1789, or as the logical completion of everything egalitarian in the Enlightenment. It is necessary, in other words, to conceptualize the prerevolutionary period as a dynamic yet self-sufficient culture.

An act of conceptualization is meaningful only in relation to already existing schemes of classification to which it provides an alternative. So it will be useful to discuss some of the important interpretations in which the dynamics of the absolute monarchy are narrated solely in order to account for the advent of the Revolution. For many historians the Revolution is, so to speak, the only divining rod used to detect the currents of change within the absolute monarchy. This is particularly true of Marxist historians, whose primary interest is in class conflict and revolution. In the Marxist paradigm, the eighteenth century was a period of growing class tensions, generated by the rise of capitalism within a feudal order. Marxism always focuses on what might be called "structurally based animosity," and Marxists writing on prerevolutionary France generally assume that the nation was divided into mutually exclusive classes that increasingly hated each other. Albert Soboul's survey of the institutions of the absolute monarchy in his three-volume work, *La Civilisation et la révolution française*, is typical in this respect. The volume on the monarchy is divided into chapters corresponding to distinct and opposed groups: Peasantry, Bourgeoisie, Aristocracy, Urban Proletariat. Since Marxists see conflict as the motor of history, Soboul does not recognize the existence of intergroup practices and ideals through which class consciousness might have been transmuted into other forms of identity. Following the example of Georges Lefebvre, another Marxist historian of the Revolution, Soboul places the whole philosophy of the Enlightenment squarely in the chapter on the bourgeoisie, as if to say that the new ideas existed only to serve the exclusive interests of that class.[47]

Many scholars have come to shed the Marxist conception of economically determined class hatred. But they often continue to believe that the production of animosity is the key, as if the answer to the question "Who disliked whom the most and why?" is the only thing that could explain where revolutions come from. The belief that revolutions stem from intergroup resentment is not limited to Marxists, for Tocqueville also focused on the dynamics of group differences. These were the differences of "isolated self-regarding groups,"[48] created not by the rise of new economic institutions

[47] Albert Soboul, *La Civilisation et la révolution française* (Paris, 1970), vol. 1. On Lefebvre's view of the Enlightenment, see William Doyle, *The Origins of the French Revolution* (Oxford, 1980), 26.

[48] Alexis de Tocqueville, *The Old Regime and the French Revolution* (New York, 1955), 81.

but by the decline of old political ones. Tocqueville believed that before the emergence of a centralized monarchy, representative bodies in the French constitution included members of different orders. He believed that political life in the medieval age was highly democratic and based on a de facto mingling of the orders in spite of the privileges that separated them de jure. With the growth of a powerful royal administration, these intergroup encounters declined. Each group now "minded its own business" and "lived only for itself." Paradoxically (and this is the most subtle part of Tocqueville's argument), French people tended to become more and more alike in the presence of a state that sought to reduce its subjects to an equal condition of political impotence. The absence of a common meeting ground, however, created a spirit of suspicion among the orders. Unfamiliarity bred contempt: "Every day the rift between them widened until, by the eighteenth century, nobleman and bourgeois never met except by chance in private life. And by then, the two classes were not merely rivals, they were foes."[49] Tocqueville argued that this isolation of Frenchmen from political affairs and from each other generated a new political mentality—the Enlightenment. A nation that had no experience in the art of negotiation and compromise became enthralled with "abstract, literary politics."[50] Utopianism became the order of the day and broke down all respect for existing institutions.

According to Tocqueville, Enlightenment ideas "were not merely antecedent to the French Revolution; they formed part and parcel of it and, in the light of subsequent events, can be seen to be its most fundamental, durable, and authentic characteristics."[51] This description of the Enlightenment as an attribute of the event that came after it is problematic because it falsely implies that Enlightenment discourse was generally protorevolutionary. Many who sought to turn politics into a literary and philosophical genre of writing were not utopian, egalitarian, or even highly critical of the idea of absolute monarchy. Tocqueville certainly knew a lot about eighteenth-century thought, but he was first and foremost a political philosopher interested in the variants of democracy—and he could not overcome his tendency to see democratic culture everywhere. His idealization of the Middle Ages is particularly revealing. When he wrote *The Old Regime and the French Revolution* in the 1850s, Tocqueville had already written *Democracy in America* and praised the New England town meeting as an institution that forged a moderate and virtuous citizenry out of egoistic individuals. Somehow it occurred to him in writing *The Old Regime and the French Revolution* that the democratic town meeting was a practice inherited from the Europe of medi-

[49] Ibid., 86, 96.
[50] Ibid., 139.
[51] Ibid., 6.

eval times, a feudal residue that the colonists, who had left Europe before the consolidation of the absolutist state, preserved and injected into American life.

> General assemblies were convened from time to time in both [i.e., in medieval France and contemporary America] and at these the townsfolk, acting in concert, elected their own officials and passed orders on matters affecting the interests of the community. In short the French and American systems resembled each other—in so far as a dead creature can be said to resemble one that is very much alive.
>
> For these two systems of local government, though their ways soon parted, had in fact a common origin. Transported overseas from feudal Europe and free to develop in total independence, the rural parish of the Middle Ages became the township of New England. Emancipated from the seigneur, but controlled at every turn by an all-powerful government, it took in France the form which we shall now describe.[52]

Tocqueville used this dubious historical connection between European feudalism and American democracy to establish that the French Revolution was an inevitable consequence of the absolutist state's departure from the nation's democratic traditions. The point he sought to make was that by suppressing the representative bodies of the Middle Ages, the monarchs eliminated the only mechanism that was capable of creating a free and harmonious community. According to Tocqueville, the Enlightenment and the French Revolution issued from the ignorance and tensions within a populace that was never allowed to convene.[53] The democratic ideals that emerged in the eighteenth century were immoderate and impracticable because the French, instead of reclaiming their past, repudiated it entirely, for they saw it only in its absolutist guise.

In spite of the political wisdom that accompanies so much of Tocqueville's writing, it appears that the outlines of his history are misleading. They exaggerate not only the democratic character of political life in the Middle Ages but also the isolated character of private life under the absolute monarchy. Tocqueville stated that "nobleman and bourgeois never met except by chance in private life."[54] But the rising participation of the nobility in commercial projects and the growth of intermarriage among nobles of the sword and recently ennobled members of the bourgeoisie do not support

---

[52] Ibid., 48.

[53] This is, I believe, the key argument of Parts 2 and 3 of *The Old Regime and the French Revolution*. See especially Part 2, Chapter 10, entitled, "How the Suppression of Political Freedom and the Barriers Set Up between Classes Brought On Most of the Diseases to which the Old Regime Succumbed."

[54] Ibid., 86.

this view.[55] Nor does the growth of Masonic lodges, academies, public libraries, reading groups, cafés, salons, and other areas of interaction that were open to people of diverse ranks.[56] Within the confines of the well-policed state, the eighteenth century experienced a blossoming of convivial life, and this effervescence of interclass activity drew much commentary. "Most of our writers brag about our nation's spirit of society [*esprit de société*], and indeed, foreigners see us as the most sociable [*la plus sociable*]in Europe," wrote Bernardin de Saint-Pierre.[57] He was right. One example is a guidebook for travelers in Paris, published in Holland in 1727. The anonymous author recommends a Parisian vacation to everyone, including students, merchants, and nobles. In describing various places in Paris that are worth visiting, he never tells his readers that some of these sites are off limits to certain classes of people. The reader has a sense of Paris as a set of open and homogeneous spaces, a city with an "infinite number" of cafés, billiard rooms, libraries, newsstands, and other zones of voluntary association that anyone could freely enter.[58] Joseph Addison, the great English proponent of the clubbish spirit, described the French as "very sociable" and possessing a "communicative temper."[59] Diderot concurred when he described France as possessing an "extreme *sociabilité*," which he characterized as follows:

[55] On noble marriages, see the review essay by J.H.M. Salmon, "Storm over the Noblesse," *Journal of Modern History* 53 (June 1981):242–57. I discuss the commercial nobility later in this chapter.

[56] On Masonic lodges, see Maurice Agulhon, *La Sociabilité méridionale: Confréries et associations en Provence* (Aix-en-Provence, 1966); Ran Halévi, *Les Loges maçonniques dans la France d'Ancien Régime: Aux Origines de la sociabilité démocratique* (Paris, 1984); Margaret C. Jacob, *Living the Enlightenment: Free Masonry and Politics in Eighteenth-Century Europe* (New York, 1991). On libraries and reading groups, see Roger Chartier and Daniel Roche, "Les Pratiques urbaines de l'imprimé," in *L'Histoire de l'édition française*, ed. Roger Chartier and Henri-Jean Martine (Paris, 1984), 2:402–29. On academies, see Daniel Roche, *Le Siècle des lumières en province*, 2 vols. (Paris, 1978), and *Les Républicains des lettres: Gens de culture et lumières au XVIIIe siècle* (Paris, 1988). On salons and cafés, see Dena Goodman, "Enlightenment Salons: The Convergence of Female and Philosophic Ambitions," in *Eighteenth-Century Studies*, vol. 22, no. 3 (Spring 1989), 329–50; Roger Picard, *Les Salons littéraires et la société française, 1610–1789* (New York, 1943); Carolyn C. Lougee, *Le Paradis des Femmes: Women, Salons, and Social Stratification in Seventeenth-Century France* (Princeton, 1976); Alfred Franklin, *La Vie privée d'autrefois*, vol. 13: *Le Café, le thé, et le chocolat* (Paris, 1893). For discussion of these institutions as part of an emergent "public sphere," see Anthony J. La Vopa. "Conceiving a Public: Ideas and Society in Eighteenth-Century Europe," *Journal of Modern History* 64 (1992):76–116.

[57] Jacques-Henri Bernardin de Saint-Pierre, *Etudes de la nature* (Paris, 1804; first published, 1784), 1:29.

[58] Anonymous, *Séjour de Paris, c'est à dire instructions fidèles pour les voiagers de condition, comment ils se doivent conduire, s'ils veulent faire un bon usage de leurs temps et argent . . .* (Leiden, 1727), 111, 282ff.

[59] Joseph Addison, *The Spectator*, ed. Donald F. Bond (Oxford, 1965), issue of June 18, 1714, 4:499.

There is no nation that is more like a single family. A Frenchman swarms about in his town more than ten Englishmen, fifty Dutchmen, or a hundred Moslems do in theirs. The same man in the same day will be at court, in the center of town, in the countryside, at an academy, a salon, a banker's, a notary's, a barrister's, a solicitor's, a great seigneur's, a merchant's, a workman's, at church, at the theatre, and with the call girls. Everywhere he is equally free and familiar. One would say that he had never left his home and that he had simply changed rooms.[60]

In the following chapter, I will analyze images of France as a "sociable" nation and the theories that made such images important to writers. In this chapter, I am more concerned with the concept of "sociability" as a tool for studying the institutional dynamics of the absolute monarchy. It is important to note that the word *sociabilité* was coined in the eighteenth century and became a key term in literature and philosophy (see Chapter 2). The same word, however, has gained currency in historical writing as a descriptive label for the spirit of voluntary association and the egalitarian mixing of ranks under the absolute monarchy.[61] There is potential for confusion when one does not distinguish clearly between the prerevolutionary language of sociability and the present historiographical language of sociability. The two languages resemble each other in that the term "sociability" in both cases refers to a mode of exchange that is free of the ritualistic constraints of corporate hierarchy. But the two languages differ in that the prerevolutionary usage did not attach radical or democratic significance to the term, while the present historiographical usage often does. An argument could be made that the institutional history is misconstrued because its lexicon is not synchronized with prerevolutionary usage, but this is not the argument I wish to develop here. Instead, I would like to assess the institutional history of sociability in its own right. How did sociable exchange fit within the corporate regime? How was it sustained, and what was its status in the well-policed state? Such questions are interesting in themselves. Moreover, the answers will necessarily shape the way we approach the intellectual history of the period.

Like the study of class conflict, the study of conviviality under the absolute monarchy is often subordinated to the study of the origins of the Revolution. While the followers of Marx and Tocqueville see the Revolution as an outcome of the dynamics of intergroup hostility, historians in the

---

[60] Denis Diderot, *Réfutation de l'ouvrage d'Helvetius intitulé L'Homme*, in *Oeuvres complètes* (Paris, 1975; first published, 1774), 2:382.

[61] Three works in which the term figures in the title are Agulhon, *La Sociabilité méridionale: Confréries et associations en Provence*; Halévi, *Les Loges maçonniques dans la France d'Ancien Régime: Aux Origines de la sociabilité démocratique*; and Etienne François, ed., *Sociabilité et société bourgeoise en France, en Allemagne, et en Suisse* (Paris, 1986). The word sociability is often used in the works listed in note 56.

school of "democratic sociability" see the origins of revolutionary culture in the dynamics of intergroup fellowship. Tocqueville believed that radical criticism of the monarchy took root in a nation of isolated and politically inexperienced castes. In *Les Origines intellectuelles de la Révolution française* (The Intellectual Origins of the French Revolution), Daniel Mornet affirmed just the opposite: that radical criticism emerged in a milieu of rich communication.

> Those who assemble [in voluntary associations] to read, reason, and discuss are more prone to reason about the Estates General, and then about the constitution, and then about the Republic, than the quiet petit-bourgeois occupied above all with the affairs of his family and trade.[62]

François Furet and Ran Halévi have deepened Mornet's argument by emphasizing the profoundly novel character and radical significance of intergroup solidarity within a regime based on the principles of differentiation and particularism. Furet describes the voluntary organizations that blossomed in the eighteenth century as "laboratories where new values were produced," values that stood in opposition to the corporate regime and that presaged the Revolution.[63] Halévi evaluates the rise of sociable groups—literary circles, reading clubs, academies, and Masonic lodges—in similar terms.

> This phenomenon appears totally new in the context of a society where all political representation is "holistic." The life of men moved in a framework of time-honored and unalterable solidarities—the family, the parish, the corporation, the order. Traditions, privileges, customs, festivals, and processions, were just so many affiliations, always communitarian, which organized life while confining it to the most narrowly local framework. It was this framework that democratic sociability enlarged . . . before exploding it in 1789.[64]

Both Furet and Halévi have been inspired by Augustin Cochin, the idiosyncratic historian, brilliant inventor of sociological ideal types, and critic of democratic totalitarianism. Writing shortly before the First World War, in which he died, Cochin was the first historian of eighteenth-century France to appreciate deeply the difference between a corporate group based on privileges and a voluntary association based only on the will of its members.[65] The latter he called a *société de pensée* (philosophical society). Cochin

---

[62] Daniel Mornet, *Les Origines intellectuelles de la Révolution française* (Paris, 1933), 313.

[63] François Furet, *Interpreting the French Revolution* (Cambridge, 1981), 180.

[64] Halévi, *Les Loges maçonniques*, 11.

[65] Augustin Cochin, *Les Sociétés de pensée et la démocratie moderne* (Paris, 1978); Cochin, *La Révolution et la libre-pensée* (Paris, 1978). These volumes reprint essays and incomplete sketches by Cochin, some of which he published during the years 1904–1913 and others that were first published posthumously in the 1920s. An interesting and neglected interpretation of Cochin's

intended this term to apply not merely to scholarly or intellectual meetings but to any group that was self-instituting. "Every society whose members *govern themselves* and where the *present will* of the collectivity is the law is necessarily a *société de penseé*," he wrote.[66] The purpose of this concept was to highlight the similarity between the sociability of salons and Masonic lodges under the absolute monarchy and the radical political sociability of Jacobinism.

Cochin's analysis was informed by his metaphysical, almost Platonic sensibility and by his sensitivity to the contradictions of democratic culture. Prior to the eighteenth century, he argued, spiritual ideals were rooted in the belief in the reality of self-subsistent ideas, such as the idea of God, the Good, and Justice. Reality was prior to social organization; truth was necessarily independent of the declaration of belief. The challenge to the philosophical and religious disposition was to overcome the world of sensations and conventions, to attain a distance from the prejudices embedded in everyday life, and to perceive transcendent truths. Cochin believed that the inner logic of voluntary association transformed the way people imagined the ontological relation between truth and collective organization. "Truth" became the product of sociability, the result of communication among the members of a group. The distinction between truth and opinion dissolved in prerevolutionary *sociétés de pensée* because the participants, refusing to ground their identity in anything anterior to their own association, were bound to treat the subjectivity of the group as an unquestionable finality. The truth was now what emerged as clear and comprehensible to all after the free exchange of opinions had taken place. "Every idea, every intellectual effort exists here only through consensus. Opinion determines being. Reality is what others see, truth what they say, good what they approve of."[67] Cochin paradoxically emphasized the loss of insight that occurred through the free play of ideas. "Each submits to what he believes is believed by all. Opinion follows its own shadow, and from illusion a reality is born."[68]

Cochin claimed that Enlightenment philosophers and those who frequented the salons and Masonic lodges were ardent defenders of the new concept of collectively generated truth. He also made the remarkable assertion that this confidence in the collectivity meant that the freethinkers did not in fact have a philosophy. Unlike a monk, who experiences a sense of insight or revelation *before* joining a monastery, the *philosophes* and enlightened elites of the eighteenth century joined a *société de pensée* in order to see

---

thought is Antoine de Meaux, *Augustin Cochin et la genèse de la révolution* (Paris, 1928), but the most sophisticated analysis is by Furet, *Interpreting the French Revolution*, 164–204.

[66] Cochin, *La Révolution et la libre-pensée*, 75 (Cochin's emphasis).

[67] Cochin, *Les Sociétés de pensée*, 15.

[68] Ibid., 23. See also Furet's exposition of Cochin's concept of ideology, 176–79.

what truths would emerge *after* the process of free communication. "They were united *for* and not *by* the truth," Cochin was fond of saying.[69] These freethinkers deferred more absolutely to human authority because they had no credo, no conviction or verity that they cherished apart from the opinion forged by the collectivity. This is what Cochin meant when he called the Enlightenment "a social, not a moral or intellectual phenomenon."[70] The *philosophes* did not offer a substantive view of life but only a naive confidence in the *société de pensée*—a complete acceptance that the present decision of a group of equals has an absolute value.

Cochin was searching for the origins of the Reign of Terror of 1793–94, a period in which thousands were killed in the name of democracy. He thought of the *société de pensée* as a miniature form of democratic totalitarianism, and he wished to portray it as the model of the Jacobin regime. He argued that the members of salons and Masonic orders invented the moral and epistemological fallacy that participation in a system of exchange is more important than the private search for meaning. Those who entered these organizations, Cochin believed, gained one kind of freedom, a freedom from their particularistic identity as defined by the traditional regime of estates and orders. But they lost their freedom vis-à-vis the new group of which they were members. And the new bondage was worse than the old. Having entered an association without a definite conviction about what its results should be, having pledged allegiance to the collective production of truth, the individual no longer had any grounds for opposing decisions that the group made—or that a charismatic leader might make in the name of the group. According to Cochin, the concept of freely produced opinion inevitably became an easily manipulated myth during the Revolution, a tool used by tyrants to impose their own program upon a public in search of its own message.[71]

Cochin's critique of the tyranny of freedom under Jacobinism is insightful, but there is no clear causal or analogical relation between the expansion of voluntarism under the absolute monarchy and revolutionary democracy. Cochin was especially interested in Freemasonry as a form of proto-Jacobin culture, but he did not study the Masons outside of France. Margaret C. Jacob's comparative study of European Masonry suggests that the principles of Masonic organization were similar across Europe, yet France alone got the Jacobins.[72] Though the principle of voluntarism is a common point

---

[69] Cochin, *La Révolution et la libre-pensée*, 39, 49.

[70] Ibid., 49.

[71] Ibid., 27–31, 127–28.

[72] See Margaret C. Jacob, *Living the Enlightenment*, especially p. 18. Jacob portrays Masonry as a form of association based on egalitarian principles, especially the principle of merit. But she argues that this egalitarianism was part of an ethical rather than a democratic activism. It was accompanied by a desire to promote domestic virtue, religious feeling, and philanthropy rather than a desire to institute popular sovereignty.

between small sociable associations and radical democracy as a political system, it does not follow that the members of sociable groups under the absolute monarchy desired the Revolution or provided a model for the revolutionaries. It does not even mean that the sociable associations exhibited the same spirit as the revolutionaries on a smaller scale, for to enjoy the voluntary spirit of a small group within a hierarchical regime is not the same thing as to wish to reconstitute the whole regime on the basis of popular will. Cochin did not consider all the possible ways in which the members of a relatively free association could formulate their identities vis-à-vis the relatively unfree regime that they inhabited. By focusing on the internal dynamics of the *sociétés de pensée* and how they reveal a structural similarity to democracy when both are classified in opposition to Christian and Platonic metaphysics, Cochin prematurely concluded that the practitioners of sociability were harbingers of democracy. He did not consider that the members of an egalitarian microcosm may take pride in their mode of association without seeking to undermine the hierarchical macrocosm. They may even prefer to live in a regime that is generally hierarchical, because without this hierarchical backdrop, the small theater of equality would lose the tone of transgression and excitement.

How can we conceptualize the rise of "sociable" institutions under the absolute monarchy without using the Revolution to define their essential meaning? To provide alternative perspectives, it might be useful to outline a series of ideal types whose purpose is not to link sociability and democracy but to show how sociability was stimulated by absolutism and coexisted with it. Each of these ideal types stands for a way of imagining sociable action that is not protorevolutionary in character. I do not offer these ideal types as a substitute for empirical research into institutions. Moreover, I could not have defined some of them without the important studies that already exist. To outline a series of ideal types, however, will help to make explicit some alternatives to the story of "democratic sociability" and the tendency to treat the prerevolutionary period in terms of revolutionary origins. These rubrics will also provide some categories for the analysis of the intellectual history of sociability in the ensuing chapters.

Five Ideal Types

The bare definition of sociability is egalitarian interaction among individuals with different corporate standing. The question is, What meaning can such egalitarian mixing have in an absolute monarchy?

1. *Sociability as the love of exchange.* Sociability may be nothing other than the pursuit of convivial interaction for the immediate pleasure it affords. Sociability in this sense is a form of play, a pure love of fellowship that has no political significance and that precludes political activism. A political party,

for example, is not sociable because it has functions and goals in relation to the outer world and does not stem from the pure desire for exchange within the group. A sociable organization, in the specific sense implied by sociability as the play-form of human interaction, is one that meets solely in order to give its members an opportunity to enjoy the commerce of the organization itself. People are truly sociable when they follow a set of rules designed to preserve this exchange.

Georg Simmel suggested that a commitment to this kind of sociability, to the enjoyment of interaction per se, necessarily entails equality. The first rule of a sociable gathering is to behave so as to maintain exchange. One's own desire for exchange dictates that one grant to others the right to share in whatever activity makes up the life of the group.

> Sociability . . . creates an ideal sociological world in which the pleasure of the individual is closely tied up with the pleasure of the others. In principle, nobody can find satisfaction here if it has to be at the cost of dramatically opposed feelings, which the other may have.[73]

The participants must adhere to a transactional ethos that requires each individual to recognize the desire of others to participate. For example, if conversation is the pleasure one seeks, one must yield to others the right to speak, or else the exchange of words will cease. If one attempts to monopolize the proceedings, this tyranny will destroy the source of one's own pleasure. This is what Simmel meant when he referred to the inherently "democratic" structure of sociability: the sociable person must be egalitarian, but this egalitarianism is limited to the sociable environment that produces it. "Democratic," in this context, does not imply a wish to apply the idea of equality to all spheres of life. Rather, it means the willingness of each of the participants in a particular system of exchange to play the role of receiver as well as the role of transmitter. As Simmel notes, the elimination of hierarchy within a sociable group is not the result of a "superimposed ethical imperative." Rather, "it [inequality] is excluded by the intrinsic principle of the social form itself."[74]

2. *Sociability as the propagation of absolutism.* Cochin argued that sociability was inherently at odds with corporatism. He also assumed that anything antithetical to corporatism was subversive in character. But the centralizing tendency and welfare orientation of the well-policed state were also at odds with corporate traditions. It is possible, then, that sociability and absolutism operated on the same plane. The growth of voluntary societies, which was concentrated in the towns, would not have been possible without officials like Delamare, who secured order and helped to make citizens

---

[73] Georg Simmel, "Sociability," in *The Sociology of Georg Simmel*, ed. Kurt H. Wolff (Glencoe, Ill., 1950), 47–48.
[74] Ibid., 48.

confident that they could interact safely with people outside of their family or corporate milieu. More importantly, the notion of royal sovereignty reconfigured the terrain of public and private life in such a way as to legitimize certain kinds of interaction among members of different orders.

Every hierarchical society is based on a set of important boundaries that keep individuals of different ranks apart. When an inferior crosses a boundary, it is an audacious insult. When a superior crosses one, it is a shameful act of derogation. Traditional boundaries in France were corporate in nature, and their purpose was to prevent any mixing of ranks that might lead to confusion about their separate positions within the chain of being. The absolutist state was also hierarchical, but the boundary that it emphasized was the single boundary between private and public, not the multiple boundaries that kept the orders apart.[75] It was now an audacious insult for private citizens (such as the inhabitants of Troyes whom Delamare threatened) to concern themselves with the general welfare. It was an act of derogation for public officials to disobey the monarch and act on the basis of private interest (as Delamare claimed the Counts had done in the tenth century). This tendency for the state to displace the multiple distinctions between privileged groups with the all-important distinction between public and private spheres stimulated interaction among people of different ranks in both the public and private domains.

In the public sphere of the state, many officials were chosen on the basis of merit rather than corporate affiliations. A new service elite arose whose members had something in common in spite of their different backgrounds: a dedication to the king and the general welfare. The state itself thus became a zone of intergroup solidarity. Some institutions of sociability, notably the royal scientific academies, became areas in which the service elite pursued intellectual inquiry and discussion that revolved around the themes of public welfare and progress.[76]

[75] Weber discusses how bureaucracy makes possible "the conceptual separation of private and public" in *From Max Weber*, 239. See also Jürgen Habermas, *The Structural Transformation of the Public Sphere: An Inquiry into a Category of Bourgeois Society* (Cambridge, Mass., 1989), 11: "'Private' designated the exclusion from the sphere of the state apparatus; for 'public' referred to the state that in the meantime had developed, under absolutism, into an entity having an objective existence over against the person of the ruler."

[76] Roche, *Le Siècle des lumières*, and La Vopa, "Conceiving a Public," 89–90. In a review of Roche's *Le Siècle des lumières*, Keith Michael Baker states, "Academic discourse constituted for this group a domain of sociability which was not exclusively defined either in terms of the old principles of privilege and particularism or in terms of the newer principles of equality and universalism. . . . The pursuit of knowledge in the service of public utility satisfied the claims of local pride and of loyalty to the monarchical state, while transposing the aristocratic ideal into the image of an enlightened elite cultivating the greatest happiness of the greatest number." Keith Michael Baker, "Enlightenment and Revolution in France: Old Problems, Renewed Approaches," *Journal of Modern History* 53 (1981):295.

A state concerned more with welfare than corporate hierarchy was bound to abdicate its role of enforcing the spirit of separation in the private domain as well. The elaborate series of progressive tax brackets that accompanied the capitation of 1695 is interesting to consider in this light. The capitation system mixed individuals by classifying them in twenty-two groups according to their ability to pay rather than their honorific rank and corporate privileges.[77] This particular mixing of ranks, of course, was a matter of administrative classification, not actual interaction. But the point is that the state was increasingly apathetic about violations of hierarchy when these violations served its fiscal needs and did not represent an encroachment of private individuals into the public sphere. In this context, it is also interesting to note two aspects of state policy in the seventeenth and eighteenth centuries: its liberal granting of exemptions to the rules of derogation with respect to commerce, and its toleration of voluntary associations that were technically illegal.

As jurists argued up to the seventeenth century, nobles who engaged in trade ran the risk of having their nobility revoked, because laboring for profit debased their spiritual dignity and brought them lower on the scale of being. In his famous *La Noblesse commerçante* (The Commercial Nobility, 1756), the abbé Coyer ignored the ideology of the chain of being and treated nation-states, not estates and orders, as the fundamental units of human organization. Coyer also saw nation-states as parts of a competitive milieu—balance-of-power politics—instead of parts of a natural hierarchy ordained by God. This highly political rather than spiritual or cosmic system of classification put nobles and commoners into a common space, France, instead of separating them according to dignity and order. Nobles and commoners should work side by side for the good of the French state, Coyer claimed. Commerce, he insisted, could be seen as a noble activity because it contributed to population growth and the financing of a strong army that could guarantee the world power of the French state. Coyer was not a government servant, but his legitimation of commerce was consonant with the political and economic goals of the royal administration. For beginning in the middle of the sixteenth century, and particularly from the time of Colbert onward, a series of royal edicts lifted the laws of derogation and encouraged the nobility to engage in trade of various kinds.[78] With its emphasis on "utility" (*utilité*) as opposed to the spirit of honor and distinc-

---

[77] See Bluche and Solnon, *La véritable hiérarchie*, 99–114, for the 1695 text outlining the tax brackets.

[78] On the traditional concept of derogation and the royal edicts of the seventeenth and eighteenth centuries designed to efface it from French culture, see Mousnier, *The Institutions of France*, 1:131–33; Marcel Marion, *Dictionnaire des institutions de la France, XVIIe–XVIIIe siècles* (Paris, 1984), 116–17, and above all, Henri Lévy-Bruhl, "La Noblesse de France et le commerce à la fin de l'Ancien Régime," *Revue d'Histoire Moderne* 8 (1933):209–35.

tion (which he calls mere "opinion" and "fashion"), Coyer's discourse is clearly indebted to the well-policed state.[79] Commercial sociability was compatible with absolutism and was even promoted by it.

As for the laws restricting association outside of corporate bodies, these were of very long standing. In 1305, Philip the Fair enjoined the *prévot* of Paris to publish ordinances against any assembly of more than five people that met without explicit royal approval in an open or confined place and at any time of day. Prohibitions such as these were supposed to prevent the formation of a "republic" in France. They were also designed to maintain the spirit of hierarchy by ensuring that interaction took place through the rituals prescribed by law. The ordinances were reissued in the seventeenth and eighteenth centuries so that salons and Masonic lodges were, strictly speaking, illegal. But although the government's coercive power was greater than before, it rarely suppressed these gatherings,[80] for it was less concerned with convivial action that defied the chain of being than with unruly action that defied the chain of command. Far from being antithetical to the status quo, sociability fit within the private domain brought into existence by the well-policed state.

3. *Sociability as a bond among strangers*. In traditional France, an individual in a village or small town could quickly infer much about the corporate standing of others by examining their clothing and other external indicators of birth and status within the local hierarchy. According to Charles Loyseau, "Each order usually has its particular mark, insignia, or ornament," such as a robe, cloak, hood, fanon, stole, miter, staff, gloves, ring, hat, coat of arms, spurs, gold chain, or cornet.[81] A large city like Paris, however, constantly saw the influx of people who were seeking to rise in the world. Such people were not eager to externalize their status in relation to a fixed hierarchy. "To tell the truth," wrote Antoine de Montchrétien in 1615, "it is almost impossible to distinguish people by their exterior. The shopkeeper dresses like a gentleman. The latter can be recognized only by his good reputation and fine conduct. If these were to disappear, goodbye to all distinctions [*adieu la*

[79] Gabriel-François Coyer, *La Noblesse commerçante* (London and Paris, 1756). On population, see especially 46–48; on balance of power and geopolitical influence of the French state, see especially 148–59; on *utilité*, see 207ff.

[80] On the laws of association under the absolute monarchy, see Olivier-Martin, *Histoire du droit français*, 340; Georges-Denis Weil, *Le Droit d'association et le droit de réunir* (Paris, 1983), 3–5; Paul Nourrisson, *Histoire de la liberté d'association en France depuis 1789* (Paris, 1920), 1:51–53, 73, 81–83. The loose enforcement of the laws is evident from the proliferation of Masonic lodges and other groups, especially after 1750. For discussion of the state's increasing leniency, see Jacob, *Living the Enlightenment*, 3–6; and Roche, *Les Républicains des lettres*, 250. Roche states that the Crown, preoccupied with its struggles against the Parlements, developed a policy of toleration toward voluntary groups and philosophical activities that did not openly oppose royal sovereignty.

[81] Loyseau, *Traité des ordres*, 10–11.

différence]."[82] The city was a scene of impersonation, with people disguising their origins and aggrandizing their appearance as part of a theatrical strategy for impressing others.[83] As a result, one could not be sure who others were and how one should communicate with them. Yves Castan writes:

> While in the [traditional] world of honor and courtesy everyone knew what he owed to others, in the urban world, people rubbed shoulders with each other, confronted each other, and frequented each other without knowing what their duties to each other were. . . . There was no *a priori* and determined connection between them, no precise means of recognition or precise classification of the relationships. . . . It was necessary at all times to find some way of establishing equilibrium with an unexpected and often unknown interlocutor.[84]

The state also contributed to the unsettling of familiar hierarchical frames of reference through the sale of offices and the promotion of a service elite based on merit rather than corporate status. In a complex regime in which traditional hierarchical norms conflicted with new utilitarian ones, people were unsure about how they should display their personal tastes and achievements in the presence of others.

One way of approaching the development of clubs and lodges in pre-revolutionary France is to see them as sanctuaries of secure interaction within a culture that tended to estrange people from each other—not because it was so hierarchical but because it was so indeterminate. The Cochin school has presumed that individuals found the salon or the lodge attractive as a means of escape from the rigid hierarchies of corporate life. It seems no less likely that people found them attractive as sources of orderly association within a world that was devoid of fixed conventions.[85] Sociability was a means of instituting stable norms. The fixed conventions of the group allowed one to classify both oneself and others according to a consistent scale of values. So long as it did not reinstate corporate privileges or force people to reveal their origins, the specific content of these values might have been unimportant to the participants, who were simply looking for a stable system within which they could represent themselves and interact with others. The essence of sociability in this context is not opposition to the monarchy but the effort to establish a determinate mode of interaction within it.

[82] Antoine de Montchrétien, *Traité de l'oeconomie politique*, ed. Th. Funck-Brentano (Paris, 1889), 60.

[83] This is one of the great themes of Richard Sennet's *The Fall of Public Man: On the Social Psychology of Capitalism* (New York, 1978), Part 2: "The Public World of the Ancien Régime." This book has been unduly neglected by historians of the eighteenth century.

[84] Yves Castan, *Honnêteté et relations sociales en Languedoc (1715–1780)* (Paris, 1974), 26.

[85] A very suggestive study of the notion of convention and how people will spontaneously establish repetitive patterns of interaction in the absence of clear rules is David K. Lewis, *Convention: A Philosophical Study* (Oxford, 1986).

4. *Sociability as socialization and education.* Socialization is the process through which individuals become accustomed to the norms of a particular group or milieu. This process usually requires the acquisition of information, the mastery of ceremonial forms, and the development of communication skills that allow one to pass oneself off as a competent member of the group in question. Socialization usually begins in the family and is completed in secondary education. Because French secondary education offered little besides theology and classics, it is plausible to think of institutions of sociability as centers of adult education in which people of different backgrounds acquired whatever was necessary to supplement their knowledge. This perspective is all the more compelling when one considers that the activities of at least one sociable institution, the salon, revolved around the cultivation of speaking, reading, and writing skills. By conversing with men of letters, the women who attended the salons had an opportunity to supplement the meager formal education that was available to them.[86] The men of letters who attended the gatherings already possessed intellectual facility, but if they came from outside the nobility, they probably lacked the facility in manners that a writer needed in order to blend into the company of the rich and powerful. And it was not just a question of poets and dramatists wishing to acquire a polished exterior so they could curry favor from noble patrons; it was also a question of satirists, economists, journalists, and political theorists who lived in an age without television or highly informative daily newspapers and who wanted to be constantly updated about the most important events. In order to learn about the doings of the powerful, they had to know how to conduct themselves smoothly in the presence of the elites who could inform them.

As for the nobility of the sword, it had to learn how to control its warrior pride as the state sponsored a conception of the elite based more on productivity and administrative service than on birth and military service. When a hereditary and military elite becomes more open, its culture must become more egalitarian. A new genre of courtesy books that appeared in the seventeenth century emphasized that boasting about one's birth or about the military exploits of one's ancestors was uncouth (see Chapter 3). In order to gain esteem, the warrior had to learn how to cover his ferocious spirit with a veneer of refinement. The salons served, among other things, as the dressing rooms in which members of very old noble families updated their appearance and received approbation from the rest of the elite even as they abandoned the code of behavior that had marked their superiority in times past.[87]

---

[86] Goodman, "Enlightenment Salons." I discuss the salons more fully in Chapter 3.

[87] The role of the salon in blending old and new elites is the principal theme of Lougee, *Le Paradis des femmes*.

5. *Sociability as the recovery of* logos. The ideal types delineated above suggest that sociability was able to fit very easily inside the boundaries of an absolutist system. We should recognize, however, that without being a form of overt political protest, sociability could represent moral dissatisfaction with certain aspects of the well-policed state. An essential part of the absolutist project was to propagate a moral code that concentrated the highest human potential exclusively in the state and construed the relation between ruler and ruled as one of domination and discipline.[88] As Delamare's *Traité de la police* suggests, the theory and practice of *police* entailed a glorification of the bureaucratic vocation and a denigration of human nature; that is to say, the human nature of those who did not belong to the administrative apparatus. As governmental administration became not only a more efficient instrument for achieving practical goals but an idealized repository of moral excellence and authority, it came into conflict with a classical and Renaissance tradition that ascribed to all men the faculty of ethical and political deliberation. As the state progressively stripped corporate bodies of their public functions, it threatened to reduce the concept of human nature to a set of passions to be disciplined, a set of needs to be administered, not a set of faculties to be exercised. In this context, it is particularly interesting to consider the attitude toward human speech in absolutist thought. "That we can command and understand commands is a benefit of speech, and truly the greatest. For without this there would be no society (*societas*) among men, no peace, and consequently no discipline (*disciplina*)," wrote Hobbes.[89] Speech fulfills its potential in the transmission of orders from above to below. Bossuet made the somewhat different but no less authoritarian point, that power manifests itself in uncontested language, when he quoted Ecclesiastes (8:4): "Where the word of a king is, there is power; and who may say to him, What doest thou?"[90] And when Delamare wrote that a good state "prohibits people from deliberating upon whether or not the laws are just,"[91] he was also making it clear that the general citizenry was unfit for rational discussion.

The absolutist conception of speech differed radically from Aristotelian anthropology, which placed more emphasis on the distinction between men and animals than between rulers and ruled. Paul Rahe writes:

[88] Gerhard Oestreich, *Neostoicism and the Early Modern State* (Cambridge, 1982).

[89] Thomas Hobbes, *De Homine* (London, 1658), 58–59. I have used the English translation, Thomas Hobbes, *Man and Citizen*, trans. Charles T. Wood (Gloucester, Mass., 1978). Oestreich argues that Hobbesian notions of discipline were central in the practice of absolutism on the Continent. See especially 265–69.

[90] Bossuet, *Politique tirée des propres paroles de l'Ecriture sainte*, 92.

[91] Delamare, *Traité*, 1:240. See also Marc Fumaroli, *L'Age de l'éloquence: Rhétorique et "res literaria" de la Renaissance au seuil de l'époque classique* (Geneva, 1980), 238: "Les affaires de l'Etat ne sont plus prétextes à débats publics."

In Aristotle's view, human beings are set apart from the other animals not by their capacity for self-expression but rather by their capacity for rational speech (*logos*). Man possesses more than mere voice (*phone*); he can do more than just intimate that he feels pleasure or pain. Thus, his humanity is in no way constituted by his ability to speak out, to get a load off his chest, to give vent to his spleen. . . . For Aristotle *logos* is something more refined than the capacity to make private feelings public: it enables the human being to perform as no other animal can; it makes it possible for him to perceive and make clear to others through reasoned discourse the difference between what is advantageous and what is harmful, between what is good and what is evil, and between what is just and what is unjust. It is the sharing of these things, Aristotle insists, which constitutes the household and the *polis* each as a community (*koinonia*).[92]

Although the traditional corporate structure of the regime always precluded the formation of a *polis* or general sphere of political communication, classical texts and values were preserved in the standard curriculum of the *collèges*. Cicero was the uncontested model of Latinity, and the Roman Republic the model of all the virtues. Students were expected to imitate the ancients in the arts of rhetoric and declamation, even though France was not a republic.[93] Corporate bodies provided a small-scale forum for reasoned debate among their members. "Each small corps was a kind of mini-Parliament," writes David D. Bien. The members of the corps "ran their own affairs and governed themselves."[94] The growth of absolutist *police*, however, tended to strip the corps of their administrative functions. In this context, sociability may be defined as a mode of action designed to sustain or recover *logos* in the face of shrinking opportunities to exercise the faculty of deliberation. This redemption of human nature could occur within the absolutist system only through the depoliticization of *logos* itself and the elaboration of forms of rational discussion and virtue that were not threatening to the state's official monopoly on political judgment. The cult of "the art of conversation" in the seventeenth and eighteenth centuries becomes intelligible as a response to

[92] Paul A. Rahe, *Republics Ancient and Modern: Classical Republicanism and the American Revolution* (Chapel Hill, 1992), 35. Previously published as "The Primacy of Politics in Classical Greece," *American Historical Review* 89 (1984):275.

[93] For discussion of the central place of Cicero and Rome in the *collèges* run by the Jesuits and other orders, see François Lebrun, Marc Venard, and Jean Quéniart, *Histoire générale de l'enseignement et de l'éducation en France* (Paris, 1981), 2:516–17. On the place of classical values in the teaching of the humanities, see Jean de Viguerie, *L'Institution des enfants, l'éducation en France 16e–18e siècles* (Paris, 1978), 159–94; L.W.B. Brockliss, *French Higher Education in the Seventeenth and Eighteenth Centuries: A Cultural History* (Oxford, 1987), 111–84; and Fumaroli, *L'Age de l'éloquence*, 30f.

[94] David D. Bien, "Offices, Corps, and a System of State Credit: The Uses of Privilege under the Ancien Régime," in *The Political Culture of the Old Regime*, ed. Keith Michael Baker, 108, 112. See also Fumaroli, *L'Age de l'éloquence*, 427–672, on rhetorical practices within the Parlements in the seventeenth century.

the challenge of constituting a *koinonia* in an absolutist regime. Sociability was *logos* privatized. It was reason and speech turned toward philosophical, aesthetic, and moral concerns that were unrelated to the direct exercise of sovereign authority. Sociability, then, may be defined as the effort to create a sphere of behavior in which humans can be human without becoming self-governing citizens.

These ideal types are schematic, as ideal types must be. They do not perhaps do full justice to the wealth of research that has already been done on voluntary practices under the absolute monarchy. But it seems that the ways in which the facts have been interpreted are less numerous than the actual possibilities. And it is useful to have some conceptual alternatives to the predominant view that the culture of sociability holds interest only as a preface to democracy. Having cleared the ground of a narrative that would have prejudiced our efforts to understand the intellectual history of sociability, we may now turn to this history.

2

THE LANGUAGE OF SOCIABILITY

> I have had new ideas; new words have had to be found or new
> meanings given to old ones.
> (Montesquieu, *The Spirit of the Laws*)[1]

> The partisans of the new philosophy, like the literate class of
> China, have a special idiom of their own. The same word does
> not have the same implication, the same literal or figurative
> sense, in short, the same meaning in the mouth of modern
> writers as in the language of the rest of humanity, or at least
> among those who have not been initiated into their
> enigmatic formulations.
> (Edict of the Parlement of Paris condemning the abbé Raynal's
> *Histoire philosophique* to be burned.)[2]

The Enlightenment as a Lexicon

THERE IS NO detailed study of the words *société*, *social*, and *sociabilité* in French thought. Perhaps we do not need one. After all, Dr. Johnson defined the lexicographer as a "drudge that busies himself in tracing the original, and detailing the signification of words."[3] This remark, however, occurs under the entry "lexicographer" in Johnson's own dictionary and suggests that he considered the study of words (including the word designating his own lexicographical pedantry) to have some utility. Though they did not generally share the English scholar's self-deprecating irony, many French philosophers did agree that semantics was of vital importance. "Nothing," wrote Holbach, "has thrown more uncertainty into ethics than the different meanings men have attached to the words they have not taken the trouble to define well."[4] According to Morellet:

[1] Charles-Louis de Secondat, baron de Montesquieu, *De l'Esprit des lois*, in *Oeuvres complètes*, ed. Roger Caillois (Paris, 1951), 2:227 (Preface to 1757 edition).

[2] "Arrêt de la Cour de Parlement," 25 May, 1781, printed in *Recueil de diverses pièces, servant de supplément à L'Histoire philosophique et politique des établissements et du commerce des européens dans les deux Indes par Guillaume-Thomas Raynal* (Geneva, 1783), 135.

[3] Samuel Johnson, *A Dictionary of the English Language* (London, 1755).

[4] Paul-Henri-Thiry, baron d'Holbach, *Système social ou principes naturels de la morale et de la politique avec un examen de l'influence du gouvernement sur les moeurs* (London, 1773), 1:88.

The greatest service that philosophers can render to reason is to determine the meaning of terms. I would practically say that this occupation is the whole of philosophy. The solution of the most important questions for men, the discovery of the truths which are the most useful, are often the happy results of a good definition of a word and of the work of a philosophical grammarian or grammatical philosopher.[5]

The *Encyclopédie* edited by Diderot and d'Alembert was an immense dictionary, a "systematic dictionary" (*dictionnaire raisonné*) as its full title indicates, designed to replace corrupt language with a new and enlightened lexicon.[6] By clarifying the meaning of old words and by adding recently coined ones of value, the *Encyclopédie*, Diderot hoped, would "change the common way of thinking."[7] Rousseau affirmed more cynically, "Every estate, every profession has its own lexicon for expressing its particular vices in decent terms."[8] But this too was an affirmation of the importance of semantics and a call to develop a new vocabulary.

The role of lexicographer, the role of philosopher, and the role of reformer thus went together. Enlightenment philosophers believed that words contained power and that they, as philosophers, had the greatest power to define words correctly. They had a keen sense that language intervened to shape human consciousness and that they could intervene to shape language. The conviction that progress stemmed from the amelioration of definitions found its support in a theory of knowledge that combined nominalism, or a belief that signs have arbitrary origins, with scientific optimism, or a belief in the possibility of purifying signs through a rigorous empirical study of both language and the world. In the *Essay Concerning Human Understanding*, John Locke delineated a nominalist position against the doctrine that languages contain traces of an original perfect language invented by Adam when God called upon him to name the elements of creation. According to Locke, Adam received no revelation that might have allowed him to anchor a system of signs in the essential nature of reality. In regard to language, Adam was an ordinary human being, and he only did what any human can still do: he applied a set of terms not to the very essence

---

[5] André Morellet, "Sur le Despotisme légal et contre M. de la Rivière," manuscript written in 1767, printed and edited for the first time by Eugenio di Rienzo in *Individualismo, Assolutismo, Democrazia*, ed. Vittorio Dini and Domenico Taranto (Naples, 1992), 329.

[6] The full title is *Encyclopédie, ou dictionnaire raisonné des sciences, des arts et des métiers, par une société de gens de lettres*. Several other works in the Enlightenment took the form of dictionaries. The most famous was Voltaire's *Dictionnaire philosophique* (first published 1764). Voltaire's work elicited a lexicographical response from the conservative Louis M Chaudon, the author of the *Dictionnaire anti-philosophique* (1767).

[7] Denis Diderot, "Encyclopédie," in *Encyclopédie, ou dictionnaire raisonné . . .* (Paris, 1765), 5:642a.

[8] Jean-Jacques Rousseau, "Fragments politiques," in *Oeuvres complètes* (Paris, 1964), 3:558.

of things but to his particular perceptions of them. "What liberty Adam had at first to make any complex ideas of mixed modes by no other pattern, but by his own thoughts, the same have all men ever since had. . . . The same liberty also, that Adam had of affixing any new name to an idea; that same has any one still."[9]

Locke rejected the possibility of there being a perfectly natural language whose structure would correspond exactly to the structure of the world. He often described words as "knots" that tied bundles of perceptions together into an idea. In this way, he drew attention, as Hans Aarsleff says, "both to the arbitrariness of the idea and to the active role performed by the word in preserving the idea as well as in fostering the opinion that it is not arbitrary, on the mistaken assumption that there is some sort of real—and hence not arbitrary—connection between word and object."[10] For Locke, linguistic knots were conventions, created by "ignorant and illiterate people, who sorted and denominated things by those sensible qualities they found in them."[11] But even though Locke did not think that our words could ever represent anything other than our own conceptions of reality, he did believe in the possibility of ameliorating the "abuse of language"[12] through the procedures of experimentation (to make our conceptions of the world more accurate) and the procedures of linguistic analysis (to improve the system of signs by which these conceptions are expressed). In the final chapter of the *Essay*, he proposed a division of knowledge into three areas: science, ethics, and "thirdly, the ways and means whereby the knowledge of both the one and the other of these is attained and communicated." He called this last field of knowledge "semeiotica" and stated that its purpose was "to consider the nature of signs the mind makes use of for the understanding of things, or conveying its knowledge to others."[13]

After the translation of the *Essay* into French in 1700, attacks upon the "abuse of words" became a common theme in French intellectual life.[14] Observing that "language is the only root of our prejudices," Diderot crit-

---

[9] John Locke, *An Essay Concerning Human Understanding*, ed. Alexander Campbell Fraser (New York, 1959), 2:96.

[10] Hans Aarsleff, *From Locke to Saussure: Essays on the Study of Language and Intellectual History* (Minneapolis, 1982), 76, n. 37.

[11] Locke, *Essay*, 2:75; also cited in Aarsleff, *From Locke to Saussure*, 57. Consider, also, Francis Bacon, *The Advancement of Learning*, in *Works* (London, 1870), 3:396. "Let us consider the false appearances that are imposed upon us by words, which are framed and applied according to the conceit and capacities of the vulgar sort."

[12] Locke defined the rectification of the "abuse of language" as one of the main purposes of philosophy at the very outset of the *Essay*, in "The Epistle to the Reader," 1:14–15.

[13] Locke, *Essay*, 2:460–61.

[14] Concerning the theme of "the abuse of words," the following contributions are highly valuable: Ulrich Ricken, "Réflexions du XVIIIe siècle sur 'l'abus des mots,'" *Mots* 4 (1982): 29–45; and Rolf Reichardt, "Einleitung," *Handbuch politisch-sozialer Grundbegriffe in Frankreich, 1680–1820*, ed. Rolf Reichardt and Eberhard Schmitt (Munich, 1985), 1:2–12.

icized the abbé Girard's *Dictionary of Synonyms* for defining the word *bassesse* (baseness, inferiority) so as to suggest that all people of low birth lacked merit.

> A child, as soon as his memory takes in the word *bassesse*, receives a sign that will forever unleash in his understanding the idea of a lack of birth, of merit, of fortune, of rank, and [the presence] of disdain. Whether he is reading, writing, meditating, or conversing, he will never encounter the word *bassesse* without attaching to it this train of false notions.[15]

For Diderot, the level of birth of an individual and the value of an individual were two utterly separate categories that Girard's concept of inferiority tied into a pernicious knot. "He makes no distinction between imputed merit and inherent merit, and he never perceives that vice is the only thing to be despised and virtue the only thing to be praised."[16]

This kind of linguistic criticism was prevalent in eighteenth-century Europe on account of the influence of Locke's philosophy, but it was especially intense in France on account of the absolutist structure of the regime. As a corporate regime, France was divided into a variety of groups and regions that had different customs, including different linguistic practices. The process of creating a highly centralized political system, however, required that the symbols of the monarch's majesty as well as his commands (and those of his bureaucratic agents) be intelligible to all. It is no coincidence that the rise of absolutist government occurred at the same time as the movement to standardize the French language. The grammarian Louis-Augustin Alemand published a book in 1688 in which he attempted to resolve hundreds of ambiguities concerning the proper gender, spelling, and usage of words. In the Dedication of the book, Alemand drew attention to the importance of language as an instrument of rulership both at home and abroad: "With this beautiful and glorious language Louis le Grand gives laws not only to his empire but to all of Europe. . . . The French language has already established a sort of universal monarchy not only over all other languages but also over all other nations, where it serves to mark the places where our sovereigns shall one day make themselves heard and obeyed."[17]

Alemand also praised Richelieu for establishing the Académie Française and for making "our language one of the most important concerns of his ministry."[18] Richelieu had indeed been conscious of the importance of controlling language for the sake of consolidating the power of the state. In 1635 he incorporated the Académie Française and endowed it with the

---

[15] Diderot, "Bassesse," in *Encyclopédie*, 2:121.

[16] Ibid.

[17] Louis-Augustin Alemand, *Nouvelles observations, ou guerre civile des françois sur la langue* (Paris, 1688), Epistre.

[18] Ibid.

privilege of creating the official dictionary of the French language. In a memorandum submitted to Richelieu in 1634, Nicolas Faret, who became one of the original members of the Académie Française, defined the purpose of the new academy. The academicians were to serve as the arbiters of linguistic and literary taste. They were to confer upon the French language the beauty, universality, and permanence that characterized the Latin of Cicero. By contributing to the refinement of language, they were to contribute not only to the ornamentation but to the very foundation of the political edifice, for the state could not be secure without the perfecting of the language "which expresses its commands and which ought to publicize its glory."[19]

Because of this movement toward a state monopolization of the means of semantic production, French writers tended to be more defensive than English writers about the power to create linguistic knots and more vociferous about their own right to untie these knots and to form new ones. While Locke had been concerned about the prejudices embedded in language by "ignorant and illiterate" people, French philosophers were more concerned about the formation and maintenance of prejudices within the high culture controlled arbitrarily by the sovereign. Arguing that it was impossible to work for the state and to improve knowledge at the same time, Diderot directed Locke's epistemology against the absolutist mode of semantic production. As a body "salaried by the government," the Académie Française, he wrote in a letter to Etienne-Maurice Falconet in 1767, was a "slave" of the sovereign and could never improve the French language. According to Diderot:

> It is permitted only to a free, enlightened, and courageous man to say, "Everything in the understanding has entered through sensation; everything that escapes the understanding must thus find a sensible object to which it can be attached," and to apply this rule to all notions and words, treating as chimerical all those that cannot support this method.[20]

Diderot was not afraid to affirm these sentiments in public. Indeed, in the *Encyclopédie*, he made it plain that intellectual creativity could not occur under the auspices of the state.

> A monarch may, by a single word, cause a palace to rise up out of the grass; but a society of men of letters (*société de gens de lettres*) is not like a gang of laborers. An

---

[19] Faret's *Projet de l'Académie pour servir de préface à ses statuts* is cited and discussed by Roland Mousnier, in Mousnier, *L'Homme rouge ou la vie du Cardinal de Richelieu (1585–1642)* (Paris, 1992), 503. For further discussion of Richelieu's cultural policies and the role of the academies in supporting absolutism in the seventeenth century, see Roland Mousnier, ed., *Richelieu et la culture* (Paris, 1987), and Jean-Marie Apostolides, *Le roi machine: Spectacle et politique au temps de Louis XIV* (Paris, 1981).

[20] Diderot to Falconet, July, 1767, in *Oeuvres complètes* (Paris, 1875), 18:232.

encyclopedia cannot be ordered into existence. . . . Works ordered by sovereigns are never conceived in view of utility, but always in view of the dignity of the patron.[21]

Diderot was the paragon of the independent man of letters who believed that intellectual creativity should be freed from all institutionalized interests. In 1772, however, d'Alembert became the Permanent Secretary of the Académie Française, and several other contributors to the *Encyclopédie* joined its ranks in the last two decades of the Old Regime.[22] But whether they spoke as free-floating intellectuals or as the official lexicographers of a new enlightened absolutism, French writers chose their terms deliberately and coined new ones in abundance—for Locke's philosophy and the cultural policies of a centralizing government conspired to make it plain that power inhered in words.

Historical Semantics

If Enlightenment authors attributed special importance to the project of transforming vocabulary, then we must make a special effort to understand the words that they relished and that they tried to put into general circulation through their writings. Here is an especially good reason for applying the method of historical semantics. Historians of antiquity and the Middle Ages have traditionally found this method indispensable for explicating the conceptions of the world that lie buried in the coffins of defunct languages. Historians of the modern period, however, have not often applied semantics to the study of the foundational ideas of modern cultures, though they have often proclaimed its potential utility.

"A study of the connection between the history of language and history proper would certainly be revealing," Tocqueville observed.

> Thus if we were to follow the mutations in time and place of the English word "gentleman" (a derivative of our *gentilhomme*), we would find its connotation being steadily widened in England as the classes draw nearer to each other and intermingle. In each successive century we find it being applied to men a little lower in the social scale. Next, with the English, it crosses to America. And now in America it is applicable to all male citizens, indiscriminately. Thus its history is the history of democracy itself.[23]

[21] Diderot, "Encyclopédie," in *Encyclopédie*, 5:636. Dena Goodman has also informed me that Diderot read his letters to Falconet out loud in the salons.

[22] Robert Darnton has underscored the rapprochement between the Enlightenment and the academies in the last decades of the Old Regime. See Darnton, "The High Enlightenment and the Low-Life of Literature, in *The Literary Underground of the Old Regime* (Cambridge, 1982), 1–40. I have also discussed the significance of this rapprochement in Chapter 4.

[23] Alexis de Tocqueville, *The Old Regime and the French Revolution* (New York, 1955), 83.

Louis Althusser wrote:

> The realities of the class struggle are "represented" by "ideas" which are "represented" by words. In scientific and philosophical reasoning, the words (concepts, categories) are "instruments" of knowledge. But in political, ideological and philosophical struggle, the words are also weapons, explosives or tranquillizers and poisons. Occasionally, the whole class struggle may be summed up in the struggle for one word against another word. Certain words struggle amongst themselves as enemies. Other words are the site of an *ambiguity*: the stake in a decisive but undecided battle.[24]

Both Tocqueville and Althusser suggest that language reflects or sums up something that is not linguistic. For Tocqueville, a Liberal, this something is the inevitable march of democracy; for the Marxist Althusser, it is the economic conflict at the heart of every regime. Though they advocate the study of words, their conception of language as a phenomenon that reflects basic economic or political processes undermines the sense that it might be valuable to study the semantic dimension of culture. Convinced that they understood the general direction in which history was moving, both the Liberal and the Marxist believed that a close examination of words could reveal only what they already knew to be true of the historical process. For historical sociologists, semantics is a method of illustrating interpretations of history but not a method for discovering new interpretations, and so it is easy to see why they have rarely put the method into practice.[25]

It is less easy to understand why historians of ideas have sometimes advocated the method without practicing it. Arthur Lovejoy called for an inquiry into "philosophical semantics," which he defined in remarkably Lockean terms as

> a study of the sacred words and phrases of a period or movement, with a view to a clearing up of their ambiguities, a listing of their various shades of meaning, and an examination of the way in which confused associations of ideas arising from these ambiguities have influenced the development of doctrines.[26]

Yet Lovejoy never applied this method. Instead of following the thread of language over time, he preferred to focus on the history of concepts abstractly defined as "unit ideas." And in spite of the fact that intellectual historians often state, in their methodological pronouncements, that ideol-

---

[24] Louis Althusser, *Lenin and Philosophy and Other Essays* (London, 1971), 24.

[25] Perhaps this is also why Max Weber did not act on the basis of his own suggestion. "The term 'individualism' includes the most heterogeneous things imaginable," he wrote. "A thorough analysis of such an expression in historical terms would at the present time be highly valuable." Max Weber, *The Protestant Ethic and the Spirit of Capitalism* (New York, 1976), 222, n. 22.

[26] Arthur Lovejoy, *The Great Chain of Being: A Study of the History of an Idea* (New York, 1965), 8.

ogies are "languages," "language games," and "discourses," there is still little work in intellectual history that focuses on the development of the vocabulary accompanying modern visions of ethics and politics.[27]

Perhaps this neglect is due to the fact that many practitioners of modern intellectual history are more prone to discipleship than to historical analysis. Treating their favorite authors as geniuses who created their own conceptual space, they often believe that their function as scholars is to introduce the uninitiated to the insights of great thinkers. This approach tends to isolate particular authors from the rest of culture and to turn them into autonomous creators of truth as well as autonomous fields of scholarly inquiry. The method of historical semantics, however, precisely because it is not especially concerned with establishing the unique philosophical genius of particular authors, tends to open up fields of meaning instead of insulating them. For historical semantics gives primacy not to particular texts as repositories of insight but to the intertextual semantic field—the terms that appear again and again in a large corpus of writings and allow the historian to see that a specific way of construing reality is widespread among intellectuals in a given period.

Strictly speaking, this approach is not incompatible with the effort to appreciate the ideas of original authors. It underscores the originality of authors, however, not by isolating them but by considering them in relation to the field of meanings that other authors deploy. If we think of all authors as having no choice but to begin working with a set of given terms, then their creativity will most likely reside in the manner in which they play with the inflections of particular words so as to create novel utterances. Authors may also create new words in order to anchor one meaning of a multivalent term in a unique signifier. The neologism will then give the meaning a less ambiguous form of expression, and the circulation of the neologism will give the meaning a more distinct and emphatic presence in the language as a whole.[28] By focusing on the invention of new words and the changing meanings of old ones, one might be able to tangibly discuss both the originality and the influence of great thinkers.

---

[27] The most important exceptions are two collective projects that have been undertaken in Germany: Otto Brunner, Werner Conze, and Reinhart Koselleck, eds., *Geschichtliche Grundbegriffe. Historisches Lexicon zur Politische-sozialen Sprache in Deutschland* (5 vols. to date; Stuttgart, 1972–); and Rolf Reichardt and Eberhard Schmitt, eds., *Handbuch politisch-sozialer Grundbegriffe in Frankreich, 1680–1820* (10 vols. to date; Munich, 1985–). For a favorable review of these two projects and a critique of some practitioners of intellectual history who do not examine the history of words, see the following three articles by Melvin Richter: "Reconstructing the History of Political Languages: Pocock, Skinner, and the *Geschichtliche Grundbegriffe*," *History and Theory* 29 (1990):38–70; "*Begriffsgeschichte* and the History of Ideas," *Journal of the History of Ideas* 29 (1987):247–63; and "Conceptual History (*Begriffsgeschichte*) and Political Theory," *Political Theory* 14 (1986):604–37.

[28] On the historical significance of neologisms, see Georges Matoré, *La Méthode en lexicologie* (Paris, 1953), ch. 6.

Historical semantics is thus a useful method for approaching the Enlightenment because Enlightenment authors themselves viewed their role in semantic terms. It is also a useful method for approaching intellectual history in general because it provides a concrete way of referring both to intellectual innovation and to the common intellectual orientation of a large number of writers over a long timespan. The method has its limitations, to be sure, and that is why it is the organizing principle of this chapter alone.[29] But what better way to begin to trace the contours of "society" in Enlightenment thought than to focus on some of the key words denoting this imaginary field of interaction?

The Rise of "Society"

Before the late seventeenth century, the word *société* did not refer to a durable and large-scale community. Instead, it referred to small associations and to the convivial life that took place within them.[30] As late as 1694, when the first edition of the *Dictionnaire de l'Académie Française* appeared, it was possible to define *société* without evoking in any way the concept of a general field of human existence. The dictionary defines *société* as "Frequentation, commerce that men naturally like to have with each other." Here *société* appears to be more of an activity than a space; a pastime among friends rather than a network of permanent relationships among a large mass of people. A somewhat more spatial view of *société* is suggested by a second definition that appears in the dictionary of the Académie: "A company of people who assemble regularly for pleasurable parties." But here the group is small and is based on an ephemeral tie rather than a continuous bond. The dictionary also indicates that *société* can mean a contractual partnership among merchants.[31] None of these definitions points to *société* as the enduring community to which all the members of a territory belong.

Although *société* continued to denote pleasurable or select company in the eighteenth century, it also took on a distinctively new meaning as the gen-

---

[29] Quentin Skinner has pointed out some of the limitations of historical semantics; see James Tully, ed., *Meaning and Context: Quentin Skinner and His Critics* (Oxford, 1988), 55, 120–21.

[30] Walther von Wartburg's *Französisches Etymologisches Wörterbuch* (Bonn, 1922) indicates that in the late Middle Ages *société* meant communication, union, alliance, or partnership. The earliest French dictionaries similarly define *société* as partnership for a common purpose, as in a business association or religious order. They also define *société* as polite company or polite conversation. See Robert Estienne, *Dictionnaire français-latin* (Paris, 1539); P. de Brosses, *Grand dictionnaire français-latin* (Lyon, 1625); Philibert Monet, *Inventaire des deux langues française et latine* (Lyon, 1636); Randle Cotgrave, *Dictionarie of the French and English Tongues* (London, 1611).

[31] *Dictionnaire de l'Académie française* (Paris, 1694), "société." In citing dictionaries, I shall give the word defined but not the volume and page numbers.

eral field of human existence.[32] This modern meaning of *société* appeared for the first time in some dictionaries in the very late seventeenth century. In 1690, Antoine Furetière defined *société* as the field of human interdependence: "Assembly of many men in one place for the mutual satisfaction of their needs. . . . Men have entered *société* in order to live more conveniently and politely; they have made severe laws against those who trouble *société civile*."[33] Once *société* had been defined as a large-scale and basic unit of human organization, a cluster of related terms took on new significance or appeared for the first time. The word *sociabilité*, meaning the tendency of humans to embrace "society" as the essential framework of their lives, was coined in the early eighteenth century and began to appear in dictionaries in the third quarter of the century.[34] The adjective *sociable* had long been used to designate individuals who were polite and pleasant in company. But after the enlargement of *société* described above, the word *sociable* took on a second, more abstract meaning: it became a generic attribute of humankind. Furetière defined *sociable* by saying, "Man is the only naturally *sociable* animal, able to establish a bond or friendship with another for mutual support." The *Dictionnaire de Trevoux* (1704 edition) gave the following sentence as an example of the correct usage of the word *sociable*. "Man is born to be *sociable* to such an extent that this quality is just as much attached to his essence as reason is."[35]

The word *social* was used very rarely in the seventeenth century and does not appear in any seventeenth-century dictionary except for Monet's *Inventaire des deux langues* of 1636. Here it is defined simply as "in *société*, belonging to *société*."[36] In the eighteenth century, *social* was used more often. Though essentially synonymous with *sociable*, *social* was more frequently paired with actions and virtues whereas *sociable* was generally a modifier for people and their dispositions. The *Encyclopédie* of Diderot and d'Alembert defined *social* as "a word recently introduced in language to designate the qualities that make men useful in *société* or fitting for the commerce of men." As an example of its usage, the *Encyclopédie* simply gave the phrase *vertus sociales* (social virtues).[37] The *Dictionnaire de Trevoux* entered the word *social*

---

[32] Keith Michael Baker has also discussed the emergence of "society" as a symbol of the basic context of human life in a forthcoming article; see Baker, "Enlightenment and the Institution of Society: Notes for a Conceptual History," in W.F.B. Melching and W.R.E. Velema, eds., *Main Trends in Cultural History* (Amsterdam and Atlanta, forthcoming 1994).

[33] Antoine Furetière, *Dictionnaire universel* (The Hague, 1690), "société."

[34] The *Encyclopédie* of Diderot and d'Alembert (vol. 15, 1765) and the 1771 edition of the Jesuits' *Dictionnaire de Trevoux* were the first dictionaries to register the word "sociabilité." As I relate below, the word was coined in natural-law theory.

[35] Furetière, *Dictionnaire universel*, "sociable"; and *Dictionnaire de Trevoux* (1704 edition), "sociable."

[36] Monet, *Inventaire des deux langues*, "social."

[37] *Encyclopédie*, "social," 15:251. This volume was published in 1765.

for the first time in its edition of 1771. The definition reads, "A new term used to express that which relates to *société*. . . . Thus one designates as *vertus sociales* or *qualités sociales* those which make a man fit for *société* and the commerce of other men. Sweetness of character, openness without rudeness, obligingness without flattery, humanity, generosity, etc., are the *vertus sociales*."[38] In his *Dictionnaire critique de la langue française* (1788), Féraud also gave *vertus sociales* as an example of correct usage and noted, "The usage of this word . . . is almost limited to this phrase."[39]

Over the course of the eighteenth century a semantic field thus emerged in which *société* stood for the framework of human existence, *sociabilité* designated the desire of humans to participate in *société*, and *sociable* and *social* referred to the personal qualities and virtuous actions that sustained *société*. For gaining a statistical overview of the usage of the field, an invaluable source is the ARTFL database, from which one can obtain concordances for hundreds of works in literature, philosophy, and the human sciences.[40] ARTFL contains 334 texts by 93 authors for the years 1600–1699 and 488 texts by 156 authors for the years 1700–1800. In the first table, taken by centuries, the corpus provides the number of occurrences of the words in the semantic field.[41]

Word	1600–1700	1701–1800
société	620	7168
social	8	838
sociabilité	0	66
sociable	16	222

A picture of the entire semantic field by decades demonstrates a linguistic surge in the middle of the eighteenth century, the period normally associated with the beginning of the Enlightenment as an aggressive critical

---

[38] *Dictionnaire de Trevoux* (Paris, 1771), "social."

[39] Jean-François Féraud, *Dictionnaire critique de la langue française* (Marseille, 1787), "social." See also Ferdinand Brunot, *Histoire de la langue française des origines à 1900* (Paris, 1930), 6:101–5.

[40] The corpus and a word-search program are administered by the Project for American Research on the Treasury of the French Language (ARTFL), a joint project of the University of Chicago and the French Centre National de la Recherche Scientifique. The database is not, in any statistical sense, a representative sample of the whole of French literature and philosophy. Strictly speaking, statistical information obtained from the database applies only to the database itself; but on account of the great size of the corpus, the information is suggestive of general lexical trends in literary and philosophical writing.

[41] I would like to thank Mark Olsen, Assistant Director of ARTFL, for helping me obtain the information for the two tables. I have included in my search the masculine, feminine, and plural forms of all words when they exist as well as the variant spellings and use of accents (e.g., *societé*) that occurred in the seventeenth and eighteenth centuries.

movement. In addition to showing the number of times the words occur, the second table shows the frequency of the words in relation to the entire number of words in the corpus for each decade. The period 1600–1610, for example, sees 40 occurrences of all the words in the semantic field resulting in .0223 occurrences per thousand words in this decade.

Date	Occurrences	Per 1000	Date	Occurrences	Per 1000
1600–1610	40	.0189	1701–1710	74	.0880
1611–1620	27	.0385	1711–1720	87	.0750
1621–1630	12	.0043	1721–1730	105	.1156
1631–1640	13	.0156	1731–1740	553	.1246
1641–1650	12	.0126	1741–1750	357	.1735
1651–1660	93	.0527	1751–1760	1102	.2450
1661–1670	16	.0297	1761–1770	1746	.3728
1671–1680	136	.0669	1771–1780	1811	.4528
1681–1690	197	.1164	1781–1790	1047	.2445
1691–1700	98	.0530	1791–1800	1396	.6265

The numbers highlight the growing usage of the semantic field over the course of two centuries. But there are limits to what statistical series can reveal about the history of thought. It is intriguing to know that writers were increasingly talking about *société*, but such knowledge is not an end in itself. The utterance of a word has significance only in relation to the images or arguments that it helps to evoke. For the understanding of intellectual change, what truly counts is not the frequency with which the semantic field was deployed but the range of its *possible* deployment—the assortment of meanings and assumptions that were associated with the words and how these meanings and assumptions changed over time.

The Concept of Latent Sociability in Natural Law

In *Leviathan*, Hobbes wrote:

> It is true that certain living creatures, as bees and ants, live sociably one with another . . . and yet have no other direction than their particular judgements and appetites . . . and therefore some man may perhaps desire to know, why mankind cannot do the same. To which I answer . . . [42]

The answer Hobbes gave was an exposition in miniature of his entire philosophy of human nature, a treatise on the competitive fever of human beings and their natural unsuitability for collective living. Unlike the insects, hu-

---

[42] Thomas Hobbes, *Leviathan* (Harmondsworth, 1968), pt. 2, ch. 17, 225 (my emphasis).

mans are not content with obtaining their physical well-being. Each takes pleasure in "comparing himself with other men," and so "can relish nothing but what is eminent," or what sets each one above another. Human beings are constantly in search of "honour and dignity," a pursuit that generates "envy and hatred, and finally war." The wish to be superior to others is at odds with collective stability, and this opposition between human nature and peace is not helped but actually compounded by humankind's unique gifts, the gifts of reason and speech. Other animals, lacking reason, do not reflect on their mode of organization or try to change it, "whereas amongst men, there are very many, that think themselves wiser, and abler to govern the public, better than the rest; and these strive to reform and innovate, one this way, another that way, and thereby bring it into destruction and civil war." As for speech, since other animals lack sophisticated language, they do not argue about what is good or evil. But humans know the use of rhetoric. They can represent good as evil and evil as good, and through this verbal art, they unsettle their fellows and incite conflict.[43]

From these aspects of the human condition Hobbes deduced the necessity of reducing men's wills to the will of a single power. The unity that cannot be achieved through the spontaneous interaction of a multitude is achieved by totally relinquishing the rights of nature to a single person. Since humankind is not sociable, order can exist through the sovereign alone.

> This is the generation of that great LEVIATHAN. . . . For by this authority, given him by every particular man in the commonwealth, he hath the use of so much power and strength conferred on him, that by the terror thereof, he is enabled to form the wills of them all, to peace at home and mutual aid against their enemies abroad.[44]

With these arguments, Hobbes brought the issue of sociability into the heart of modern natural law.[45] Associated with the works of Grotius, Cumberland, Hobbes, Pufendorf, Thomasius, and others, modern natural law attempted to discover the basis of authority and obligation by examining the relations between three things: (1) the objective "needs" and "interests" of all human beings; (2) the subjective inclinations or "passions" of all human beings; and (3) the dynamics of human interaction as it unfolds or would unfold without the intervention of law and government. This mode of political thought was secular; it did not rely upon sacred Scripture. It was

---

[43] Ibid., 225–27.

[44] Ibid., 228.

[45] My understanding of the natural-law tradition is informed above all by the following works: Otto Gierke, *Natural Law and the Theory of Society* (Boston, 1957); Richard Tuck, *Natural Rights Theories, Their Origin and Development* (Cambridge, 1979); and Robert Derathé, *Jean-Jacques Rousseau et la science politique de son temps* (Paris, 1950).

also ahistorical; it did not draw on the histories of specific cultures and constitutions for its primary data. Instead, it focused on the generic qualities of the human species. In particular, it sought to establish that every individual has certain objective interests, notably the desire for peace and self-preservation, and it sought to determine the degree to which the passions and actions of individuals living in proximity to each other naturally combined to bring about the satisfaction of these essential interests. Government, as imagined in modern natural law, was a product of the gap between objective human needs, on the one hand, and spontaneous human interaction, on the other. The state became necessary when the passions and actions of people living in a group did not lead to the fulfillment of basic human interests. The kind of state that a particular thinker imagined to be necessary depended on the manner in which this gap was construed. For a thinker like Hobbes, the gap was so wide that only an absolutist state could make interaction compatible with the satisfaction of the most elementary human interests.

The arguments of Hobbes about humans' lack of a sociable disposition stimulated other discussions throughout Europe about the natural suitability of human nature for collective living. It was in the context of these discussions that the language of sociability first gained currency in France. Paradoxical as it may seem, absolutist writers were the first to deploy this language in France and to insist that sociability was an inherent property of the human species. Three writings from the late seventeenth and early eighteenth centuries can serve as examples.

The first is Bossuet's *Politique tirée des propres paroles de l'Ecriture Sainte* (Politics Derived from the Words of Holy Scripture).[46] The work begins on a remarkably un-Hobbesian note. The title for Book I, Article I, reads, "Man is made to live in *société*." Bossuet states that there are natural ties among human beings that give them strong grounds for loving each other. Humans incline toward collective living because they have three things in common: they are all children of God; they are all blood relatives as descendants of Adam; and they are all united by the ties of economic need.[47]

Yet Article II turns this all around with the assertion, "Human *société* has been destroyed and violated by the passions. . . . God was the bond of human *société*. The first man separated himself from God, and as just punishment discord was put in his family, and Cain killed his brother Abel."

---

[46] Bossuet was the tutor to the son of Louis XIV, the heir to the throne. He wrote this work for the benefit of his royal pupil. It was published posthumously in 1709.

[47] Jacques-Bénigne Bossuet, *Politique tirée des propres paroles de l'Ecriture Sainte* (Geneva, 1967), 5, 6, 9. When translating French quotations, I have left the words *sociable, social, société*, and *sociabilité* in French. These words are italicized throughout to indicate that they are French. The italics serve not only to highlight the semantic field but also to distinguish *sociable* and *social* from their identical English cognates.

Human nature is so corrupted by original sin that in spite of the bonds that God and nature have provided to unite men, they are now unfit for society. "It is easy to understand that this perversity renders men *insociable*. Man, dominated by his passions, only thinks of satisfying them without thinking of others."[48] Of all the creatures, a human being is the most brutal and bloodthirsty. Hence this paradox: as creations of God, humans are inherently sociable; but as creations of their own will, they have become unfit for society. "Thus human *société*, established by so many sacred bonds, is violated by the passions; and as Saint Augustine said, 'There is nothing more *sociable* than man by nature, nor nothing more incorrigible or more *insociable* by corruption.'"[49]

Article III establishes that government is necessary as "a brake on the passions." A ruler is required to overcome the confusion stemming from each person's pursuit of personal desires. Bossuet does not explain the origins of government, the mechanism by which it emerged out of the chaos of humankind's unsociable passions. He does not suggest that a contract took place. Most of the book, in fact, departs from the natural-law framework established in the opening articles of the book and rests on the assumption that the French monarchy was simply instituted by God. Yet, even though he does not explain where government originated, Bossuet's description of human nature as simultaneously sociable and unsociable does explain why government is a necessary institution. The ruler exists to complete humankind's impulses, which tend toward peace in their ideal disposition but create discord in actual practice. According to Bossuet, government forces people to do what their better nature intends them to do, and government by one person is best because "never are we more united than when under a single chief."[50]

The second work is the *Essai philosophique sur le gouvernement civil* (Philosophical Essay on Civil Government), by the Chevalier de Ramsay.[51] The third chapter of this work is entitled, "Man Is Born *Sociable*." For Ramsay,

[48] Ibid., 11–12.

[49] Ibid., 13. The quotation from Saint Augustine comes from *The City of God* (bk. 12, ch. 28): "Nihil enim est quam hoc genus tam discordiosum uitio, tam sociale natura." See Augustine, *De Civitate Dei*, ed. J.E.C. Welldon (London, 1924), 2:4.

[50] Ibid., 54.

[51] André-Michel, Chevalier de Ramsay, *Essai philosophique sur le gouvernement civil . . . selon les principes de feu M. François de Salignac de la Mothe-Fénelon*, in *Oeuvres de Fénelon* (Paris, 1843), vol. 3. The text was based on conversations that Ramsay had with Fénelon. As Jeanne-Lydie Goré says, the text is "more a 'philosophical' interpretation of Fénelon's thought than a reliable account of it." Goré also notes that Ramsay's thought was more absolutist than Fénelon's. See her *L'Itinéraire de Fénelon: Humanisme et spiritualité* (Grenoble, 1957), 675 and 677, n. 5. Andrew Michael Ramsay was born in Scotland in 1686. A Jacobite and Catholic convert, he spent most of his adult life in Paris. He was the friend and biographer of Fénelon. On Ramsay's life, see G. D. Henderson, *Chevalier Ramsay* (London, 1951).

sociable refers to the capacity of every person to engage in "a mutual commerce of friendship" with any other member of the human species. This capacity for reciprocity springs from the fact that everyone ought to be able to see that all humans resemble each other and need each other. Human fellowship has three universal foundations. The first is that we are all intelligent creatures who can recognize what is right and wrong. The second is that humans need to cooperate with each other for the sake of subsistence. The third is that the continuance of the species depends on procreation. Ramsay summarizes his position: "Men are thus born *sociable* by the common and immutable law of their intelligent nature, by bodily indigence, and by the order of reproduction."[52]

The tone of the argument changes, however, as Ramsay, rather like Bossuet, argues that "being sociable" is an ideal aspiration but not a powerful instinct in human psychology. If all persons followed the laws that flow from their nature as sociable beings, says Ramsay, no political authority would be necessary. But "such is the sad state of humanity" that very few can distinguish natural law from their own selfishness. They are guided by their passions rather than by their consciousness of their universal likeness and interdependence, so they must not be free to judge public affairs. A supreme power is needed to terminate the contests generated by the passions. Government must be absolute, and such power is best achieved by attaching sovereignty to the will of a single person.[53]

The third absolutist author is the police official encountered in the previous chapter, Nicolas Delamare. Although Delamare deployed extensive historical arguments in favor of the absolute power of Louis XIV, he also sketched a brief natural-law defense of absolutism at the outset of his *Traité de la police*. Here he declares that mankind is "destined to live in *société* with his fellows."[54] Drawing on Seneca to support his view, he paraphrases the ancient Stoic's *De Beneficia* (Book IV, Chapter 18):

> What would be the condition of the human species if each lived alone? So many men, just so many prey and victims ready for the other animals; so much blood so easily taken; in a word, weakness itself. Other animals have the necessary strength to defend themselves. All those that are wanderers and whose fierceness does not allow them to live in herds are born with weapons, so to speak; while man is endowed with weakness in every way, having neither claws nor teeth to make himself formidable. Nature, to compensate him, has given him two things, which, from an otherwise weak and miserable creature form a very

---

[52] Ibid., 357.
[53] Ibid., 358–59, 384.
[54] Nicolas Delamare, *Traité de la police*, 2d ed. (Amsterdam, 1729), 1:6. The first volume, from which all the following quotations are taken, was first published in Paris in 1705. The text is the same in the edition quoted here.

strong and powerful one. I mean reason and *sociabilité*[55] so that he who alone could not resist anything, becomes through this union the master of all. *Sociabilité* gives him an empire over all the animals, even those of the sea, which are born and live in another element. It is also *sociabilité* that helps against the onslaught of sickness, that furnishes help to old age, which softens our pains, that gives us the chance to ask assistance from others against the accidents of fortune, and that inspires us with courage to bear them. Remove *sociabilité* and you will destroy at the same time the union of humankind on which depend the conservation and happiness of life.[56]

From the sociable nature of man, Delamare goes on to deduce a set of universal laws of human conduct. These laws include the imperative to forbear from hurting others physically, to respect their property, not to inflict an injury that we would not wish to suffer ourselves, and to compensate others for any harm we may do. Delamare calls these "the natural laws of *sociabilité*," but like Bossuet and Ramsay, he does not consider sociability to be a psychological faculty or an operating principle of human action. The laws of sociability are guides for making laws to police human action; they are not powerful motives in human nature.[57] Delamare states that a small measure of sociability does reside in the human spirit. This modicum of sociability leads people to search for "an easy and tranquil life" by living cooperatively with their fellows. "But self-love, the other passions, and error soon throw up trouble and division." Government then becomes the only possible source of stability in a world dominated by the passions, and order becomes impossible "without an exact observation of the laws of police."[58]

Taken together, the three texts make it plain that theories of absolutism rested upon a definition of human passions as unsociable. Yet the theories also contain the idea that humans are indeed sociable in that they possess a potential for fellowship, a potential, however, that does not inform human action. The arguments appear unnecessarily convoluted. Why assert the

[55] Delamare uses *sociabilité* to translate Seneca's *societas*. This appears to be the first instance of the word *sociabilité* in French. Of course, one can never be certain when any word was first coined. As long as some texts remain unread, it is a theoretical possibility that the word can be found in them. Delamare's usage, however, is the earliest in the body of texts I have consulted, and it predates by about fifty years the earliest *verifiable* examples of usage given in recent etymological dictionaries of the French language. Some of these dictionaries attribute the word to Jean Chapelain's *Lettres* (1665), though without giving a quotation or page reference. I have not been able to locate the word in the text, and two works devoted to Chapelain's vocabulary do not mention it: A. Fabre, *Lexique de la langue de Chapelain* (Paris, 1889); Alfred C. Hunter, *Lexique de la langue de Jean Chapelain* (Geneva, 1967). I believe that the Chapelain reference entered into an early etymological dictionary by mistake and that the error was mechanically copied by subsequent compilers.

[56] Ibid., 6.

[57] Ibid., 6–8.

[58] Ibid., 4.

existence of human sociability only to deny that sociability has any influence over human action?

The answer is that the concept of a latent sociability in human nature had a strategic value for authors who wished to demonstrate the utility of royal sovereignty as a curb on the passions without resorting to the Hobbesian position that the state is based on a contract. In explaining how humans deliberately opted for a sovereign power to protect themselves from each other, contract theory rooted the legitimacy of the state in the rational choice of the subjects. Contract theory thus allowed rulers to claim that their authority was based on the approval of the subjects. Contract theory, however, was also potentially threatening to absolutism because it imputed a measure of intelligence to the subjects, who were at least credited with the wisdom that is required to erect a sovereign power as a solution to their own problems. In this way, contract theory added stature to the subjectivity of the populace, even though it portrayed government as a cure for human subjectivity. A contract also implies a set of conditions—the terms of the contract—with which one can judge the legitimacy of government at any time. These conditions can become the grounds for disobedience. In the Hobbesian system, the people transfer their rights to a repressive power because they see that this power is the only thing that can ensure their preservation. As Hobbes himself recognized, however, the logical implication of this system was that individuals could resist the sovereign if the sovereign directly threatened their preservation, though they could not resist for any other reason.[59] This possibility of resistance within a generally authoritarian system reveals the subversive potential of the concept of a state based on the agreement of its subjects—a potential that Rousseau would capitalize upon. In the seventeenth century, French defenders of absolutism could already see the dangerous potential of the idea of a monarchy based on contract in the works of sixteenth-century Protestant critics of absolutism, such as Philippe Duplessis-Mornay, the author of the *Vindiciae Contra Tyrannos* (A Defense Against Tyrants, 1579).[60]

Authors such as Bossuet, Ramsay, and Delamare were eager to demolish every possible foundation of resistance to monarchical authority.[61] This goal, however, presented a quandary. On the one hand, they could not

[59] On Hobbes's concept of resistance, see Tuck, *Natural Rights Theories*, 124–32.

[60] See Julian H. Franklin, ed., *Constitutionalism and Resistance in the Sixteenth Century: Three Treatises By Hotman, Beza, and Mornay* (New York, 1969), 142–99 (for the translation of the *Vindiciae*).

[61] For Bossuet's ideas on the absolute obedience owed to the sovereign, see *Politique tirée*, 92–104. Ramsay (*Essai philosophique*, 366–67) wrote that no one ever has the right to pronounce the government in error. Delamare (*Traité*, 1:240) wrote, "The best and most useful of all laws is that which prohibits one from considering if the laws are just or not, and which commands that they obtain the same obedience as if they had been established by God himself."

suggest that the citizens contractually set up the association in which they lived, because this might imply the possibility of contractual limitations on the sovereign. On the other hand, they could not suggest that humans had no inclination to see an association established, for then no state could have legitimacy in the sense of a positive relation to the desires of its subjects. The value of the argument about humans' innate but corrupted sociability was that it posited a universal desire for peaceful living while demonstrating how the perversity of the passions thwarted *this same desire*. The argument of Bossuet, Ramsay, and Delamare, in short, was the Augustinian one that people wanted order, but on account of their passions, they could not will it. With this argument the stage was set for the state to appear as a necessary check on the passions and the only means of instituting *société*. Since *sociabilité* was presumed to be embedded in the better part of human nature, government did not require the explicit approval of its subjects. The state's legitimacy rested not on the will of the subjects but on their "need" for peace and fellowship, a need that inhered in all human beings whether they appreciated it at a given moment or not.

The Amalgamation of Natural Law and Politeness

It is ironic that French authors first declared humans to be sociable beings in order to argue that sociability is merely a latent feature of humankind and not sufficient to constitute an orderly existence. If the strategic value of this approach was that it allowed absolutist authors to make quasi-Hobbesian arguments about the passions without becoming involved in the Hobbesian theory of contract, its strategic weakness was that it invited others to consider whether sociability—the capacity of humans to hang together without the intervention of sovereign authority—was in fact more than latent. The Enlightenment, in this context, may be viewed as the process through which sociability was defined not as a latent feature of human nature but as an active and operating principle of human life.

The philosophy of Samuel Pufendorf was important in this process. When Delamare quoted a portion of Seneca's *De Beneficia* on the subject of human interdependence, he was probably thinking of this German natural lawyer who, as Richard Tuck observes, was "the most famous political philosopher of his day."[62] In his *De Jure Naturae et Gentium* (The Law of Nature and Nations, 1672), Pufendorf had quoted the same portion of Seneca's work. He had also used the Latin term *socialitas* in discussing the human need for fellowship. It seems likely that Delamare, who cited Pufendorf frequently in other contexts, coined the term *sociabilité* in order to

---

[62] Tuck, *Natural Rights Theories*, 156.

provide a French equivalent for the Latin word. But even though Delamare appropriated Pufendorf's references and vocabulary, he integrated them into his own absolutist thought and ignored some of the basic postulates of the German theorist. For Pufendorf had fashioned his own concept of *socialitas* so as to refute Hobbes's argument that the state of nature was a state of war. He treated sociability as an operative force in human psychology and suggested the possibility that society was a self-sustaining entity.

Pufendorf became familiar to a broad audience in eighteenth-century France through Barbeyrac's French translation of Pufendorf's *De Jure Naturae et Gentium*. Barbeyrac's translation, which included extensive laudatory notes, ran through five editions between 1706 and 1734. The French words *sociable* and *sociabilité* abound as translations of *socialitas*, *socialis*, and *sociabilis*, and it is probable that Barbeyrac's edition of Pufendorf's book did more than any other text to inject the language of sociability into eighteenth-century French philosophy. The crucial section of Pufendorf's argument was Book II, Chapter II, "On the State of Nature." In this section Pufendorf modified Hobbes's conception of the state of nature by reasoning that there were in fact two states of nature. In the first or "pure state of nature," the individual was alone, naked and helpless. The second was "the state of nature considered in relation to others," that is, the condition of people living in proximity to each other but still enjoying their natural liberty because they had no common master or government. In this collective state of nature, were people enemies, as Hobbes claimed, or were they foes?

> A state of nature and a *sociable* life are not, properly speaking, two things opposed. For those same people who live in the state of nature can and must maintain together some relation.[63]

According to Pufendorf, people in the collective state of nature avoid conflict. The risk of violence is too great; the pleasure of killing one's enemy does not outweigh the danger of exposing one's own life. Humans see the utility of peace, and an accord arises prior to legal convention.[64] This argument already represents an extension of sociability beyond the limits established by Hobbes, Bossuet, Ramsay, and Delamare.

In Book II, Chapter III, entitled "On the Law of Nature in General," Pufendorf reiterated the concept of the collective state of nature and used it to derive natural law. In the pure state of nature, he argued, humans were

---

[63] Samuel Pufendorf, *Le Droit de la nature et des gens*, 5th ed., trans. Jean Barbeyrac (Amsterdam, 1734), 1:182.

[64] Ibid., 1:187–88. See also Istvan Hont, "The Language of Sociability and Commerce: Samuel Pufendorf and the Theoretical Foundations of the 'Four-Stages' Theory," in Anthony Pagden, ed., *The Languages of Political Theory in Early-Modern Europe* (Cambridge, 1987), 265–68.

dominated by selfish drives. They desired their own conservation above all else. In describing the collective state of nature, however, Pufendorf did not emphasize the competitive passions of humans, such as the wish for relative superiority that Hobbes had underscored. Instead, he emphasized their ability to appreciate how difficult it is to survive alone and how advantageous it is to be in a collective condition rather than in the pure state of nature. When they were alone, humans were so poor and helpless against the animals and the elements that they could hardly survive. When they were together, their desire for self-conservation and their awareness of their insufficiencies as individuals led them to act peacefully.

> Man, as we have seen above, being an animal that is very much in love with his own conservation, yet poor and indigent by himself, incapable of conserving himself without the help of his fellows . . . cannot subsist or enjoy the goods appropriate to his estate here below unless he is *sociable*, that is to say, unless he wishes to live in a sound union with his fellows and act with them in such a way that he gives them no reason to think he will do harm but rather that he is engaged in maintaining or advancing their interests. . . . It follows that everything that necessarily contributes to this *sociabilité* must be held to be prescribed by natural law; just as what troubles it must be deemed to be prohibited by the same law.[65]

As Pufendorf describes it, the movement toward society is not an instinct for companionship but a rational choice flowing from practical necessity. He makes it clear that sociability is not to be confused with an instinct for gregariousness.

> Our *sociabilité* is not that disposition which leads us to form private *sociétés*. . . . Instead it is the general disposition of a person toward every other, in consequence of which he views them as united together by the bonds of peace.[66]

Nor does sociability mean benevolence in the sense of an innate moral disposition to prefer the well-being of others over our own well-being. In setting out to refute Hobbes, Pufendorf kept to the Hobbesian premise that individuals pursue only their own interests. His goal was to show that considerations of self-interest will lead humans to establish stable social bonds even before government orders them to do so.

The political implications of Pufendorf's concept of sociability are not easy to discern in his treatise.[67] It is clear that in refuting Hobbes, his

---

65 Pufendorf, *Le Droit de la nature*, 1:222.

66 Ibid., 1:223.

67 Tuck states that Pufendorf developed "a genuinely muddled theory" of authority and obligation. See Tuck, *Natural Rights Theories*, 158. Leonard Krieger, in *The Politics of Discretion: Pufendorf and the Acceptance of Natural Law* (Chicago, 1965), 119–20, 143–46, 260–64, also noted the inconsistencies of Pufendorf's deductions from the principle of sociability.

purpose was not to glorify natural rights or to demonstrate that government is unnecessary. In somewhat inconsistent terms he claimed that the state of nature was too dangerous to continue on its own. He envisaged a contract leading to the establishment of a monarch who would be endowed with a high degree of unquestionable authority. The king would have a duty to obey natural law but would be accountable principally to God rather than to the inhabitants of his realm. Nevertheless, Pufendorf did deduce from the law of sociability some constitutional checks on the monarch and a few rights of resistance. In his notes to the French edition, Barbeyrac heightened the importance of Pufendorf's strictures on absolutism and tried to bring the text into alignment with the liberal political philosophy of Locke.[68]

In spite of Barbeyrac's efforts at popularization, Pufendorfian natural law had very few close imitators in the French Enlightenment. As a mode of argument, natural law was deductive and slow moving rather than literary and immediately engaging. Like the discipline of economics in our time, the maintenance of the natural-law idiom was largely the work of university professors and was most easily sustained in a university climate where students could be forced to devote an entire course to digesting a single dense treatise. Intensive discussion of Pufendorf became important in the university-based Enlightenment of Scotland, but it never took root in the salons and academies that formed the setting for the French Enlightenment.[69] Yet even though the French rarely engaged in natural law as a systematic mode of inquiry, they frequently invoked what they took to be the basic principles of Pufendorfian natural law and injected these principles into a variety of genres. They thus gave the language of sociability a life of its own, separate from the idiom in which it was invented. The language of sociability ceased to be the distinctive language of the rigorous discipline of natural jurisprudence and became a language applicable to all inquiries concerning human nature.

In the *Encyclopédie*, the article "*Sociabilité*" was written by Louis de Jaucourt, a polygraph who contributed several articles in diverse fields. Jaucourt defined sociability as a principle of natural law "engraved in the human heart." He characterized it as a disposition leading us to treat others well and to reconcile our desire for happiness with theirs. "From the principle of *sociabilité* flow all the laws of *société*," he states. The first of these laws is never to pursue self-interest when it will damage the common good. The second law is that the spirit of *sociabilité* should be universal because all humans have the same nature and are theoretically dependent on each other. The third

---

[68] Krieger, *The Politics of Discretion*, 263–64; Tuck, *Natural Rights Theories*, 175.

[69] On natural law in the Scottish Enlightenment, see Knud Haakonssen, *The Science of a Legislator: The Natural Jurisprudence of David Hume and Adam Smith* (Cambridge, 1981).

law of *sociabilité* is that all humans are equal because they have the same faculties and interests.

> We are obligated to regard each other as naturally equal. . . . On this is based the law of reciprocity as well as that rule which is so simple but of such universal usage, that we ought to be disposed toward others as we would like them to be disposed toward ourselves, and conduct ourselves toward them in the same way as we would like them to conduct themselves toward us in the same circumstances.[70]

Jaucourt thus drew upon the concept of sociability in order to secularize the Golden Rule.

In the entry for the word "*Société*" in the *Encyclopédie*, we are told that *sociabilité* is the foundation of collective order. Seneca's *De Beneficia* is cited once again: "Remove *sociabilité* and you will destroy the union of the human species on which the conservation and all the happiness of life depend."[71] This article reiterates that all humans are equal. It also states that all distinctions ought to be based only on the utilitarian considerations that led humans to form society in the first place. This is a far cry from the notion of the great chain of being that was traditionally used to justify the corporate regime. The idea of a natural hierarchy of human types is here replaced by the idea of the unity of all humans as social creatures. But instead of denying the legitimacy of estates and orders, the author affirms that a certain amount of subordination is necessary for the welfare of society. He advises those of superior status to bear in mind that others are their natural equals in the sense that all humans have the same needs and have joined society for the same reasons. On account of this community of interests, those of superior station ought to practice "compassion, generosity, and benevolence" toward others.[72] The idea of sociability thus appears in the *Encyclopédie* as a new way of conceptualizing the framework of human life, but the idea is limited to a personal ethical doctrine. *Société* is the sphere in which humans voluntarily practice this doctrine.

The notion of society as a voluntary sphere of ethical practice based upon the universal needs and interests of humankind was central in Holbach's treatise, *La Morale universelle* (The Universal Morality, 1776). This work is a kind of lexical apotheosis[73] and is worth discussing in some detail because of the ways in which it attempted to formulate moral discourse as a whole in the language of sociability. Holbach defined morality as "the knowledge of

---

[70] *Encyclopédie*, 15 (1765):251. De Jaucourt's initials can be found at the end of the article.

[71] *Encyclopédie*, 15 (1765):252. It is not clear who the author of this article was, but it appears to have been either Jaucourt again or Antoine-Gaspard Boucher d'Argis.

[72] Ibid., 15:253–54.

[73] The word *sociabilité* occurs 30 times, *social* 148 times, and *société* over 300 times in the work.

what must be done by intelligent and rational beings who wish to conserve themselves and live happily in *société*."[74] Ethics is thus rooted in society understood as the joint pursuit of well-being. Holbach stressed that the desire for self-preservation and happiness is universal. It is the "general point" that makes all humans alike in spite of other differences. All humans also possess "reason" or the capacity to determine a plan of conduct that will secure their happiness. Finally, Holbach affirms that all humans are *sociable* because the exercise of reason informs them that they can secure happiness only in cooperation with others.[75] Holbach's logic is close to Pufendorf's, for he never departs from the axiom that sociability is rooted in the individual's personal interests. Defining *intérêt* as that which one desires because one believes it to be necessary for one's own well-being, Holbach affirms that everyone acts, and can only act, on the basis of interest. "To act without interest would be to act without motive." The intelligent person understands, however, that one can advance one's own interests only by contributing to the happiness of others; for "others will contribute to his happiness only in view of the happiness they expect from him."[76]

In a large section of the treatise on *vertus sociales*, Holbach attempted to show that all of the key terms traditionally used to denote the basic moral virtues—terms such as "prudence" and "temperance"—are simply ways of expressing the primary concept of social virtue understood as the pursuit of self-interest within the framework of society.[77] He defined "prudence" as the habit of examining the various methods available for realizing a particular interest and choosing the one that does the least harm to society. "Temperance" is the habit of restraining the appetites that disrupt our well-being and the happiness of those upon whom we depend. "Humanity," he writes, is the "quintessential human virtue." It is "the affection that we owe to beings of our species as members of the universal *société*." Humanity, in short, is reciprocity. Holbach argues that the sentiment of humanity should be universal. "A truly great soul embraces the whole human race in its affection and desires to see all men happy." Holbach condemns those who refuse to recognize the principle of humanity—the patriotic zealots who

---

[74] Paul-Henri-Thiry, baron d'Holbach, *La Morale universelle, ou les devoirs de l'homme fondés sur la nature* (Amsterdam, 1776), 1:1.

[75] Ibid., 1:10, 12.

[76] Ibid., 1:23, 25.

[77] Victor Riquetti, marquis de Mirabeau, the economist and father of the famous revolutionary, had already affirmed that all the virtues derived from *sociabilité* in *L'Ami des hommes, ou traité de la population* (Avignon, 1756), 3:456. Voltaire had also stated that the only truly virtuous actions were "those which are useful to *société*." *Dictionnaire philosophique* (Paris, 1954; first published, 1764), 82. Holbach was thus systematizing a conception of virtue that was already in circulation in France.

engender "national antipathies" and the vain grandees who believe "that they are beings of a different species from others."[78]

The same section of the book that converts the names of the basic virtues into variants of sociability concludes with a subchapter entitled, *"De la douceur, de l'indulgence, de la tolérance, de la complaisance, de la politesse, ou des qualités agréables dans la vie sociale"* ("On gentleness, indulgence, tolerance, obligingness, politeness, or the agreeable qualities in social life"). Most of these terms had been important for over a century in the French courtesy literature on "the art of conversation." Not only *politesse* but also *douceur*, *indulgence*, *agréable*, and *complaisance* were words that denoted central ideals in etiquette manuals for the salon milieu.[79] Holbach's thought amalgamated the older language of politeness and the newer language of natural law. He defined *complaisance* as "a habitual disposition to conform to the just wills and reasonable tastes of the beings with whom we live." *Douceur* he defined as "a flexibility that is conducive to making us liked." He defined *politesse* broadly as "the sentiments and regards which beings united in *société* owe each other reciprocally."[80]

Holbach himself was a salon host and was famous for his refined manners and sparkling conversation.[81] The difference between his definitions of the virtues and those found in the older courtesy literature is that Holbach defined politeness and the other agreeable qualities as constitutive of "social life" or "society" as a general field of human interaction, whereas the courtesy literature had defined the same qualities as constitutive of a select company of refined individuals. The "universal morality" that Holbach described was nothing other than politeness writ large with the help of the language of natural law. It was against this amalgamation of natural law and politeness that Rousseau was protesting when he made remarks such as this:

> The savage lives within himself; the sociable man [*l'homme sociable*], always outside of himself, knows how to live only in the opinion of others, and it is so to speak, from their judgement alone that he draws the feeling of his own existence.[82]

Rousseau sought to construe politeness as something artificial, not natural. His critique of manners was premised on his anti-Hobbesian belief that

[78] Holbach, *Morale universelle*, 1:92–95, 117, 122.

[79] I discuss the etiquette manuals in Chapter 3.

[80] Holbach, *Morale universelle*, 1:145–48.

[81] See the accounts of Holbach in Dominique-Joseph Garat, *Mémoires historiques sur la vie de M. Suard* (Paris, 1820), 1:206, and André Morellet, *Mémoires sur le XVIIIe siècle et sur la Révolution* (Paris, 1988), 129–30. Alan Kors, *D'Holbach's Coterie: An Enlightenment in Paris* (Princeton, 1975), gives an account of the membership and activities of Holbach's salon.

[82] Jean-Jacques Rousseau, *Discours sur l'origine . . . de l'inégalité parmi les hommes*, in *Oeuvres complètes* (Paris, 1964), 3:193.

conflict characterizes only civil life, not the state of nature. The primitive or natural being has very few needs and no competitive passions, so coexistence is in no way problematic. No special acts of mutual accommodation are required. Rousseau's critique of politeness was also premised on his anti-Pufendorfian belief that personal autonomy is more important than personal security. Freedom is more important than peace.[83] In this philosophical framework, politeness is neither a necessity nor a virtue.

For Holbach, on the contrary, it is both. Much of his treatise, in fact, focused on the art of conversation, the classic topic of *la politesse mondaine*. Holbach's maxims on this subject echoed the conventional precepts of salon etiquette, though he tried to extend their field of application beyond the scope of the salons and into the whole sphere of human interdependence. "The great art of conversation consists in not wounding or humiliating anyone," Holbach wrote. "A truly *sociable* life" is based on creating good will toward oneself by being attentive to others. The essence of good conversation is inclusiveness and affability. Even if one is superior by birth to others, one must curb one's own desire to establish superiority within the gathering. "A high opinion of oneself constitutes pride and is displeasing, even when accompanied by merit, because it usurps the rights of *société*."[84] Holbach derided the obsession with formality (*l'orgueil de l'étiquette*) at the royal court. He rejected the idea that "good tone" lies in the maintenance of hierarchy within human interaction. "Good tone," he suggested, "is that which maintains *harmonie sociale*." No one is "less *sociable* and gay" than those "who arrogate for themselves the exclusive title of good company."

> These persons are courtiers by estate, enemies of each other, who cover their ulcerated souls beneath the externals of an affected politeness. They are nobles infatuated with their prerogatives, ever ready to make others feel the haughtiness of their pretensions.[85]

Holbach's concept of sociability was egalitarian. He stated that nobles with titles must strive "to forget and to make others forget" their superior degree of birth.[86] In advocating equality as a form of polite theater, however, he did not claim that legal privileges should be abolished. Holbach's concept of sociability hinged on a distinction between the legal structure of a regime and its ethical and convivial structure. The duty of the philosopher, he affirmed, is not "to propose to suppress the nobility but to put before its eyes its duties toward *société*."[87] According to Holbach, the leveling of ranks,

[83] See Derathé, *Jean-Jacques Rousseau*, 106–10.
[84] Holbach, *Morale universelle*, 1:264–65, 267–68.
[85] Ibid., 3:192–94.
[86] Ibid., 3:193.
[87] Ibid., 2:111.

which he calls "democratic equality" (*égalité démocratique*), is contrary to natural law, for it would lead to anarchy.[88] Rousseau, as Holbach understood him, had called for the abolition of all privileges in order to recapture the simplicity of primitive life. Exhorting his readers to reject the principles of Rousseau's *Discourse on the Origins of Inequality*, Holbach writes:

> Let us not listen to the maxims of a disgruntled and jealous philosopher who, under the pretext of revivifying justice, . . . would like to annihilate all ranks in order to bring into *sociétés civilisées* a chimerical equality that does not even exist among the most savage hordes.[89]

Sociability, it is clear, did not mean political equality. It did, however, mean equality in the domain that Holbach called "private life" (*la vie privée*).[90]

Holbach's discussion of sociability resembled the definitions of *sociabilité* and *société* in the *Encyclopédie*. The purpose of this language was to define a sphere of practice that was based on the egalitarian premises of natural law, yet was compatible with the hierarchical legal foundation of the French regime. By portraying politeness as the essence of *société*, Holbach defined the project of the Enlightenment to be the cultivation of a spirit of reciprocity within the boundaries of a regime that was officially based on a lack of reciprocity. *Société* was the domain in which individuals "forget" about the hierarchical distinctions and deferential norms stemming from corporate life and respect each other as equals in order to institute a mutually beneficial "private life."

Holbach's *Morale universelle* was typical in the use it made of the language of sociability. In several other works of moral philosophy in which the terms *société*, *sociabilité*, and *social* denoted key moral principles or idealized zones of conduct, the arguments consistently revolved around a definition of civil behavior as the practice of benevolence within the pursuit of happiness.[91] Diderot's *Principes de philosophie morale* is an important example. First pub-

---

[88] Ibid., 2:112. See also Holbach, *Système social*, 2:41.

[89] Ibid., 2:112. See also Holbach, *Système social*, 1:145.

[90] The entire last volume of the work is entitled "The Duties of Private Life" (*Les Devoirs de la Vie Privée*). I have not done a systematic study of the term *vie privée*, but I believe this term was still rare in the eighteenth century. I am not aware of any other philosophical treatise in which the term is used so prominently. In any case, the term "private life" helped Holbach to suggest that the norms that should govern sociable exchange are not the same norms that should shape the legal and political sphere.

[91] Some titles (apart from the works I discuss in some detail below) are Jean d'Alembert, "Elémens de philosophie," in *Oeuvres et correspondances inédites*, ed. Charles Henry (Paris, 1887); Charles Pineau Duclos, *Considérations sur les moeurs* (Paris, 1751); François Adrien Pluquet, *De la Sociabilité* (Paris, 1767); Claude-François-Nicolas Le Maître de Claville, *Traité du vrai mérite* (Paris, 1736); Anonymous, *L'Homme sociable et lettres philosophiques sur la jeunesse* (London and Paris, 1772).

lished in 1745, this text injected the word *social*, and particularly the phrase *vertu sociale*, into the French Enlightenment.[92] The work is a translation of Shaftesbury's *Inquiry Concerning Merit and Virtue*, but Diderot modified the text by adding lines and notes to the original and by absorbing Shaftesbury's vocabulary into his own semantic structures.[93] As part of his argument that humans possessed an innate moral faculty, Shaftesbury had called benevolent inclinations the "natural affections." These he opposed to selfish inclinations or what he called the "self affections."[94] Apparently believing that these terms made self-interest appear unnatural, Diderot ignored the opposition implied in Shaftesbury's terminology and referred to both self-interest and benevolence as *affections naturelles*.[95] He also used the terms *affection sociale*, *passions sociales*, *inclinations sociales*, and *vertu sociale* throughout the text to signify the dispositions of individuals who understand that they can achieve their happiness only by expressing good will toward others.[96] *Social* thus denoted a psychological field in which self-interest and altruism were mutually constitutive.

The idea of social virtue as the crossing ground of selfishness and benevolence became popular in the Enlightenment because it mediated between a number of radically opposed alternatives. Holbach's *Morale universelle* shows that the language of sociability was congenial for those seeking an alternative both to the hierarchical regime of estates and orders and to the idea of a purely democratic polity. The language of sociability was also congenial to those who wished to deploy the methodological individualism of natural law but who did not wish to relinquish the traditional ideal of

[92] It will be remembered that in 1765 the *Encyclopédie* stated that *social* was a new word in the French language. The ARTFL database shows only two other authors using the word before Diderot: Pierre Charron, in *De la Sagesse* (Bordeaux, 1601), with five occurrences, and René Aubert de Vertot, in *Histoire des révolutions* (Paris, 1719), with six occurrences. The word *social* occurs sixty-five times in Diderot's *Principes de philosophie morale*, and it appears frequently in many works after the publication of the text.

[93] The complete title is *Principes de philosophie morale, ou essai de M. S*** sur le mérite et la vertu avec Réflexions*. The text has been printed alongside Shaftesbury's *Inquiry Concerning Virtue and Merit* in vol. 1 of Denis Diderot, *Oeuvres complètes*, ed. Roger Lewinter (Paris, 1969). All references are to this edition. Gordon B. Walters has identified many of the significant changes or additions in Diderot's version in Walters, *The Significance of Diderot's Essai sur le mérite et la vertu* (University of North Carolina Studies in Romance Languages and Literatures No. 112, Chapel Hill, 1971).

[94] For a full discussion of Shaftesbury and the language of politeness in early-modern England, see Lawrence Klein, "The Rise of 'Politeness in England, 1660–1715" (Ph.D. diss., Johns Hopkins University, 1983).

[95] Walters, *The Significance of Diderot's Essai*, 93. See also Holbach, *Système social*, 1:48–49, where Holbach criticizes Shaftesbury for believing in an innate moral faculty that was opposed to self-interest. It will be recalled that Pufendorf had insisted that sociability was not an instinct for benevolence but a self-interested decision to perform benevolent actions.

[96] Diderot, *Principes*, 82, 84, 86, 146, 165–66, 178, 214; these are just some examples of Diderot's usage of the terms mentioned. See also Walters, *The Significance of Diderot's Essai*, 88.

service to others. Benevolence toward others became meaningful as a policy or set of manners that one adopted in order to reap the advantages of exchange. In reconfiguring the concept of morality in this way, Enlightenment philosophers made it difficult to justify those extraordinary virtues, such as religious martyrdom or patriotic self-sacrifice in war, that had no apparent advantages for the individual in this life. For the most part, however, they were content to articulate an ideal of moderate virtue that operated within the confines of ordinary life.[97]

In this context, it is important to observe that Enlightenment authors did not set out to exalt self-interest or to suggest that order was a consequence of avaricious pursuits. In political theory and the philosophy of history, it has become too common to see Adam Smith's principle of the invisible hand of the free market as the quintessential expression of eighteenth-century European thought—in spite of the fact that this principle is not enough to account even for the thought of Smith himself.[98] In *The Great Transformation*, Karl Polanyi defined modern culture as based on the "segregation of the economic aspects [of human life] and the sacrosanct role of the market." Louis Dumont has followed Polanyi by affirming that with the decline of hierarchical modes of thought, the only conceivable way of representing human relationships in early-modern Europe was the "mechanical" discourse of free-market economics.[99] For both Polanyi and Dumont, the eighteenth century was the period in which modern materialism took over the philosophical representation of human life. Hannah Arendt's discussion of the "rise of society" in eighteenth-century thought is somewhat more nuanced, but her main purpose was to indicate a stark contrast between the Greek conception of the public sphere as a locus of communication and virtue and the Enlightenment conception of civil society as a network of "laborers and jobholders."[100] To redefine "civil society" as a space between the political and economic domains has become a vital task for some political philosophers, who do not seem to appreciate fully that their efforts are consonant with Enlightenment thought, not antithetical to it.[101]

Diderot, Holbach, and others did not see man as *homo economicus*. They

---

[97] Henry C. Clark has discussed the notion of "moderate virtue" in "Passions, Interests, and Moderate Virtues: La Rochefoucauld and the Origins of Enlightenment Liberalism," *Annals of Scholarship* 7 (1990):33–50.

[98] For discussion of how Smith's concept of the invisible hand was embedded in his religious and moral views, see Laurence Dickey, "Historicizing the Adam Smith Problem: Conceptual, Historiographical, and Textual Issues," *Journal of Modern History* 58 (1986):579–609.

[99] Karl Polanyi, *The Great Transformation: The Political and Economic Origins of Our Time* (Boston, 1957), 6; Louis Dumont, *From Mandeville to Marx: The Genesis and Triumph of Economic Ideology* (Chicago, 1977), 10.

[100] Hannah Arendt, *The Human Condition* (New York, 1958), 35–45.

[101] See Jean L. Cohen and Andrew Arato, *Civil Society and Political Theory* (Cambridge, Mass., 1992).

expected humans consciously to regulate their own conduct in accordance with the needs of others. The argument that morality was rooted in the pursuit of one's own well-being did not imply that all ways of pursuing gratification were moral.[102] Even in French economic discourse, pure self-ishness was considered problematic. The marquis de Mirabeau, one of the pioneers of liberal economics, insisted upon the difference between *cupidité* and *sociabilité*. The former meant raw egoism. The latter was the basis of what Mirabeau called *commerce*, which included not only economic activity but also family relations, friendship, politeness, and benevolence among the members of a village community.[103] "Commerce," he wrote, "is the useful and necessary relationship that every *sociable* being has with his fellow. In this sense ethics is on its territory as well as economics and everything is commerce in this world."[104] One reviewer was astonished by Mirabeau's use of the word "commerce." "Has anyone ever called commerce all the ties and relations that beings have with each other? Why remove from things the distinct notions that philosophy has attached to them? This simplification only creates confusion."[105] Mirabeau himself, however, emphasized the importance of defining words clearly,[106] and he deliberately used *commerce* to denote a broad range of relationships involving mutual support. By employing *commerce* to denote the entire field of sociable relations, he made *commerce* synonymous with *société*. In this way he suggested that economic production and trade were not acquisitive activities based on raw greed but civilized activities based on the rational quest for happiness within a field of human interdependence.

Another set of radically opposed alternatives that the language of socia-bility allowed one to bypass was the absolutist distinction between anarchy and sovereignty. The absolutist conception of order rested on the view that peace and happiness depended continuously upon "police" or the exercise of royal power. The Enlightenment conception of society as a product of politeness allowed one to imagine a sphere in which sovereignty was super-fluous. The "polite" or "polished" individual (*l'homme poli, l'homme policé*) was the individual who did not need to be coerced in order to be content, because he knew how to find happiness in reciprocity. Sociability thus meant

[102] Emphasizing that self-interest is the sole spring of action, Holbach wrote, "A man with no interests would never be disposed to care about the interests of others." But Holbach also stressed that self-interest was moral only when pursued in a social manner. "Morality is the art of living well with men. Virtue consists in making oneself happy through the happiness that one procures for others." Holbach, *Système social*, 1:25, 90.

[103] Mirabeau, *L'Ami des hommes, ou traité de la population*, 1:20, 23–24, 26, 97, 376; 3:456.

[104] Ibid., 2:9.

[105] *Supplément aux Journaux des Sçavans et de Trevoux ou Lettres critiques sur les divers ouvrages périodiques de France* (Amsterdam, February 1758), 85–86.

[106] Mirabeau, *L'Ami des hommes*, 3:453–54.

self-police.[107] This was not to deny that sovereign power was necessary for the punishment of crimes, the collection of taxes, the administration of foreign policy, and other vital functions. The point was not to usurp the whole power of the state but to delineate an area of interaction in which human nature checked or redeemed itself autonomously.

Self-Centered Cosmopolitanism

Mirabeau declared that the *"vertus sociables"* are "more natural to us than to any other nation." And he added:

> That nobility of morals which flowed from the antique independence of our fathers has without doubt declined . . . but urbanity and politeness have taken their place and these exterior virtues, though less noble in their principle than those they have replaced, are nevertheless more supple, easier to govern, and better fitted to cement *société*.[108]

According to Mirabeau, the purpose of government is to sponsor the sociable disposition.[109] Instead of operating as an exogenous control upon the passions, the state now appears as an instrument that helps the human capacity for self-control to run its natural course.

Implicit in this argument was the idea that some nations are more sociable than others and that the role of government ought to vary accordingly. Montesquieu dealt with the question of the relation between governmental policy and manners in Book 19 of *The Spirit of the Laws*. In Chapter 5 of Book 19, called "On the Degree to Which One Must Be Careful Not to Change the General Spirit of a Nation," Montesquieu suggested that when a nation, such as France, has a "sociable temperament" (*humeur sociable*), it is unwise to regulate its manners through law. "If in general the character is good, what do a few faults matter?" In Chapter 6, entitled "That One Should Not Try to Correct Everything," he affirmed, "Let us be left just as we are. . . . Laws constraining our *humeur sociable* would not be appropriate."[110] This positive image of France as an especially sociable nation also

---

[107] See the discussion of the difference between "l'homme sauvage" and "l'homme policé" in Holbach, *Système de la nature* (London, 1770), 1:4–5. On the notion of self-police, see also Peter France, *Politeness and Its Discontents, Problems in French Classical Culture* (Cambridge, 1992), 60–64.

[108] Mirabeau, *L'Ami des hommes*, 2:386.

[109] Ibid., 3:456–57. On the priority of the social over the political, consider also these statements by Holbach: "The principles of politics, in order to be useful, should be based on nature, that is, they should conform to the essence and goal of *société*" (*Système de la nature*, 1:152). "A sovereign is not the master but the minister of *société*" (*Système social*, 2:6).

[110] Montesquieu, *De L'Esprit des lois*, in *Oeuvres complètes*, 2:559 (for both quotations).

figured in the ideology of the royal academies. As seen in d'Alembert's introduction to a collection of his academic *éloges*, the idea of sociability allowed the academician to harmonize his status as a member of a royal institution with his identity as a liberal reformer.

> We will readily agree that it is more necessary for the state to have laborers and soldiers than an Académie Française. But we will first ask if in a flourishing nation, whose taste is studied and whose language is learned by all of Europe, it is not necessary to have a body designed to maintain the purity of language and taste. We will ask if the perfecting of these two objects is not essential to the charms of *société* in a nation that has *sociabilité* as its principal characteristic and that has carried further than all others the talent for enjoying and the art of living.[111]

This passage suggests that the purpose of the Académie is not to assist the monarch as a tutelary power but to assist in the "perfecting" of a community that is already more perfect—that is, more sociable—than any other.

D'Alembert's vision is simultaneously liberal and snobbish, and so it points to yet another opposition that the language of sociability managed to dovetail, the opposition between the universalistic implications of modern natural law and the elitist suppositions of French classical culture. Aristocratic ideals of politeness in the seventeenth century were, of course, premised on the belief that some people possessed more refinement than others. The most common term used to describe superior cultivation was *honnête*, which meant convivial, genteel, well-bred, and morally decent all at once. The word *sociable*, as noted earlier, was a relatively rare term prior to the rise of Pufendorfian natural law in the late seventeenth century. To the extent that it was employed, its usage was consistent with the basic postulate of French classical culture that grace and moral refinement could vary immensely from person to person. *Sociable* stood for a distinction, not a quality inherent in human nature. In a poem addressed to the comte de Candale, Théophile de Viau used *sociable* in characterizing Candale's superior manners.

> Tes regards sont courtois, tes propos aimables,
> ton humeur agréable, et tes moeurs *sociables*.[112]

Vincent Voiture wrote about Jean-Louis Guez de Balzac:

> He is one of the two persons in the world with whom I would most like to spend the rest of my life. . . . Without mentioning his intelligence, which is

[111] Jean d'Alembert, *Eloges lus dans les séances publiques de l'Académie Française* (Paris, 1779) 1:xiii. D'Alembert italicizes the word *sociabilité* in the text.

[112] "Your expressions are courteous, your remarks pleasant, / your disposition agreeable, and your manners sociable." Théophile de Viau, *Oeuvres poétiques* (Geneva, 1951; first published 1621), 1:72.

beyond description, there is no man under the sun who is a better friend, a better man, more *sociable*, more agreeable, or more generous.[113]

With the rise of the natural law idiom, however, it became axiomatic that all humans were essentially identical. Hobbes and Pufendorf did not dwell on the distinctive characteristics of particular individuals or particular groups of people. Nevertheless, even though Enlightenment authors grounded society in a universalistic conception of human nature, as Pufendorf had done, the particular inflection that Holbach and others gave to the content of sociable behavior allowed them to suggest that some regimes contained more society than others. In its meaning as politeness, sociability referred to the disposition and manners of humans who understood that their interests were intertwined with the interests of others. Eighteenth-century writers believed that the principles of sociability were simple and intelligible to everyone. But they also believed that false philosophy, especially in the form of religion, could distort a people's conception of happiness and the proper means of pursuing it. With religion and other myths obstructing the growth of sociability, the degree of sociability varied from people to people and required time to achieve perfection, even in the relatively polite nations of Europe.

It was common to affirm in the Enlightenment that France was the model of sociability to the rest of the world. The aristocratic ideal of a polite individual was transposed with the help of natural law into the Enlightenment ideal of a polite nation. "Most of our writers brag about our nations's spirit of *société*," wrote Bernardin de Saint-Pierre.[114] In the Dedication in his play *Zaïre*, Voltaire wrote:

> Since the reign of Anne of Austria they [the French] have been the most *sociable* and polite people on earth, and this politeness is not something arbitrary. . . . It is a law of nature that they have fortunately cultivated more than other peoples.[115]

In Montesquieu's *Persian Letters*, Uzbec, the Persian visitor in Paris, writes back to his homeland:

> It is said that man is a *sociable* being. On this score it seems to me that a Frenchman is more human than anyone else. He is man *par excellence* for he seems to be made uniquely for *société*. Moreover, I have noticed people among them who are not only *sociable* but who are in themselves a universal *société*. They multiply in every corner; they populate in an instant the four quarters of

[113] Vincent Voiture, *Lettres*, in *Les Oeuvres* (Paris, 1654) 1:386.

[114] Jacques-Henri Bernardin de Saint-Pierre, *Etudes de la nature* (Paris, 1804; first published, 1784), 1:29.

[115] Voltaire, "Epître Dédicatoire à M. Falkener," in *Zaïre* (Paris, 1889), 22. The dedication was composed in 1736.

the town. A hundred men of this kind abound more than two thousand citizens.[116]

"The general character of the French nation is gaiety, activity, politeness, *sociabilité*," wrote Holbach.[117] Statements like this are signs of an outlook that might be called self-centered cosmopolitanism. Enlightenment philosophy defined France as a superior culture, but it claimed to do so from a point of view outside of French culture—the universalistic point of view of natural law. The alleged superiority of France stemmed not from its culturally unique features but from its enlargement of society as a forum of purely human action. In this way, the Enlightenment sustained the ideals of *la politesse mondaine* but integrated them into a geocultural framework that resembled, and perhaps constituted the origins of, the modern theory of "developed" and "underdeveloped" nations. In seventeenth-century literature, politeness was taken to be the distinctive trait of the gentleman and his circle. In the eighteenth century, politeness appeared as the organizing principle of an imaginary network of relations in which "reason" was to be applied to the satisfaction of human "interests." The supposed superiority of one country, such as France, came from its having already evolved into what all countries must become in order to achieve happiness.

The Religion of Society

Although this self-centered cosmopolitanism was chauvinistic, it was not nationalistic in any primordial sense. It did not portray the nation as the ultimate unit of association. Civility transcended nationality. The writers who praised French sociability believed that nations were shells in which *société* developed. They were boundaries around systems of sociability that might be geographically remote from each other but were comparable in type and capable of being joined. "Nations are merely the individual units of the universal *société* of the human species," wrote Holbach.[118] The idealized space was not the *patria* or fatherland; it was *société* as the only system that embodied natural law and fulfilled the generic potential of humankind. "Les hommes se civilisent par la *société*" ("Men become civilized through society"),[119] wrote Mirabeau. If men were superior to the animals, this superiority stemmed not from their unique relationship to God but from their unique relationship to each other as members of society. "It is to *société*,

---

[116] Charles-Louis de Secondat, baron de Montesquieu, *Lettres persanes* (Paris, 1929; first published, 1721), 35.

[117] Holbach, *La Morale universelle*, 3:107. See also Duclos, *Considérations sur les moeurs*, 171: "The Frenchman is the most *sociable* of all men."

[118] Holbach, *Système social*, 1:109.

[119] Mirabeau, *L'Ami des hommes*, 1:420.

which unites us with other men, that we directly owe, as I just said, our moral ideas and most of our purely speculative notions," wrote d'Alembert. "In order to be convinced of this," he added, "we need only reflect on the great difference found between savages and civilized peoples [*peuples policés*]. . . . Is it not probable that lack of *société*, more than any other cause, reduces animals to so narrow and limited a circle of ideas?"[120]

"Of all the nations, France is the one that has most experienced *société*," affirmed Voltaire.[121] This is rather like a Catholic saying that a certain nation contains the greatest congregation of the faithful. Indeed, an important feature of the language of sociability is that it translated the theoretical universality of the Catholic Church into a new secular space. *Société* came to signify the ultimate horizon of all individual aspirations, the only domain in which human nature could develop, and the only context in which particular institutions, including religion itself, could have meaning. The result was what Ernst Cassirer called "an exchange of index symbols"[122] between the human and the divine. Instead of being viewed as a subsystem within a cosmic unit based on divine principles, human life, now designated as *société*, became the cosmos—the system of being within which everything else, even the sense of the sacred, took on value.

This subordination of the concept of religion to the concept of society was logically implicated in the structure of modern natural law. By taking the "needs" and "interests" of humans as the primary data of reflection, authors such as Grotius and Pufendorf inevitably discussed religion in terms of its capacity to satisfy such needs and interests rather than its capacity to usher humans into a higher plane of reality. For the natural lawyers, religion might be a necessary social institution but it was not a necessary metaphysical orientation. In *De Jure Belli ac Pacis* (The Right of War and Peace, first published 1625), Grotius argued that religious belief helped to sustain peaceful manners and obedience to the law. He suggested that those who denied the existence of God should be punished for disturbing the peace. This was a secular defense of religion that did not require any theological suppositions. The point was that most humans would practice the laws of nature more diligently if they believed that God had instituted these laws.

---

[120] D'Alembert, "Eléments," 207.

[121] Voltaire, Dedication, in *Zaïre*, 20.

[122] Ernst Cassirer, *The Philosophy of the Enlightenment* (Princeton, 1968), 159. "An exchange of index symbols takes place, as it were. That which formerly had established other concepts, now moves into the position of that which is to be established, and that which hitherto had justified other concepts, now finds itself in the position of a concept which requires justification. Finally even the theology of the eighteenth century is affected by this trend. It gives up the absolute primacy it had previously enjoyed; it no longer sets the standard but submits to certain basic norms derived from another source." Keith Michael Baker also discusses the "social gospel" of the Enlightenment in "Enlightment and the Institution of Society."

The laws of nature were true in themselves, however, and would be valid, as Grotius said, "though we should even grant, what without the greatest wickedness cannot be granted, that there is no God, or that he takes no care of human affairs."[123]

Pufendorf's position on the relation between natural law and religion was similar, but he placed more emphasis on the need to affirm God's existence in order to add binding force to the principles of sociability. The rules of sociability, he wrote, have "manifest utility" and do not require theological justification. According to Pufendorf, however, a rule has the greatest binding force on humans when they believe not only that it is a good rule but also that an authority has promulgated it and will punish them for transgressing it. In order to give the norms of sociability the greatest force, we should presume that God has commanded all humans to perform whatever their reason determines to be natural law.

> [I]t is necessary to presuppose that God exists, and by His providence rules all things; also that He has enjoined upon the human race that they observe those dictates of the reason, as laws promulgated by Himself by means of our natural light. For otherwise they might, to be sure, be observed perhaps, in view of their utility, like the prescriptions of physicians for the regimen of health, but not as laws; since these of necessity suppose a superior, and in fact one who has actually undertaken the direction of another.[124]

This is less a proof for the existence of God than a proof for the social utility of affirming the existence of God. Pufendorf does not describe God as an efficacious force sustaining society; rather, he describes human religious subjectivity as a buttress of social order. The passage is remarkable because it encourages individuals to sacralize society and to assume that God automatically approves of whatever is conducive to the satisfaction of human needs and interests through social exchange. Religion, from this perspective, adds nothing to the range of moral principles discernable through reason. It only serves to make these principles more binding. "The ultimate confirmation of duties toward other men," wrote Pufendorf, "comes from religion and fear of the Deity, so that man would not be sociable (*sociabilis*) either, if not imbued with religion."[125] Religion is thus the guarantee that

---

123 This quotation comes from the English translation of Barbeyrac's 1724 edition of *De Jure Belli ac Pacis*, *The Right of War and Peace* (London, 1738), xix (Preliminary Discourse, XI). For discussion of the significance of the quoted passage in Grotius's thought, see Leonard Besselink, "The Impious Hypothesis Revisited," *Grotiana*, n.s., 9 (1988):3–63; and Richard Tuck, "Grotius, Carneades, and Hobbes," *Grotiana*, n.s., 4 (1983):43–62.

124 Pufendorf, *De Officio Hominis et civis*, trans. Frank Gardner Moore (New York, 1927), 2:19. Pufendorf wrote this work in 1673.

125 Ibid., 2:21 (and 1:24 for the Latin). Pufendorf's arguments about religion as a necessary foundation of society appear in a more technical form in *De Jure Naturae et Gentium*, bk. 1, ch. 2.

humans will practice sociability, but religion no longer promotes any aspirations outside the boundaries of the social field.

As I suggested earlier, virtually no French authors developed the natural-law idiom as thoroughly as Pufendorf did. A variety of writers, however, took up some of the key principles of Pufendorfian natural law and used them as a framework for theorizing about politeness. A tendency to equate politeness and religion is evident in all of these works.[126] A good example is Claude Buffier's *Traité de la société civile et du moyen de se rendre heureux, en contribuant au bonheur des personnes avec qui l'on vit* (Treatise on Civil Society and the Means of Achieving Happiness by Contributing to the Happiness of the Persons with Whom One Lives, 1726). The terms *société* and *société civile* appear on virtually every page. In a manner consistent with Pufendorf's philosophy, these terms signify the sphere of interdependence in which self-interest induces humans to practice benevolence.[127] Buffier, a Jesuit, did little to direct the attention of his readers to anything beyond the secular domain of society. He acknowledged that the "happiness" that humans pursue in society does not compare to the "sweetness" of life in heaven.[128] But he never considered the possibility that the means of obtaining entrance into heaven might differ from the means of achieving happiness in "civil society." In fact, he insisted that every virtue was advantageous for "the happiness of *société*" and every vice militated against it.[129] He defined morality as "the science of living with other men in *société civile* in order to procure, as much as we can, our own happiness in concert with the happiness of others."[130] He thus made "civil society" the ultimate reference point of right and wrong.

Buffier described his text as a "treatise on civility [*civilité*] derived from general principles and reason."[131] The work is indeed an encyclopedia of the rules of *politesse* and *savoir vivre* (these being words that Buffier uses interchangeably with *civilité*). The single most important subject is the art of conversation, because conversation, as Buffier says, is the principal form of human interaction and "the sweetest bond" of social life.[132] One of Buffier's maxims is to avoid hostile argumentation. He advised his readers never to speak about religion in order to "prevent the inconveniences that such a

---

[126] Robert Mauzi observed the tendency of eighteenth-century writers to equate piety and politeness in *L'Idée du bonheur au XVIIIe siècle* (Paris, 1960), 186.

[127] The first chapter of the book is especially Pufendorfian. It is entitled, "Du caractère et de l'usage de la raison naturelle qui doit nous conduire au bonheur dans la société civile."

[128] Claude Buffier, *Traité de la société civile* . . . (Paris, 1726), 6.

[129] Ibid., 1:38–39, 177. See also 2:103ff., where Buffier defines the cardinal virtues as forms of sociability.

[130] Ibid., 1:3.

[131] Ibid., 1:Avertissement.

[132] Buffier treats the art of conversation over the course of several chapters (*Traité*, 1:71–148).

legitimate subject of contestation would engender."[133] He thus drew attention to conversation as the constitutive activity of "civil society" and argued, surprisingly for a priest, that religion had no place within conversation. The implication was that religious discourse tends to be uncivil. By calling religion a "legitimate" topic of contestation, Buffier suggested that religion was a matter upon which humans naturally tended to disagree and around which they could not easily coordinate the collective pursuit of happiness.

Paradoxically, Buffier concluded his work with a defense of religion, and Christianity in particular, as the foundation of "civil society." Although religion "is not absolutely necessary to establish the laws of purely moral virtue and of human *société*," religion, he stated, is necessary to help fix these laws in the minds of individuals.[134] There are, Buffier contended, certain times when our passions are so strong that we lose sight of what reason advises us to do. We are then inclined to pursue our own interest without thinking about others. Without the sobering threat of divine punishment, we would damage society. The rational effort to preserve civil society, Buffier argued, leads one to appreciate the necessity of having a religion: "It is reason itself that leads necessarily to religion in order to make it [religion] the solid rule of our conduct."[135] Of all the religions, according to Buffier, Christianity is the one whose principles are best suited for the perfection of civil society. Buffier claimed that Christian nations are the most "cultivated" (*cultivé*) because Christian morals are most conducive to "the perfecting of politeness" and the maintenance of "the economy of human *société*."[136]

Buffier's social justification of religion contains some revealing contradictions. He suggests that Christian theological concerns do not belong within civil society when he urges people not to converse about religion. Yet he also argues that the Christian religion is an important support for civil society. The convolution stems from the fact that Buffier, like Pufendorf, treated religion as a sanction but not as a source for morality. The true source of morality for these authors was the natural law of sociability. They invoked religion merely to add weight to natural law. In doing so, they treated religion less as a truth than as an incentive. Instead of standing for the absolute, religion exists only in relation to society. That Buffier himself was aware of the tension between the philosophy of sociability and the philosophy of Christianity is evident in his tortured discussion of lying. Buffier criticized Pufendorf for suggesting that the telling of a lie is bad only when it hurts society.[137] Bearing false witness was proscribed in the Ten Command-

---

[133] Ibid., 1:98.
[134] Ibid., 2:118.
[135] Ibid., 2:113.
[136] Ibid., 2:119–20.
[137] Ibid., 1:241–42. Buffier correctly specifies Pufendorf's *De Officio Hominis et Civis* (bk. 1, ch. 10) as the place where Pufendorf defended the use of "fictitious and figurative language"

ments, and so it was a vice that Buffier could not comfortably redefine in purely social terms. Yet he was unable to articulate a principle that would both prohibit false testimony under any circumstances and be consistent with his theory of civil society as the essential context of human life. In the end, he admitted his inability to formulate a theory of lying, an activity that "may in no way be opposed to human *société*" yet "does not accord with the divine law." "This is an issue for theology," he concluded, "and is not part of my province."[138] Buffier's inability to resolve the issue of lying within the terms of his own treatise reveals the tension between the language of sociability and the language of Christianity. Though he suggested that the issue of lying could be resolved better in a purely theological treatise, the truth is that he had outlined a new theology of society within which it was impossible to reformulate many of the traditional principles of Catholic morality. His hesitations concerning lying reflect the confusion of a priest in the presence of the secular implications of his own choice of a moral language, a moral language based on the terms "happiness" and "society" rather than "salvation" and "heaven."

Buffier's text reveals a tension concerning the place of "religion" within the language of sociability. More precisely, it reveals a tendency to make society sacred even as one argued that a sense of the sacred was necessary for society. This tension carried over into the second half of the eighteenth century and ultimately resolved itself through the divinization of society and the outright denigration of religion.

The position of Pufendorf and Buffier, that religion is a buttress of sociability, was the moderate position established in the article "*Société*" in the *Encyclopédie*—moderate, because even though it departed from Christian metaphysics, it nevertheless ascribed importance to belief in the divinity and treated Christianity as a kind of superior social glue.[139] A movement toward a more radical position was already evident in Diderot's *Essai sur le mérite et la vertu*. This was the text in which Diderot repeatedly employed the word *social* in order to dissolve Shaftesbury's distinction between the

---

in cases where truthful language would injure another. Buffier writes: "According to them [philosophers such as Pufendorf], the common good of *société* being the primitive and universal measure of every purely moral virtue, there can be nothing vicious in anything [such as a lie] that creates an advantage for *société*." (Buffier, *Traité*, 1:141)

[138] Ibid., 1:246–47.

[139] "However plausible the maxims of morality may be and whatever utility they may have for the sweetness of human *société*, they would contain nothing to bind us permanently without religion. Although reason alone generally makes us cognizant of the manners which contribute to the sweetness and the peace that we owe to others in *société*, it is nevertheless true that it is not enough, on certain occasions, to convince us that our interest is always joined to that of society." "Société," in *Encyclopédie*, 15:254. Although the author of this article does not explicitly acknowledge Buffier, the article contains at least two passages lifted verbatim from Buffier's *Traité de la société civile*. Compare Buffier, 1 and 15, to "Société," 252.

selfish and the benevolent inclinations. A fuller consideration of the additions that Diderot made to the original text of Shaftesbury shows that one of his aims was to establish that virtue can exist without religion, and that religion can exist without virtue.

In the Dedication of the work, Diderot underscored the evil effects that religious passions could have by evoking the French religious wars of the previous two centuries.

> But recall the history of our civil troubles and you will see one half of the nation bathing itself, out of piety, in the blood of the other half and violating, in order to sustain the cause of God, the first sentiments of humanity; as if one had to stop being a man in order to prove that one was *religious*.[140]

Shaftesbury himself had argued that atheism was not necessarily immoral and that religion sometimes justified inhumane practices, though he drew his examples primarily from the religions of the new world rather than from Christianity. Diderot gave the English philosopher's critique of religion an anti-Christian focus by adding comments against the Christian ideal of celibacy and ascetic contemplation. In traditional Christian thought, hermits and ascetics were ranked near the top of the scale of human characters. Though they contributed nothing to the everyday life of the community, they helped to maintain human life by sustaining its ontological link to the divine and by affirming the proper order of priority between worldly and spiritual concerns. Having repudiated the human world in order to become closer to God, they stood, in the opinion of a metaphysically traditional jurist like Loyseau, at the pinnacle of the very world they disavowed—the highest ranking order of the first estate.[141] Diderot, however, treated "happiness" within society as the only meaningful aspiration for every individual.[142] In passages that he added to Shaftesbury's text, he described the monastic life as *insociable*, a treason against *société*, and harmful to "the economy of *social* inclinations."[143] Finally, he elevated the sociable person to the rank of a god.

> Avoir les affections *sociales* entières, ou l'intégrité de coeur et d'esprit, c'est suivre pas à pas la nature; c'est imiter, c'est representer l'Etre suprême sous une forme humaine.

---

[140] Diderot, *Essai sur le mérite*, 17 (Diderot's emphasis).

[141] Charles Loyseau, *Traité des ordres* (Paris, 1613), 45.

[142] Diderot, *Essai sur le mérite*. See the footnote he added to his translation of Shaftesbury's text on pp. 134–35: "Each person in *sociéte* is like a part within an organized whole. Measurement of time is the essential property of a watch; the happiness of individuals is the principal end of *société*. These effects will not be produced or will be produced poorly without a perfect coordination among the parts of the watch and among the members of *société*."

[143] Ibid., 59–60 (see footnote), 149. See also Walters, *The Significance of Diderot's Essai*, 56–60, and Franco Venturi, *Jeunesse de Diderot, 1713–1753* (Paris, 1939), 61–62, for discussion of Diderot's critique of monastic ideals in the footnotes.

(To have the social affections entirely, or integrity of the heart and mind, is to follow the course of nature; it is to imitate, it is to represent the supreme Being in a human form.)[144]

Pufendorf and Buffier had contributed to the secularization of religion by arguing that the main purpose of faith in the divinity was to instill respect for the laws of sociability. Diderot went a step further by suggesting the possibility of dispensing with religion and divinizing the sociable human being.

The anti-Christian ideas that Diderot embedded in his translation of Shaftesbury, first published in 1745, were expressed more openly and vehemently as the decades passed. Increasingly, writers used *sociabilité* as an explicit measure of religious doctrines—or as a means of suggesting that *société* itself was a god. "*Sociétés* have their birth in purely human motives," wrote d'Alembert. "Religion plays no role in their first formation; and though religion is destined to reinforce the tie, one can still say that it exists principally for man considered in himself."[145] The author of the article "Philosophe" in the *Encyclopédie* developed the concept of a purely secular morality and announced that for the well-bred philosopher, "*Société civile* is, so to speak, a divinity on earth."[146] The abbé Raynal also outlined a cult of society in his popular *Histoire philosophique et politique des établissements et du commerce des européens dans les deux Indes* (Philosophical and Political History of the Establishments and the Commerce of the Europeans in the East and West Indies, first published in 1770). Reprinted over twenty-five times prior to 1789, this work was without doubt one of the most popular and notorious texts of the late Enlightenment. The Parlement of Paris condemned this work for its "impious declamations" and "indecent sarcasms . . . regarding everything having to do with the Christian religion."[147] The Faculty of Theology at the University of Paris also condemned Raynal for "the implacable hatred he has shown for religion."[148]

Raynal purported to describe the foreign cultures discovered by European explorers in the East and West Indies. Like many Enlightenment authors, however, he actually referred to exotic countries fictitiously, as a pretense for describing and criticizing institutions that his readers could

[144] Ibid., 183. Shaftesbury's text simply reads, "And to have this entire affection or integrity of mind, is to live according to nature, and the dictates and rules of supreme wisdom." Diderot thus added the part about becoming divine.

[145] D'Alembert, "Elémens," 127.

[146] *Encyclopédie*, 12 (1765):510. On the complex question of the authorship of this article, see Herbert Dieckman, *Le Philosophe: Texts and Interpretation* (St. Louis, 1948). On God and society, see also Voltaire's *Traité de métaphysique*, Chapter 8, "De L'Homme considéré comme un être sociable," and Chapter 9, "De la Vertu et du vice," in *Oeuvres de Voltaire* (Paris, 1829), vol. 37.

[147] "Arrêt de la Cour de Parlement," in *Recueil de diverses pièces*, 131.

[148] "Determinatio sacrae facultatis parisiensis in librum cui titules Histoire philosophique . . . ," in *Recueil de diverses pièces*, 156.

recognize as European. Thus, his discussion of Japanese Buddhism had nothing to do with Japanese religion and everything to do with Catholicism. The Japanese religion, Raynal says, makes people "ferocious in human *société*" because of its emphasis on the monkish virtues and because the clergy encourages unnatural feelings of guilt in the populace regarding sexuality. Raynal writes a veritable sermon against celibacy, decrying those who would ruin "the bonds of *société*" by thwarting human sexuality.[149]

While Raynal claimed to detest Japanese Buddhism, he found Chinese Confucianism to be the most sociable form of belief on earth. Raynal idealized China in order to present the reader with his own conception of a perfect nation. "In this nation of wise men, everything that connects and civilizes men is religion, and religion itself is only the practice of the *vertus sociales*."[150] Superstition had no authority in China because the government was controlled by philosophers, the mandarins. It was a philosopher, Confucius, who formulated the country's national religion according to the principles of "natural law" and "for the sake of *société*." As a result, Raynal affirmed, the entire nation possessed "*moeurs sociales* (social mores)."[151] Raynal says nothing about the gods of the Chinese religion. What he idealizes is a religion that is not a religion—an adoration of the bonds of society, a cult of social virtue promoted by an intellectual priesthood.

Perhaps the most sustained attack on Christianity through the language of sociability occurs in Holbach's *Système social*. Holbach viewed the ideals of monasticism as the essence of Christianity, and he emphatically rejected these ideals as contradictory to "real virtue and the good of *société*."[152] Holbach even declaimed against Jesus: "This misanthropic God, in his dismal and *insociable* lessons, appears to have completely forgotten that he was speaking to men living in *société*."[153] Every revealed religion, Holbach states, has "made men *insociable*" by separating its adherents from the rest of humanity and convincing them that they constitute a superior group of beings. "The religious spirit was and always will be incompatible with moderation, sweetness, justice, and humanity. Thus religious morality can never serve to render mortals more *sociable*."[154]

Though his rhetoric was unusually strong, Holbach's vocabulary and conceptual system were essentially the same as that of all the philosophers,

---

[149] Guillaume-Thomas-François Raynal, *Histoire philosophique . . . des européens dans les deux Indes* (Paris, 1778), 1:161–63. This was one of the sections that the University of Paris cited when it condemned Raynal's book. Several other passages that were cited and condemned contained the words *social* and *sociabilité* (see "Determinatio," 258, 334, 365, 379).

[150] Raynal, *Histoire philosophique*, 1:131.

[151] Ibid., 1:143–46, 151.

[152] Holbach, *Système social*, 1:87–88

[153] Ibid., 1:29.

[154] Ibid., 1:31. See also Holbach, *Système de la nature*, 2:382, and *La Morale universelle*, 3:225.

from Pufendorf onward, who took society as the only meaningful framework of human life. The essence of traditional Christianity was an ideal of perfection and immortality pursued by cultivating contact with a being who transcended every system of human interaction. The language of sociability, in contrast, was deployed to show that everything worth pursuing was located within a system of reciprocal engagements serving human interests. In the language of sociability, religion could only be defined as a veneration of the bonds of society. And the word God, if it meant anything at all, could only refer to a highly abstract being who told humans not to look beyond the social field. Saint Cyprian's dictum, "Outside of the Church there is no salvation," was abandoned. The new motto, one might say, was, "Outside of society there is no happiness," or "Outside of society there is no salvation, no purpose, for religion."

Though European thought had been touched by secular conceptions of virtue and well-being prior to the Enlightenment, the value of transcendence had not been called into question systematically before. The Renaissance humanists who defended the *vita activa* over the *vita comtemplativa* had weighed the relative merits of a life of political service and a life of ascetic self-cultivation. They sometimes found the former to be preferable, but they did not proclaim the latter to be illegitimate. "The often voiced praise of the lay citizen did not mean that the solitary life of the monk or of the scholar were explicitly or even implicitly rejected," says Paul Oskar Kristeller. "The humanists and their contemporaries were fully aware of the fact that different styles and ways of life coexisted legitimately, and that the choice among these alternatives belonged to the individual person."[155] When, however, the imagined framework of human existence became *société*, a radically critical attitude toward religion became possible. It was no longer a question of weighing asceticism and civic commitment against each other as two viable modes of life. Modern natural law provided the framework for a metaphysical reduction of the world, a complete repudiation of the ascetic pursuit of transcendent communication, and a sacralization of "happiness" achieved through mundane interaction. *Société* was a god. Henceforth in French thought, the fate of every religious idea was to experience the pressure of these two unhappy possibilities: either to be radically reformulated in terms of "social" utility, or to be rejected altogether.

[155] Paul Oskar Kristeller, "The Active and the Contemplative Life in Renaissance Humanism," in Brian Vickers, ed., *Arbeit, Musse, Meditation* (Zurich, 1985), 142. See also Jill Kraye, "Moral Philosophy," in Charles B. Schmitt et al., eds., *The Cambridge History of Renaissance Philosophy* (Cambridge, 1988), 336, and (in the same volume) Brian Vickers, "Rhetoric and Philosophy," 731.

3

THE CIVILIZING PROCESS REVISITED

At the heart of true politeness you will find one sentiment,
which is the sentiment of equality. But there are many ways of
loving and comprehending equality . . .
(Henri Bergson, "La Politesse." Speech delivered to the
graduating class of the Lycée Henri-IV, 1892.)[1]

The Varieties of Civility

IN 1671, Antoine de Courtin, a diplomat in the service of Louis XIV, published his *Nouveau traité de la civilité qui se pratique en France parmi les honnêtes gens* (New Treatise on the Civility Practiced in France among Well-Bred People). Courtin's precepts of civility are largely concerned with the rules of speech. Throughout the treatise he emphasized the importance of talking to others according to their "quality" or rank. We should never try to join a conversation among people whose rank is higher than our own, unless someone in the group "bids us to confirm what he says as a witness or wishes us to say something that is to his advantage and that he would be embarrassed to say himself." When invited to enter a conversation, we should always address our remarks to the "person who is eminent in dignity." We should never contradict a grandee, unless it is on a practical point of information, such as the whereabouts of another person, and even in this instance we must preface our remark with the words, "I ask you to excuse me." (*Je vous demande excuse*).[2]

In 1677, Courtin was able to boast that his book was known throughout France.

> We are into the fifth edition, without including the pirated editions which can be found in many towns of the realm; and because the great war has blocked the distribution of works . . . into foreign countries, these editions have certainly all been sold in France.[3]

---

[1] Henri Bergson, *Mélanges*, ed. André Robinet (Paris, 1972), 320.

[2] Antoine de Courtin, *Nouveau traité de la civilité qui se pratique en France parmi les honnêtes gens*, 2d ed. (Paris, 1672), 37–38, 50.

[3] Antoine de Courtin, *Traité de la paresse* (Paris, 1677), 182.

By the end of the century at least seven more editions had appeared, and nine more followed in the early years of the eighteenth century, leaving little doubt that Courtin had indeed produced a best-seller. The popularity of this work, however, does not mean that it was the definitive expression of French courtesy in the seventeenth and eighteenth centuries. In 1675, a Jesuit, Dominique Bouhours, attacked Courtin in a popular work of his own entitled *Remarques nouvelles sur la langue française* (New Remarks on the French Language).[4] "That man who has meddled in the composition of rules of civility as it is practiced in France among well-bred people does not know what he is talking about," Bouhours declared. "Our fine French civility," he continued, "never to contradict except after having asked to be excused!" "If he [Courtin] had consulted well-bred people who know how to live and speak politely, or if he knew how to live and speak politely himself, he never would have given this advice to those who approach persons of high rank." Bouhours called the phrase *je vous demande excuse* a piece of "grandiloquence" and even doubted that it was correct French (he preferred the phrase *je vous demande pardon*). Bouhours ridiculed Courtin's effort to systematize the smallest details of personal comportment. "This new master even teaches a method for paying compliments in all kinds of encounters, and the only thing that is left for him to do is to give rules for how to laugh correctly."[5]

Courtin responded to Bouhours by dubbing him "the banal master of the *prétieuses*" and by insisting that the habit of excusing oneself before contradicting a grandee "does not, I admit, agree with the natural pride of certain persons . . . but it is appropriate for well-bred men."[6] The dispute between these two codifiers of refined living illustrates a point that is plain yet not always appreciated: manners were a subject of debate in early-modern France. Authors disagreed with each other not merely about particular conventions but about the very purpose of manners. In doing so, they argued about the goals of intimate exchange and about the structures of collective life that were worthy of being ratified through small-scale interaction. The dispute between Courtin and Bouhours was, in fact, a sign of a profound institutional rift between them. Courtin was influenced by the courtly milieu in which hierarchy was the supreme norm. A constant sense of "above" and "below" was imperative at court, where the spirit of precedence served the double purpose of imbuing the king with sovereign power

---

[4] *Remarques nouvelles* went into seven editions before 1700. Bouhours was also the author of the popular *Les Entretiens d'Ariste et d'Eugene* (1671) and *La Manière de bien penser dans les ouvrages de l'esprit* (1687). Each went into at least thirteen editions.

[5] Dominique Bouhours, *Remarques nouvelles sur la langue française* (Paris, 1675), 42, 44–46.

[6] Courtin, *Traité de la paresse*, 175–76, 181.

and the nobility with ceremonial honor. Bouhours, though a Jesuit, spent more time at the salon of Mlle. de Scudéry than he did at his *Collège de Clermont.*[7] He composed his works for a noncourtly milieu that aspired to free itself of the rigid stratification of the court and to establish a more sociable mode of living, one in which good manners, instead of merely acknowledging power and status, could be a source of status in themselves and function to promote pleasurable exchange.

It would be unnecessary to point out the existence of divergent views of manners were it not for some scholarly trends. Prior to the late 1960s, French literary scholars tended to view courtliness as just one model of politeness in French classical culture.[8] More recently, however, the theories of Norbert Elias have shaped the interpretation of manners in French classical culture. Elias treated the court as a symbol of French culture as a whole. In his two influential works, *The History of Manners* (vol. 1 of *The Civilizing Process*) and *The Court Society*, he greatly exaggerated the power of the court as a model of refined behavior.[9] One of the remarkable features of his writing—a feature that has received little criticism—is a comparative historical outlook that clearly owed something to the nationalistic tendencies of German thought in the Weimar period.[10] Elias's central thesis was this: in contrast to Germany, where moral ideals were constructed in the process of criticizing courtly elites, French culture fell under the complete hegemony of the court on account of the successful "diffusion of courtly-aristocratic manners, the tendency of the courtly aristocracy to assimilate and, so to speak, colonize elements from other classes."[11] The courtly aristocracy was receptive to the assimilation of new layers of the population; these new elements accepted the court as a cultural model. Even those who never attended the court absorbed the courtly ideology and its rigorous code of deference that was structured to preserve a sense of hierarchy in all aspects of

---

[7] Georges Doncieux, *Un Jésuite homme de lettres au dix-septième siècle: Le Père Bouhours* (Paris, 1886), 6–7, 25–26.

[8] Two studies stand out by their scholarly comprehensiveness: Roger Lathuillère, *La Preciosité: Étude historique et linguistique* (Geneva, 1966), and Maurice Magendie, *La Politesse mondaine et les théories de l'honnêteté en France au XVIIIe siècle*, 2 vols. (Paris, 1933). Georges Mongredien, *La Vie de société au XVIIe et XVIIIe siècles* (Paris, 1950) is less rich but also useful.

[9] Norbert Elias, *The History of Manners* (first published in German in 1939 as vol. 1 of *Über den Prozess der Zivilisation*; my references are to the English edition, New York, 1978); *The Court Society* (first published in German in 1969; my references are to the English edition, Oxford, 1983).

[10] The only other discussion of how national biases have influenced the historiography on courts and manners is, so far as I am aware, C. Stephen Jaeger's *The Origins of Courtliness: Civilizing Trends and the Formation of Courtly Ideals, 939–1210* (Philadelphia, 1985), 260–71. Some interesting general remarks on the history of the tendency of German intellectuals to define their own nation in opposition to France appear in Isaiah Berlin, *The Crooked Timber of Humanity, Chapters in the History of Ideas* (New York, 1992), 35–37.

[11] Elias, *The History of Manners*, 21.

life. Through the process of diffusion made possible by the printing of courtesy books, the attributes of courtliness became the attributes of the French "national character,"[12] and this process occurred without being challenged by any other code of politeness.

> And even if, with the stronger upsurge of the middle class from the mid-eighteenth century onward—or, stated differently, with the enlargement of aristocratic society through the increased assimilation of leading middle-class groups—behavior and manners slowly changed, *this happened without rupture* as a direct continuation of the courtly-aristocratic tradition of the seventeenth century.[13]

Because Elias's ideas have had an impact not only on the interpretation of early-modern courtesy codes but also on the conceptualization of French history as a whole, it is worth being precise about the suppositions of his analysis.

Elias's historical sociology revolves around two axes of comparison, the one temporal, the other spatial. The temporal axis is evident in his attempt to define modernity in opposition to the Middle Ages by historicizing the Freudian concept of the superego.[14] Beginning in the Renaissance, the rules of everyday interaction required a high degree of self-scrutiny and self-repression. These prohibitions, which concerned table manners, sexual conduct, and the bodily functions, became increasingly strict. The sentiment of embarrassment became more frequent through a constant intensification of the prerequisites of "good behavior." The spatial axis appears in Elias's concern to define the essential differences between France and Germany within modernity. Here the traces of a national bias are evident in his use of the distinction between *Zivilisation* and *Kultur*.

When Elias was a student in Heidelberg in the 1920s, Karl Jaspers encouraged him to write one of his first seminar papers on Thomas Mann's critique of French "civilization."[15] During the First World War and through the early 1920s, Mann was a conservative and a nationalist. In *Betrachtungen eines Unpolitischen* (Reflections of a Nonpolitical Man, 1918), he took up the old distinction between "civilization" and "culture" in order to denigrate France and create a German sense of pride. Mann praised Germany's musical, metaphysical, and subjective "culture," contrasting it with the more technical, political, and external "civilization" of France.[16]

---

[12] Ibid., 36.

[13] Ibid., 36 (my emphasis).

[14] Ibid., 301–2, n. 81.

[15] Stephen Mennell, *Norbert Elias: Civilization and the Human Self-Image* (Oxford, 1989), 12.

[16] Thomas Mann, *Reflections of a Nonpolitical Man*, trans. Walter D. Morris (New York, 1983).

His book is filled with effusive declamations concerning this distinction. For example:

> In Nietzsche's literary remains, an interpretation of the *Meistersinger* was found that is unbelievably full of intuition. It says: "Meistersinger—*antithesis of civilization, German tradition against the French.*" The statement is invaluable. Here in a blinding flash of ingenious criticism there appears for a second the antithesis that this whole book struggles with—the antithesis that for cowardly reasons has been much denied and disputed, but that is nevertheless immortally true.[17]

Some of Mann's claims, such as his assertion that the French middle class took its ideals from the nobility without adding anything of its own,[18] appear to have influenced the substance of Elias's historical sociology. More importantly, the normative balance of Elias's comparative framework resembles Mann's: Germany appears superior because it has something, "culture," that France lacks.

Elias was aware of the nationalist implications of the German concept of *Kultur.*

> It is clear that the function of the German concept of *Kultur* took on new life in the year 1919, and in the preceding years, partly because a war was waged against Germany in the name of "civilization" and because the self-image of the Germans had to define itself anew in the situation created by the peace treaty.[19]

Yet, even though he was aware of the nationalist implications, Elias himself used the culture/civilization antithesis rather uncritically to frame his principal arguments about comparative cultural history. He stated, for example, that German intellectuals, from the eighteenth century to the twentieth century, would not have insisted on the distinction between culture and civilization "had not the development of the French bourgeoisie followed, in certain respects, exactly the opposite course from the German."[20] Elias thus believed that the objective differences between the two nations, as well as the subjective nationalism of Germany, produced the German consciousness of its superior "culture." According to him, the French never extricated the ideal of intellectual, artistic, or religious "accomplishment" from the ideal of outwardly polished "behavior."[21] The crucial period of divergence between France and Germany was the eighteenth century. At this time, the German intelligentsia and bourgeoisie rejected the aristocratic-courtly emphasis on external refinement and emphasized "the inner enrichment" of the

---

[17] Ibid., 18.

[18] Ibid, 33.

[19] Elias, *The History of Manners*, 8.

[20] Ibid., 35; see 74 for a similar comment that dichotomizes France and Germany

[21] Ibid., 4.

personality. In France, the centralization of cultural life under the absolute monarchy produced a more unitary regime. The intellectuals and the bourgeoisie were drawn into court society, and the entire nation came to honor the external refinements of courtly *civilité*.[22]

It is ironic that Elias, who was to flee from Germany to France and England following the National Socialists' accession to power in 1933, imbibed some of the more nationalistic modes of self-representation that were current within the German intellectual world. I say some of the *more* nationalistic modes of self-representation, for not all German intellectuals who used "culture" and "civilization" as key categories in the study of comparative national traditions proceeded to elevate Germany above other countries. A good example is Ernst Robert Curtius's *Die Französische Kultur* (1930). "We rate *Kultur* higher than *Zivilisation*. France places *Zivilisation* higher than *Kultur*," Curtius wrote. But while emphasizing, to some extent, the more superficial character of French *Zivilisation*, Curtius also insisted that the ideals signified by this term were more democratic and universal than the ideals of German *Kultur*.[23] Elias made no such claims.

The supreme irony, however, is that some French social scientists have taken Elias's ideas at face value, thus transmuting his nationalist antipathy toward France into a kind of sociological self-defamation. "With the aid of Norbert Elias's analyses," writes Pierre Bourdieu, "I do indeed emphasize the particularity of the French tradition, namely, the persistence, through different epochs and political regimes, of the aristocratic model of 'court society.'"[24] Moreover,

> as Norbert Elias very clearly shows, bourgeois intellectuals were much earlier and much more completely integrated into the world of the court in France than in Germany. The conventions of style and forms of civility which dominate the educational system and all its products, in particular the attention given to language and to intellectual propriety, derived in the case of France, from court society, whereas in Germany the intelligentsia, especially in the universities, set itself up in opposition to the court and the French models it was importing, summing up its vision of "high society" in the antithesis between "Civilization," characterized by frivolity and superficiality, and "Culture," defined by seriousness, profundity and authenticity.[25]

Here, as in Elias, we see the antithesis between culture and civilization treated as if it "sums up" the differences between the two nations, when it should actually be treated as a construct in German intellectual history.

[22] Ibid., 26–28, 35; see also Elias, *The Court Society*, 36.

[23] Ernst Robert Curtius, *Die Französische Kultur* (Berlin, 1930), 4, 21, 24–25.

[24] Pierre Bourdieu, *Distinction, A Social Critique of the Judgement of Taste* (Cambridge, 1984), xi.

[25] Ibid., 73–74.

Roger Chartier, in a recent book in which he acknowledges that his vision of cultural history "is largely indebted to the work of Pierre Bourdieu,"[26] devotes an essay to Elias's contribution to the discipline of cultural history. Here he suggests that to read Elias's books properly, one must understand the intellectual milieu of Weimar Germany in which they were conceived. Yet Chartier does not consider the importance of "culture" and "civilization" in Elias's work and the centrality of these concepts in earlier German thought. The only significant Weimar influence he detects is Max Weber's innocuous theory of ideal types.[27] Chartier has also written an essay on French civility in the early-modern period in which he makes some subtle distinctions between different types of civility but adheres overall to Elias's view that civility served hierarchy. The rules of civility, he writes, functioned to "assure an adequate and readable translation of the hierarchy of estates."[28] In another recent article, Jacques Revel detects a more egalitarian form of politeness in the salons of the very early seventeenth century. But he quickly adds that this egalitarianism "had no future"—the courtly model soon installed itself as the only important pattern of courtesy in France.[29]

What is remarkable in these accounts is the degree of servility that is ascribed to the French character. It is as if the court nobility, having been domesticated by the French monarchs, proceeded to domesticate the entire nation without resistance. Chartier has theorized upon this process, and his ideas are worth considering more closely. He perceives a continuous cycle of "distinction and divulgation"—a process by which the norms of upper-class comportment became publicly known through courtesy books and consequently became imitable by the lower orders. When the upper classes perceived that their manners were being copied by others, they redefined the norms of civility so as to reappropriate their monopoly on refined comportment. These new norms were divulged once again to a broader public through the courtesy literature, and the cycle began anew.

This idea of a continuous cycle of popularization and redefinition is interesting, but it is not really compatible with the argument that the essential purpose of French civility was to etch the hierarchy of estates onto the surfaces of everyday interaction. The theory presumes that the popularization of civility was inherently threatening to the elite's sense of distinction. Otherwise, there would be no need for genteel people to change their behavior in response to this popularization. The content of elite civility must have been something other than the hierarchically construed respect

[26] Roger Chartier, *Cultural History, Between Practices and Representations* (Ithaca, 1988), 15, n. 3.

[27] Chartier, "Social Figuration and Habitus, Reading Elias," in Ibid., 75–76.

[28] Roger Chartier, "Distinction et divulgation: La Civilité et ses livres," in *Lectures et lecteurs dans la France d'Ancien Régime* (Paris, 1987), 45.

[29] Jacques Revel, "The Uses of Civility," in *A History of Private Life*, vol. 3: *The Passions of the Renaissance*, ed. Roger Chartier (Cambridge, 1989), 168, 194.

that writers like Courtin advocated, for the dissemination of such respect could only enhance, rather than threaten, the elite's status. Thus, even within the framework of an interpretation that defines civility as essentially a form of distinction, there are grounds for believing that the culture of civility created a space of its own outside the hierarchy of estates.

A tendency to equate hierarchy and distinction is evident in the work of Elias and his followers, and the apparent equivalence of these two things is perhaps the main obstacle to formulating new views of the sociological significance of the early-modern preoccupation with polite manners. Although it may be true that the cultivation of manners always serves a group's need to achieve a sense of superiority, it is not necessarily true that the cultivated forms of distinction are hierarchical in content. In the case of Courtin's *Nouveau traité*, and courtly civility in general, hierarchy is indeed the structure within which the quest for distinction plays itself out. In a courtly milieu characterized by degrees of precedence, civility was inevitably characterized by degrees of obligation. As Courtin wrote:

> If we should be civil toward our equals . . . we should be all the more so toward people who are above us in rank, even if the difference is small. And if we should be civil toward them, we should be even more so toward those whose rank is eminently above ours . . . and finally much more so toward crowned heads.[30]

As this passage suggests, the essence of courtly civility was its asymmetrical structure. The rules of polite behavior, such as the injunction not to contradict a superior, simultaneously established a potential duty (not to interrupt) and a potential privilege (not to be interrupted). Whether it was in fact a duty or a privilege depended on whether one was in the presence of a superior or an inferior. Respect flowed upward but not downward. Courtin noted that his manual established no rules for the civil treatment of inferiors. "The requirements of systematic presentation would have led us to say something more precise about the forms of decorum which a superior should observe toward an inferior. But because this would be to prescribe rules to those who make them, we can dispense with it."[31]

Other models of civility, however, emphasized reciprocity as the basis of distinction. In this case, groups outside the court took pride in their superior moral and aesthetic habits, and in the egalitarianism which they alone embraced. Elizabeth C. Goldsmith observes that the salons of the seventeenth century were "exclusive," yet the culture of the salons was designed to sustain "the illusion of a world where hierarchy does not exist."[32] Here, in

[30] Courtin, *Nouveau traité*, 253.

[31] Ibid., 233.

[32] Elizabeth C. Goldsmith, *Exclusive Conversations: The Art of Interaction in Seventeenth-Century France* (Philadelphia, 1988), 69. Paradoxically, Goldsmith also argues that salon interaction "directly derived from the courtly notions of polite conversation" (45). She appears to treat the court and the salon as constituting a single elite culture. I would agree that a

the philosophical space in which the spirit of distinction merged with the spirit of universalism, we are on a territory that has been left uncharted by Elias, a territory that contains the roots of what I have called the "Self-Centered Cosmopolitanism" of the Enlightenment.[33] It is this territory that I would like to explore.

The Rules of Irrelevance

"The character of an encounter is based in part upon rulings as to properties of the situation that should be considered irrelevant, out of frame, or not happening," writes Erving Goffman.

> An effortless unawareness will be involved, and if this is not possible then an active turning-away or suppression will occur. Heroic examples of this quite fundamental process—the operation of rules of irrelevance in social interaction—can be discovered in mental hospitals, where patients can be found immersed in a game of bridge (or affecting this immersion) while . . . the whole table is surrounded by the clamor of manic patients. Here it can be clearly seen that an engaging activity acts as a boundary around the participants, sealing them off from many potential worlds of meaning and action.[34]

Goffman has not written about the history of courtesy codes, but he has developed a set of concepts for analyzing manners. Central in his perspective is the belief that every institutional microcosm can become a distinctive macrocosm. The subgroup rarely embodies the same principles of organization as the larger social universe. The "encounter" is sui generis. It does not reproduce the life of the whole; it constitutes a discrete site within it. This space is maintained by rules that establish a "boundary" around the actors, thus "sealing them off" from an outside world that may be highly structured or highly chaotic but in either case is "irrelevant" to the situation at hand.

Elias and his followers have treated civility as a set of forms designed to make all encounters hierarchical. They see hierarchy as the general principle of the French regime, and they see the court as a subunit that fully embodied this principle. The courtly rules of civility "colonized" the rest of the regime and came to supply the meaning of all coded encounters. Goffman, in contrast, suggests the possibility that the rules of "good manners" served an anticolonial function by releasing encounters from the grip of external

---

preoccupation with good form was important in both milieus, but the forms themselves were different. The court was not a source of the egalitarian "illusion" that Goldsmith aptly describes.

[33] See Chapter 2.

[34] Erving Goffman, *Encounters* (Indianapolis, 1961), 25.

structures. The encounter is a kind of game or theater. It is a separate "field for fateful dramatic action, a plane of being, an engine of meaning, a world in itself, different from all other worlds except the ones generated when the same game is played at other times."[35]

Especially interesting in this regard is Goffman's concept of "transformation rules." Like the rules of irrelevance, transformation rules relate to what is not supposed to happen or count within a gathering. "Thus, a game of checkers played between two strangers in a hospital admissions ward may constitute orderly interaction that is officially independent of sex, language, socio-economic status, physical and mental condition, religion, staff-patient hierarchy, and so forth."[36] In actuality, Goffman notes, external credentials are given some place in most encounters. "The classic phrase of England's gentry, 'Anyone for tennis?' did not quite mean *anyone*; it is not recorded that a servant has ever been allowed to define himself as *anyone*, although such doubtful types as tutors have occasionally been permitted to do so."[37] Transformation rules act like a sieve: they establish a suspension of ordinary norms by which participants in a gathering cut themselves off from externally based hierarchies, but they allow a few externally based matters to seep into the gathering. Goffman notes that external criteria seem more frequently to decide who is allowed to participate in a gathering than how the game is played once the participants have been selected.[38] This observation seems especially true for certain theorists of politeness in France.

The most prolific author of guides to polite behavior in the age of Louis XIV was Jean-Baptiste Morvan de Bellegarde (1648–1734). Bellegarde, who once described himself as "a man who has no status or authority in the world,"[39] was born into a poor noble family in Bretagne. He studied with the Jesuits in Paris under Bouhours.[40] Around 1690, Bellegarde became inspector of books at the private printing press of the duc de Maine. Of the sixty or so books of his own that he published in the ensuing twenty years, about one third were translations of early church fathers, one third original manuals of Christian piety, and one third guides to the art of polite living. Several of the works in the last category went into five editions or more during Bellegarde's lifetime and continued to appear after he was dead. The titles of these works give a clue to their purpose and subject matter: *Réflexions sur ce qui peut plaire et déplaire dans le commerce du monde* (Reflections on

---

[35] Ibid., 26–27.

[36] Ibid., 29.

[37] Ibid., 29–30.

[38] Ibid., 30.

[39] Jean-Baptiste Morvan de Bellegarde, *Lettres curieuses de littérature et de morale* (The Hague, 1702), 67.

[40] Biographical and bibliographical information comes from the article in three parts by Olivier de Gourcuff, "Un Moraliste Breton: L'Abbé de Bellegarde," *Revue de Bretagne* 2 (1887):447–56; 3 (1888):46–54, 132–45.

What Is Pleasing and Displeasing in the Commerce of The World),[41] *Suite de Réflexions sur ce qui peut plaire ou déplaire dans le commerce du monde* (Continuation of Reflections on What Is Pleasing and Displeasing in the Commerce of the World), *Réflexions sur le ridicule et les moyens de l'éviter* (Reflections on Ridicule and the Means of Avoiding It), *Réflexions sur l'élégance et la politesse du style* (Reflections on Elegance and Polite Style), *Modèles de conversations pour les personnes polies* (Models of Conversation for Polite Persons), and *Réflexions sur la politesse des moeurs* (Reflections on Polite Manners). If one can measure popularity by the number of editions, then Bellegarde was surely one of the most popular French authors on civility in the seventeenth and eighteenth centuries.

One French literary scholar has suggested that Bellegarde would be worth knowing better,[42] but no one has taken his cue. So long as Elias's monolithic interpretation of courtesy as a form of hierarchy was accepted, there was no reason to flesh out the ideas of a little known theorist of courtesy. Hierarchy, however, was not what Bellegarde sought to institute. The anonymous English translator of one of Bellegarde's works observed, "This author not only takes all occasions but sometimes goes out of his way to speak of the natural freedom and equality of mankind."[43] This comment is accurate for Bellegarde's theological writings as well as for his courtesy treatises. The two genres, in fact, must be considered in tandem in order to understand Bellegarde thoroughly. For the moment, however, it will be useful to focus on the practical rules of polite behavior outlined in Bellegarde's courtesy books in order to grasp what "freedom" and "equality" meant in the context of civil encounters.[44]

Bellegarde's works on politeness are very repetitive, and it is possible to point to a common set of themes. He consistently made it clear that politeness was a sign of personal distinction, but that this distinction had no relation to an already existing hierarchy. Nobility did not automatically

---

[41] The term *le monde* is remarkably difficult to translate. It can mean the world, the worldly (i.e., secular) departments of life, convivial company, and aristocratic society. Often, it carries two or more of these associations. In Bellegarde's works, the second and third are the most pronounced.

[42] Jean-Pierre Dens, "L'Honnête homme et l'esthétique du paraître," *Papers on French Seventeenth-Century Literature*, no. 6 (1976–77), 72.

[43] *The Letters of Monsieur l'Abbé de Bellegarde* (London, 1705), translator's introduction. The work translated was Bellegarde's *Lettres curieuses de littérature et de morale*.

[44] As my terminology in this sentence implies, I shall be using the words "civility," "politeness," and "courtesy" (and their adjectival forms) interchangeably. In my usage, all of these words refer to a concept or code of good manners, but none denotes a specific style of good manners. These words will indicate specific styles when I use them with adjectives, as in "courtly politeness," "salon politeness," "egalitarian civility," and "hierarchical civility." I reserve the term "courtliness," however, for the hierarchical model of polite interaction practiced at the French court. And I use the term "sociability" to refer only to the more egalitarian form of politeness associated with the salons and Enlightenment philosophy.

confer prestige; nor did it automatically deserve deference. Value was not given from without but was constituted within the polite gathering. "The merit of a man is decided on the basis of how he acquits himself in conversation. . . . He is judged according to the impression that he gives of his person in *le commerce du monde*."[45] Bellegarde even affirmed that many grandees were so infatuated with their own rank that they were incapable of politeness.

> The choice of the persons whom one will frequent is one of the things that must be studied the most. But it would be false delicacy or excessively vain to want to associate only with people of rank while spurning persons of low birth. Personal merit should be preferred to rank. It is not with the greatest seigneurs that commerce is the most agreeable. Their manners do not always correspond to their high birth. With the titles of Viscount and Marquis one often has much that is vulgar (*roture*) in the soul.[46]

According to Bellegarde, many grandees believed that their birth was enough to confer prestige upon them; but in fact, most members of the nobility did not possess "those easy manners" and "that delicate style" that were the signs of politeness.[47] Bellegarde assured those who were not nobles that they could compensate for their low birth by cultivating "a genteel air" and "good manners" (*un air honnête, les belles manières*)—things that "emit more honor and much more charm than everything given by birth and fortune."[48]

For Bellegarde, the constitutive activity of politeness, the activity that was essential to master if one sought to be truly genteel, was conversation. He was concerned with the *art de plaire*, the technique by which pleasure was created in communication. In one work he defined *politesse* itself as "a certain attention which, through our words and manners, makes others happy with us and themselves."[49] The supposition that pleasure was the goal of exchange was the foundation of Bellegarde's egalitarianism. This pleasure-oriented approach makes Bellegarde's concept of politeness similar to Georg Simmel's concept of sociability. Simmel suggested that when exchange was pursued as a form of sociability, that is, as an intrinsically enjoyable activity, the norms of interaction tended to become more egalitarian than they usually were.[50] Simmel's concept of sociability resembles Goff-

[45] Jean-Baptiste Morvan de Bellegarde, *Modèles de conversation pour les personnes polies*, 5th ed. (Amsterdam, 1709), Avertissement.

[46] Bellegarde, *Réflexions sur le ridicule et sur les moyens de l'éviter* (Paris, 1696), 247–48.

[47] Bellegarde, *Réflexions sur ce qui peut plaire ou déplaire dans le commerce du monde* (Paris, 1690), Epitre. See also Bellegarde's *Réflexions sur la politesse des moeurs* (Paris, 1698), 23.

[48] Bellegarde, *Réflexions sur ce qui peut plaire*, Avertissement.

[49] Bellegarde, *Réflexions sur le ridicule*, 23.

[50] See my discussion of Simmel and the ideal types of sociability in Chapter 1.

man's concept of the rules of irrelevance, and the following passage from Simmel is in fact cited by Goffman.

> The fact is that whatever the participants in the gathering may possess in terms of objective attributes—attributes that are centered outside the particular gathering in question—must not enter it. Wealth, social position, erudition, fame, exceptional capabilities and merits, may not play any part in sociability. At most they may play the role of mere nuances of that immaterial character with which reality alone, in general, is allowed to enter the social work of art called sociability.[51]

In the same spirit, Bellegarde stated that communication had to be unconstrained. He believed it should be spontaneous, not in the sense that people should say everything they felt, but in the sense that the flow of the group's conversation should be unplanned and should have a wide latitude for development. No one could control the agenda of discussion. "Conversation requires nothing studied or constrained. Chance, contingencies, the situation of the minds composing the circle, should give birth to the subjects treated."[52] "It is necessary that the occasion engender conversation and that it be conducted by chance."[53] "One should go along with the current" (*Il faut se laisser au torrent*).[54]

Bellegarde dismissed the obsession with trivial ceremonies, an obsession he associated with the court. He condemned those whose speech was nothing but a shower of "formalities" and who would argue interminably about pointless matters of precedence, such as who had the right to pass through a door first.[55] "A free, easy, and natural air is much more commodious," he stated. The absence of freedom ruins conversation, "for when freedom [*franchise*] is banished from conversation, it is no longer anything but an embarrassment and a kind of little war."[56] He felt that one should also be tolerant of the differences of others: "Let others live in their own way."[57] Those who insisted that others agree with their own ideas were enemies of good conversation.

> This is, however, the privilege of conversation: everyone is permitted to say his sentiment, and we must suffer with good grace those who contradict us. It would be an insupportable tyranny to wish to fix the thought of others under one's own opinion. Kings, with all their authority, have no jurisdiction over the

---

51 Georg Simmel, *The Sociology of Georg Simmel*, trans. K. H. Wolff (Glencoe, Ill., 1950), 45–46; also cited by Goffman, *Encounters*, 21.

52 Bellegarde, *Modèles de conversation*, Avertissement.

53 Bellegarde, *Réflexions sur le ridicule*, 59.

54 Bellegarde, *Lettres curieuses*, Avertissement.

55 Bellegarde, *Réflexions sur ce qui peut plaire*, 208–9.

56 Ibid., 209, 211.

57 Bellegarde, *Réflexions sur la politesse des moeurs*, 41.

sentiments of their peoples, and individuals should not claim to be more absolute than kings.[58]

No one should strive to dominate the group, for "everyone must contribute to the pleasure of the conversation." According to Bellegarde, "The great secret of pleasing is to give others time to say what they know and to applaud them when they say something good."[59]

Bellegarde insisted that the polite individual was one who desired "to give pleasure to everyone." Conversation was not supposed to be a competitive game. The good conversationalist did not feel frustration when someone else spoke eloquently or received praise. This was the habit of the court, whose members, as Bellegarde described them, treated conversation as a zero-sum game in which "they [were] in despair at the elevation of their competitors."[60] In a discussion of the role of humor in conversation, Bellegarde stated that it was better not to engage in pleasantries at all than to risk insulting others by making mirth of their imperfections. He also underscored the principle of reciprocity when he said that although one should not react violently to a light joke made at one's expense, one might respond in kind to an outright insult—regardless of the rank of the insulter—

> as did that young seigneur of Greece who had come to the court of Augustus. He was presented to the emperor, and it was observed that this young man resembled him [the emperor] exactly. Laughing, Augustus asked him if his mother had ever been to Rome. "No, sir," he answered without registering any surprise, "but my father has been here."[61]

Bellegarde suggested that those who wished to be pleasing should cover their own speech with a film of modesty and gentleness (*douceur*, a key term in Bellegarde's thought). They should avoid talking about themselves and especially avoid referring to themselves as superior beings or as part of an exclusive order. The polite person should never brag about family name, lineage, or estate. The idea was to purge one's discourse of those irrelevant considerations. "However illustrious be the blood from which one has issued, it is always proper to have modest sentiments and one must never be infatuated with or brag about one's rank."[62] Instead of trying to impose one's status (as given by the hierarchy of estates and orders) upon others, one ought to conform to the norms of politeness and leave it to others to

[58] Bellegarde, *Réflexions sur ce qui peut plaire*, 183. See also Bellegarde, *Réflexions sur le ridicule*, 159.

[59] Bellegarde, *Réflexions sur ce qui peut plaire*, 155, 173. See also p. 12 of the same work as well as *Réflexions sur le ridicule*, 34–35, and *Réflexions sur la politesse des moeurs*, 163.

[60] Bellegarde, *Réflexions sur ce qui peut plaire*, 18, 64–66.

[61] Ibid., 155–56.

[62] Ibid., 115–16; see also 258. For other examples of emphatic transformation rules concerning birth, wealth, and lineage, see Bellegarde, *Réflexions sur le ridicule*, 2, 74, and *Réflexions sur la politesse des moeurs*, 109.

determine one's value. "Leave to the public [*le publique*] its suffrage," Bellegarde declared. "It is up to it to decide what glory you deserve."[63]

The "public" makes its appearance here as a sphere of independent judgment, a sphere in which individuals interact, define each other, and evaluate each other without reference to the hierarchies observed elsewhere in the regime. The exact location of this "public" and the conditions of admission into it are left ambiguous, though it is clear that the "public" is not identified with the court. At times, Bellegarde appears to write for the new elite created by the growth of the royal bureaucracy—an elite of nobles, financiers, newly titled administrators, and writers. As Carolyn C. Lougee has shown, seventeenth-century salons in Paris acted as a convivial meeting ground of these elements of the new service elite. The members of the salons, who upheld state service and wealth as the basis of distinction, saw personal refinement as something that could be learned rather than something given by birth. Noble members updated their sense of superiority by casting it in the form of a less haughty but more pleasing courtesy, while the bourgeois or recently ennobled members certified their status through their cultivated manners.[64]

That Bellegarde wrote primarily for the salons seems evident when he says:

> Although these reflections are useful to all kinds of people, it must be admitted that most of the maxims are intended for the use of those who see *le grand monde* and who find themselves in its fine conversations.[65]

The expression *le grand monde*, however, does not have a clear institutional or class referent. In none of his writings does Bellegarde mention specific orders, families, salons, or other particular settings. (His most specific institutional reference is "the court," which he criticizes.) His intended audience is indeterminate even when it is restricted. There is no exact correspondence between his imagined readership and a given class of people. *Le grand monde*, then, is not so much an institution as a way of behaving. It is the space of sociability within the hierarchical regime.

Bellegarde's conversational maxims were not novel. In fact, he only systematized the egalitarian precepts that had already been elaborated in the late seventeenth century by other theorists of polite behavior, such as Méré, Scudéry, and Callières. An examination of the works of these authors reveals that the preference for an inclusive politeness came decisively from within the aristocracy.

---

[63] Bellegarde, *Réflexions sur le ridicule*, 83.

[64] See my discussion of the ideal types of sociability in Chapter 1.

[65] Bellegarde, *Réflexions sur ce qui peut plaire*, Avertissement.

The Chevalier de Méré (1610–1685) was one of the most influential theorists of courtesy for the salon milieu.[66] Méré spent most of his life publicizing himself as an impeccable example of leisured gentlemanliness and deriding others who falsely posed as cultivated.[67] In his *Lettres*, he flamboyantly mocked the "artificial world" of the court.[68] Méré rejected the suggestion that the court was the one place a person had to frequent in order to observe and acquire personal refinement. In an essay entitled "De la Conversation," he wrote:

> It is good to remember that this court which is taken as a model is a crowd of all sorts of people; and that some are there only in passing, others have not been there long, and the majority, though they were born there, are not to be imitated.[69]

Méré praised Socrates, who was not too haughty to speak freely with artisans. On a less populist note, he affirmed that one had to be a member of the more polished circles (*le monde*) to be a truly accomplished speaker. "For to learn the graces of conversation, one must be in *le monde* and one must be a true *honnête homme*."[70] Méré's *le monde*, however, resembled Bellegarde's *le grand monde* and should not be confused with the courtly elite or any other class whose composition was strictly limited. It is true that some authors in the period employed *le monde* or *le grand monde* to signify either the court itself or a larger milieu for which the court was the model. Pierre de Villiers wrote in his *Réflexions sur les défauts d'autrui* (Reflections on the Faults of Others, 1690):

> The court is the school in which one learns the science of *le monde* and one is more or less polite in accordance with one's distance from the court.[71]

[66] According to Jean-Pierre Dens, Méré "incarnates better than anyone the spirit of the salons of the epoch, on which his whole work is a sort of commentary." "L'Art des agréments: Le Chevalier de Méré et la sensibilité mondaine" (Ph.D. diss., Columbia University, 1971), 2.

[67] For biographical information on Méré, see the editor's introduction to the first volume of Antoine Gombaud, Chevalier de Méré, *Oeuvres complètes du Chevalier de Méré*, ed. Charles H. Boudhours (Paris, 1930).

[68] Antoine Gombaud, Chevalier de Méré, *Lettres de Monsieur le Chevalier de Méré* (Paris, 1689), 197 (letter 35); see also 299 (letter 65). Méré's diary also contains anticourtly jibes, such as, "I notice that those who have been at the court for forty years are as stupid as when they arrived." See "Divers propos du Chevalier de Méré en 1674–1675," *Revue d'histoire littéraire de la France publiée par la Société d'Histoire littéraire de la France*, 19 (1922), 85.

[69] Méré, "De la Conversation," *Oeuvres complètes*, 2:128. This essay was first published in 1677. See also 122: "As for the royal residences . . . people go there less for discussion than to be seen. . . . Hence the majority, who go there for the sake of their private interest, are tiresome careerists instead of good company."

[70] Méré, *Lettres*, 428 (letter 110).

[71] Cited in Dens, "L'Art des agréments," 49. Other examples of this type of usage appear in Erich Auerbach, "La Cour et la Ville," in *Scenes from the Drama of European Literature* (Man-

Méré, in contrast, wrote:

> Many people, because they are from the court, imagine themselves to be of *le grand monde* . . . but there is quite a difference between the two. This court, though the finest and perhaps the largest on earth, has its faults and limits. But *le grand monde*, which extends everywhere, is more accomplished, so that for those who are concerned with those manners of living and behaving which are favored, it is necessary to consider the court and *le grand monde* separately, and to be aware that the court, through either custom or caprice, sometimes approves of things that *le grand monde* will not permit.[72]

The significance of a passage such as this can scarcely be overestimated. A distinction between state and civil society is implicit in the explicit distinction between the court and *le grand monde*. By rejecting the notion that the court was the best model of cultivation, Méré rejected the symbolic field under the immediate supervision of the absolute monarch.[73] In its place, he championed the standards of an autonomous sphere.

What were these standards? Méré's conception of good company and conversation was, like Bellegarde's, eudaemonistic. This is not to say that Méré was a utilitarian who believed that pleasure of any kind was inherently good. Rather, he believed that some pleasures were more noble or refined than others. Nevertheless, Méré saw the production of certain kinds of pleasure as the end of cultivated manners. This notion that manners existed to *produce* a form of subjectivity was profoundly different from the courtly notion that manners existed to *recognize* preexisting hierarchies. Méré claimed that he "was the first to disabuse *honnêtes gens*" of the importance of condolence calls and other acts of pure protocol.[74] He also rejected the formalities stemming from respect for superior rank. The purpose of good breeding was to make enjoyable interaction possible. "He who speaks, if he desires to be liked and considered good company, should hardly think about anything except making his listeners as happy [*heureux*] as he can. For everyone wishes to be happy."[75]

The kind of happiness or pleasure that Méré had in mind was that which comes from the exchange of well-formed sentiments and ideas. The speakers' thoughts should be interesting, and their words should aptly pub-

---

chester, 1984), 133–82. Auerbach focuses on those writers who treated *le monde* as an amalgamation of court and town but failed to notice that many writers in the late seventeenth century devalued the court in the course of praising *le monde*.

[72] Méré, "De la Conversation," 111.

[73] This point has already been made by Lawrence E. Klein in a well-conceptualized article, "Politeness in Seventeenth-Century England and France," *Cahiers du dix-septième* 4 (1990): 97–100.

[74] Méré, *Lettres*, 356–59 (letter 87). See also Méré, "De la Conversation," 103.

[75] Méré, "De la Conversation," 103.

licize their thoughts. Méré's view of conversation was thus highly intellectual. Language, as he understood it, was not merely sonorous stimulation; it was an instrument of representation.

> For words only please inasmuch as they are fit for expressing our sentiments, and it would signify an absence of *esprit* to look for words before having found the things [*de chercher les mots avant que d'avoir trouvé les choses*].[76]

From this it followed that the essence of good conversation and the aesthetic source of pleasure was clarity.[77] The goal of cultivated speakers was to make their perceptions "intelligible" to others.

Since obscurity was ugliness,[78] the *honnête homme* was skillful in transforming the most difficult thoughts and subtle sentiments into clear expressions. This translation did not take place by means of a fixed set of rules. Rather, it took place by "accommodating," as Méré often said, one's ideas and words to the particular listeners at hand. The audience was thus internal to the procedure of clarification, rather than the mere recipient of a message purified according to exogenous rules. The speaker, Méré said, must "put himself in the place of those whom he wishes to please," adopting such metaphors and examples as will be intelligible to them.[79] When the speakers in a group mutually accommodated their forms of expression to each other's intelligence, mood, and character, they achieved what Méré called *conformité* and *sympathie*.[80] This reciprocally sustained understanding was the true source of the collective enjoyment of conversation. "It is *conformité* that allows us to please each other and to love each other with a reciprocal affection."[81]

Méré offered no precise technique for creating conformity and sympathy, but he did state:

> It is necessary to observe what goes on in the heart and mind of the persons with whom one is communicating and to be accustomed from the start to recognizing sentiments and ideas by their nearly imperceptible signs.[82]

Méré's principle of the *je ne sais quoi* (the indefinable quality that a refined person has) underscored the impossibility of laying down a fixed method for tailoring one's ideas and sentiments to the ideas and sentiments of others.

---

[76] Méré, "De l'Eloquence et de l'entretien," in *Oeuvres complètes*, 3:107. This essay was first published posthumously in 1700.

[77] On the theme of "clarity" in French literature in the period as a whole, see Daniel Mornet, *Histoire de la clarté française, ses origines, son évolution, sa valeur* (Paris, 1920).

[78] Méré, "De l'Eloquence et de l'entretien," in *Oeuvres complètes*, 3:118.

[79] Méré, "Divers propos," 91, and "De l'Eloquence et de l'entretien," 118.

[80] Méré, "De la Délicatesse dans les choses," in *Oeuvres complètes*, 3:132–33 [first published posthumously in 1700].

[81] Méré, "De la Conversation," 106.

[82] Ibid., 107.

The *je ne sais quoi*, which appears to be an elitist idea, was actually meant to promote a rapprochement between souls. The challenge was to conform to the "particular mood," "nature," and "inclination" of others.[83] Méré could not give concrete rules for how this was to be done: "This art seems to have a bit of sorcery in it."[84] But in spite of the ambiguity concerning the means, Méré sustained an ideal of civility that was clearly different in its goal from the hierarchical courtly civility. In place of "rank," "condition," and "quality" (the attributes that commanded deference at court), he substituted "mood," "nature," and "inclination." The categories of hierarchical organization were replaced by the variations of individual personality.

Like Bellegarde, Méré emphasized the importance of maintaining a feeling of spontaneity in the conversational circle. The speaker should adopt an agreeable tone and not pay too much attention to the order of ideas ("to what goes before and what comes after").[85] Many of his maxims had the purpose of sustaining the conversational group as a circuit of free communication and preventing it from freezing into a ritualistic order of ceremony. He rejected the "constrained posture" of the court and advocated a "free posture: and "natural air."[86] "Conversation must not appear studied; and the more one can make it free and easy, the better it seems to me."[87]

The goal of freedom did not imply the absence of imperatives. Freedom, which in this context meant the flow of communication, the play of freely moving discourse,[88] required certain rules. The accomplished speaker was to avoid boisterous laughter, for it might alienate those who were not equally amused. One also had to avoid a somber bearing because extreme seriousness could weigh down the discussion.[89] Daydreaming was forbidden for the obvious reason that conversation required attention and participation.[90] The individual had to be engaged: "When one goes into *le monde*, it is necessary to be open and ready to communicate."[91] In intellectual discussions, the refined speaker was never to make complex points or scholarly references that others could not understand. And instead of trying to judge things definitively, one should only seek to make an interesting contribution that pleased others with its freshness (*naïveté*).[92] The person who

---

[83] Méré, "De la Délicatesse," 132.

[84] Méré, "De la Conversation," 107.

[85] Ibid., 105.

[86] Ibid., 110, 121.

[87] Méré, "De la Délicatesse," 137.

[88] "The play of freely moving discourse" is a phrase I have taken from Michael Moriarty's interesting *Taste and Ideology in Seventeenth-Century France* (Cambridge, 1988), 19. Moriarty discusses Bouhours in this context, but his remarks about the idea of freedom in Bouhours's theory of polite conversation apply well to Bellegarde and Méré.

[89] Méré, "De la Conversation," 103.

[90] Ibid., 108.

[91] Ibid., 121.

[92] Ibid., 106–8, 113–14.

adhered to these rules and who could "say good things about everything and say them agreeably" had reached the high point of refinement. "The mind can go no further, and this is the *chef-d'oeuvre* of intelligence."[93]

Not all noble theorists of the art of conversation in the late seventeenth century were as anticourtly and egalitarian as Méré. It is important to observe, however, that some of them were *more* so. A good example is François de Callières (1645–1717), who published two successful works on civility, *Des mots à la mode et des nouvelles façons de parler* (On Fashionable Words and the New Ways of Speaking, first published in 1692) and *De la Science du monde et des connaissances utiles à la conduite de la vie* (On the Science of Good Company and the Knowledge Useful for the Conduct of Life, 1717). The books are written in the form of a dialogue between a group of nobles who meet regularly to discuss the nature of *le beau langage*. The discussion, which is continuous across the two volumes, begins when one figure, a "Commander" who has recently returned after twenty years of military service abroad, shows surprise at the fashions of speaking that have become common in France during his absence. In spite of his long absence from France, he quickly establishes himself as the authoritative voice in the circle on matters of linguistic usage—a kind of Socrates in a Platonic dialogue.

In his treatment of these dialogues in *The History of Manners*, Elias cited the voice of another figure in the dialogues, a noble woman, as if she represents the views of the author. The snobbish lady repeatedly suggests that it is important for the nobility to distance itself from the bourgeoisie by cultivating a distinct vocabulary.[94] But the concept of distinction achieved through linguistic differentiation is precisely what the Commander rejects. He describes the courtly vocabulary as "a strange jargon"[95] and affirms that the purpose of language is to facilitate communication, not separation. "Would you thus like noble people to speak like ordinary people?" the lady asks with apprehension. "Yes, without doubt," the Commander responds, "when ordinary people speak well and make themselves understood; and I believe I would renounce my rank if it entailed a loss of good sense."[96] "As for me," the snobbish lady says later, "I am quite convinced that noble people must distinguish themselves from the bourgeois through language as they are distinguished from them by birth." The Commander does not soften his response, "It is, Madame, by speaking precisely and by speaking well that one distinguishes oneself through language and not by affecting new and extraordinary manners of expressing oneself."[97]

[93] Ibid., 119.
[94] Cited by Elias in *The History of Manners*, 93, 109.
[95] François de Callières, *Des Mots à la mode et des nouvelles façons de parler* (Paris, 1696), 20. As noted above, the first edition appeared in 1692.
[96] Ibid., 29–30.
[97] Ibid., 74.

At the beginning of *De la Science du monde*, all of the characters now appreciate the Commander's wisdom and thank him for having corrected their previous misconceptions about refined language. They ask him to define in greater detail the manners "which can contribute to form an agreeable, polite, obliging, and gracious man."[98] The Commander responds with a set of precepts designed to negate hierarchy. His basic principle is that anyone striving to be polite must be more concerned with showing decorum (*les bienséances*) to others than with exacting it from them.

> People who do not know how to live generally require too many pains from their friends and do not return them enough. This is due to the fact that they almost never journey outside of themselves in order to reflect on their duties.[99]

To live politely is to "journey outside" oneself, to take on a second self that fulfills the needs of the interactive circle instead of one's own pride as a privileged member of a hierarchical regime. In the *Nouveau traité*, Courtin told the grandees that they need not worry about their obligations to their inferiors. Callières, in contrast, told the grandee to "go outside himself" in order to show respect and give pleasure to others.

> He who wishes to please must shed his own disposition (*humeur*) in order to be accommodating to that of others. . . . He must, so to speak, go outside of himself in order to put himself in the place of the one he wishes to please.[100]

"A free and natural air must reign," says the Commander.[101] A polite person will not be offended by people who are ignorant of fashionable words or who speak with unfamiliar accents.[102] It is not at all important to speak or expect others to speak with the accent of the court, for the majority of courtiers speak badly.[103] The polite person, moreover, is never self-righteous about his own opinions.

> One must get accustomed to proposing one's sentiments only as likely opinions and not as decisions to which everybody must be subjected; for [to do the latter] would be to remove from the people with whom one communicates the right that they naturally have to judge for themselves the things in question.

According to the Commander, the polite person must possess "a disinterestedness (*désinteressement*) such that he is always ready to abandon dispute."[104]

[98] François de Callières, *De la Science du monde et des connaissances utiles à la conduite de la vie* (Paris, 1717), 4–5.
[99] Ibid., 8–9.
[100] Ibid., 21.
[101] Ibid., 37.
[102] Ibid., 37, 47.
[103] Ibid., 47–49, 54.
[104] Ibid., 69–70.

For the Commander, politeness is a tool for creating a common ground of sociable interaction. To the extent that he sees politeness as a form of distinction, the distinction lies in being able to sustain this common ground. The Commander cites and rejects a maxim attributed to a Spanish noble, "All is well as long as we are not equal."[105] Instead, he says, "We must become accustomed to speaking to our equals as if they were our superiors and to our inferiors as if they were our equals."[106] This formulation is a perfect example of a "transformation rule," for it exhibits a consciousness of two orders of being. The first is the world outside of the polite gathering in which people are ranked differentially as "equals," "superiors," or "inferiors." The second is the order of sociability, in which others are systematically treated as if they were one degree higher than they actually are, that is, as if they were at least our equals.

The Public Sphere in Apolitical Form

Madeleine de Scudéry (1607–1701) offered a vision of politeness that was similar to that of Méré and Callières. She is of special interest, however, partly because she was a woman and the organizer of a salon, and partly because her general definitions of "conversation" are suggestive for understanding the relation between politeness and politics. One of the leading novelists in the decade following the Fronde, Scudéry enjoyed a second wave of popularity in the 1680s and '90s thanks to her numerous *Conversations*, a series of dialogues on the art of civilized living.[107] Victor Cousin called these works "so many little masterpieces of politeness and good taste." In the conversations represented in these volumes, with their "natural and free allure and happy spontaneity of speech," Cousin detected the existence of freedom under the absolute monarchy and a proof for his conviction that "our country is profoundly monarchical and profoundly liberal at the same time."[108]

Scudéry maintained a salon for several years that did indeed have a certain "liberal" character. In her home on the rue de Beauce in the Marais, she promoted a relatively egalitarian form of conviviality that ran against the grain of the corporate regime. The composition of her salon has been

[105] Ibid., 97–99.

[106] Ibid., 95.

[107] Her *Conversations* appeared in ten volumes during the years 1680–92: Madeleine de Scudéry, *Conversations sur divers sujets*, 2 vols. (Paris, 1680); *Conversations nouvelles sur divers sujets*, 2 vols. (Paris, 1684); *La Morale du monde, ou conversations*, 2 vols. (Paris, 1686); *Nouvelles conversations de morale*, 2 vols. (Paris, 1688); *Entretiens de morale*, 2 vols. (Paris, 1692).

[108] Victor Cousin, *La Société française au XVIIe siècle d'après le Grand Cyrus de Mademoiselle de Scudéry* (Paris, 1905), xvi, 14.

studied, and the mixing of ranks appears as one of its salient features.[109] The salon included the wives of financiers and several men of letters of humble birth. Their status in the gatherings held by Sappho, as Scudéry was called, did not suffer on account of their origins. Scudéry herself was noble, yet she never lived at court.[110] Georges Mongredien called her salon "bourgeois," meaning not that its membership was entirely middle-class but that it contributed to the rise of a fashionable urban milieu separate from the court at Versailles.[111]

Scudéry's colloquies consist of subtle discussions among a small number of speakers about the requirements of gentility. The tone of her dialogues is always tranquil. The speakers, who usually number about six, rarely disagree for long. Their consideration of every issue moves peacefully toward consensus. Several of the conversations focus on the nature of good conversation itself. The content of civil conversation is frequently its own form. This self-discussion has the effect of suggesting that the norms of conversation are not arbitrary or coercive but are defined consensually through the communicative dynamic of the gathering. One of the dialogues, entitled "De la Conversation," begins when a speaker named Cilenie[112] proposes that conversation is "the bond of all human society [société], the greatest pleasure of well-bred people, and the most usual means of introducing not only politeness but also the purest morality."[113] The members of the circle give assent to Cilenie's proposition and agree to pursue collectively a more precise definition of polite speech.

They begin by noting its nonpractical character, its isolation from professional duties and motives. "For when people speak only on account of the practical requirements of their affairs, this cannot be called [conversation]," says Cilenie. "Indeed," another responds, "a plaintiff who speaks of his case before the judges, a merchant who negotiates with another, an army general who gives orders, a king who talks about politics in his council—none of this is what should be called conversation." For all these people speak about "their interests and their affairs," whereas conversation is speech for the sake of conversation itself, which is "the sweetest charm of life."[114]

Having established that conversation exists for sociability (in Simmel's

[109] Nicole Aronson, *Mademoiselle de Scudéry ou le voyage au pays du tendre* (Paris, 1986), 216; Mongredien, *La Vie de société*, 119ff.; Cousin, *La Société française*, iv.

[110] Aronson, *Mademoiselle de Scudéry*, 17.

[111] Mongredien, *La Vie de société*, 119ff.

[112] Scudéry designates speakers by their first names alone, thus making it impossible to identify their family or estate. This device adds an egalitarian and almost liminal flavor to the dialogues.

[113] Scudéry, "De la Conversation," reprinted in *La Société française au dix-septième siècle*, ed. Thomas F. Crane (New York, 1907), 240. The dialogue was first published in Scudéry, *Conversations sur divers sujets*, vol. 1.

[114] Ibid., 240.

sense), the speakers proceed to enumerate the faults that can ruin it. The chief vice is the tendency of people to talk vainly about their private possessions. Self-centered discourse, the speakers agree, is never amusing. Too many women talk about their bodies and appearance—their clothing, jewels, and other "boring trifles." Too many men talk about their genealogies and estates. Pleasurable conversation cannot be rooted in what is particular to any given participant. The characters in the dialogue unanimously condemn women whose imagination is centered on the family, "on all their little domestic concerns . . . such as the good qualities of their children."[115]

In Scudéry's effort to differentiate conversation from the domestic sphere on the one hand, and from business, law, and politics on the other, we can discern the outlines of a kind of *aristocratic feminism*—a critique both of the domestic sphere to which women were relegated and the professional sphere from which women were excluded. This aristocratic feminism can be distinguished from *modern feminism* in that the latter, while critical of the professional and political domains, also seeks to include women within them. Scudéry's definition of conversation simply makes the professional and political domains irrelevant to cultivated pursuits. "Conversation" stands for a zone in which women can achieve distinction without struggling for sovereign power or economic equality. Instead of calling for the abolition of existing inequalities, Scudéry espoused an art in which the inequalities did not count. The logic of aristocratic feminism helped to give the concept of conversational politeness its distinctively apolitical but egalitarian flavor.

For Scudéry, the most important element in good conversation was variety, a mixture of topics discussed as well as a mixture of people discussing them. Nobody, male or female, was to dictate the topics or prevent the flow of conversation in new directions.

> Since conversation should be free and natural, and since all who form the company have an equal right to change it as it seems good to them, it is irksome to find those obstinate persons who leave nothing unsaid on a topic and who always return to it, no matter how much one tries to interrupt them.[116]

All subjects of general interest, including science, love, and politics, were legitimate subjects of conversation. "There is nothing which cannot enter [conversation]; it must be free and diverse."[117] Political matters might thus enter as the content of sociable discourse, though sociable discourse was not politically pragmatic or instrumental in its intent. Everything could be included in conversation, so long as the form in which it was expressed was

[115] Ibid., 241, 244, 246.
[116] Ibid., 256.
[117] Ibid., 258–59.

designed to give pleasure to the members of the group. The key thing was to say nothing that others would find unpleasant or shocking. The purpose of form was to moderate content. One was to speak "nobly of low things, [and] rather simply of elevated things." The style should be "natural" and "without hurry or affectation."[118] Scudéry espoused evenness and tranquillity. Conversation was to be diverse yet stable, free to wander yet controlled. Spontaneity and self-control went together. "Thus I would like one never to know what one is going to say and always to know what one is saying."[119]

In another of Scudéry's dialogues, "De la Politesse," the speakers agree that politeness consists in something very much like the Golden Rule.

> It [politeness] is never to express a rude or uncivil word to anyone. It is to say nothing to others that you would not wish them to say to you. It is the absence of a wish to be the tyrant in conversation, to be always speaking without letting those to whom you are speaking speak themselves.[120]

Scudéry's dialogue called "De Parler trop ou trop peu et comment il faut parler" (On Speaking Too Much or Too Little and How One Should Speak) reiterates the critique of people who talk too much and offers the rule of "*laisser parler ceux avec qui l'on est*" (let the others speak). The person aspiring to be civil had to know that "society [*société*] should be free; that there should be no tyranny in conversation; that everyone has a part and the right to speak in turn."[121] The dialogue ends with an ideal image of a free salon.

> In all countries there are certain homes that one finds much more agreeable than others simply because their owners do not constrain any of their guests. Here, indeed, one daydreams [unlike Méré, Scudéry permits daydreaming in conversation], one speaks, one laughs, one sings, one communicates with whomever one wants, one goes in and out without saying anything; and one passes the time there with a liberty that has something so sweet in it that one prefers [these homes] to others.[122]

Pleasure is here identified with a lack of constraint, the possibility of entering and leaving the conversational milieu at will. The joy of sociability flows from the exercise of choice and from spontaneous engagement.

Scudéry's ideal domestic habitat, with its rejection of "tyranny" and its

---

[118] Ibid.

[119] Ibid., 260.

[120] Scudéry, "De la Politesse," in *Conversations nouvelles sur divers sujets*, 1: 65.

[121] Scudéry, "De Parler trop ou trop peu et comment il faut parler," in *Choix de conversations de Mlle. de Scudéry*, ed. Phillip J. Wolfe (Ravenna, 1977), 27; first published in *Conversations sur divers sujets*, vol. 1.

[122] Ibid (ed. Wolfe)., 38–39.

emphasis on "liberty," appears to be an example of what Jürgen Habermas called "the public sphere in apolitical form" in *The Structural Transformation of the Public Sphere*.[123] Habermas used the concept of an apolitical public sphere to explain how democracy could begin to develop within an absolutist regime based on hierarchical principles. The process began when members of the regime transcended differences of hierarchy by meeting in settings that were deliberately cut off from politics. "The decisive element was not so much the political equality of the members but their exclusiveness in relation to the political realm of absolutism as such: social equality was possible at first only as an equality outside the state."[124] Private persons came together to constitute a free audience "behind closed doors." The salon "replaced the celebration of rank with a tact befitting equals." It "established the public as in principle inclusive." Strategically confining itself to the domestic sphere, this public would later dare to emerge in the open light and seek to transform the absolutist state.[125]

Habermas's description of the egalitarianism of the salon is accurate, but his effort to integrate the rise of inclusive politeness into an account of the fall of absolutism makes his interpretation similar to the interpretation of Cochin. This interpretation is open to the criticism that it prematurely politicizes the content of private life, making every mode of nonhierarchical interaction meaningful only as a foreshadowing of democratic politics instead of a self-sufficient cultural form.[126] Habermas's interpretation, however, is not exactly the same as Cochin's. While Cochin wished to explain the origins of Jacobinism and totalitarian democracy, Habermas was concerned with explaining the rise of liberal democracy in which property rights are central. As a result, Habermas did not associate the most radical modern political tendencies with prerevolutionary sociability. Indeed, the problem of the origins of Jacobin democracy does not figure in his study. Nevertheless, Habermas regards the growth of salon politeness as an anticipation of subsequent political movements. Civility was a "training ground"[127] for the bourgeois political imagination, a place where citizens could become familiar with equality in an intimate setting, where they could exercise reason in a highly focused milieu, before directing their critical understanding against the sovereign power.

It is worth remembering that the concepts of open political debate, political participation, and political equality predated the seventeenth century as

---

[123] Jürgen Habermas, *The Structural Transformation of the Public Sphere, An Inquiry into a Category of Bourgeois Society*, (Cambridge, 1989), 29.

[124] Ibid., 35.

[125] Ibid., 35–37.

[126] See Chapter 1 for a critique of Cochin.

[127] Ibid., 29.

part of the classical and Renaissance republican tradition.[128] These ideals did not require a period of incubation in protopolitical institutions in order to develop into an intelligible political alternative to absolutism in the late seventeenth century. In fact, it makes more sense to see egalitarian politeness as a postdemocratic ideal rather than a protodemocratic one. Habermas's expression, "the public sphere in apolitical form," becomes an appropriate description of egalitarian politeness when we consider that the authors who advocated it, instead of seeking to pave the way toward political action, were in fact repudiating political action by investing the concept of a nonpolitical public with value. The concept of politeness, in other words, implied the superiority of the private life of sociable *gens du monde* over the political life of sovereign agents. It was accompanied by a sense that the culture of antiquity emphasized the legislative assembly and the army as the contexts of great action, but that these spheres were not adequate for the cultivation of the higher faculties. The apolitical sphere of *le monde* was championed as the area in which the highest public ideals (equality, rational communication, virtuous action) could be effectively realized.

This repudiation of the political domain in favor of the private domain was first expressed explicitly and emphatically by Jean-Louis Guez de Balzac (1597–1654) in his essay "De la Conversation des romains."[129] Balzac claimed to be an admirer of the ancients, but he sought to reveal what he considered to be a previously neglected dimension of their existence, "their private life" (*leur vie intérieure*).[130] Although every age may have a private life, the notion of "private life" as an idealized context of existence does not exist in every age. Balzac's use of the expression "private life" is significant as a sign of the effort of salon intellectuals to depoliticize the sphere in which humans achieve excellence.[131] His essay is written in the form of a letter to Madame de Rambouillet, the famous salon hostess. Balzac pretended that Madame de Rambouillet had asked him to describe some of the great attributes of the ancient Romans that are not displayed in their political histories.

[128] See J.G.A. Pocock, *The Machiavellian Moment: Florentine Political Thought and the Atlantic Republican Tradition* (Princeton, 1975), and Paul A. Rahe, *Republics Ancient and Modern: Classical Republicanism and the American Revolution* (Chapel Hill, 1992), on the history of republicanism from antiquity to the eighteenth century.

[129] Balzac's "La Conversation des romains" appeared in *Oeuvres diverses* (Paris, 1644). Eighteen more editions of the *Oeuvres diverses* appeared prior to 1665, the date of the publication of *Les Oeuvres de Monsieur de Balzac* (Paris, 1665). "La Conversation des romains" appeared in volume 2 of this 1665 edition. This is the source I cite when quoting the essay.

[130] Balzac, "La Conversation des romains," 435.

[131] See Roger Chartier, ed., *A History of Private Life*, vol. 3: *The Passions of the Renaissance*. The issue of the origins of privacy as a philosophical category is not treated, but the volume contains suggestive essays on the turning inward of consciousness. See especially Orest Ranum's essay, "The Refuges of Intimacy," 207–64.

Madame, you wish me to show you the Romans in their hidden places and to open the doors of their retreat. Having seen them going about their official duties, you would like to see them in conversation, to know if that upright and elevated grandeur was able to descend from practical affairs to games and diversions.[132]

Balzac's goal, one might say, was to feminize the ancients—to depict their actions in such a way that they would appear interesting and imitable to a genteel lady. He admitted that there was scant evidence for constructing the Romans' private life.

How unfortunate to know about the majority of their battles, the order of their militia, and to be unaware of their tranquil gatherings and the method by which they discussed things together; to be witnesses at their solemn festivals, their great ceremonies, and to have no part in their familiar dealings or the affairs of their homes.[133]

Yet he moved forward and confidently developed an image of the Romans' conversation based on a few anecdotes from Plutarch and what he called "my suspicions."

Balzac portrayed Scipio as a conversationalist and *littérateur*. He suggested that the valiant general was not "outside of his greatness" when he politely discussed literary manuscripts in genteel company. Roman conversation in general, according to Balzac, was marked by "a sweetness and easiness in manners" and "a naive frankness and a custom of saying the truth."[134] A key term in Balzac's essay was the new French word "urbanity" (*urbanité*). It is not clear who was the first to use this term, but Balzac's contemporary, Pierre Costar, claimed that it was Balzac who "naturalized" it.[135] The word went on to become prominent in theories of politeness for a noncourtly audience. As Sainte-Beuve observed, it came to signify "not only a quality of language and wit but also a kind of virtue and . . . a moral quality that makes a person amiable and embellishes and sustains the commerce of life."[136] "Urbanity" was one of the lexical products of Balzac's effort to find a more sociable and less militaristic and political image of the ancients. He defined urbanity with reference to the old Latin word *urbanitas*. "This is how, Madame, they [the Romans] denoted that amiable virtue. . . . It means the science of conversation and the ability to please in good company."[137] He thus presented to his modern readers an ideal that

[132] Balzac, "De la Conversation des romains," 429.

[133] Ibid., 435.

[134] Ibid., 432.

[135] See Jean Jehasse, *Guez de Balzac et le génie romain* (Saint-Etienne, 1977), 416.

[136] Charles-Augustin Sainte-Beuve, "Mme de Caylus et de ce qu'on appelle *urbanité*," in *Causeries du lundi* (Paris, 1862), 3:69.

[137] Balzac, "De la Conversation des romains," 434.

was allegedly ancient in origin but that was actually fitted for contemporary associations such as Rambouillet's salon.

Balzac belittled rhetoric, or the exercise of speech in a political forum, and he idealized private discourse.[138] He compared the Romans' political life to their conversational life and found the latter alone to be the realm of liberty and authentic communication. After "thundering and invoking the heavens and the earth" in legal debates, the Romans practiced a "more humane" style of interaction in private gatherings. Here they could abandon their "fake exclamations and artificial heats of anger" and "enjoy a state where they could speak of themselves as they truly were."[139] Politics was deceit; only private conversation was genuine.

> It was here [in conversation] . . . that Cicero was neither a sophist nor rhetorician, neither an idolater of this man nor a furious enemy of that one, a man of neither this party nor that: he was the real Cicero and often made fun in private of what he had adored in public.[140]

The sentiments that "came from the heart" were "hidden in the great assemblies." But in conversation, the Romans spoke openly, without ulterior political aims. Freedom existed in the small-scale forum, not the political arena.

> And if it has been said of some of them that they became rulers every time they exerted their influence on the souls of men [in political debate], it can be said of these same men that in conversation they returned the liberty which they had removed in their harangues, that they put at ease the same minds that they had just pressured and tormented, and that they inspired admiration among the people they had agitated, making them feel a sweet transport, and ravishing them with less force.[141]

Specialists on Balzac disagree as to whether or not he deliberately distorted the contours of ancient culture so as to realign it with the pleasure-oriented aspirations of salon culture.[142] Regardless of the intention, however, the redefinition of "antiquity" in accordance with contemporary concerns is unmistakable. French authors had long admired the ancients as virtuous legislators and soldiers or as poets and architects—either collectively for their law and politics or individually for their aesthetic creations, but not socially.[143] By claiming to discover a new dimension of the Romans, their

---

[138] See my discussion of the privatization of *logos* as an ideal type of sociability, in Chapter 1.

[139] Balzac, "De la Conversation des romains," 435.

[140] Ibid., 435.

[141] Ibid.

[142] See Roger Zuber, *Les "Belles Infidèles" et la formation du goût classique* (Paris, 1968), 402; and Zobeidah Youssef, *Polémique et littérature chez Guez de Balzac* (Paris, 1972), 376.

[143] Zuber, *Les "Belles Infidèles,"* 401–2.

private life, Balzac offered a new conception of ancient civilization and hence a possible basis of legitimacy for conversational practices that were apolitical.

In 1646, when Méré first read Balzac's essay, he sent the author an ambiguous letter of praise.

> I principally admire the many new things you say about the ancient Romans; and because you have ordered me to speak sincerely, I will say that the portraits you have made of the conversations, *bon mots*, and urbanity of your Romans are more agreeable than the originals. . . . For truly, their good sayings, when examined closely, were not so good. Better ones are spoken in France.[144]

Méré believed that the ancients, in fact, were hardly interested in the art of private conversation.

> It is true that the things they say about [speech] are more appropriate for those who speak in public than for the private commerce of life; and on the subject of conversation, they have neglected to uncover their sentiments to us. This is because they put little store by those familiar interchanges, and the most eloquent of these masters (*De Oratore*) assures us that it is mere play in comparison to public harangues.[145]

In a letter to the duchesse de Lesdiguières, Méré claimed that he had forced Balzac to confess that "he did not believe in half of the fine qualities which he had given to the ancient Romans."[146] Méré did not disagree with Balzac about the nature of good conversation. He, and others after him, only wished to dispense with the fiction of ancient models. In the wake of Méré's critique of Balzac's pseudohistory of sociability, various authors praised Balzac's ideal of *urbanité* but without mentioning the alleged ancient forerunners.[147] Bellegarde went so far as to attack the ancients for lacking "humane sentiments." The Romans, he observed, were an iniquitous people who launched a series of vicious wars. "They ravished, they killed, they performed a thousand cruelties; they violated all the rights of civil society [*société civile*] through cruel injustices." Modern people, he claimed, are "more peaceful, more polite, more humane."[148]

An appreciation of the attitude toward classical values in the courtesy literature makes it possible for us to see the ideal of sociability as a form of historical consciousness. Theories of the art of conversation, one could say,

---

[144] Méré, *Lettres*, 267–68 (letter 56).

[145] Méré, "De l'Eloquence et de l'entretien," 105. Méré is referring to Cicero when he mentions *De Oratore*.

[146] Méré, *Lettres*, 18 (letter 4).

[147] A good example is Scudéry's discussion of *urbanité* in "De la Politesse," 65.

[148] Bellegarde, *Modèles de conversation*, 19–20, 94, 130–31. See also Bellegarde, *Lettres curieuses*, 57, 126, 216, 235–36, for further criticism of the ancients.

were competing not only "synchronically" against the court but also "diachronically" against the classical inheritance. The two crucial oppositions that constituted the egalitarian courtesy literature I have been describing are thus: (1) the distinction between hierarchy and reciprocity (the former being associated with the court and the latter with an indeterminate salon milieu or "civil society") and (2) the distinction between politico-military life and private life (the former being associated with antiquity and the latter with modernity). The ideals of Bellegarde and his forerunners can be described as the ancient ideal of *vita activa* reduced to the scale of private life, or as modernity (i.e., a preoccupation with aesthetic cultivation) restricted to a specifically sociable purpose. This classification helps to explain how the "art of conversation" managed to become so important in French culture in the seventeenth and eighteenth centuries. "Conversation" resonated with the ideals of the ancients but in a uniquely modern key. It also implied an opposition to modern courtliness but not a rejection of the modern pursuit of refinement in manners. It thus captured both the past and the present in a unique form of historical consciousness.

This historical consciousness is important for understanding why Bellegarde and other authors approached the "art of conversation," an apparently frivolous subject, as a serious matter. But to understand fully the intellectual allure of the "art of conversation," it is necessary to consider one of its dimensions more closely, the ethical or Christian dimension.

The *Douceur* of the Gentleman

It is common to see the seventeenth-century literature on manners as an "aesthetic" rather than an "ethical" literature. The separation of politeness and morality is the great theme of Maurice Magendie's standard history of *la politesse mondaine* in seventeenth-century France. In the first half of the century, Magendie argued, Christian moral qualities, such as sincerity and humility, were predominant in the definition of the *honnête homme*. Morality had priority over wit and smooth gestures; piety took precedence over the ability to be pleasing. By 1660, however, *honnêteté* signified an ideal of good manners that was purely aesthetic. Moral virtues were replaced by the art of displaying brilliant external accomplishments.[149] In an essay that confirms Magendie's thesis, Jean-Pierre Dens distinguishes the standards of virtue and the standards of politeness. The latter relate only to what gives pleasure, not to what is true or right. "It is no longer a question of knowing

---

[149] Magendie, *La Politesse mondaine*.

if our actions are intrinsically good or bad but only if they please, that is, if they answer favorably to the exigencies of worldly etiquette."[150]

This formulation is insightful, but it perhaps overemphasizes the distinction between pleasure and morality. It is true that the goal of sociable conversation was pleasure, but not only for oneself. Because one's own enjoyment depended on the goodwill and communicability of others, the aesthetic (that is, pleasure-producing) function merged with the moral one. The reciprocity that made sociable conversation possible also became the foundation upon which writers could describe politeness as a form of morality. The arguments of writers on the art of conversation were similar to those made by natural lawyers, such as Pufendorf, with respect to the satisfaction of human "needs" and "interests" in the state of nature.[151] The concept of *le monde* resembled the concept of the state of nature in that both were the sites of an ethic of reciprocity practiced for the sake of self-fulfillment.

The "appearance" that the good conversationalist was required to maintain included the showing of respect for the "being" of others, the essential humanity that lay beneath the accidents of birth and corporate status. Kant later made this point well in his *Anthropology from a Pragmatic Point of View*, in which he described polite conversation as the "highest ethico-physical good," that is, the activity that succeeds best at simultaneously realizing the pursuit of pleasure and the duty to adhere to the moral law of altruism—two things which, according to Kant himself, are more often than not radically opposed to each other. The motive of the sociable conversationalist, Kant observed, is the wish for pleasure. But the rules of sociability, which exist "to save the open exchange of ideas" and to sustain "the refreshing play of thoughts," elicit consideration for the autonomy of others, so that ethical duty is fulfilled in the process. "It cannot be disputed at all that an inclination of such a nature [toward sociable interaction] must also have an influence on the ready willingness in rendering services, helpful benevolence, and the practical development of human kindness." Kant also claimed, "The French nation stands out among all others by its taste for conversation, in which it is the model for all the rest."[152] Apparently, Kant was well read in French courtesy literature, and his remarks show that a highly analytical mind could detect an ethical law at the heart of sociability.

---

[150] Jean-Pierre Dens, "L'Honnête Homme et l'esthétique du paraître," *Papers on French Seventeenth Century Literature*, no. 6 (1976–1977), 72. Another important study of the aesthetics of politeness is Domna C. Stanton's *The Aristocrat as Art: A Study of the Honnête Homme and the Dandy in Seventeenth- and Nineteenth-Century French Literature* (New York, 1980).

[151] See Chapter 2.

[152] Immanuel Kant, *Anthropology from a Pragmatic Point of View*, trans. Victor Dowdell (Carbondale, Ill., 1978), 185–89, 228.

As the courtesy writers themselves maintained, politeness meant that one had to be committed to preserving the whole system of exchange that made possible both one's own happiness and that of others. Authors such as Scudéry and Bellegarde presented the rules of conversation as moral rules, and their readers recognized them as such. In the *Nouvelles de la république des lettres* (October, 1684), Pierre Bayle commented on Scudéry's *Conversations nouvelles sur divers sujets*: "Here one finds judicious remarks on all things, a great deal of politeness, and a highly sensible morality that can be very useful to those who live in *le grand monde*."[153] Two years later (July 1686), in response to Scudéry's *La Morale du monde, ou conversations*, he wrote again:

> The public seems highly satisfied with all these conversations, and this should oblige that illustrious woman to communicate to *le monde* everything that she may have developed on this kind of morality.[154]

As Scudéry herself saw it, polite conversation was moral not only because it was based on mutual respect but also because it subjected the interlocutors to criticism, and through criticism, growth. Liberty and diversity, which she advocated as sources of refreshment and pleasure in sociable life, were also supposed to create self-knowledge. In the dialogue "De la Connaissance d'autrui et de soy-mesme" (On Knowledge of Others and of Oneself), the speakers ridicule the rampant flattery that exists in royal courts. They agree that within a highly ceremonious environment, it is impossible to criticize others or to receive criticism from them. And without polite criticism, people never become aware of their faults. The result is that kings, courtiers, and royal ministers lack what private individuals (*les particuliers*) can attain: self-knowledge. "For one acquires this knowledge of oneself in the commerce of *le monde*."[155] In this way, Scudéry formulated the boundary between *la cour* and *le monde* in ethical terms. The court appears as an area that has, so to speak, no mirrors. Ambition, servility, and ritual make it imperative to portray the grandees as they wish to be seen, not as one actually sees them.

Interestingly enough, the most popular seventeenth-century courtly writers themselves highlighted the amoral character of courtly life and made only feeble efforts to portray the courtier as a character ideal. Authors such as Scudéry, authors who did write in moralistic terms, were appropriating a function that European courtly writers had exercised prior to the seven-

---

[153] Pierre Bayle, *Nouvelles de la république des lettres*, in *Oeuvres diverses* (Hildesheim, 1964), 1:150.

[154] Ibid., 1:608. Scudéry's most avid nineteenth-century reader, Victor Cousin, also described her dialogues as "a veritable school of morality." See Cousin, *La Société française*, 14.

[155] Scudéry, "De la connaisance d'autrui et de soy-mesme," in *Conversations sur divers sujets*, 1:164–65.

teenth century but that French courtly writers consciously relinquished in the seventeenth century. The first expositors of courtly ideals were medieval clerics who emphasized the spiritual responsibility of the courtier to "correct" the lay ruler when he went astray.[156] In the Renaissance, Baldassare Castiglione presented a secular version of the courtier. The courtier was now a gentleman and no longer a priest, but the courage to oppose the ruler's opinions and even a willingness to disobey him "in dishonorable things" were still a part of the courtier's qualifications.[157] These qualifications reflect the Platonic element in the Renaissance ideal of the courtier— the belief in a transcendent, absolute conception of the good that the wise person is supposed to embody in the presence of an audience that may be ignorant of it. Castiglione's perfect courtiers, of course, were fashionable dressers. They were also adept at worldly pastimes, such as dancing and playing tennis. These external concerns, however, did not displace their philosophical *raison d'être*. In fact, the courtier's good manners and worldly accomplishments were supposed to create an aura of prestige and favor around his person, an aura that would make him compelling when he adopted a moral posture.

> Therefore, I think that the aim of the perfect Courtier, which we have not spoken of up to now, is to win for himself, by means of the accomplishments ascribed to him by these gentlemen, the favor and mind of the prince whom he serves that he may be able to tell him, and always will tell him, the truth about everything he needs to know, without fear or risk of displeasing him; and that when he sees the mind of his prince inclined to wrong action, he may dare to oppose him and in a gentle manner avail himself of the favor acquired by his good accomplishments, so as to dissuade him of every evil intent and bring him to the path of virtue.[158]

With the growth of absolutism in seventeenth-century France, particularly in the years following the Fronde, royal ministers propagated courtesy codes to subdue a nobility that had acted with so much "discourtesy" during the civil war.[159] Docility and hierarchy then became the supreme norms of courtliness. From this time onward, the instrumental relation between courtliness and state power posed an insuperable obstacle to French authors who wished to construe the courtier as a spiritual ideal. For courtliness now had reference to a hierarchy that was flat, that had no Christian or Platonic "beyond." The ideal courtier was expected to defer to the scale of precedence within the court and not to appeal to transcendent

---

[156] C. Stephen Jaeger, *The Origins of Courtliness*, especially 99.
[157] Baldassare Castiglione, *The Book of the Courtier* (New York, 1959), 117, 289–90, 293.
[158] Ibid., 289. See also 117, 290, and 293 on the courtier's duty to contradict a bad prince.
[159] Orest Ranum, "Courtesy, Absolutism, and the French State," *Journal of Modern History* 52 (1980):426–51.

standards. This flattening of the chain of being into a purely worldly hierarchy entailed what Marcel Gauchet calls "the ontological independence of the political body" and "the extrication of the visible world from its invisible source."[160] Instead of functioning to preserve inherited distinctions that were legitimated in the language of medieval cosmology, the king's will now acted as the absolute starting point for the creation of a new cosmos of distinctions within the regime. A non-Christian (i.e., pagan) imagery was evoked in courtly theater and art in order to ratify this divinization of the human—to create a new symbolic milieu in which courtiers could worship the king's will in ways that would have been sacrilegious within a Christian framework.[161]

The manner in which the king's will acted as the source of value, rather than as the preserver of ontologically anterior values, is evident in such concrete courtly rituals as the *lever du Roi*. This royal awakening and dressing ceremony was part of a spectacle that conferred prestige upon all who were allowed to take part. Access to the body of the king was a privilege, but the king freely violated the traditional scale of privilege in granting admission. As the German observer Ezéchiel Spanheim commented, "Princes of the blood, cardinals, and other great seigneurs [are] present in the antechamber, but they do not have the right of the *première entrée*."[162] The king simply admitted whomever he wished to admit, and in so doing, he affirmed that courtly hierarchy issued directly from his personal preferences.

Spanheim described the court as a system of arbitrary conventions in which "interest" and "fear" induced the courtiers to obey the monarch in all things.[163] As a foreign observer, Spanheim made no effort to idealize the court. One might expect a different picture from French authors of guides to courtly civility. The question would then be, How did systematizers of courtliness portray the court as a sphere of moral action? But the fact is, these authors made very little effort to reconcile courtly hierarchy with a spiritual ideal because the essential rule of courtly life, to defer to superiors in all things, was so obviously incompatible with Western moral traditions. Formal codes of courtly politeness were pragmatic; they outlined the rules for success without regard to moral considerations.

Eustache de Refuge's *Traité de la cour* (Treatise on the Court, first published in 1616 and republished at least fifteen times in the seventeenth

[160] Marcel Gauchet, *Le Désenchantement du monde, une histoire politique de la religion* (Paris, 1985), 65, 70.

[161] The use of non-Christian imagery to aggrandize the monarch is one of the main themes of Jean-Marie Apostolides, *Le Roi-Machine, spectacle et politique au temps de Louis XIV* (Paris, 1981). Also valuable is Marie-Christine Moine, *Les Fêtes à la cour du roi soleil, 1653–1715* (Paris, 1984). For thinking theoretically about the state and the court, I have found Arthur Hocart's *Kings and Councilors* (Chicago, 1970) very useful.

[162] Ezéchiel Spanheim, *Relation de la cour de France en 1690* (Mayenne, 1973), 128–29.

[163] Ibid., 133.

century)[164] is a case in point. In order to make a successful career at court, according to Refuge, one had to cultivate the favor of the ruler. There are three kinds of rulers, he said: "melancholy," "cheerful," and "phlegmatic." Refuge outlined how the clever courtier could obtain the favor of each. The three types required different strategies, but flattery and obedience lay behind the courtier's method in all cases. "A courtier must be committed to following all the inclinations of princes, which are not usually reasonable or upright." Anyone concerned with the state of his soul should avoid the court. "Indeed, he who wishes to lead a wholly innocent life . . . would do better never to embrace the court, which is (if we may be allowed to say so) a great whore who will corrupt the healthiest and most chaste of men."[165]

Not all guides to courtly living were so explicitly cynical, but they all reveal the insurmountable difficulties in developing the concept of the courtier as a character ideal. Magendie pointed to Nicolas Faret's *L'Honnête homme, ou l'art de plaire à la cour* (The Gentleman, or the Art of Pleasing at Court, first published in 1630 and republished fourteen times in the seventeenth century), as the supreme example of the moralistic approach to politeness that prevailed in the first half of the century. Faret's purpose was indeed to show "that a good man can live in the corruption of the court without being tainted." The notion of goodness in question, however, was a truncated one. Observing that "the good of the prince is not separate from that of the state," Faret linked obedience to the ruler with service to the general good.[166] And in spite of some preliminary remarks about "religion" and "virtue" as prerequisites for being a good courtier, Faret, like Refuge, made the art of courtliness consist in conformity to whatever happened to be the ruler's temper. If the king is a lover of warfare, the courtier should speak only of bold invasions. If the king is a lover of peace, the courtier should offer plans for ensuring tranquillity. If the king is a lover of study, "Let he who wishes to be pleasing observe which branch of knowledge he prefers, and let him apply himself particularly to studying it."[167] Faret's courtier was not a true adviser to princes. He was a mere servant, a chameleon who changed color easily to please the ruler. The courtier should "never play the wise man with his master." And he should never contradict the ruler, for the king was as jealous of his own opinions as he was of sovereignty itself.

---

[164] The text was published in thirteen editions between 1616 and 1665. An English translation of part of the book appeared in 1652 under the title *Arcana Aulica, or Walsingham's Manual of Prudential Maxims for the Statesman or Courtier*. This English version was translated back into French and published twice in the 1690s.

[165] Eustache de Refuge, *Traité de la cour* (n.p., 1616), 103–4.

[166] Nicolas Faret, *L'Honnête homme, ou l'art de plaire à la cour*, ed. Maurice Magendie (Paris, 1925), 36. The text is based on the 1630 edition.

[167] Ibid., 51.

> For extreme power is usually accompanied by such sensitivity that the least word of resistance makes a wound and it [sovereign power] seems to desire that its opinions comprise a part of its authority.[168]

Faret reiterated this advice when telling the courtier how to behave in the presence of great nobles. The courtier "must yield without resistance to the opinions and wills of those who are above."[169]

In spite of its moralistic pretense, Faret's book degenerated into a guide for currying favor. The most popular guide to courtly civility in the late seventeenth century, Courtin's *Nouveau traité*, also made it clear that the courtier should not contradict a grandee. This work also failed to offer a clear definition of the courtier as a character ideal and took the form of a list of rules to be observed at court—simply because they happened to be the rules at court. Refuge, Faret, and Courtin, the three most popular French authors of guides to courtliness in the seventeenth century, thus abandoned Castiglione's ideal of the upright courtier who regenerates the ruler. Courtliness contained no space for critical discussion. Scudéry's notion that the individual undergoes spiritual improvement through polite exchange is nowhere present in the courtly literature. This fact suggests that Magendie may have erred when he divided seventeenth-century courtesy literature into moral and amoral periods. The difference was institutional rather than chronological. An amoral courtly literature coexisted with a more moralistic salon literature. And the latter, far from losing its ethical dimension as the seventeenth century approached its end, actually became more moralistic. Scudéry's *Conversations* were more moralistic than Méré's writings. And Bellegarde, a theologian, was particularly concerned to show that *le monde* was a good forum for the cultivation of virtue.

As the anonymous English translator of Bellegarde's *Lettres curieuses* wrote:

> In all that our author has writ, tho his chief design is to observe the errors of conversation and to improve civil society; and tho there is a peculiar freedom in all his reflections, yet his maxims are so far from being inconsistent with the solid rules of morality and religion, that, on the contrary, he keeps these still in his view and never varies from that compass.[170]

Bellegarde himself described *politesse* as "a précis of all the virtues" in one of his guides to conversation.[171] In his theological writings as well, he attempted to forge a link between piety and politeness. While his worldly writings moralized society, his theological writings socialized religious devotion.

---

[168] Ibid., 54.
[169] Ibid., 88.
[170] Bellegarde, *The Letters of Monsieur l'Abbé de Bellegarde*, translator's introduction.
[171] Bellegarde, *Réflexions sur la politesse des moeurs* (Paris, 1698), 1–2.

To understand the moral and religious dimensions of Bellegarde's thought, it is important to focus on how he reconciled sociability—that is, the pursuit of interactive pleasure—with the old Christian distinction between body and soul. In the classic formulation of the body/soul distinction, the body was seen as the source of man's sensual appetite, a motor for the pursuit of enjoyments that were frowned upon by God—such things as drunkenness, sex, and gambling. The soul was viewed as the seat of the individual's consciousness of God. It was believed to engender humility, self-control, and a higher happiness—the sweet joy of salvation. The distinction between the sinful pursuit of multiple sensual *plaisirs* and the Christian pursuit of the *douceur* of pious cultivation runs throughout Bellegarde's religious writings. But where do the pleasures of refined company and conversation fit into this scheme?

In the seventeenth century, it was not unusual to treat all forms of convivial action as emanations of man's bodily nature. Conversation in particular was considered to spring from that dangerous instrument implanted in the body by the devil—the tongue. Many theologians viewed speech as the vehicle by which the mind directed its attention away from God and toward the vain concerns of secular life. In place of the "art of conversation," such thinkers advocated the "art of keeping silent." Commenting on the extensive seventeenth-century literature on "the art of keeping silent," two French scholars have written:

> The superiority of silence over speech in the ordinary conduct of life was thus based on an ideal of self-conversation which draws its resources from immobility and which sees in speech a risk [of corruption].[172]

The anonymous author of *Conduite pour se taire et pour parler, principalement en matière de religion* (Guide for Keeping Silent and for Speaking, Principally in Religious Matters, 1696), wrote:

> Never does man possess himself more than in silence; beyond it, he seems to be dispersed, so to speak, outside of himself and to become dissipated through discourse so that he is less for himself than for others.[173]

---

[172] Jean-Jacques Courtine and Claudine Haroche, "Silences du langage, langages du visage à l'âge classique," introductory essay to Abbé (Joseph Antoine) Dinouart's *L'Art de se taire* (Paris, 1987), 37. Dinouart's work was first published in 1771, but Courtine and Haroche, the editors, show that its contents came from works on the theme of silence that were written in the seventeenth century, when this genre was most popular.

[173] Anonymous, *Conduite pour se taire et pour parler, principalement en matière de religion* (Paris, 1696), 8. As Courtine and Harouche mention in "Silences du langage," there is a tradition of attributing this work to Bellegarde. But the style and content are very different from his works. In addition, the catalogues of Bellegarde's works that appear at the beginning of many of his books do not mention *Conduite pour se taire*. The catalogue of the Bibliothèque Nationale suggests the possibility that the work was written by du Rosel (first name not given).

And Pierre Nicole explained:

> Our failures usually come from our false judgements; our false judgements from our false impressions; and these false impressions from the commerce we have with each other through language. This is the unhappy chain that precipitates us into hell.[174]

Bellegarde was not of this persuasion. "I believe that nothing precludes having a heart loyal to God and observing the customs of *le monde* at the same time," he wrote in one of his courtesy books.[175] In his theological writings, he developed this position further. While pouring a steady stream of moralistic disdain on sensuality and worldly activity, he nevertheless created a space for the practice of sociable exchange within a life of piety.

Like the authors just cited, Bellegarde condemned those who "concern themselves uniquely with procuring all sorts of pleasure." He believed that the pursuit of bodily pleasure was the road to suffering in the afterlife. Even in this life, sensual pursuits were less rewarding than pious ones. "If worldly persons had tasted the sweetness [*douceur*] of service to God, all the pleasures [*plaisirs*] of the world would appear stale to them."[176] But unlike Nicole, who believed that interaction necessarily pushed man's inherently corrupt soul more deeply into sensuality and perversion, Bellegarde did not believe that the individual per se was corrupt; rather, the individual became corrupt through exchange with corrupt people. He thought people were good or bad in accordance with the company they kept, for "we generally resemble the persons whom we frequent."[177]

For Bellegarde, the court was the supreme example of a milieu that corrupted those who participated in it. Hatred of the court, in fact, was even more pronounced in his religious writings than in his courtesy books. Courtiers were people who "speak to princes only to flatter them and to applaud their projects, however unreasonable they may be."[178] The grandees at court also displayed their corruption by their refusal to submit to relations of equality. They expected humility from others but showed no respect in return.

> The grandees are too formalistic [*formalistes*] and always think that we fail to show sufficient respect for their person or dignity. . . . Naaman, covered with leprosy, was dissatisfied that the Prophet Elisha did not come before him to

---

[174] Pierre Nicole, *Essais de morale*, 5th ed. (Paris, 1679), 62–63.

[175] Bellegarde, *Suite de réflexions sur ce qui peut plaire ou déplaire dans le commerce du monde* (Amsterdam, 1699), 180.

[176] Bellegarde, *Sentiments que doit avoir un homme-de-bien sur les vérités de la religion* (Paris, 1704), 295, 311.

[177] Ibid., 134.

[178] Ibid., 190–91.

show him honors that would have in no way contributed to his cure. This prophet offered him an easy and agreeable remedy to cure him of such an infamous disease; however, this proud courtier complained of the incivility of the prophet, who had neglected the little formalities.[179]

Here one can detect a common ground between Bellegarde's theory of polite conversation and his theological ethics. Both reject the hierarchical formalism associated with the court and posit a gentle reciprocity as the supreme norm.

While urging his readers to avoid the court, Bellegarde did not urge them to avoid company in general. Gatherings in which humans practiced reciprocity and *l'art de plaire* were compatible with religion.

> To fulfill our duties exactly, it is necessary to please both God and men. Faith subjects us to God; it captures our understanding and leads us to the practice of his law. Gentleness [*douceur*] renders us agreeable to men. To have obligingness and regards for them is a sure means of pleasing them.[180]

This passage shows that Bellegarde embedded the sociable art within a religious ethos. In his view, religion decreed not only that one cultivate an awareness of God but that one also cultivate a gentleness (*douceur*) toward other humans. According to Bellegarde, faith in God and obligingness toward humans were both means of "pleasing" others. In this way, Bellegarde fused the language of politeness and the language of religion. The term *douceur* was at the center of this synthesis. This word was already a stock term in the vocabulary of salon courtesy. It signified amiability—the willingness to melt into a gathering as opposed to the wish to dominate it. Bellegarde used the term *douceur* to signify both the pleasure of sociability and the satisfaction that stems from pursuing spiritual rather than sensual things. He also used it to translate the Latin word *mansuetudo* (meekness) in his commentaries on the Vulgate.[181] *Douceur* thus stood for the religious virtue of gentleness, a means of pleasing the company one keeps, and a legitimate form of pleasure that one can experience in polite gatherings. It was the concept in which everything—religion, ethics, aesthetics—came together.

Bellegarde sponsored a highly interactive type of Christianity. "The Christian life," he writes, "is a kind of commerce."

> It is necessary for each person to contribute his share to maintain this society. . . . Those who are good only for themselves, who relate everything to their particular interest, and who at the same time would like everyone to serve them,

---

[179] Ibid., 102–3. The biblical story commented upon here can be found in 2 Kings 5.
[180] Bellegarde, *Livres moraux de l'Ancien Testament* (Paris, 1701), 2:10.
[181] Ibid., for example.

are very far from having the sentiments that Christian charity inspires. They are not even men.[182]

Convivial interaction (which Bellegarde calls *commerce*, *société*, or *société civile*) was a gift from God to man.

> Society [*société*] is a remedy that God has given to soothe us and to console us for our failures, which are quite frequent. Our vexations are softened [*adoucis*] by the presence and the words of our friends.[183]

As defined in Bellegarde's writings, the true Christian was one who had faith in God and who believed that all were equal in the eyes of the Creator. The Christian avoided the court and other places where haughty individuals claimed to be more than equal and where slavish careerists pandered to the haughty. The commerce of life, however, was not to be disdained. The practice of polite conversation was an innocent pleasure and an important part of a life infused with *douceur*. The Christian was to have "a gentle disposition [*une humeur douce*], an obliging mind, an affability in his words, and a politeness of discourse [*la politesse du discours*]."[184] In this way, Bellegarde welded the idea of civility onto the idea of the holy.

Politeness and the Lineage of the Enlightenment

"One day, the French people, almost to a man, were thinking like Bossuet. The day after, they were thinking like Voltaire. No ordinary swing of the pendulum, that. It was a revolution." This is how Paul Hazard described the dramatic appearance of the Enlightenment in France. According to Hazard, the intellectual mutation that produced the Enlightenment was the most sudden in history.

> Never was there a greater contrast, never a more sudden transition than this! A hierarchical system ensured by authority; life firmly based on dogmatic principle—such were the things held dear by the people of the seventeenth century; but these—controls, authority, dogmas, and the like—were the very things that their immediate successors of the eighteenth held in cordial detestation. The former were upholders of Christianity; the latter were its foes.[185]

Hazard's conception of eighteenth-century thought as a sudden repudiation of seventeenth-century culture remains a common view of the Enlight-

---

[182] Bellegarde, *Pensées édifiantes et Chrétiennes pour tous les jours du mois* (Paris, 1715), 11.

[183] Ibid., 196–97.

[184] Bellegarde, *La Morale des ecclésiastiques et des cléres* (Paris, 1691), 147–48. Bellegarde wrote this book for priests, but he says in the preface that the parts dealing with good speech and manners are designed for priests and laymen alike.

[185] Paul Hazard, *The European Mind, 1680–1715* (Middlesex, 1964), 7.

enment. But the works of Méré, Scudéry, Balzac, Callières, and Bellegarde do not fit into a scheme in which the seventeenth century stands for hierarchy and the eighteenth century for equality. The whole preoccupation with the art of conversation in the late seventeenth century, in fact, constitutes the key element in the gradual transformation of aristocratic thought into Enlightenment philosophy. It is worth noting that it was only after 1789 that the Enlightenment came to be seen as an instantaneous upsurge of egalitarianism. The revolutionaries traced their own genealogy no further back than the generation of Voltaire and Rousseau. Because they saw their Revolution as the overthrow of a thoroughly corrupt culture, it was necessary for them to attribute to the Revolution a very short intellectual lineage. Otherwise, the roots of enlightened understanding would appear to go back deeply into the prerevolutionary period, and this would in turn suggest that enlightenment and absolutism were compatible with each other—a proposition that radical opponents of absolutism could not admit.

Reactionaries who opposed the Revolution were compelled by a similar logic to view the Enlightenment as an innovation of the last years of the monarchy. For them, the absolute monarchy was good and the Revolution bad. The philosophy that presaged 1789 must have emerged in the minds of evil conspirators very shortly before 1789, rather than from the depths of the monarchy. For if the intellectual roots of 1789 lay far back in the past, that would mean that the monarchy was structurally flawed, that it had produced and accommodated the source of its own destruction.

Revolutionaries and counterrevolutionaries alike presumed that the Revolution did have an intellectual lineage, that there was a continuity of spirit between what transpired during the years 1789–94 and what transpired in the most active minds of the previous decades. They were mistaken. Most egalitarian thinkers, even in the two decades prior to 1789, were not democratic. Most of them, moreover, saw themselves as the heirs of the sociable gentlemen of the seventeenth century. The article entitled "Philosophe" in the *Encyclopédie* states that the true philosopher is an *honnête homme* for whom "civil society [*la société civile*] is, so to speak, a divinity on earth."[186] The social religion of Bellegarde developed into a secular cult of society, and this was an important change; but the belief that society rested upon civility (*civilité, honnêteté, politesse*) remained constant, as did the conception of civility operative in this belief.

Civility, in the writings of Balzac, Méré, Scudéry, Callières, and Bellegarde, stood for the qualities that made possible the "art of conversation," which was understood to be an ideal system of verbal reciprocity—a mode

---

[186] Article entitled "Philosophe" in *Encyclopédie, ou dictionnaire raisonné des sciences, des arts, et des métiers* (Neuchâtel, 1765), 12:510. On the complex question of the authorship of this article, see Herbert Dieckman, *Le Philosophe: Texts and Interpretation* (St. Louis, 1948).

of interaction that sustained pleasure, intelligence, morality, and beauty. As the next two chapters will show, on the basis of the metanorms of exchange developed in seventeenth-century theories of conversation, eighteenth-century thinkers imagined other, not necessarily verbal, activities as forms of civility. In this way, prerevolutionary egalitarianism, which began with the "art of conversation," continued to evolve and to expand, though always within, not directly against, the absolute monarchy.

4

SOCIABILITY AND UNIVERSAL HISTORY: JEAN-BAPTISTE SUARD AND THE SCOTTISH ENLIGHTENMENT IN FRANCE

Je ne crois pas qu'il y êut dans toute notre société un homme
plus accompli.
(Diderot on Suard)[1]

. . .l'homme de lettres français qui réunit au plus haut degré le tact
de la littérature à la connaissance du grand monde.
(Mme. de Staël on Suard)[2]

Universal History

THE RULES of sociable conversation that had been spelled out in the seventeenth century by Méré, Scudéry, Callières, and Bellegarde were repeated in many eighteenth-century guides to the art of refined living.[3] But although there is ample evidence to show that seventeenth-century conversational norms endured in the eighteenth century, it is the new use of the idea of sociable communication, not its mere preservation, that is important for understanding the Enlightenment. In the eighteenth century, "conversation" and "civility" ceased to be the special concern of authors producing a courtesy literature for urban elites. They became important ideals in all domains of philosophical reflection, and especially in the writing of universal history, or the "history of society" as it was often called. Many men of letters now portrayed sociable communication not merely as the tone of *le monde* but as the defining characteristic of modern nations. In

---

[1] Diderot to Sophie Volland, 18 January 1766. Denis Diderot, *Lettres à Sophie Volland*, ed. André Babelon (Paris, 1930), 3:20.

[2] Anne-Louise-Germaine Necker, baronne de Staël-Holstein, *Considérations sur les principaux événements de la Révolution française* (Paris, 1845; first published, 1818), 430.

[3] Some examples are Anonymous, *Tablettes de l'homme du monde* (Paris, 1715); Nicolas Trublet, *Essais sur divers sujets de littérature et de morale* (Paris, 1735); François de Moncrif, *Essais sur la nécessité et sur les moyens de plaire* (Paris, 1738); Anonymous, *Manuel de l'homme du monde* (Paris, 1761); Anonymous, *L'Homme sociable* (London and Paris, 1772). The frequent anonymity and textbookish character of such works suggest that "the art of conversation" was becoming the code of politeness for the French upper classes in general, rather than a literary genre for a select milieu.

the parlance of the time, the rise of sociability was a "revolution" that separated "civilization" from "barbarism."

As the idea of sociability migrated from seventeenth-century natural law and courtesy to eighteenth-century historiography, the meaning of the idea and the range of activities to which it referred expanded. Writers continued to idealize conversation, but they also placed other forms of action under the rubric of "sociable" and "polite." In the natural-law discourse of Pufendorf, *socialitas* signified the capacity of human beings to coordinate their activities without the commands of a sovereign agent. It thus stood for cooperative exchange in a broad sense, not just courteous speech. With the unrigorous blending of meanings taken from the courtesy literature and natural-law theory (this mixing of idioms, as I have already suggested, being highly characteristic of the French Enlightenment as a whole), a variety of activities, some verbal and some not, came to stand together as the constituent activities of "civil society."

Montesquieu is a revealing figure in this context. On the one hand, he appears as a *bel esprit* in the tradition of Méré. His writings seem to be designed for the salon milieu, for he emphasizes the importance of receiving an education in aesthetics and the *art de plaire*, an education which is gained only by frequenting *les gens du monde*.[4] Even *De L'Esprit des lois* (1748), Montesquieu's most systematic work, belongs to the genre of polite literature. Madame du Deffand, a salon hostess, characterized it as "De l'esprit sur les lois," a witty performance having law only as its nominal subject matter.[5] In his writing style, Montesquieu cultivated a tone of familiarity— "le ton de la conversation," as his son called it.[6] His use of short chapters, some no more than two sentences long, was designed to impart a feeling of freshness and repartee, brevity and new departures, to his lengthy treatise.[7]

On the other hand, Montesquieu's interest in politeness was part of a universalistic political philosophy. It was part of his greater fascination with *les moeurs and les manières*, which he defined as "the usages that laws have not established, or that they have not been able, or have not wanted to establish."[8] By distinguishing manners and morals from the juridical use of force, he drew a distinction between the state, the source of authoritative commands, and society, a domain of self-sustaining interaction. Polite conversa-

---

[4] Montesquieu, "Essai sur les causes qui peuvent affecter les esprits et les caractères," in *Oeuvres complètes*, ed. Roger Caillois (Paris, 1951), 2:57; and *De L'Esprit des lois*, in *Oeuvres complètes*, 2:263 (bk. 4, ch. 2). See also Melvin Richter, "Montesquieu, the Politics of Language, and the Language of Politics," *History of Political Thought* 10 (1989):77–88.

[5] Cited by Peter France, *Rhetoric and Truth in France, Descartes to Diderot* (Oxford, 1972), 81.

[6] *Eloge historique de Monsieur de Montesquieu par Monsieur de Secondat, son fils*, in Montesquieu, *Oeuvres complètes*, ed. D. Oster (Paris, 1964), 17.

[7] France, *Rhetoric and Truth.* 91.

[8] Montesquieu, *De L'Esprit des lois*, 566 (bk. 19, ch. 16).

tion was one type of self-sustaining interaction. But because Montesquieu subsumed manners under the broader heading of customs and conventions not established by law, conversation occupied the same conceptual ground as other "usages" that were independent of legal authority. In this way, economic commerce emerged as an analogue of polite conversation.

In the *Essai sur les causes qui peuvent affecter les esprits et les caractères* (Essay on the Causes which Can Affect Minds and Characters), Montesquieu wrote:

> Our temperament [*génie*] is formed to a large extent by those with whom we live. The commerce of cultivated people [*le commerce des gens d'esprit*] provides a constant education; a different kind of commerce makes us lose what we have already attained. We enrich ourselves with the first; we impoverish ourselves with the others. . . . Moderate people instill in us gentleness [*douceur*]; impetuous people, unrest.[9]

Here, Montesquieu describes polite conversation metaphorically as a "commerce" that enriches us. In *De L'Esprit des lois*, conversely, he describes economic trade as a kind of conversation that civilizes us.

> Commerce cures destructive prejudices, and it is an almost general rule that everywhere there are gentle mores [*moeurs douces*], there is commerce; and everywhere there is commerce, there are gentle mores.[10]

Montesquieu thus created a close lexical and sociological bond between economic activity and polite behavior. His use of the term "commerce" when describing polite conversation drew attention to its transactional nature. His use of the adjectival form of *douceur*[11] when describing economic trade drew attention to its peaceful nature. Albert Hirschman has observed that the *doux commerce* metaphor was an important means of conferring legitimacy upon economic activities previously censured by theologians and moral philosophers. "There was much talk from the late seventeenth century on, about the *douceur* of commerce: a word notoriously difficult to translate into other languages . . . it conveys sweetness, softness, calm, and gentleness and is the antonym of violence."[12] Hirschman sees Montesquieu as the most influential exponent of the doctrine that commerce brings moral improvement to those who engage in it. But although Montesquieu did help to popularize the *doux commerce* metaphor, his thought also contains many critical remarks about commerce. His writings helped to make a staunchly procommercial ideology possible, yet they did not embody that ideology.

[9] Montesquieu, *Essai sur les causes*, 62.

[10] Montesquieu, *De L'Esprit des lois*, 585 (bk. 20, ch. 1).

[11] See my discussion of the conceptual significance of the term *douceur* in Chapter 3.

[12] Albert Hirschman, *The Passions and the Interests: Political Arguments for Capitalism Before Its Triumph* (Princeton, 1977), 59.

"Commerce corrupts pure mores, and this was the subject of Plato's complaints; it polishes and softens [*polit et adoucit*] barbarous mores, as we see every day."[13] As this passage suggests, Montesquieu considered the effects of commerce to vary according to the nature of the regime in which it grows. He believed that in a regime where "pure mores" or virtue was widespread, commerce brought about degeneration of patriotic feeling. In a "barbarous" regime where political fragmentation and violence reigned, commerce could unite individuals and sweeten their dispositions. Montesquieu's sociological vision was thus comparative: he was interested in the different effects that the same phenomenon could have within different types of collectivity. Far from idealizing commerce per se, he only underscored an irony: commercial pursuits, which were inherently destructive of austere virtue, could have a positive influence in a regime that was not marked by virtue at all. Montesquieu supported the growth of commerce in France because he saw France as emerging out of a "barbarous" (i.e., feudal) condition. Yet he did not idealize commerce per se as a human activity. He argued that the value of commerce was not absolute but relative to the constitutional and moral traditions of a country. Even within a nation such as France, commerce was inappropriate for some people. "It is against the spirit of monarchy for the nobility to engage in commerce,"[14] he wrote. Since commerce would ruin the nobles' military spirit and sense of honor, the state should prevent them from engaging in commercial pursuits. Montesquieu also believed that the economic utility of commerce was relative to the condition of the rural economy. In a chapter entitled "Those Nations for Whom It Is Disadvantageous to Engage in Commerce," he argued that nations that are poor in movable wealth are inevitably impoverished if they carry out commerce with other nations. Citing the example of Poland, he claimed that in a nation in which the majority of farmers were extremely poor because they did not own their own land, the people would benefit from a prohibition on foreign trade. The land-owning nobles would then be unable to procure luxuries from abroad with the grain harvested by their serfs. "These grandees, with too much grain on their hands, would give it to their peasants to eat. Extremely large estates would become a burden to them and they would divide them among their peasants. . . . The grandees, who always love luxuries and who could only get them from their own country, would encourage the poor to produce them."[15]

Montesquieu's analysis of commerce was saturated with a sense of contingency. Such a measured approach could give way to an outright glorification of trade only when a shift in historical vision took place: when the method of comparative sociology was replaced by the method of evolutionary his-

[13] Montesquieu, *De L'Esprit des lois*, 585 (bk. 20, ch. 1).
[14] Ibid., 598 (bk. 20, ch. 21).
[15] Ibid., 600–601 (bk. 20, ch. 23).

tory. Montesquieu tried to classify systematically the differences between nations, but he did not account for these differences in temporal terms. Although he sometimes observed a process of transition from "barbarous" to "gentle" mores within the different kinds of regimes—monarchical, aristocratic, and democratic—he provided no general evolutionary scale for the sum total of regimes. But when other authors streamlined the diverse nations into a single evolutionary succession, the meaning of "commerce" changed. It ceased to be an *institution* whose utility was relative to the collectivity in which it occurred. It became instead a *historical moment*—a stage in the grand movement from barbarism to civilization. In this context, the context of universal history, "commerce" took on a more powerful normative force as the motor of human progress.

Evolutionary views of human history clearly predate the eighteenth century. Anthony Pagden has shown that the advent of evolutionary anthropology dates back at least to the sixteenth century, when Spanish theologians and jurists confronted the issue of how to treat the natives of America. Rejecting the Aristotelian view that human beings differ from each other in their essential nature (a view that gave the "superior" the right to enslave the less endowed members of the species), some of these Catholic thinkers affirmed the universality of human nature. They explained the "barbarous" practices of the Indians as a result of their stage of development in the general history of the human race.[16] In this way, differences of time were substituted for biological differences as the means of explaining cultural variation.

A study of the history of universal history from the Spanish thinkers to Marx would be very useful. It would undoubtedly reveal many fascinating continuities in the ideologies of Catholic theologians, Enlightenment liberals, and revolutionary communists. This chapter deals with one part of the story: the writing of universal history in the Scottish Enlightenment and the meaning that it acquired within the French absolute monarchy.

France and the Scottish Enlightenment

In the second half of the eighteenth century, Scotland, as Tobias Smollet observed, was "a hotbed of genius."[17] The thinkers associated with this

[16] Anthony Pagden, *The Fall of Natural Man: The American Indian and the Origins of Comparative Ethnology* (Cambridge, 1982).

[17] Tobias Smollet, *The Expedition of Humphrey Clinker*, ed. L. M. Knapp (Oxford, 1966), 233. In characterizing the Scottish Enlightenment, I have benefited especially from the following studies: T. C. Smout, *A History of the Scottish People* (London, 1969); Istvan Hont and Michael Ignatieff, eds., *Wealth and Virtue: The Shaping of Political Economy in the Scottish Enlightenment* (Cambridge, 1983); Richard B. Sher, *Church and University in the Scottish*

movement—Adam Smith, David Hume, William Robertson, John Millar, and Adam Ferguson, to name only a few—were original in a variety of domains, but especially history, politics, and economics. A common goal united most of the Scottish thinkers and stimulated their creativity in the human sciences. This goal was, in the words of Nicholas Phillipson, "to help ordinary men and women to lead happy, useful, and virtuous lives in an increasingly complex, commercial society."[18] The issue was practical: how to contribute to the economic development of a provincial country. But it also involved a philosophical problem: how to make economic pursuits and the concept of a commercial nation dignified enough to inspire people to become engineers, industrial scientists, bankers, and merchants. According to Richard B. Sher, the Scottish thinkers inherited a Calvinist theology that had to be modified in order to make the happiness of the nation, rather than its salvation, the object of people's concerns. "Without explicitly rejecting Calvinist doctrine, they sought to shift the emphasis of Scottish Presbyterianism from predestination and election to individual and social morality. And without surrendering the fundamental Christian ideal of salvation, they attempted to supplement this otherworldly goal with ethical and ideological objectives designed to increase virtue and happiness."[19] Phillipson argues that classical and Renaissance republicanism was also an important element in the Scottish inheritance and that republican ideology, with its emphasis on political virtue over private gain, was an obstacle to the formation of a commercial ethos.[20] The Scottish thinkers, then, faced the challenge of imbuing commerce with spiritual and civic meaning. They sought to embed economic activity in a vision of life whose meaning went beyond economics. This new cult of commercialism was grounded, to a great extent, in the idea of sociability.

A quintessential expression of the new outlook was Hume's essay, "Of Refinement in the Arts" (1752). The essay presented an optimistic account of how the rise of commerce is necessarily accompanied by the rise of

---

Enlightenment: The Moderate Literati of Edinburgh (Princeton, 1985); John Clive and Bernard Bailyn, "England's Cultural Provinces: Scotland and America," *William and Mary Quarterly* 11 (1954):200–213; Alan William Swingewood, "The Scottish Enlightenment and the Rise of Sociology," (Ph.D. diss., University of London, 1968); Nicholas Phillipson, "The Scottish Enlightenment," in *The Enlightenment in National Context*, ed. Roy Porter and Mikulas Teich (Cambridge, 1981), 19–40.

[18] Phillipson, "The Scottish Enlightenment," 20.

[19] Sher, *Church and University*, 35.

[20] Phillipson, "The Scottish Enlightenment," 21–22. Phillipson is more inclined than Sher to see the Scottish conception of the socioeconomic field as a departure from classical and Renaissance republicanism. Sher suggests that the Scots did not reject republicanism but blended it with Presbyterian and procommercial elements (see Sher, *Church and University*, 324–28).

learning and humane sentiments. "Another advantage of industry and refinements in the mechanical arts," Hume explains,

> is that they commonly produce some refinements in the liberal; nor can one be carried to perfection, without being accompanied, in some degree, with the other. . . . We cannot reasonably expect, that a piece of woolen cloth will be wrought to perfection in a nation, which is ignorant of astronomy, or where ethics are neglected.

The growth of the arts, both commercial and intellectual, draws people out of their lethargic backwardness and stimulates communication.

> The more these refined arts advance, the more sociable men become: nor is it possible, that, when enriched with science, and possessed of a fund of conversation, they should be contented to remain in solitude, or live with their fellow-citizens in that distant manner, which is peculiar to ignorant and barbarous nations. They flock into cities; love to receive and communicate knowledge; to show their wit or their breeding; their taste in conversation or living in clothes or furniture.

The rise of commerce and the sciences makes people more industrious, both economically and intellectually. People become more energetic, "eager to think as well as to act, to cultivate the pleasures of the mind as well as those of the body."

> Particular clubs and societies are everywhere formed: Both sexes meet in an easy and sociable manner; and the tempers of men, as well as their behavior, refine apace. So that, beside the improvements which they receive from knowledge and the liberal arts, it is impossible but they must feel an increase of humanity, from the very habit of conversing together, and contributing to each other's pleasure and entertainment. Thus *industry*, *knowledge*, and *humanity*, are linked together by an indissoluble chain.[21]

In this way, Hume, and other Scottish writers after him, welded commerce, communication, politeness, and ethics into a single image of civilized society.

To what extent were French writers aware that the Scots were designing a new commercial humanism? To what extent did they even know that Scottish thinkers were not identical in nationality and outlook to their English counterparts? Diderot, for one, had no conception of Scotland or Scottish culture as a distinct entity. And Peter France has shown that Diderot was typical. Even the *philosophes* who greatly admired Scottish authors generally

---

[21] David Hume, "Of Refinement in the Arts," in *Essays, Moral, Political, and Literary* (Indianapolis, 1987), 270–71 (Hume's emphasis). In some later editions of the *Essays*, the essay was called "Of Luxury."

saw them as "anglais."[22] Yet there was at least one great exception. "I regard Edinburgh as the great school of philosophy," wrote Jean-Baptiste Suard to William Robertson in 1772.

> It is only there that one can find together a Robertson, a Hume, a Ferguson, a Lord Kames, a Smith and other men who are, no doubt, equal to their association. The English presently appear lost in politics, led astray by the spirit of faction, and corrupted by ambition and cupidity; letters and taste are languishing in their country, and philosophy is silent. It is from Scotland that all the good works which have been published in your language during the past several years have come.[23]

Suard took a keen interest in Scottish thought and worked to publicize in his own country what he saw as distinctively Scottish ideas. To understand why he did so, it is necessary to appreciate the affinity between the political situation of the Scots and the situation of Suard, a moderate *philosophe* who wished to define a middle ground between absolutism and democracy.

The Scottish situation was defined by the Act of Union of 1707. Instead of enacting a federal government that would have preserved the Scottish Parliament, the Act of Union abolished the Scottish Parliament and stipulated that Scotland could send sixteen peers to the House of Lords and forty-five representatives to the House of Commons in London. The small number of representatives, the slowness of communication between London and Scotland, and the susceptibility of the Scottish MPs to control by court patronage, all made "the Parliament of Great Britain," as it was now called, a poor symbol of civic pride. As Phillipson has stressed, the need to create a positive vision of their depoliticized country was one of the reasons that Scottish writers explored the nature of commerce and private life so profoundly.[24]

A Parisian *philosophe*, such as Suard, was in a similar situation. True, he was in the capital of a large state, the hub of European culture. But this state was an absolute monarchy, and in an absolute monarchy of the bureaucratic kind that was developing in France, most people were provincials, in the sense of being isolated from the seat of sovereign power, the state. As the French kings curtailed the authority of the Parlements and other judicial corps, some French writers responded by defending the traditional rights of the magistracy. This was Montesquieu's chief concern. Others, inspired by

---

[22] Peter France, "Diderot et l'Ecosse," in *Diderot, les dernières années, 1770–84*, ed. Peter France and Anthony Strugwell (Edinburgh, 1985). Voltaire called Milton, Congreve, Bolingbroke, Robertson, and Hume "compatriots." See Laurence Bongie, "Hume en France au XVIIIe siècle" (Ph.D. diss., University of Paris, 1952), 196.

[23] Suard to Robertson, 6 April 1772, The papers of William Robertson, National Library of Scotland, ms. 3942, 118–19.

[24] Phillipson, "The Scottish Enlightenment," 22.

ancient models of republicanism, formulated a more radical alternative to absolutism. This was the democratic ideology of Rousseau, Mably, and numerous "patriots" who generated a steady stream of pamphlets against the monarchy from the late 1760s on.[25] Suard, who did not like politics, wished to dispense with both the conservative and the radical critiques of absolutism. Bypassing the judicial traditions of France as well as the possibility of constructing a new democratic citizenry, he looked for inspiration across the channel and beyond the Tweed, finding his ideal in a worldview that glorified communication and private life—a worldview in which issues concerning the location of sovereignty in the nation were subordinated to questions concerning the cultivation of sociability in "civilization." Although the political cultures of the two countries were utterly different—in Scotland, not enough state; in France, too much—the problems produced by these contexts were the same: how to construe a domain of ethically significant exchange outside of the political sphere, and how to depoliticize virtue so that life without sovereignty could have meaning.

Storm over Suard

Jean-Baptiste Suard produced few writings of his own. His contribution to French literature was mainly in the realm of translation, a seemingly second-rate occupation. Yet few of the *philosophes* begrudged Suard the trappings of literary glory that he accumulated—a luxurious array of titles, pensions, and editorial posts. When the Académie Française welcomed Suard into its ranks in 1774, its spokesman was not embarrassed to point to Suard's translation of Robertson's *History of the Reign of the Emperor Charles V* as a major work.[26] Even more strangely, Dominique-Joseph Garat, who attended the same salons as Suard in the 1780s, and who made Suard the central figure in a book he wrote on the Enlightenment in 1820, considered Suard to be a model *philosophe*. Garat declared that the translation of *Charles V* "placed Suard, as a writer among the best in our language."[27]

The acclaim that Suard received appears to be well out of proportion to his deserts. Robert Darnton, who has appreciated this, regards Suard as a typical posh man of letters in a post-*Encyclopédie* Enlightenment for which intellectual originality and revolutionary action no longer counted. According to Darnton, Suard was committed to maintaining the institutional

---

[25] Simon Schama, *Citizens: A Chronicle of the French Revolution* (New York, 1989), Part 1.

[26] See "Réponse de M. Gresset, Directeur de l'Académie française, au discours de M. Suard," *Discours prononcés dans l'Académie française, le jeudi 4 août à la réception de M. Suard* (Paris, 1774), 25.

[27] Dominique-Joseph Garat, *Mémoires historiques sur le XVIIIe siècle et sur M. Suard* (Paris, 1820), 1:332.

structure of the absolute monarchy. Suard "wrote little and had little to say—nothing, it need hardly be added, that would offend the regime." His entire generation, the generation of *philosophes* who came into their own in the 1770s, acted as a "prop" for the existing hierarchy in France. In return for their loyalty, they received the choicest honors and pensions that the monarchy could bestow.[28]

Darnton outlines the path of Suard's career in order to illustrate the self-satisfied mediocrity of this representative of the elitist "High Enlightenment." Suard left the provinces at the age of twenty and arrived in Paris, where family connections helped him to support himself for a few months until his good looks and refined manners were discovered by the abbé Raynal, the man "who functioned," Darnton notes, "as a sort of recruiting agent for the socio-cultural elite known as *le monde*." (Darnton does not point out that this agent of the "elite" wrote the *Histoire philosophique ... des deux Indes*, the most radical critique of European slavery in the eighteenth century.) "Having made it into *le monde*, Suard began to make money." Darnton sketches the variety of Suard's pensions, some of which came from the government and others from friends. He received 10,000 livres for taking over the administration of the *Gazette de France*; 800 livres annually as a gift from the Neckers; and 900 livres annually in salary as a member of the Académie Française.[29]

Suard's accumulation of riches seems to confirm that he was not a critical intellectual. It is doubtful, however, that raw information about pensions and institutional status can tell us who the man was. Was the pursuit of institutional success a substitute for philosophy, or did it form a part of a new philosophy? The issues at stake are both substantive and methodological. Following the method of "the social history of ideas," Darnton classifies Suard and other members of the "High Enlightenment" not on the basis of their categories of thought but on the basis of institutional position and financial success.[30] His account of the haves and have-nots within the literary world is suggestive. But without an account of the writers' institutional language—without an explanation of how writers construed institutions and defined the meaning of their own activities within them—it is impossible to define any period of intellectual history.[31]

[28] Robert Darnton, "The High Enlightenment and the Low-Life of Literatures," in *The Literary Underground of the Old Regime* (Cambridge, Mass., 1982), 3, 7, 11–12, 14–15.

[29] Ibid., 4–6.

[30] For Darnton's conception of "the social history of ideas," see Robert Darnton, *The Literary Underground*, viii, and "The Social History of Ideas," in Darnton, *The Kiss of Lamourette: Reflections on Cultural History* (New York, 1990), ch. 11.

[31] Elizabeth L. Eisenstein, in *Grub Street Abroad: Aspects of the French Cosmopolitan Press from the Age of Louis XIV to the French Revolution* (Oxford, 1992), offers a critique of practitioners of "the social history of ideas" and what she sees as their tendency to denigrate the study of texts and conceptual structures; see 22–35. See also William G. Palmer, "Exploring the Diffusion of Enlightened Ideas in Prerevolutionary France," *The Eighteenth Century: Theory*

The Achilles' heel of using the social history of ideas as a method for approaching the Enlightenment in particular is that it tends to reify a concept—the concept of the social—that was invented in the period which the method is meant to explain. In Darnton's account, categories integral to Suard's worldview are sometimes treated as if they were things, not ideas. One example is his reference to *le monde* as the "sociocultural elite" of France, as if *le monde* were a unified and objective stratum of the regime. It is true that Suard and his circle of literary friends were welcome in certain salons whose members dubbed themselves *le monde*. But that does not mean that they were part of a monolithic elite committed to preserving hierarchy in all aspects of life. Nor does it mean that all who styled themselves members of *le monde* approved of men of letters like Suard. In 1785, a conservative gentleman's magazine called *Journal des Gens du Monde* attacked Suard for being part of a "*clique philosophique*," a circle of liberal intellectuals.[32] The term *le monde*, then, should not be used to conjure up the image of a single elite, for it was used normatively in the eighteenth century by different people to idealize the particular milieu to which they belonged. One of the reasons that Suard is worth studying is that he managed to symbolize to many *philosophes* a particular conception of *le monde* that they found appealing. He stood for the egalitarian conception of *le monde* that writers such as Méré and Bellegarde had championed earlier. For him, *le monde* was an ideal of sociable living, not a hierarchical establishment. In his institutional imagination, *le monde* encompassed some privileged bodies, such as the Académie Française, but it also excluded others, notably the court. *Le monde* stood for the elite not within the regime of estates and orders but within *la société civile*: the people who provided a model of communication for everyone else who wished to cultivate the bonds of sociability. *Le monde* was thus a component of Suard's philosophy and not merely the privileged ground of his existence.

On a less methodological, more substantive plane, it is important to observe that controversial episodes in Suard's life suggest that he was not merely an opportunist. As a student at the University of Besançon, Suard took a stand against the bullying of fellow students by members of the army.

---

and Interpretation 26 (1985):63–72, for a defense of the study of "various and competing political languages" in the Enlightenment and a critique of the social history of ideas. In *Grub Street*, Eisenstein also draws into question Darnton's substantive distinction between "High Enlightenment" and "Literary Low-Life" by examining the careers of several journalists; see 131–55. For further debate about the distinction between High Enlightenment and Low-Life, see Jeremy Popkin, "The Prerevolutionary Origins of Political Journalism," in *The French Revolution and the Creation of Modern Political Culture*, vol. 1: *The Political Culture of the Old Regime*, ed. Keith Michael Baker (Oxford, 1987), especially 204; and Leonore Loft, "*Le Journal du Licée de Londres*: A Study in the Pre-Revolutionary French Press," *European History Quarterly* 23 (1993), especially 13.

[32] *Journal des Gens du Monde*, 80 (1785):154–56.

According to his wife, Suard was an excellent swordsman and easily defended himself against a noble officer who tried to humiliate him by shouting, "Bourgeois, get off the sidewalk!" In this encounter, Suard's greatest challenge was to avoid killing the inept officer. A few months later, he served as a witness at a duel in which one of his classmates killed another officer. For his complicity, Suard was imprisoned for a year and a half.[33]

Later in life, Suard was involved in controversy when Louis XV refused to validate his election to the Académie Française. Suard had been elected by a majority of only one vote in 1772. The king's nullification of the election indicates that a battle was going on for control of the Académie and that Suard was not associated with the more conservative side. Louis XV refused to state the reasons for his exclusion of Suard, but it is clear that the opposition of the duc de Richelieu and the duc d'Aiguillon was important. The former, the leader of the conservative prelates and courtiers within the Académie, sought to obstruct the admission of philosophers and scientists into an academy traditionally devoted exclusively to belles lettres. The latter, the Minister of Foreign Affairs, sought to punish Suard for an indiscretion he had committed as editor of the *Gazette de France*. Suard had embarrassed the English government by writing about the secret marriage of the Duke of Gloucester before the English king had publicly acknowledged the marriage.[34] Richelieu and Aiguillon also advised Louis XV that Suard was a particularly unsuitable candidate on account of his participation in the *Encyclopédie*. As Grimm astutely noted, Suard had never actually written for the *Encyclopédie*, but his "voice" was recognizably that of one who identified with the encyclopedists and kept a critical distance from the court.[35] Suard was elected again in 1774, and this time ratified by the new king, Louis XVI. But the episode of exclusion suggests that he was a figure of some controversy, a person whose affiliations made him suspect to certain members of the royal administration.

Given some of Suard's foreign connections, the suspicion had even more foundation. On December 28, 1763, John Wilkes, the English radical re-

[33] Amélie Suard, *Essais de mémoires sur M. Suard* (Paris, 1881), 119–24.

[34] The most thorough discussion of Suard's exclusion from the Académie is by Charles Nisard, "Portefeuille d'un académicien du XVIIIe siècle: Exclusion de Delille et Suard de l'Académie Française en 1772," *Revue Contemporaine* 25 (1856):622–49. Nisard gathers the relevant minutes from the Académie's sessions and several contemporary letters stating the reasons for Suard's exclusion. See also Alfred Hunter, *J.B.A. Suard, un introducteur de la littérature anglaise en France* (Paris, 1925), 128–29, and Louis Petit de Bachaumont, *Mémoires secrets pour servir à l'histoire de la république des lettres* (London, 1780–89), entries for May 8–13, 1772, 6:133–35.

[35] Friedrich Melchior von Grimm, *Correspondance littéraire, philosophique et critique*, July 1772, 10:19–20. Suard's unpublished letters reveal that he was, in fact, commissioned to write for the *Encyclopédie*. But when the project was banned in 1759, his charge was suspended before he made any contribution. Suard to Dussert, 22 March 1759, Bibliothèque Nationale, ms. (N.A.F.) 10844, 56.

former, arrived in Paris, having fled from his own country to escape persecution for printing his notorious *Essay on Women*. Wilkes was promptly taken into a circle of men of letters that convened in baron d'Holbach's salon and that included Suard. Suard and Wilkes became friends. Suard, at this time, was planning the *Gazette Littéraire de l'Europe*. Wilkes offered to make contributions to the new journal and did in fact submit a number of manuscripts on literary subjects to Suard.[36] Although Suard never accepted the Englishman's political views, the two maintained an amicable correspondence for years after Wilkes left France.[37]

Who, then, was Jean-Baptiste Suard? A contradiction when viewed only from the outside. A man who wrote little but achieved recognition as a writer. A journalist who consorted with radicals but was never radical. A *philosophe* who did not philosophize but somehow symbolized *philosophie* to many of his contemporaries. Suard's elusive identity is a sign of how little we still know about the Enlightenment in the last decades of the Old Regime.

The Virtues of Being Lazy

"Monsieur Suard a beaucoup plus causé qu'il n'a écrit," wrote Garat.[38] Suard chatted more than he wrote. Here is one of the great clues to his success. Suard became a symbol of enlightenment by projecting an image of unproductive affability. In an age in which intellectuals were trying not only to grasp truth but also to reform the order of things by making truth public, in an age in which they were trying to bring philosophy down from the heavens and into the drawing rooms of polite company, the new literary republic needed not only critical *gens de lettres* but also urbane *gens du monde*. It needed individuals who could simultaneously exude intelligence and elegance, individuals who concentrated in their physical presence the viability of a public philosophy. Suard fulfilled this role. By harmonizing learning and likableness in his character, he was the walking proof that philosophy has a "civilizing" effect on humankind.[39]

The *Journal des Gens du Monde*, in criticizing Suard, noted that his many pensions "encourage his laziness, for no one likes work less than he."[40] Yet

[36] Louis Bredvold, "The Contributions of John Wilkes to the *Gazette Littéraire de l'Europe*," *University of Michigan Contributions in Modern Philology* 15 (1950):1–36.

[37] Gabriel Bono, ed., *Lettres inédites de Suard à Wilkes* (Berkeley, 1932).

[38] Garat, *Mémoires historiques*, 1:173.

[39] John Mullan makes a similar point with regard to Hume, Richardson, and Sterne in his *Sentiment and Sociability: The Language of Feeling in the Eighteenth Century* (Oxford, 1988), 2: "For all three of these authors, the conception of harmonious sociability was dramatized not only in the books they produced but also in their self-conscious efforts actually to live out models of social being."

[40] *Journal des Gens du Monde*, 80 (1785):154.

laziness was part of Suard's own self-image. He deliberately cultivated the air of a man of letters who was more interested in discovering and enjoying what he had in common with others than in advancing highly complex theories. To his friends, his celebrated laziness was a virtue. It signified his unwillingness to pursue any project at the expense of his own pleasure or the pleasure of those around him. Laziness was a sign of his mediocrity, but it was also a sign of his sociability.

The word "lazy" (*paresseux*) began to enter into Suard's self-description as soon as he arrived in Paris from Besançon. In 1751, he wrote back to an acquaintance in Besançon, "You will still find me, my dear, as lazy as ever."[41] This was a modest way of giving assurance that he was doing fine in his new environment, that he was not caught up in the race for subsistence, and that he had time for convivial pleasures. The letter continues:

> My great pastime is to go to a café where I amuse myself and get bored by turns. These places are always filled with people of more than one species. Some have a cup of coffee, others play a game of chess or ladies, still others are courting the nymph of the café, and the rest talk about literature, morality, politics, philosophy, or deride the new plays, or recount the scandalous gossip of Paris.[42]

Later in his life, Suard used the word "laziness" (and others used it to describe him) to suggest that he was above factional dispute and extreme philosophic "enthusiasm." The term implied the opposite of that complete absorption in self or in systems of thought which can harm relations with others. Laziness was not selfishness. It was an ever-present availability for others. Suard wished to convey a kind of feminine being-for-others rather than the traditional masculine being-for-oneself. The absence of the spirit of self-importance in his character made him appealing to women and men alike. To his wife, Suard's laziness symbolized his hatred of work, his domestic geniality, his attentiveness to others, especially herself. "He is the most amiable man and the most delicate husband and lover," Madame Suard wrote to the marquis de Condorcet.[43] She did have some concerns that his idleness would render him completely unproductive and ruin his career. "His laziness still distresses me," she complained in another letter to Condorcet. Yet she added in the same breath that he amused her with "his marvelous talent for catching flies and crackling leaves in his hand."[44] Other women adored him too. It was with Suard in mind that Madame de Vaisne outlined her ideal of the voluptuous man:

[41] Suard to Dussert, 19 December 1751, Bibliothèque Nationale, ms. (N.A.F.) 10844, 6.

[42] Ibid.

[43] Madame Suard to Condorcet, April 1771, *Correspondance inédite de Condorcet et Madame Suard, 1771–1791*, ed. Elisabeth Badinter (Paris, 1988), 29.

[44] Madame Suard to Condorcet, September 1771, ibid., 51.

In my opinion, the lazy man is the lover *par excellence*. I love the most loveable and lazy of men. His laziness does harm to most of his talents and serves only my pleasure. . . . Oh you whom I love just as you are, conserve forever that laziness which is the charm of my life.[45]

Above all, Suard's laziness was perceived as an aspect of his superb presence in the salons. Diderot, who encountered Suard often in various salons, described him to Sophie Volland as "lazy," but added:

I love Suard. He is considerateness itself. He is one of the most beautiful and tender souls I know, full of *esprit*, taste, knowledge, familiarity with *le monde*, politeness, and delicacy. I do not think there is a more accomplished man in our whole society [*société*].[46]

Jean-François Marmontel called Suard "naturally indolent," while praising "his fine, supple, and just mind, his pleasant character, his gentle and engaging commerce [*commerce doux et liant*]."[47]

Suard's "laziness" helps to explain why many *philosophes* liked him and supported his career. As a man who did not write much and who had a highly polished exterior, his existence made it possible to refute charges that the *philosophes* were subversive radicals. His excellent manners also made him a symbol of civility—the capacity of human beings to police themselves. In other words, he represented the possibility of sociability displacing sovereign authority as the source of order in human life. Amélie Suard's account of her husband's demeanor in the Académie Française shows that Suard impressed others with his ability to bring self-moderation and reciprocity into a royal institution.

One of his colleagues at the Académie informed me that his conversation there revealed the most instructed *homme de lettres* and the most polite *homme du monde*. . . . He had a remarkable capacity for seeing and making others see a question from all sides. Whatever the nature of the discussion, he never elevated his voice above ordinary pitch, and he always knew how to make himself heard. Whether he was praising or criticizing, he added to his praise or blame something indefinably delicate and fine, which removed all bitterness from his criticism and all mawkishness from his praise. He was not the one ever to make a literary discussion degenerate into dispute. When a subject that had given rise to a conflict was exhausted, he was to be seen chatting amicably with those of his colleagues who had most combatted his opinion, proving by a politeness that

[45] Cited by Maxine Druhen, ed., in "Mlle. de Lespinasse et Suard, correspondence inédite," *Académie des Sciences, Belles-Lettres et Arts de Besançon, Procès-Verbaux et Mémoires*, 1927, 4.

[46] Diderot to Sophie Volland, 18 January 1766. Diderot, *Lettres à Sophie Volland*, 3:20.

[47] Jean François Marmontel, *Mémoires*, ed. John Renwick (Clermont-Ferrand, 1972), 1:153. The *Mémoires* were first published in 1805.

was in no way affected, that he was above the petty resentments of dispute and of wounded vanity.[48]

Suard's speeches within the Académie also indicate that he saw this institution not as an instrument of hierarchy and royal power, but as a part of *le monde*—the center of civil society. In his reception speech of 1774, he declared, "I shall find in your assemblies the persons whose society [*société*] I seek in *le monde*, whose conversation delights and instructs me, whose talents I admire and whose virtues I respect."[49] In another speech of 1784, he defined the Académie as an upholder of the norms of politeness that helped to make free communication possible in the nation as a whole.

> In a nation where a continuous communication reigns between the two sexes, between persons of all estates, and between minds of all sorts . . . it is necessary to set some limits to the movements of the mind as well as those of the body and to observe the feelings of those to whom we speak in order to temper the sentiments or thoughts that would shock their beliefs or injure their pride.[50]

Suard saw the Académie as an arbiter of the polite code of behavior that made possible "*la grande sociabilité de la nation*."[51] In this way, he defined the function of the Académie not in relation to the state but in relation to an imaginary civil society.

In the 1784 speech, Suard proceeded to define politeness in terms that show the continuing influence of the seventeenth-century salon tradition. Politeness is motivated by "*le désir de plaire*" and the wish to preserve the flow of convivial interaction. It is "the art of veiling with a light gauze what may be too free in our images and ideas." "From this," he added, "has been formed that tone of *le monde*, which consists in speaking of familiar things with nobility and of grand things with simplicity."[52] Suard continued his panegyric of *le monde* by discussing how, in truly polite gatherings, philosophy was transformed into an elegant and public discourse, while, conversely, genteel conversation was infused with learning and intelligence. The role of men of letters in *le monde* was to inject intellectual matters into the stream of conversation: to make knowledge intelligible to "frivolous minds" by using a language "in which grace is united with the greatest clarity," a language "simple in its forms, and precise in its terms."[53]

From these words it is evident that Suard's conception of the Académie

---

[48] Amélie Suard, *Essais de mémoires*, 246.

[49] Jean-Baptiste Suard, *Discours prononcés dans l'Académie Française le jeudi 4 août à la réception de M. Suard* (Paris, 1774), 4.

[50] J.-B. Suard, *Discours prononcés dans l'Académie Française le 15 juin 1784 à la réception de M. Montesquiou* (Paris, 1784), 26–27.

[51] Ibid., 29.

[52] Ibid., 26–27.

[53] Ibid., 27–28.

was complex, for he treated it as a part of a greater whole, *le monde*, which he in turn construed as the wellspring of politeness for the entire nation. Suard was indeed an elitist, but the elite class that he admired was one whose communicative competence supposedly helped to maintain free exchange. His ideology added luster to a privileged institution, the Académie, but it also put down others, such as the court, which he described as a place "where each person brings only his passions and particular views and has no concern with general utility."[54] This exclusion of the court from the positively charged entity called *le monde* is reminiscent of Méré and the seventeenth-century conversational tradition. It suggests that Suard should be viewed not merely as the occupant of a privileged slot in an objective social hierarchy but as the purveyor of a distinctive idiom that transformed the idea of privilege into the idea of sociable culture.

But did Suard do more than perpetuate this idiom? Did he modify it or develop it in any way? Suard's thought is elusive. Most of his efforts took the form of translations. The issue, then, is how to interpret the acts of a cultural intermediary, a man who tried to popularize Scottish works in France. The meaning of Scottish thought for French *philosophes* has yet to be examined, so it will be useful to treat Suard as a case study and to examine his relations with the Scots in detail. These relations were primarily with three characters: Ossian, Robertson, and Hume.

Ossian: The Savage Poet

In 1759, a Scot named James Macpherson traveled to the Scottish Highlands to investigate the isolated culture of the clans. He soon claimed to have discovered a people who had lived apart from the rest of the world for many centuries, who did not know writing or any of the arts of "civilized" society—who were, in short, a primitive people. Macpherson was especially interested in the poetry of the region and claimed to have made a number of transcriptions of recitations by local bards. These bards maintained an oral tradition that had supposedly been established in remote antiquity by the first great poet, a kind of Scottish Homer named Ossian.

Macpherson transcribed the poems, written in a language that he called "Erse," and also translated them into English. With encouragement from some of Edinburgh's leading men of letters, he published them in June of 1760 under the title, *Fragments of Ancient Poetry, Collected in the Highlands of Scotland and Translated from the Galic or Erse Language*. So began the craze over Ossian that lasted well into the nineteenth century.

Hugh Blair, the renowned professor of rhetoric at the University of

---

[54] J.-B. Suard, "Notice sur la personne et les écrits du duc de la Rochefoucauld," in *Maximes et réflexions morales du duc de la Rochefoucauld* (Paris, 1782), xv–xvi.

Edinburgh and an indefatigable champion of the poems of Ossian, wrote the preface to the first volume of translations. Blair affirmed that the poems unquestionably dated from "an era of the most remote antiquity" and that they "abound with those ideas, and paint those manners, that belong to the most early state of society."[55] Blair, however, did not know Erse. Nor did anyone else. The poems were a forgery, as Dr. Johnson suspected.[56] But the forgery was not definitively established until the next century, and most of the literati of Glasgow and Edinburgh saw Ossian as a national treasure.[57] Blair's dating of the poems to "the most remote antiquity" was based not only on a misplaced confidence in the existence of Erse bards but on a set of assumptions about how the language and manners characteristic of a primitive people shape its poetry. Ossian was interpreted, by Blair and others, through the categories of a preexisting understanding of the evolution of discourse. The same was to be true in France.

The poems of Ossian were introduced to French readers in the 1760s through the *Journal Etranger*. Founded in April 1754, this journal struggled under a series of editors and finally died away in December 1758. The *Journal Etranger* claimed to be a review of foreign publications, but it generally reviewed only foreign works already published in French translation. In January 1760, it began anew with Suard's friend François Arnaud as general editor and Suard himself as the editor of the English section.[58] This time it truly became a journal of recent foreign literature, with lengthy reviews and translations of non-French writings.

In September 1760, an article in the journal began with these words:

> Here, gentlemen, are two pieces which appear to merit a place in your journal. They are two fragments of ancient poems, composed originally in the Erse language spoken by the Highlanders of Scotland.

This was Ossian's debut in France. The author of these words was none other than Anne-Robert-Jacques Turgot, the French encyclopedist and Intendant (and later, finance minister), who translated two fragments of Ossianic poetry for the journal and added an essay on their philosophical significance.[59] For some years Turgot had already been interested in the historicity of poetic norms and of language in general. In the 1750s, he had developed

[55] Hugh Blair, preface to James Macpherson, *Fragments of Ancient Poetry, Collected in the Highlands of Scotland and Translated from the Galic or Erse Language* (Edinburgh, 1760), 1.

[56] Sher, *Church and University*, 252.

[57] Ibid., 242–61. See also Hugh Trevor-Roper, "The Invention of Tradition: The Highland Tradition of Scotland," in *The Invention of Tradition*, ed. Eric Hobsbawm and Terence Ranger (Cambridge, 1983), 16–18.

[58] "Prospectus du nouveau *Journal Etranger*," *Journal Etranger*, January 1760, xxxix, mentions that Suard was an editor.

[59] Anne-Robert-Jacques Turgot, "Lettre adressé aux auteurs du Journal Etranger," *Journal Etranger*, September 1760, 3–20.

a theory of universal history based on the idea that all collectivities move through the same stages of socioeconomic development: the hunting, shepherding, and agricultural stages, each with its own superstructure of language, laws, and customs.[60] In a critique that he wrote in 1750 of a book by Maupertuis on the origin of language, Turgot stated:

> Thence arose the different languages, according to whether the people were hunters, shepherds, or husbandmen. . . . The hunters would have few words, very vivid, not closely linked together, and progress would be slow; the shepherd, with his peaceful life, would construct a gentler and more refined language; the husbandman, one that was colder and more coherent.[61]

Turgot's essay on Ossian in the *Journal Etranger* did not explicitly employ the three-stages theory, but it did evaluate Ossian's poems in the framework of universal history. Turgot began by observing that the poems were written in a style commonly called the "Oriental style," one characterized by figurative language and "rapid and disconnected passages." But Ossian's poems, he observed, proved that this style was not peculiar to the Orient. He noted that some authors had attributed the "Oriental style" to the hot climate of the East, others to the despotic government of Eastern nations. According to Turgot, the very existence of Ossian's poems in the cold climate and politically decentralized communities of the Highlands refuted the Orientalist thesis.[62] He attempted to demolish the practice of classifying language and literature in accordance with geographical origins, substituting instead a framework based on temporal location.

Turgot affirmed that the figurative style was the result of a people's linguistic simplicity, itself a product of an early stage of historical development. He believed that people in this early stage had few regular contacts with each other; their language was devoid of complex terms because their relations with each other were intermittent and simple, and the impressions of nature upon their minds were strong and direct, unmediated by abstract discourse. This closeness to nature, he suggested, gave rise to the figurative style:

> The fewer terms a people has for expressing abstract ideas, the more it is obliged, in order to make itself understood, to find help at every turn in images and metaphors. . . . The less a people has made progress in the arts, the more its writers are forced to draw from nature—which is all the more easy for them,

---

[60] See Ronald L. Meek's introduction in *Turgot, on Progress, Sociology, and Economics*, ed. Ronald L. Meek (Cambridge, 1973), 5–6. See also Meek's *Social Science and the Ignoble Savage* (Cambridge, 1976), ch. 3, "The French Pioneers of the 1750s." As Meek says, Turgot was one of the few French thinkers who independently came up with the three-stages view of history, with its emphasis on the modes of economic production.

[61] Cited by Meek, *Social Science and the Ignoble Savage*, 69. Also relevant is the essay "On Universal History," translated by Meek in *Turgot* (see especially 85–86, 90–92).

[62] Turgot, "Lettre adressé," 4.

since her [nature's] great pictures and the details of rustic life are familiar to them from infancy.[63]

Turgot continued by describing how the advancement of civilization brought with it the loss of poetic genius.

> In civilized peoples [*les peuples policés*], on the contrary, the objects [of nature] become foreign to all those who enjoy the leisure necessary to cultivate poetry, almost all of whom live in towns. There, constantly occupied with abstract ideas, surrounded by a thousand ingenious inventions of the arts, their imaginations cannot fail to become impoverished at the same time that their minds become enriched.

Turgot did not lament the decline of the poetic faculty. Universal history for him was not a story of the progress of all of humankind's gifts, but it was still a story of progress. The loss of figurative language was offset by the rise of "the tranquil language of reason," a language that allowed people "to create the finest and most delicate nuances." This "polite language" was superior to "savage language," because even though it could not represent things with enormous force and imagination, it could represent things with the utmost precision.[64]

Following Turgot's contribution, Suard translated several of Ossian's poems for the *Journal Etranger*, prefacing them with his own interpretations.[65] Ossian, he wrote, was of interest to those "who would like to go back to the very sources of the arts and to follow the first steps of the human mind in societies that are still barbarous [*les sociétés encores barbares*]."[66] Like Turgot, he affirmed that great poetry was to be found more in *peuples barbares* than in *peuples civilisés*.[67] The savage conserved all the "impetuosity" of untamed nature and spoke "the language of the imagination and the passions." In more developed communities, according to Suard, "the habit of reflection and thought blunts the sensitivity of the imagination and moderates the activity of the passions." Suard went beyond Turgot by giving a more subtle account of the relation between signifier and signified in savage and civilized language. In this account, he emphasized the importance of the invention of writing.

> In the formation of languages, words, being made only for the ear, had to be addressed directly and more sensibly to the organ and awaken therein the

[63] Ibid., 6–7.

[64] Ibid., 7, 8.

[65] Poems by Ossian translated by Suard appeared in the *Journal Etranger*, January and December of 1761, and January, February, April, July, and September of 1762. Suard also translated several poems in the *Supplément à la Gazette Littéraire de l'Europe*, 4 November 1764.

[66] J.-B. Suard, remarks accompanying his translation of Ossian's "Comala," *Journal Etranger*, September 1762, 211.

[67] J.-B. Suard, "Fragments de poésie Erse," *Journal Etranger*, January 1761, 4.

physical image of the thing they designate. When signs were fixed by writing, the character of the sounds must have been altered; that delicate analogy between word and object was destroyed in proportion as languages evolved from their original state. The very terms that were figurative in their formation gradually lost, through usage, the trace of the physical image and no longer represented anything but abstract ideas. This is what has happened to all of the evolved languages, and especially to ours.

The French language, Suard concluded, was the one that most abounded in abstract terms and precise words. Hence, it was the language whose structure "most conforms to the march of reason."[68]

Suard's last contribution to the analysis of Ossian was a synopsis, in the *Gazette Littéraire*, of Hugh Blair's *Critical Dissertation on the Poems of Ossian*. Blair had published the *Dissertation* first in 1763 and again in 1765 as part of a two-volume edition of Ossian's works. Suard wrote, "We are going to give the substance of his [Blair's] work and expose his ideas while compressing them."[69] A reading of the English original shows that Suard gave an accurate synopsis. Blair had a number of ideas that neither Suard nor Turgot had articulated in their own interpretations, and Suard included these in his synopsis. One of these was the four-stages view of history, which was similar to Turgot's three-stages view, but which Blair had borrowed from Adam Smith.[70]

> One can distinguish four periods in the history of human societies [*sociétés*]. Men began to live by hunting; the pastoral life followed; agriculture came next and was followed by commerce. The poetry of Ossian presents a picture of the first of these periods.[71]

Blair's essay emphasized that primitive man, the hunter, was a loner "dispersed amidst solitary and rural scenes." He was close to nature but insular with respect to humankind. This creature, whose passions were not hemmed in by conventions, was sullen and explosive. Delicacy of manners was absent. The slightest cause produced quarrels, "which is the case with all savage peoples." A single insult led to war among bands of hunters.

> Gaiety is a benefit we owe to civilized society [*la société policée*]: the savage and solitary man is always serious, except for those sudden and violent explosions of joy which sometimes escape from him in dances and festivals.

Only in civilized societies, the essay continued, do people disguise their passions "as the exterior manners become formed on the common model of

[68] Ibid., 6–7.

[69] J.-B. Suard, "Dissertation de M. Blair sur les poésies d'Ossian," *Gazette Littéraire de l'Europe*, 1 July 1765, 104.

[70] Meek, *Social Science*, ch. 4, "The Scottish Pioneers of the 1750s."

[71] J.-B. Suard, "Dissertation de M. Blair," 114.

politeness." Moderation of the passions cuts down "warmth of spirit" but increases "precision" in language as well as peace in relationships.[72]

By introducing Frenchmen to Ossian and by glossing the mythical bard with his own thoughts and those of Blair, Suard was promoting a particular type of historical consciousness in France. The constituent attributes of this consciousness were the principles of cosmopolitanism, modernism, and sociability. Cosmopolitanism was evident in the very words "civilized" and "savage," which figured so prominently in the discussion of Ossian. These terms were designed to cut across national boundaries; to refer to generic states of time, not particular territorial states. Modernism was the belief in the value of "civilization," a sense of the superiority of the present over the primitive. Scholars have seen the poems of Ossian as the basis of a romantic cult of primitive energy,[73] but Suard used the poems to underscore the advantages of modernity's placid culture. The principle of sociability, finally, was evident in the way Suard, following Turgot and Blair, focused not on forms of government but on language, manners, and modes of subsistence. In his writings on Ossian—in fact, in all of his translations and writings— Suard ignored the disquisitions of French jurists and the research of French constitutional historians. He was mute on the conflict between the advocates of the *thèse royale* and the supporters of the *thèse nobiliaire*. In fact, he expressed no opinion at any time about the historical legitimacy of particular political institutions. His reflections on Ossian encouraged his readers to ignore historically grounded ideologies about the nature of sovereign power in France and to view the past in terms of what would now be called social psychology. He thus directed the focus of historical thought away from politics and toward the evolution of mentalities and systems of exchange, especially verbal exchange. As part of his effort to establish an alternative to both Hobbesian absolutism and parlementary contestation, Suard portrayed the mentality of the modern individual as both rational and apolitical. Let others argue about where sovereign power was ideally located in the French constitution. No matter who was right in that debate, the fact remained that France was a "civilized" nation. And the identity of the modern individual lay in the possibilities for expression in the sphere of sociability. This is the message Suard sought to propagate.

Robertson: The Progress of Refinement

When Suard was inducted into the Académie Française in 1774, his translation of William Robertson's *History of the Reign of the Emperor Charles V* was

---

[72] Ibid., 104, 105, 114, and "Suite de la Dissertation de M. Blair sur les poésies d'Ossian," *Gazette Littéraire de l'Europe*, 1 August 1765, 236.

[73] Especially Philippe Van Tieghem, *Ossian en France* (Paris, 1917).

cited as his most important literary work. Although Suard was only the translator, the French version of *Charles V* was viewed as a creative achievement, not a derivative effort. To the members of the Académie and to other admirers of Suard, it did not matter that Suard was not an original European thinker. What mattered was that through his personality and his publications, he found a variety of ways of upholding the ideals of free communication and self-police in a country in which the monarch officially had the authority to control the entire culture. Translating Robertson's work was one of the ways in which Suard sustained and enriched the discourse of sociability in absolutist France.

In January 1769, in the midst of translating *Charles V*, Suard wrote to Robertson:

> The more I advance in the translation of your work, the more I am enchanted by it. I have long recognized in the history of Charles V a writer, ever wise, elegant, intelligent, and full of sense and the graces.[74]

In August of the previous year, Robertson had informed Suard that the part of the text that had taken the most work, and the part that he considered "the most estimable," was the lengthy introduction, "The Progress of Society in Europe from the Subversion of the Roman Empire to the Beginning of the Sixteenth Century."[75] In his letter of January, Suard singled out Robertson's lengthy introduction for special praise:

> I find in the introduction a profound philosopher who streamlines everything, who describes with sagacity all the effects of each cause, who goes back to the forms of manners, opinions, laws, and above all, who looks for the sources of the revolutions of societies [*sociétés*] in the natural progress of the human mind . . . instead of attributing them to anecdotal events, to the passions or caprices of a few men, or to other fortuitous and partial circumstances.[76]

Suard praised Robertson for representing the uniform development of "societies" rather than narrating the unique and contingent events in a given nation's history. He admired Robertson for producing a history consonant with the evolutionary framework that he himself had already used to analyze the poems of Ossian, a framework based on the universal development of civilization rather than on the emergence of distinctive constitutional or national traditions. Suard told Robertson that he believed that the "usages and prejudices of nations" had "general causes" that were not

---

[74] Suard to Robertson, 19 January 1769, National Library of Scotland, Papers of William Robertson, ms. 3942, 73.

[75] This letter from Robertson to Suard, dated 4 August 1768, is printed by Charles Nisard in "Portefeuille d'un académicien du XVIIIe siècle: Histoire littéraire," *Revue Contemporaine* 25 (1856):28.

[76] Suard to Robertson, 19 January 1769, Papers of William Robertson, ms. 3942, 73.

specific to any given nation, though the progress of a nation could be "retarded or accelerated by accidental circumstances."[77] In the Notice to his translation of *Charles V*, Suard underscored the importance of Robertson's introduction, describing it as "one of the finest works that this century has produced . . . never has the philosophical spirit made a happier use of erudition."[78]

The purpose of Robertson's introduction was to trace the evolution of Europe from the fall of the Roman Empire to the sixteenth century. Robertson saw these centuries as the period that gave birth to "refinement," a term Suard generally translated as *civilisation*. Because Robertson's story was about Europe, it was not universal history in a global sense; but the writing of universal history in the Enlightenment rarely was. The universality of universal history consisted not in the extent of its explicit coverage but in its subordination of particular collectivities to a small number of types. These types were defined in terms of their position within an evolutionary scheme that presumably applied to peoples all over the world. By writing about the general evolutionary process, Robertson took the spotlight off the distinctive laws and customs of European nations and placed it upon the emergence of "refinement" as a feature of Europe as a whole.

Robertson declared:

> It is not my province to give a minute detail of the progress of government and manners in each particular nation whose transactions are the object of the following history.

His goal instead was

> to mark the great steps by which they advanced from barbarism to refinement [*de la barbarie à la civilisation*] and to point out those general principles and events which, by their uniform as well as extensive operation, conducted all of them to that degree of improvement in policy and in manners which they had attained at the period when Charles V began his reign.[79]

---

[77] Ibid.

[78] William Robertson, *L'Histoire du règne de l'Empereur Charles-Quint, précédé d'un Tableau du progrès de la société en Europe, depuis la destruction de l'Empire Romain jusqu'au commencement du seizième siècle*, trans. Jean-Baptiste Suard (Amsterdam and Paris, 1771), 1:xxii–xxiii (Avertissement du Traducteur). Further evidence that Suard attached special importance to the introduction is found in a letter to Robertson, in which he writes: "We are going to publish the introduction separately in two volumes . . . it is a sublime portrait which forms a complete work in itself and which is an introduction to all the histories of the recent centuries of Europe." Suard to Robertson, 2 September 1769, Papers of William Robertson, ms. 3942, 102.

[79] William Robertson, *The History of the Reign of the Emperor Charles V* (Boston, 1857), 13–14; Robertson, *L'Histoire du règne de l'empereur Charles-Quint*, 15–16. Double page references separated by a semicolon from now on refer to the English version and Suard's translation, respectively. Because it would be awkward and confusing to translate Suard's translation of Robertson back into English, all quotations from Robertson are taken from the original

This assimilation of the facts of European history to the universalistic language of barbarism and refinement is evident at the outset of Robertson's narrative, in his description of the tribes that invaded Rome.

> Civilized nations [*Des peuples civilisés*], which take arms upon cool reflection, from motives of policy or prudence, in order to guard against some remote contingency, carry on their hostilities with so little rancor or animosity, that war among them is disarmed of half its terrors. Barbarians [*Les barbares*] are strangers to such refinements. They rush into war with impetuosity, and prosecute it with violence. Their sole object is to make their enemies feel the weight of their vengeance; nor does their rage subside until it be satiated with inflicting on them every possible calamity. It is with such a spirit that the savage tribes [*les sauvages*] in America carry on their petty wars. It was with the same spirit that the more powerful and no less fierce barbarians in the North of Europe and of Asia fell upon the Roman empire.[80]

Here the conflation of "barbarian" and "savage," European and American, shows that Robertson worked with a simple system of classification. For him, there were essentially two kinds of community: barbarous and civilized. The purpose of history, regardless of its geographic focus, was to explain the transition between the two.

What made *Charles V* novel was the fact that Robertson focused on the dynamics of civilization in the already civilized part of the world, Europe. He wished to instill in his readers a sense that refinement was of fairly recent origin, and that the progress of civilization was still in the making. He thus emphasized that Europeans were themselves barbarous until the relatively recent past. In this context, his concept of the "feudal" way of life took on crucial significance.

During the years following the invasions of Rome, a mode of life was established "with little variation, in every kingdom of Europe." This was the "feudal system" (*le système féodale*).[81] The concept of feudalism as a set of customs pertaining to the fief was not new.[82] But Robertson did not use "feudal" in this narrow sense. He used it to refer to an insularity—an absence of exchange and civility—throughout Europe in the Middle Ages. The feudal system was shaped by the preeminent concern of the tribes that conquered the Roman territories: self-defense, both against the Roman inhabitants whom they had spared and against new invaders who sought to

---

English text. I have in all cases verified that Suard translated these passages literally. In this quotation and elsewhere I have added French terms in brackets to show how Suard rendered certain phrases.

[80] Ibid., 10; 12.

[81] Ibid., 15; 17.

[82] J.Q.C. Mackrell, *The Attack on "Feudalism" in Eighteenth-Century France* (London, 1973).

displace them. In the new system, the king or general who led the people in conquest distributed land to his subordinates. Each one of these became his vassal by promising to supply him with a number of troops in proportion to the extent of the land granted. The vassals imitated the example of their sovereign, distributing portions of their territory on similar conditions. "Thus a feudal kingdom resembled a military establishment, rather than a civil institution."[83]

Though established for the sake of order, the feudal system was not conducive to domestic peace. Conflicts between the monarch and his vassals, and among the vassals themselves, were rampant. Charlemagne managed to pacify those living under him, but his success was partial and short-lived, for the violence of the feudal system did not stem merely from the absence of a strong state; it stemmed from the absence of manners, a defect that state power was not sufficient to rectify. Europeans in the Middle Ages were "strangers to the arts which embellish a polished age [*les siècles policés*]." They had "not attained that degree of refinement [*civilisation*] which introduces a sense of decorum and propriety [*honnêteté*] in conduct, as a restraint on those passions which lead to heinous crimes." The feudal period was filled with "deeds of cruelty, perfidy, and revenge, so wild and enormous as almost to exceed belief."[84]

Robertson's account of the emergence of refinement out of this backward state was the key part of his narrative and was, in all likelihood, the part of the story that interested Suard the most.[85] Robertson explained the emergence of refinement out of feudalism as a consequence of three events or trends: the Crusades, urbanization, and commerce. The Crusades were inspired by religious fanaticism, but their outcome was extraneous to the motives that initiated them. Like his compatriot, Adam Ferguson, Robertson believed that great historical revolutions stemmed from the unintended consequences of human action. In his *Essay on the History of Civil Society* (1767), Ferguson wrote: "Mankind, in following the present sense of their minds, in striving to remove inconveniences, or to gain apparent and contiguous advantages, arrive at ends which even their imagination could not anticipate, and pass on, like other animals, in the track of their nature, without perceiving its end. . . . Nations stumble upon establishments which are indeed the result of human action but not the execution of human

[83] Robertson, *The History of the Reign of the Emperor Charles V*, 15–16; Robertson, *L'Histoire du règne de l'empereur Charles-Quint*, trans. Suard, 18–19.

[84] Ibid., 23–24; 27–28.

[85] In the *Journal Etranger*, Suard had already translated extracts from other historical works by Robertson and Hume dealing with the decline of feudal relations and the emergence of modern refinement. See the extract from Robertson's *History of Scotland* in the *Journal Etranger*, June 1760, and from Hume's *History of England*, May 1762.

design."[86] With regard to the Crusades, Robertson wrote: "But from these expeditions, extravagant as they were, beneficial consequences followed, which had neither been foreseen nor expected." It was the unanticipated interaction between Christians and non-Christians, not the Christians' attempt to impose their beliefs on others, that ushered in progress. The "close intercourse" between East and West that subsisted during the three centuries of the Crusades helped to civilize the Christians. The Crusades broadened the horizon of European experience by forcing Europeans to communicate with people unlike themselves. The manners of the Moslems were also more elegant than those of the Europeans, who "must have been sensible, on many occasions, of the rusticity of their manners when compared with those of a more civilized [*policé*] people."[87]

Robertson saw the growth of cities as a product of royal policies that created municipal bodies to counterbalance the nobility. An urban life developed outside of the context of the feudal system, providing space for a blossoming of exchange, which in turn led to the "greater refinement in manners, and in the habits of life [*plus de politesse dans les manières et plus de douceur dans les moeurs*]."[88] The growth of commerce, however, was the most important factor in the emergence of civilization. Robertson treated commerce as a form of sociability rather than a selfish pursuit. The emphasis was on communication as the distinctive aspect of the commercial life. "Commerce" thus signified the opposite of "the feudal system." It represented the movement of the self outward, while the feudal system represented provincialism and intransigence. Just as Blair had depicted Ossian and his fellow savages as leading a solitary life, so Robertson portrayed the feudal system as a collection of small and insular groups. "Europe was broken into many separate communities. The intercourse [*communication*] between these divided states ceased almost entirely during several centuries." Even within a single kingdom, Robertson affirmed, "communication was rare and difficult." Locked up in its limited sphere of action, each locality remained enclosed in its particular variant of barbarism.[89]

---

[86] Adam Ferguson, *An Essay on the History of Civil Society*, ed. Duncan Forbes (Edinburgh, 1966), 122.

[87] Robertson, *The History of the Reign of the Emperor Charles V*, 29–31; Robertson, *L'Histoire du règne de l'empereur Charles-Quint*, trans. Suard, 34–36.

[88] Ibid., 38; 41. See also 44; 48.

[89] Ibid., 90; 108. Robertson's conception of medieval Europe as a world without communication was widely reiterated in both Scotland and France. As examples, see John Millar, *Observations Concerning the Distinction of Ranks in Society*, 2d ed. (London, 1773), 204–6; Antoine Thomas, *Essai sur les Eloges, ou Histoire de la littérature et de l'éloquence appliqués à ce genre*, in *Oeuvres* (Paris, 1773), 2:8. The bibliographer A.-E. Barbier (*Dictionnaire des ouvrages anonymes*, Paris, 1964), attributed an eighteenth-century French translation of Millar's work to Suard. But I find no evidence to support this attribution in the translation itself, in Suard's

The invention of the mariner's compass, according to Robertson, unleashed new possibilities of travel and trade. Robertson discussed the effects of commerce in a glowing section that drew directly on Montesquieu's idea of *doux commerce*. But the difference between the two, as I have already suggested, is that Montesquieu saw commerce as an institution that was frequently, but not always, beneficial, whereas Robertson treated it as a moment in universal history, the inauguration of modernity. Commerce, according to Robertson, dissolved national prejudices by acquainting people with foreign ways. It accustomed merchants to diversity and to a supranational medium of interaction.

> Commerce tends to wear off those prejudices which maintain distinction and animosity between nations. It softens and polishes the manners of men [*il adoucit et polit les moeurs des hommes*].[90]

Commerce was the true source of civilization in Europe.

> In proportion as commerce made its way into the different countries of Europe, they successively turned their attention to those objects, and adopted those manners, which occupy and distinguish polished [*policés*] nations.[91]

Robertson was pleased with Suard's translation of *Charles V*. In the preface of the first edition of his *History of America*, he thanked "M. Suard, to whose elegant translation of the *History of the Reign of Charles V* I owe the favorable reception of that work on the continent."[92] According to Garat, Suard himself gained much prestige from the work. "After this translation of the *History of Charles V* . . . all eyes, and especially those of the most distinguished members of the Académie Française, were focused on him for one of the first places which became vacant."[93] Suard was, in fact, elected to the Académie in the year following the publication of the French version of *Charles V*. He continued the association with Robertson by translating Robertson's *History of America*. This time he had Robertson send him the English proofs of the book prior to their publication, and *L'Histoire de l'Amérique* appeared in 1778.[94] This history, for the most part, is not written in the broad sociological mode that characterizes "The Progress of Society," Robertson's introduction to *Charles V*. Instead, it is a detailed narrative of

---

letters, or in other contemporary references to Suard's activities, including the memoirs by his wife and Garat.

[90] Robertson, *The History of the Reign of the Emperor Charles V*, 95; Robertson, *L'Histoire du règne de l'empereur Charles-Quint*, trans. Suard, 113.

[91] Ibid., 96; 114.

[92] Robertson, *The History of America* (London, 1777), xiii.

[93] Garat, *Mémoires historiques*, 1: 322.

[94] Suard was assisted by André Morellet in the translation of Books 1–4. The rest of the work was translated by Suard's assistant, H. Jansen. See Hunter, *J.B.A. Suard*, 180.

the voyages of various explorers to the New World. The exceptions are two important portions of the text—a large section of Book 1 and the whole of Book 4—-in which Robertson returned to the discourse of universal history in order to outline the stark differences between "civilized" Europe and "savage" America at the time of the discovery of the New World.

In Book 1, Robertson retold the story of "The Progress of Society" in a condensed form (he referred his readers back to *Charles V* for the details). He again emphasized the parceling of Europe after the Fall of Rome; the decline of communication in an age in which "the names of *stranger* and of *enemy* became once more words of the same import"; and the rise of "a new species of correspondence among men" in the form of commerce.[95] In Book 4, Robertson described the culture of the Indians and its place in universal history. His analysis is an interesting effort in sociological objectivity, but it reveals the inevitable tendency to present life in America as the diametrical opposite of European refinement. Robertson was sensitive to the phenomenon of cultural chauvinism:

> For in every stage of society [*dans les différents degrés de sociabilité*], the faculties, the sentiments and desires of men are so accommodated to their own state, that they become standards of excellence to themselves, they affix the idea of perfection and happiness to those attainments which resemble their own, and wherever the objects and enjoyments to which they have been accustomed are wanting, confidently pronounce to be barbarous and miserable. Hence the mutual contempt with which the members of communities, unequal in their degree of improvement [*civilisation*] regard each other.[96]

Nevertheless, he affirmed that the Indians were "so extremely rude, that the denomination of *savage* [*sauvage*] may be applied to them all."[97] Here the terms "rude" and "savage" are not purely judgmental. They have a kind of technical status because they designate a particular stage in the process of historical evolution, a stage that Robertson calls "the infancy of social life [*l'enfance de la vie sociale*]" and "that state of primeval simplicity, which was known in our continent only by the fanciful description of poets."[98] Ossian's poems offered glimpses into the beginnings of history, but the Indians alone provided the living spectacle necessary "to complete the history of the human mind."[99]

In order to complete the history of the human mind, Robertson sketched

---

[95] William Robertson, *The History of America* (New York, 1839), vol. 1 (bk. 1), 17, 27–30; William Robertson, *L'Histoire de l'Amérique*, trans. J.-B. Suard (Paris, 1778), vol. 1 (bk. 1), 4, 50–54. Double page references separated by a semicolon will henceforth refer to the English and French editions, respectively.

[96] Ibid., vol. 1 (bk. 4), 138; vol. 2 (bk. 4), 220.

[97] Ibid., 138; 219.

[98] Ibid, 138; 217.

[99] Ibid., 137; 215.

the contours of Indian culture. But what is striking about this sketch is how contrived it is, how closely it resembles what Robertson thought he already knew not only from Ossian's poems but also from his own research into the nature of the "feudal system." Indeed, his portrait of the Indians hardly differs in its essentials from his portrait of the barbarism of the Middle Ages. The concepts of "savage" and "barbarous" are barely distinguishable, even though they appear to signify different historical stages (barbarism coming after savagery). As a result, Robertson's universal history is essentially a binary account of the differences between savagery and barbarism on the one hand and refinement on the other. Just as Robertson described the feudal system as fragmented and uncommunicative, so he described the American continent. America "was possessed by small independent tribes." The personality of the individual took shape in the absence of broad interaction with others. "The character of a savage results almost entirely from his sentiments or feelings as an individual."[100] Robertson believed the Indians to be unsociable beings, marked by "that taciturnity which is so disgusting to men accustomed to the open intercourse of social conversation [*la libre communication de la vie sociale*]."

> When they are not engaged in action, the Americans [Indians] often sit whole days in one posture, without opening their lips. When they go forth to war, or to the chase, they usually march in a line at some distance from one another, and without exchanging a word. The same profound silence is observed when they row together in a [canoe].[101]

So unaccustomed were they to the "liberal communication of their own sentiments," so strong was their "pride of independence," according to Robertson, that they had none of the more delicate or tender affections for their fellows. They were hard of heart. Each was "indifferent about the manner in which his actions may affect other men."[102] Robertson notes that they were particularly indifferent about the effects of their actions on women. The Indians venerated physical strength, so they despised and degraded their women. Only in modern nations are women treated well.

> Whether man has been improved by the progress of art and civilization in society [*par les progrès des arts de la civilisation*], is a question, which, in the wantonness of disputation, has been agitated among philosophers. That women are indebted to the refinements of polished manners [*la politesse des moeurs*] for a happy change in their state, is a point which admits of no doubt.[103]

[100] Ibid., 132; 192.
[101] Ibid., 192; 488.
[102] Ibid.
[103] Ibid., 153; 294–95.

Robertson thus adduced savage misogyny as an argument against Rousseau's primitivism.

With characteristic moderation, Robertson rounded out his description of the Indians with gestures in their favor. The mind of the American had an inimitable "consciousness of its own freedom." The Indians could be observed to act at times "with astonishing force, and perseverance, and dignity." Robertson admired their zeal for honor and concluded:

> Thus, in every situation where a human being can be placed, even in the most favorable, there are virtues which peculiarly belong to it; there are affections which it calls forth; there is a species of happiness which it yields.[104]

The recognition that every culture had a distinctive "species of happiness" was a moment of relativism within the nonrelativistic scheme of universal history. This recognition did not outweigh Robertson's belief that commercial life was better than savage life, but it was a small trace of tragedy within the theory of refinement. It was similar to the way in which Turgot and Suard acknowledged that modern language could never be as fervent as primitive language, though it had the advantage of being clearer. The tragedy was that individuals were more peaceful in modern times than in primitive times, but the primitive individual had more energy, more pride, more poetry—was more of an individual. The sense of tragedy, however, did not include a yearning to go back. Robertson considered it proper that the savage was content with his own species of happiness, but he never suggested that it was either possible or desirable for civilized people to relinquish the benefits of sociability.

A close examination of Robertson's historical vision makes it easier to understand how Suard was able to gain respect from other *philosophes* merely by translating the works of a Scottish historian. Robertson had elaborated a grand scheme that transposed sociability into a historical key. By representing commerce as a particular species of *interaction* and by insisting that interaction in general was the motor of civilization, Robertson created a conceptual space into which urbane French men of letters could insert their own conversational ideals. Indeed, to Suard, Robertson's image of modernity must have looked like a vast salon—a network of "correspondence" and "communication" yielding increasing "refinement." French authors of guides to polite conversation had already observed that when the aristocratic warrior left the military camp and entered the salon, he ceased to be a man of iron and fire and softened his manners through communication.[105] Robertson took these personality types, the warrior and the communicator, and turned them into sociological ideal types—barbarism and

---

[104] Ibid., 193; 492–94.
[105] This was particularly the theme of Chalesme [first name unknown], *L'Homme de qualité, ou les moyens de vivre en homme de bien, et en homme du monde* (Paris, 1671).

refinement. In this way, his works provided materials with which Suard and his associates in the Académie and salons could assign grand historical significance to their conversations and their efforts to refine the French language. And this is always the function of universal history—to establish the value of a particular mode of action (whether it be politeness, as in Robertson's history, or revolution, as in Marx's) by presenting it as the means for bringing into being the highest stage in world history. Suard's translation was an achievement because he recognized a connection between his own communicative milieu and Robertson's image of a historically evolving refinement. He capitalized on Robertson's work to portray sociability as the essence of the present and to show its advantages over the past. He also capitalized on Hume's work to portray France as the most sociable country in the present.

Hume: The Elimination of Politics

In October of 1763, David Hume arrived in Paris in the service of the English ambassador to France, the earl of Hertford. He had already sojourned once in France, from 1734 to 1737, during which time he composed his *Treatise of Human Nature*. The *Treatise* was Hume's deepest philosophical work, and it was a flop in the literary marketplace. It "fell *dead born from the press*, without reaching such distinction, as even to excite a murmur among the zealots," Hume observed.[106] The work, along with Hume's later epistemological writings, also drew no attention in France (the *Treatise*, in fact, was not translated into French until 1878). Yet by the time of his second arrival in France, Hume was a celebrity, thanks to the popularity of his essays and histories.[107] The Scottish skeptic was welcomed into the salons of Madame Geoffrin, Mademoiselle de Lespinasse, and baron d'Holbach.[108] In his short autobiographical memoir, "My Own Life," Hume emphasized how much he enjoyed these Parisian circles, even if he did not enjoy being treated as an object of fashion.

> Those who have not seen the strange effects of modes will never imagine the
> reception I met with at Paris, from men and women of all ranks and stations.
> The more I recoiled from their excessive civilities, the more I was loaded with

---

[106] David Hume, "My Own Life," in *Essays, Moral, Political, and Literary* (Indianapolis, 1985), xxxiv. Hume's emphasis.

[107] The reputation that Hume eventually achieved as a historian in France is indicated by Bachaumont's comment in 1777: "Since the death of M. Hume, Robertson is the most esteemed historian among the English" (Bachaumont, 24 June 1777, 10:159). As described below, Suard played a key role in introducing French readers to Hume's writings in the 1760s. For information on all the French translations of Hume's works in the eighteenth century, see Bongie, "Hume en France."

[108] Bongie, "Hume en France," 3.

them. There is, however, a real satisfaction in living at Paris, from the great number of sensible, knowing, and polite company with which that city abounds above all places in the universe. I thought once of settling there for life.[109]

With these words, Hume reveals much about his attitude toward the French. It was no small compliment to say that Paris surpassed "all places in the universe" in learning and politeness. Hume simply loved *le monde*. And Suard, who translated "My Own Life,"[110] wanted French readers to love Hume.

There is no evidence to suggest that Suard formed a close relationship with Hume during the latter's stay in Paris in the 1760s. While it is certain that the two must have encountered each other in the salons named above, all of which Suard attended, there is no extant correspondence between the two. Nevertheless, Suard became Hume's greatest champion in France. In the bitter conflict between Hume and Rousseau, Suard served as the conduit through which Hume defended himself before the French reading public. The story began in 1762 when the Parlement of Paris condemned Rousseau's *Emile* because of its religious views and issued a warrant for Rousseau's arrest.[111] Rousseau first found asylum in Switzerland, but in January 1766 he accepted a retreat in England arranged by Hume. When Hume thought of soliciting a pension for Rousseau from George III, he wrote to Rousseau to see if the idea was agreeable to him. Rousseau rejected the offer and failed to respond to Hume's subsequent efforts to change his mind. At the same time, Rousseau became convinced that Hume had played a part in the circulation of a satirical letter about himself written by Horace Walpole. In this letter, which was avidly read in the salons in December 1765 and published in Grimm's *Correspondence Littéraire* in January 1766, Walpole pretended to be Frederick the Great inviting Rousseau to take asylum in Prussia.

> My dear Jean-Jacques,
> You have renounced Geneva, your native soil. You have been driven from Switzerland, a country of which you have made such boast in your writings. In France you are outlawed: come then to me. . . . It is high time to grow prudent and happy; you have made yourself sufficiently talked of for singularities little becoming a truly great man: show your enemies that you have sometimes common sense: this will vex them without hurting you. . . . If you persist in perplexing your brains to find out new misfortunes, choose such as you like

[109] Hume, "My Own Life," xxxix.

[110] David Hume, *La Vie de David Hume, écrite par lui-même*, trans. J.-B. Suard (London, 1777).

[111] The best account of the Hume-Rousseau affair is Dena Goodman, "The Hume-Rousseau Affair: From Private *Querelle* to Public *Procès*," *Eighteenth Century Studies* 25 (Winter 1991–92):171–202.

best; I am a king and can make you as miserable as you can wish; at the same time, I will engage to do that which your enemies never will, I will cease to persecute you, when you are no longer vain of persecution.

Your sincere friend,
Frederic[112]

In June, when Hume again tried to communicate with Rousseau about the royal pension, Rousseau finally answered, accusing Hume of launching a plot against him. Hume asked for an explanation, and Rousseau responded with a long letter that flatly accused him of conspiring to ruin his reputation in France and England. Rousseau wrote, "In a moment a ray of light discovered to me the secret cause of that touching and sudden change, which I had observed in the public respecting me; and I saw the plot which was put in execution at London."[113]

In an insightful interpretation of this episode, Dena Goodman writes:

> Just as an earlier epiphany had shown Rousseau that the history of humanity was a history of corruption, this one caused him to rewrite his own history as one of betrayal. He now went back and reinterpreted Hume's every word and action since they had departed from France in this new light. . . . He accused him of actions that ranged from giving him a strange look to intercepting and opening his mail.[114]

Communication between the two principals ceased, but then, as Goodman says, "the private affair began to be transformed into public scandal, the private quarrel into a public debate."[115] Hume wrote to friends about Rousseau's crazy ingratitude, while Rousseau offered justifications in letters of his own. As these letters were circulated, the affair became widely discussed and soon gained a place in the periodicals. When Hume decided to defend himself by circulating the letters that he had exchanged with Rousseau, he was urged by d'Alembert and Mademoiselle de Lespinasse to publish the materials. When Hume agreed, the job of translating and editing the letters fell to Suard, who had already translated several writings by Hume.[116]

---

[112] *Exposé succinct de la contestation qui s'est élevée entre M. Hume et M. Rousseau avec les pièces justificatives*, ed. Jean-Baptiste Suard (London, 1766); translated into English as *A Concise and Genuine Account of the Dispute Between Mr. Hume and Mr. Rousseau* (London, 1766). I have cited from Walpole's letter as given on pp. 20–21 of the English version (also cited by Goodman, "The Hume-Rousseau Affair," 174–75).

[113] *A Concise Account*, 59.

[114] Goodman, "The Hume-Rousseau Affair," 177.

[115] Ibid.

[116] Suard had translated extracts from Hume's historical writings in the *Journal Etranger*, May 1762 and July 1762. But his most important translations were his renditions of Hume's essays, which I discuss in detail below.

The *Exposé succinct de la contestation qui s'est élevée entre M. Hume et M. Rousseau* (Concise Account of the Dispute Between M. Hume and M. Rousseau) appeared in October 1766. In his Notice, Suard clearly sided with Hume, praising his "sweet" (*doux*) manners, his "moderation," and the lack of "polemical spirit" in his writings.[117] It is not difficult to establish why people like Suard, d'Alembert, and Lespinasse favored Hume over Rousseau. Apart from the fact that Rousseau's accusations were a fraud, Hume was more appealing because he was a recognized defender of politeness and civilization, whereas Rousseau was their greatest critic. Like Robertson's histories, Hume's writings, especially his essays, presented resources with which French *philosophes* could think optimistically about themselves. In Hume's thought, Suard found excellent tools for deepening the ideology that he and other members of the salons and Académie wished to propagate, an ideology that evaded questions concerning the location of sovereignty in the community and that focused instead on the cultivation of private sociability.

Hume's preoccupation with sociability was deeply rooted in his theory of knowledge and his conception of the role of the philosopher in the world. With a skeptical epistemology, he did not believe that philosophers could generate discourses completely free of the suppositions of ordinary life and language. As Hume showed in the *Treatise of Human Nature*, the efforts of pure reason to build autonomous sources of authority necessarily fail because Pyrrhonian doubts about the existence of the world, the reliability of sense experience, and the nature of causality cannot be overcome through reason alone. "The understanding, when it acts alone, and according to its most general principles, entirely subverts itself, and leaves not the lowest degree of evidence in any proposition, either in philosophy or common life."[118] In Hume's "post-Pyrrhonian philosophy,"[119] reason does not attempt to ignore or transcend the conventions of everyday action and discourse, which Hume calls "common life." Instead, it aims to sift through and organize the experience of common life, elevating, whenever possible, the coherence of our ordinary thoughts, yet without repudiating all of our elementary suppositions: "philosophical decisions are nothing but the reflections of common life, methodized and corrected."[120]

According to Hume, philosophers cannot defend their own conceptions through reason alone, so they have no right to demand that ordinary indi-

[117] *Exposé succinct*, Avertissement, iii, v.

[118] Hume, *A Treatise of Human Nature*, ed. L. A. Selby-Bigge and P. H. Nidditch (Oxford, 1978), Treatise, 267–68.

[119] This appellation comes from Donald W. Livingston, *Hume's Philosophy of Common Life* (Chicago, 1984).

[120] David Hume, *David Hume's Enquiries Concerning Human Understanding and Concerning the Principles of Morals*, ed. L. A. Selby-Bigge (Oxford, 1975), 162 (from *Enquiry Concerning Human Understanding*).

viduals do so. The philosopher, however, can pose new questions for the ordinary person to consider, questions that arise logically out of the ordinary person's commitments or prejudices. The philosopher can point out contradictions and clarify the meaning of the decisions one must make on the basis of what one already believes. And the philosopher can introduce a more refined set of terms for discussing experience, though the experience in question is still the experience of "common life." As Donald W. Livingston explains:

> Common life for Hume is an order of passion, prejudice, custom, and tradition. It is in this world that the philosopher has his being. He is, however, never entirely at home in it. But unlike Descartes, Hume does not, methodologically, view the customs and prejudices of common life as barriers to understanding. Rather he views them as the only instruments through which we can understand the real, however darkly and obscurely.[121]

Although it is unlikely that Suard fully appreciated the epistemological depth of Hume's thought (the *Treatise* and other epistemological writings, as mentioned, had drawn little attention), he did appreciate Hume's interest in sociability, which was one of the consequences of his epistemology. Hume advocated a special brand of empiricism. By definition, empiricism is the belief that "experience" is the basis of knowledge. But Hume did not conceive of experience in a Lockean or individualistic way; that is, as the mind's clarification of its own sensations. He conceived of experience as something rooted in interaction, something generated "in the common course of the world, by men's behavior in company, in affairs, and in their pleasures."[122] This "public notion of experience," as Livingston calls it, was the foundation of Hume's interest in sociability, an interest that he sustained in his lighter essays. Thus, in his self-descriptive essay entitled "Of Essay Writing," Hume condemned those philosophers "who never consulted experience in any of their reasonings, or who never searched for that experience where alone it is to be found, in common life and conversation." He believed that the isolation of the philosopher from "the conversible world" had "a very bad influence both on books and company." Company that showed disdain for learning and philosophical reflection became mere gossip. And learning that was secluded from the "world" (Hume uses this term in a very French way, as in *le monde*) became "totally barbarous" and devoid of "manners" as well as of the "facility of thought and expression, which can only be acquired by conversation." Once again we find a Scottish thinker associating seclusion with barbarism and establishing that communication is the motor of civilization. Hume defined his own function as a mediator between two domains:

121 Livingston, *Hume's Philosophy*, 31.
122 Hume, *A Treatise of Human Nature*, xix.

In this view, I cannot but consider myself as kind of resident or ambassador from the dominions of learning to those of conversation; and shall think it my constant duty to promote a good correspondence betwixt these two states, which have so great a dependence on each other. I shall give intelligence to the learned of whatever passes in company, and shall endeavor to import into company whatever commodities I find in my native country for their use and entertainment. . . . The materials of this commerce must chiefly be furnish'd by conversation and common life: The manufacturing of them alone belongs to learning.[123]

Unlike Rousseau, who set himself up as a critic standing wholly outside the field of convention, Hume believed that the identity of the philosopher could not and should not be extricated from existing systems of interaction. Even philosophical books should draw readers into conversation, instead of isolating them from the world.

Hume was fascinated by the dialogue form as a means of bridging learning and conversation within the world of the text. In his view, philosophical issues about which

human reason can reach no fixed determination . . . lead us naturally into the style of dialogue and conversation. Reasonable men may be allowed to differ, where no one can reasonably be positive: Opposite sentiments, even without any decision, afford an agreeable amusement: And if the subject be curious and interesting, the book carries us, in a manner, into company; and unites the two greatest and purest pleasures of human life, study and society.[124]

Hume believed that the job of the writer was to imitate the pluralistic discourse of conversation while raising it to a higher level of precision than it achieved in a real oral exchange. The writer, in other words, should not only take advantage of the written word to develop systematic reflections but should also recreate the sense of difference—of unresolvable but politely maintained disagreement—that characterized good "company" and that was consistent with skeptical epistemology. "I have often thought," Hume wrote in a letter to Gilbert Eliot in 1751, "that the best way of composing a dialogue would be for two persons that are of different opinions about any question of importance, to write alternately the different parts of the discourse, and reply to each other. By this means, that vulgar

---

[123] Hume, "Of Essay-Writing," *Essays*, 534–35. See also the excellent discussion by Livingston, *Hume's Philosophy*, 45.

[124] David Hume, *Dialogues Concerning Natural Religion*, ed. Norman Kemp Smith (Indianapolis, 1947), 128. Again, see the insightful discussion by Livingston, *Hume's Philosophy*, 39–40. Livingston also argues that even Hume's *Treatise*, which is a work of exposition and not literally a dialogue, is in fact constructed as an exchange of viewpoints rather than as an authoritative monologue.

error would be avoided of putting nothing but nonsense into the mouth of the adversary."[125]

Hume's philosophy could be described as an epistemologically more profound version of the French theory of the art of conversation. His assimilation of writing to the orality of "the world" could only have been congenial to Suard, a man whose identity was rooted in the conversations of *le monde*. But to understand in exact terms what Suard saw in Hume, we must consider more carefully the writings that he translated.

One thing is clear: Suard liked Hume because Hume liked France. Hume sought to improve the status of France in British political discourse by emphasizing its "civilized" private life rather than its unfree political life. Indeed, Hume was far more effective than any French writer in developing a new description of France in accordance with a system of classification based on the kinds of society rather than the kinds of sovereignty. One of the results of his new description was that he appeared to be a Francophile. In a postscript that Suard appended to his translation of Hume's essay, "Of Civil Liberty," Suard wrote:

> M. Hume, though English, republican, and Protestant, has always spoken of the French with esteem, of Kings and Catholics with moderation; and this singular habit may have wounded a nation too accustomed to seeing in monarchies nothing but a horde of slaves and in Papists nothing but a league of fanatics, and recognizing neither liberty nor virtue nor philosophy in any government other than its own.[126]

Suard praised Hume for not condemning France simply for being an absolute monarchy.

> However, M. Hume does not at all mean by *absolute government* a despotic government, as one sometimes means. This expression for him simply means a government where the people has no part in legislation and where it [legislation] resides completely in the Sovereign. He has avoided confusing the monarch with the despot. He is the first English writer who has dared to write that monarchies are about as favorable to the progress of the arts, of reason, and of commerce as are republics.[127]

[125] Hume to Eliot, 10 March 1751, *The Letters of David Hume*, ed. J.Y.T. Grieg (Oxford, 1932), 1:154. See also Gary Shapiro's discussion of this letter in "The Man of Letters and the Author of Nature: Hume on Philosophical Discourse," *The Eighteenth Century, Theory and Interpretation* 26 (Spring 1985), 118.

[126] J.-B. Suard, postscript to "Essai sur la liberté et le despotisme" (trans. of Hume's "Of Liberty and Despotism"), *Journal Etranger*, May 1760, 170.

[127] Ibid., 170–71. Suard refers to Hume as "English" here. I believe that he did not appreciate the distinction between English and Scottish men of letters in the early 1760s and that he recognized it only in the 1770s, after he had encountered a "critical mass" of texts by the various Scottish writers whom he mentions in the 1772 letter to Robertson cited above.

There is no doubt that Hume did cast a favorable eye on France. His autobiography, as already cited, shows he enjoyed French company and thought of settling in Paris. Suard noted, in his preface to the translation of Hume's autobiography, "M. Hume liked France and for good reason. Never has a foreigner been better received there."[128] But Hume's favorable attitude toward France was not just an outcome of his celebrity in Paris; it was an intellectual attitude, shaped by his philosophical principles. To the abbé Le Blanc he wrote: "You would have remarked in my writings, that my principles are, all along, tolerably monarchical, and that I abhor that low practice, so prevalent in England, of speaking with malignity of France."[129]

"Of Liberty and Despotism" was the first of Hume's essays that Suard translated. This piece was designed to negate the distinction between "absolute" and "free" governments. Hume began the essay by observing that the study of politics was still very far from reaching definitive conclusions on its most elementary questions. He noted that modern political philosophy was based largely on ancient thought. He felt, however, that Greek and Roman categories were inadequate and had to be updated in the light of the "revolutions" of modern history.[130] Above all, he pointed out, the rise of trade and the incursion of commercial objectives into statecraft were unknown to the ancients:

> Trade was never esteemed an affair of state till the last century and there is scarcely any ancient writer on politics, who has made mention of it. Even the Italians have kept a profound silence with regard to it, though it has now engaged the chief attention, as well of ministers of state, as of speculative reasoners. The great opulence, grandeur, and military achievements of the two maritime powers [England and Holland] seem first to have instructed mankind in the importance of an extensive commerce.[131]

As he discussed the flourishing of commerce in modern nations and the efforts of modern statesmen to stimulate commercial progress, Hume showed how the old categories of political science, especially the division between absolutist and free regimes, were invalid. According to Hume, the ancients believed that a government monopolizing sovereign power necessarily obstructed freedom in private life. He went on to say that writers have declared that "commerce can never flourish but in a free government."

[128] Hume, *La Vie de David Hume*, trans. J.-B. Suard, vii.

[129] Hume to Le Blanc, 12 September 1754, *The Letters of David Hume*, 1:194.

[130] Hume, "Of Liberty and Despotism," in *Essays*, 89; Hume, "Essai sur la liberté et le despotisme," trans. J.-B. Suard, *Journal Etranger*, May 1760, 154. As with Suard's translation of Robertson, I cite from the original English source. Page references are to the English edition and Suard's translation, respectively. French words are sometimes given in parentheses to show how Suard translated key political terms. "Of Liberty and Despotism" was entitled "Of Civil Liberty" in editions of the *Essays* after 1757.

[131] Ibid., 88–89; 153.

It must, however, be observed, that the great jealousy entertained of late, with regard to the commerce of France, seems to prove, that this maxim is no more certain and infallible than the foregoing, and that the subjects of an absolute prince [*un prince absolu*] may become our rivals in commerce, as well as in learning.[132]

Hume affirmed, "Private property seems to me almost as secure in a civilized European monarchy, as in a republic" (*Les propriétés particulières me semblent presque aussi assurés dans les monarchies civilisées de l'Europe que dans les républiques*). Though in principle the absolute monarch had free scope to exercise violence upon the citizens, this danger was not "more than we commonly dread harm from thunder, or earthquakes, or any accident the most unusual and extraordinary."[133] Hume interchanged the terms "absolute government" and "civilized European monarchy," suggesting that in countries such as France, the king's sovereignty, which made him absolute, was compatible with respect for freedom and property.

Hume made an even fuller case on behalf of France in his discussion of the progress of politeness and learning under absolute monarchies. Ancient thinkers, according to Hume, observed that culture flourished under the free republics of Greece and Rome, but that it decayed simultaneously with the decline of liberty in the same states.

> From these two experiments . . . Longinus thought himself sufficiently justified, that the arts and sciences could never flourish, but in a free government. And in this opinion, he has been followed by several writers in our own country, who either confined their view merely to ancient facts, or entertained too great a partiality in favor of that form of government, established amongst us.[134]

Hume claimed that recent history had shattered the myth that monarchical regimes were unrefined. He admitted that ancient Rome lost her liberty and her civilization at the same time. But modern Italy provided a different picture: Ariosto, Tasso, Galileo, Raphael, and Michelangelo were not born in republics.

> But the most eminent instance of the flourishing of learning in absolute governments is that of FRANCE, which scarcely ever enjoyed any established liberty and yet has carried the arts and the sciences as near perfection as any other nation. The ENGLISH are, perhaps, greater philosophers; the ITALIANS better painters

---

[132] Ibid., 92; 159–60.
[133] Ibid., 92–93; 161.
[134] Ibid., 89–90; 155–56. In a note to this passage, Hume gave Addison and Shaftesbury as examples of "eminent writers" who maintained the ancient prejudice against absolute government. For Addison's view of French absolutism, see *The Tatler*, 161 (20 April 1710). For Shaftesbury's view that France could not be a polite nation because it was an absolute monarchy, see Lawrence Eliot Klein's discussion in "The Rise of 'Politeness' in England, 1660–1715," (Ph.D. diss., Johns Hopkins University, 1983), 590–98.

and musicians; the ROMANS were greater orators: But the FRENCH are the only people, except the GREEKS, who have been at once philosophers, poets, orators, historians, painters, architects, sculptors and musicians. With regard to the stage, they have excelled even the GREEKS, who far excelled the ENGLISH. And, in common life, they have, in a great measure perfected that art, the most useful and agreeable of any, l'Art de Vivre, the art of society and conversation.[135]

In 1773, Suard echoed this theme in a letter to the Margrave of Bayreuth, clearly showing that he had grasped Hume's argument and that he considered it important.

The ancients believed that the arts could flourish only in free governments. They made their judgement in accordance with their own experience and they were wrong; but it is strange that some enlightened moderns have repeated this paradox and have forgotten that all the arts were brought to an extraordinary degree of perfection in Italy . . . and that they made great progress in France under the reign of Louis XIV.[136]

In this way, Hume (and Suard) argued that "civil" refinement could exist in the absence of "civic" liberty, in the sense of participation in the law-making institution. "Civilized monarchies" were those that respected property and provided a social space for the cultivation of politeness and the arts. Hume considered this social space to be a locus of liberty in its own right, and the purpose of his essay was to demonstrate that such a space did not have any particular form of government as its prerequisite.

Suard translated three other essays by Hume: "Of the Study of History," "Whether the British Government Inclines More to Absolute Monarchy or to a Republic," and "Of the Coalition of Parties."[137] The last is the most suggestive. Suard prefaced the essay by saying that its subject matter—political parties—could only be a matter of "curiosity" for Frenchmen. By this he meant that political parties were a futile subject of discussion in France, where the absolutist constitution precluded their existence. Suard translated the essay, however, because it was not about the necessity or advantages of a party system. In fact, Hume argued that party divisions, which appeared to be based on deep differences of principle, were unnecessary and could virtually disappear. According to Hume, parties were unnecessary because there was a set of "moderate opinions"[138] that all people

---

[135] Hume, "Of Liberty and Despotism," 90–91; "Essai sur la liberté et le despotisme," 157–58.

[136] J.-B. Suard to the Margrave of Bayreuth, 17 September 1773, *Correspondance littéraire de Suard avec le Margrave de Bayreuth*, ed. Gabriel Bonno (Berkeley, 1934), 166.

[137] Translated respectively, in the *Journal Etranger*, September 1760, October 1760, and January 1761.

[138] Hume, "Of the Coalition of Parties," in *Essays*, 493; Hume, "Essai sur la réunion des partis," trans. J.-B. Suard, *Journal Etranger*, September 1760, 22.

could rally around. Hume believed that party differences in his time were based primarily on divergent sympathies for the actors in the great constitutional conflicts of the seventeenth century. He tried to show that there was in fact nothing in the English past that made differences of allegiance necessary in the present. In a rapid excursion through the seventeenth century, he argued that both defenders and opponents of the Stuarts had maintained reasonable views about government. He seems to have believed that if Whigs and Tories in the eighteenth century could sympathetically understand the conceptions of their historic antagonists, then party strife would disappear. "The greater moderation we now employ in representing past events, the nearer shall we be to produce a full coalition of the parties."[139]

"Of the Coalition of Parties" is one of Hume's weakest essays, for he did not explain how people could see seventeenth-century royalism as a reasonable position in its time and yet be loyal to the revolutionary settlement. Nevertheless, Hume's essay was appealing to Suard, not because he liked the English political system but because Hume appeared to be saying that an important aspect of that system, party conflict, was unnatural. "Never did I hear him [Suard] express the wish to adopt the government of England," Suard's wife stated.[140] In his *Notice sur le caractère et les écrits du duc de la Rochefoucauld*, Suard affirmed that while the spirit of party might be natural in republics, it was unnecessary and harmful in monarchies.[141] Describing Suard's relations with John Wilkes, the English radical, Garat observed that the Englishman viewed with favor the existence of permanent groups in opposition to each other, whereas Suard considered "an agreement of opinions" to be necessary to avert civil war:

> M. Suard, though very convinced that it is good that the people always be alert and enlightened, could not be persuaded that a state of war was the true social state. "To be free," he used to say, "must one have alarms where there are no dangers, or even storms and clouds? Only an agreement of opinions can give a gentle and easy play to the many parts of the public domain. When this agreement exists, obedience goes before the law, and the political spheres experience only harmony like the celestial spheres."[142]

Suard considered political contestation, even when organized through legal channels, to be inherently disorderly and conducive to civil war. He was against political parties and disliked the idea of a constitution that functioned on the basis of institutionalized conflicts of interest. In this respect, his vision was consonant with French absolutist theory, which was premised on the belief that public power must be based on unity.

[139] Ibid., 500; 37–38.
[140] Amélie Suard, *Essais de mémoires*, 187.
[141] J.-B. Suard, *Notice sur le caractère*, xvi–xvii.
[142] Garat, *Mémoires historiques*, 2:94–95.

Suard departed from absolutism, however, by seeing civil society as a unified totality. This made private life, not royal power, the fountainhead of public order. All of his translations of Ossian, Robertson, and Hume suggest that he wished his contemporaries to believe that a historical process of refinement was making the "agreement of opinions" an immanent feature of modern life. Whether he believed in this fiction literally or whether he merely subscribed to it in the hope that its propagation could become a self-fulfilling prophecy is unclear. Most likely, it was a combination of conviction and hope.

The optimism about the possibility of consensus that Hume expressed in "Of the Coalition of Parties" was not characteristic of his political philosophy as a whole. With this in mind, it becomes interesting to inspect some of the essays that Suard did not translate and to compare them with those that he did in order to see which aspects of Humean political science were uncongenial to him. Suard did not translate any of the essays in which Hume conceptualized politics in terms of self-interest or the inevitability of conflict. Those which he did translate amount to a picture of modern society advancing in refinement and peace. The belief that history was a civilizing process was indeed an important element in Hume's historical vision, yet his political thought did not hinge on this belief as much as it appears from the Suard translations alone. Hume did not believe that all political wisdom could be skimmed off the surface of historical trends. Political theory was informed, but not nourished exclusively, by an understanding of the progress of civilization. Hume believed that the historian could be an optimist but that the political theorist had to be a cynic. This intellectual schizophrenia is clearest at the beginning of Hume's essay, "Of the Independency Of Parliament."

> Political writers have established it as a maxim that, in contriving any system of government, and fixing the several checks and controls of the constitution, every man ought to be supposed a *knave*, and to have no other end, in all his actions, than private interest. By this interest, we must govern him, and, by means of it, make him, notwithstanding his insatiable avarice and ambition, co-operate to public good. Without this, say they, we shall in vain boast of the advantages of any constitution, and shall find, in the end, that we may have no security for our liberties or possessions, except the good-will of our rulers; that is, we shall have no security at all.[143]

What Hume here calls a "maxim" is to be understood as an axiom of political theory, a form of discourse that he took to be separate from the empirical study of civilized nations. The maxim that every man is a knave, he stated, was false "in fact," yet true "in politics." This seeming paradox stemmed

---

[143] Hume, "Of the Independency of Parliament," *Essays*, 42–43.

partly from Hume's belief that people tended to act more selfishly in their "public capacity" than in their private social lives[144]—an interesting denial of the republican belief that the public sphere brings out the best in man. At the same time, Hume, as a skeptic and conservative, was more interested in enjoying the present liberties afforded by the English constitution than in dreaming about how civilized beings could construct a perfect regime. Hence, he wished to ground political philosophy in prudential consider-ations and to insulate it from the optimistic discourse of universal history, including even his own optimism about the rise of commercial society. He wished to separate constitutional thought from history, not because the data of history were unpromising, but because he considered it *safer* for the preservation of existing liberties to ascribe passions and interests to humans instead of reason and refinement.

For Suard, however, the distinctively prudential element was unimpor-tant. He evaded the dictum that every man ought to be supposed a knave, relegating it to the obscurity of untranslated material. He translated "Of the Coalition Of Parties" with its hope of consensus, and he ignored not only "Of the Independency of Parliament" but also "Of Parties in General," in which Hume argued that deep divisions of interest were a necessary fact of political life. In Britain, Hume wrote, the nobles and the people "naturally follow a distinct interest; nor can we reasonably expect a different conduct considering that degree of selfishness implanted in human nature."[145] Un-like Hume, Suard, anticipating Marx, completed the circuit between history and politics. The fusion of two idioms (politics and universal history) into a single one, the reduction of political thought to a description of the civiliz-ing process, the explanation of public order in terms of private life—these were the key elements of Suard's Scottish corpus.

With this corpus he offered a distinctive vision of things to his French readers. According to absolutist thinkers, the inherent divisions stemming from human unsociability made it necessary to have a sovereign being who was above private interests or who could at least use force to impose his will on a divided community. Scottish liberalism, if we may take Hume as its representative, articulated a conception of modern sociability, but without completely injecting the idea of sociability into the political imagination. The political art was the art of maintaining constitutional arrangements that tempered the effects of human selfishness and competition. The true source of order, then, was neither the monarch nor human civility but good institu-tions. Suard, in contrast to both French absolutism and Scottish liberalism, dissolved the absolutist problem of order into the depoliticizing solution of "civilization." In doing so, he not only undermined the pessimism that

[144] Ibid., 43.
[145] Hume, "Of Parties in General," in *Essays*, 59. See also "Of the Parties of Great Britain," in *Essays*, 64–65.

formed the intellectual basis of French absolutism but also took historical optimism to a point where he could ignore the constitutional questions that were important in British liberalism. For him, the very concept of civilization implied refinement and "an agreement of opinions." This style of thinking was based on the assumption that the sovereign state, whether residing in the hands of the king, the people, or any other agent, played no crucial part in the maintenance of modern society.

This remarkable confidence in the power of history and the social world that history creates was well expressed in Suard's reception speech to the Académie Française in 1774. The speech was a defense of critical men of letters against their detractors, who claimed that the rise of *philosophie* had done harm to belles lettres, to religion, and to government. Suard said that it might be true that *philosophie* tended to displace older forms of eloquence with a more abstract jargon. This was "an inevitable misfortune," however, because "philosophy is the necessary effect of the progress of the human mind," and there could be no turning back to the past.[146] According to Suard, the "infancy" of society, when the imagination was virile, when souls were sensitive to nature, and language extravagant and beautiful, had to give way to the age of intellect.[147] Suard did not mention Ossian, but it is clear he was reiterating the evolutionary ideas that he, Turgot, and Blair had formulated about the mythical bard. As for the critics who claimed that philosophy was destructive of religion, Suard's response was that ignorance and self-isolation, not philosophy, were the scourges of religion. To prove his point he evoked an image of the Middle Ages à la Robertson. The absence of communication in medieval times, he affirmed, had contributed greatly to the absurd opinions and "crude morals" that had generated so much conflict and bloodshed among Christians.[148]

Finally, Suard considered the charge that philosophy was the enemy of governmental authority. Here, the influence of Hume is unmistakable. Philosophy could not subvert the monarchy, Suard argued, for although philosophers were defenders of liberty, "they know how to distinguish civil liberty [*liberté civile*], which consists in obeying only the laws, from political liberty, which calls each citizen to the formation of the laws; they know that civil liberty is the only one which contributes to the happiness of men and that it can be found in a monarchy as in a republic."[149] Moreover, philosophers appreciated that manners were becoming increasingly polite and that the best form of government was not a republic but a limited monarchy, a monarchy "tempered above all by manners."[150] With the growth of polite-

[146] Suard, *Discours . . . à la réception de M. Suard*, 6–7.
[147] Ibid., 7–8.
[148] Ibid., 11–12.
[149] Ibid., 13.
[150] Ibid., 14.

ness and communication, the "barbarous" ferocity of the Middle Ages had been left behind for good and a new source of order and peace had emerged. This new phenomenon was "public opinion" (*opinion publique*). "Of this opinion one must say that it governs the world, for everything obeys its power. It governs the laws themselves, tempering or destroying their action." Public opinion, Suard declared, was "more powerful than the public force charged with the execution of laws."[151]

What, precisely, is public opinion? How is it formed? How does it exercise its omnipotent and beneficial power over the state ("the public force charged with the execution of laws")? There are no answers to these questions in Suard's speech or in any of his writings. It is evident, however, that Suard envisioned "public opinion" as an outcome of the growing civility in private life—the collective consciousness of polite human beings. Paradoxically, "public opinion" was the linchpin of political order, yet it was located outside of the political constitution, in the private sphere. Vague as the idea may appear, it played the crucial role of binding together the two main impulses in Suard's thought, optimism concerning history and indifference with regard to constitutional questions about the location of legislative sovereignty. It was as if public opinion, which "governs the world," made sovereign power an instrument of society rather than its master. The particular *form* of government (monarchy, democracy, etc.) was now irrelevant, because the *content* of its laws would flow superstructurally from civil society. Implicitly, government itself was merely a residue of a prior epoch, when barbarous men needed a coercive agent to restrain them. Modern people, in this vision, appeared as self-governing creatures. This is not to say that they were active in party management, voting, and office holding; for their self-government was not one of politics but of manners, of restraint and polish acquired through conversation. Suard's notion of "public opinion," and the Scottish ideas on which he established it, made up a grand myth. His remarkable success in the late Enlightenment was due to his facility in offering this ideal of a consensual, apolitical community to a literary republic whose members generally sought to envision life without either Hobbes or Rousseau. The men of letters wished to be free, but they wished to be free as men of letters and sociable creatures, not as sovereign agents. Suard's urbane character became a symbol of sociability, of virtue without passion, and of literary achievement without political struggle. The images that he presented of the growth of civility and consensus in universal history were showered with praise, and he reaped all the honors due to a writer who managed to blend utopianism and acceptance of the regime.

As a second-generation *philosophe*, Suard was too young to die before the French Revolution. He was forced to witness events that were not part of

---

[151] Ibid., 16–17.

universal history as he understood it. Suard's belief that France was the most civilized nation, a nation marked by "an agreement of opinions," was destroyed by the contentious and bloody efforts of Frenchmen to institute democracy. After the Revolution, Madame Suard expressed bafflement that such violence could have erupted in the polite culture of France.

> France, which for so long had served as the model of politeness and urbanity . . . this France was ruined in the opinion of Europe by the bloody routes it took to arrive at liberty, and it was at the very moment when enlightenment was the most widespread throughout the nation.[152]

Suard himself had no constitutional philosophy, and in 1787–88 he was neither for nor against the meeting of the Estates General. Once the king agreed to convene it, however, Suard presumed that it would meet in a civilized fashion. In October of 1788 he wrote to Robertson that the impending events should prove "worthy of furnishing an interesting [new] section to the immortal introduction of the history of Charles V."[153]

But Robertson had celebrated the centuries-old death of the "feudal system" and praised the gradual development of commercial manners. The men of 1789 clamored to annihilate the *ancien régime* and swiftly install a completely new order of things. The sense of immediate temporal proximity to the object of hatred was what separated revolutionary discourse from the evolutionary discourse of Suard and the Scots. According to Robertson, the "feudal system" had begun to decay in the late Middle Ages as a result of the Crusades. According to the Revolutionaries, the *ancien régime* was still in full force in 1789. The revolutionaries sought to abolish legal inequality and to instill the kind of virtue that Rousseau admired and that he personified in his quarrel with Hume—a disdain for financial profit, a repudiation of external manners in favor of inner sincerity, a belief in the existence of evil plots that become the counterpoint for the affirmation of one's own moral purity. In the revolutionary climate, Suard's urbanity, to make an understatement, was no longer progressive. He began by defending the monarchy in newspaper articles. He briefly joined the national guard, patrolling in support of the king. After the massacres of September 1792, however, he retired to the countryside and managed to live quietly throughout the rest of the revolutionary years.[154]

It did not take Suard long to confess that his early hopes had been misplaced, that the Revolution had broken out of the civilizing process as he had imagined it. In the spring of 1791 he again wrote to Robertson:

---

[152] Amélie Suard, *Essais de mémoires*, 188.
[153] J.-B. Suard to Robertson, October 1788, Papers of William Robertson, National Library of Scotland, ms. 3943, 259.
[154] Amélie Suard, *Essais de mémoires*, 188–203.

The incomprehensible revolution operating here was foreseen by the philosophers . . . but it is operating in a manner that I think must astonish all the philosophers of the world. No political revolution can be compared to this one: no one has ever seen such a vast and solid edifice demolished.[155]

But although the Revolution had surprised the philosophers, Suard did not lose his confidence in philosophy. He simply saw a need "to undertake a new analysis of the principles of political science."[156]

Suard himself never undertook such an analysis. Lacking a gift for original speculation and unaccustomed to thinking about governmental forms and policies, he was not up to the task. The events demanded a fresh analysis of political ideas and institutions—of sovereignty, democracy, representation, party conflict, and terror. As a thinker of only moderate talents, and as one who had devoted his efforts to articulating a notion of civilization in which the state was not central, Suard was simply unequipped to provide a meaningful analysis of the postrevolutionary situation. As always, he emerged polite in his manners and successful in his career, for in the Napoleonic period he enjoyed his last years as a member of the Institut de France and as the host of his own salon. But he no longer had anything important to say.

What is striking about Suard's experience during the revolutionary years is that he continued to feel confidence in his original source of knowledge. Nothing better indicates how enthusiastic he had once been about his Scottish inspirations than the continuing faith he expressed even after the Revolution had destroyed his entire creed:

I wish that all the instructed men of Europe would communicate their enlightenment and their opinions on what we have done and what we ought to do, not with the exaggerated declamations of M. Burke, but with the gravity and conscience of a William Robertson. I would also like the opinion of M. Stewart, of M. Millar, of all you sages of Scotland, for there, especially at Edinburgh, is the sanctuary of philosophy.[157]

[155] J.-B. Suard to Robertson, 21 March 1791, Papers of William Robertson, ms. 3944, 39.
[156] Ibid., 40.
[157] Ibid., 40–41.

5

ANDRÉ MORELLET AND THE END OF THE
ENLIGHTENMENT

"Why," I was asked, "were you gay before August 10, and why
have you been sad since?"
*(From Morellet's account of his interrogation during the
Reign of Terror)*[1]

Form versus Substance

THE PHILOSOPHIC career of André Morellet (1727–1818)
spanned more than sixty years and embroiled him in many of the
great ideological struggles of his time. Born in Lyons, he studied for
the priesthood and was licensed by the Sorbonne in 1752. It was in the
library of this institution that he discovered the works of Locke, Bayle,
Leibniz, Cudworth, and Voltaire. "I lived in the library," he recounted later
in his memoirs. "I went out only to hear theses and to go to the dining
hall."[2] As his reading took a secular turn, the young theology student began
to imagine the possibility of heaven on earth: "[I was] firmly convinced that
this world would develop inexorably, through the progress of enlightenment and virtue, into a sanctuary of peace and perfect happiness."[3] After
leaving the Sorbonne, Morellet became a professional reformer. His numerous books, brochures, and translations advocated a variety of new policies, including religious toleration, smallpox inoculation, the abolition of
torture, freedom of the press, and freedom of trade. A nineteenth-century
French encyclopedia states, "Morellet wrote much; more than anyone else,
he contributed to the diffusion of the theories of the *philosophes* in the
eighteenth century."[4]

Morellet achieved fame under the absolute monarchy not only through
his publications but through a remarkably broad range of friends, patrons,

---

[1] André Morellet, *Mémoires sur le dix-huitième siècle et sur la révolution*, ed. Jean-Pierre
Guicciardi (Paris, 1988), 384. The date mentioned in the quotation, August 10, 1792, was the
day of the popular uprising in Paris that forced the Legislative Assembly to suspend the king's
powers. A fuller account of the interrogation follows in this chapter.

[2] Ibid., 52.

[3] Ibid, 51–52.

[4] "Morellet, André," in *La Grande encyclopédie* (Paris, 1886), 24:333.

and correspondents. Among his manuscript papers he left a "List of notable persons whom I knew and with whom I have had relations." The list contains the names of eighty distinguished philosophers, artists, and statesmen, both French and foreign.[5] Morellet, who dubbed Rousseau "the unsociable man" (*l'homme insociable*)[6] was himself one of the more sociable philosophers of the Enlightenment. During the 1760s and '70s he could be found on Mondays at the salon of Madame Geoffrin, Tuesdays at the salon of Madame Helvétius, Wednesdays again at Geoffrin's, Thursdays at the salon of Holbach, Fridays at the salon of the Neckers, and Sundays again at Holbach's.[7]

Morellet reached the peak of his career as a reformer of absolutism in the 1780s, a decade in which most of the great *philosophes* were either dead or dying. After 1789, with both his intellectual comrades and the absolutist system gone, he attempted to forge a new identity as a critic of democracy. Recognizing the breadth of Morellet's writings, the scope of his contacts, and the precariousness of his fate in a democratic regime that was less tolerant of its critics than the absolute monarchy had been, Pierre Edouard Lémontey, who was elected to Morellet's seat in the Académie Française after Morellet's death, declared him to have been "a monument of endurance" and "the representative of that century which engendered us."[8] What exactly Morellet endured and what exactly he represented—as well as what he inflicted upon others and what he did not represent—are questions that are worth considering, questions for which there are no readily available answers. Morellet's *Mémoires*, his letters, and his *Prospectus d'un nouveau dictionnaire du commerce* (Prospectus for a New Dictionary of Commerce, 1769) have been recently republished.[9] Yet his career as a whole has not

---

[5] Among them are Beccaria, Buffon, Chamfort, Condillac, Condorcet, d'Alembert, d'Holbach, Diderot, Franklin, Galiani, Garrick, Geoffrin, Helvétius, Hume, Lord Shelburne, Loménie de Brienne, Malesherbes, Necker (Monsieur and Madame), Paine, Piccinni, Raynal, Suard, Trudaine de Montigny, Turgot, and Voltaire. The list is appended to the second edition of Morellet's *Mémoires* (Paris, 1822), 2:507–8.

[6] Morellet, *Mémoires* (1988 edition), 116. I will occasionally cite the 1822 edition, which contains supplementary documents, but unless otherwise indicated, all references to the *Mémoires* will be to the 1988 edition.

[7] Morellet, *Mémoires*, 96–97, 129–35, 143–44.

[8] Pierre Edouard Lémontey, "Eloge de l'Abbé Morellet," in Morellet's *Mémoires* (1822 edition), ii.

[9] See note 1 for reference to the *Mémoires*; *Lettres d'André Morellet (vol. 1) 1759–1785*, ed., Dorothy Medlin, Jean-Claude David, and Paul Leclerc (Oxford, 1991; the editors are preparing further volumes of his letters); *Prospectus d'un nouveau Dictionnaire de commerce*, with a preface by Jean-Claude Perrot (Munich, 1980). The original manuscript of the *Mémoires*, which I will be citing often, has been lost. References by Morellet to his age or to events at the time of his writing indicate that he composed the work in patches between 1797 and 1805. The memoirs are an autobiography, yet as the title suggests, they are meant to be a history of the "eighteenth century and the revolution," so it is not surprising that they stop in 1803, the year before Napoleon became emperor. The text was first published posthumously in 1821.

received much critical attention, and so he remains a symbol without a meaning, a monument to an unspecified achievement.[10]

Morellet was not a writer of genius, so there is little challenge or reward in merely summarizing any particular aspect of his thought. At the same time, he was more than a dull diffuser of other people's ideas. He was truly a philosopher, for his mind always had a tendency to double back upon itself—initially through analysis, to explain its own presuppositions, and later through narrative, to tell its own history.

Under the absolute monarchy, Morellet delineated the theoretical foundations of his own vocation as a liberal man of letters. When he propagandized, he also reflected on the activity of being a propagandist. In fact, Morellet was perhaps the only eighteenth-century French writer to provide an extended account of that entity to which most political propaganda was addressed in the last three decades of the absolute monarchy—"public opinion." In the same spirit of self-explication, Morellet not only flourished in the convivial atmosphere of the Parisian salons but also wrote about the psychological sources of politeness and the nature of conversation as a sign of "civilized society."

After the Revolution, Morellet's idealism turned into nostalgia. On the title page of his memoirs he placed a maxim from the Roman epigrammist Martial, "To be able to draw pleasure from considering one's earlier life is to live twice."[11] Here, in the memoirs, he created a space in which, so to speak, from beyond the grave, he could describe the death of the Enlightenment. He portrayed the prerevolutionary "republic of letters" as a world in which a man such as himself, of humble birth, could attain wealth and recognition for his service to the cause of freedom and progress. And he described how the republic of letters died by describing how he lost his wealth and his rhetorical influence in the new republican climate. His hatred of the Revolution was thus personal, but it was also intellectual. He opposed it not only because it robbed him of his livelihood but also because it did not implement the ideals that he believed he shared with the greatest minds of prerevolutionary France.

---

[10] The only books on Morellet were written early in this century and do not raise the analysis to a very high level: Daniel Delafarge, *L'Affaire de l'abbé Morellet en 1760* (Paris, 1912); Auguste Mazure, *Les Idées de l'abbé Morellet* (Paris, 1910); and Pierre Proteau, *Etude sur Morellet considéré comme auxiliaire de l'école physiocratique* (Laval, 1910). A recent article by Dorothy Medlin, though brief, does effectively sketch Morellet's entire career: "André Morellet and the Idea of Progress," *Studies on Voltaire and the 18th Century*, 189 (1980):239–46. I am also grateful to Professor Medlin, one of the editors of the fine edition of Morellet's correspondence, for supplying me with information about Morellet's manuscripts. I wish to thank Jeffrey Merrick for sending me his bibliography of Morellet scholarship. Several articles, too numerous to cite here, deal with specific aspects of Morellet's thought. Collectively, they attest to the breadth of his preoccupations, but none offers a general interpretation of the structure and evolution of his philosophy.

[11] Morellet, *Mémoires*, 39.

The Enlightenment, as Morellet conceptualized it after 1789, was a critique of despotism, but it was also a part of the *ancien régime* that the revolutionaries abolished. It was a chapter in the history of the absolute monarchy, not a preface to democracy. This conception of the Enlightenment as a finite episode set Morellet apart not only from the revolutionaries themselves but also from their conservative critics, such as Edmund Burke and Joseph de Maistre. For all of these believed that the spirit of the Enlightenment (whether understood as a progressive age of reason or a pernicious age of hyperrationalism) marked the beginning of a new phase of history, a modernity characterized by criticism and creative destruction. Morellet saw the Enlightenment as modern, but not the violent modernity that his country had embarked upon in 1789. He was one of the very few thinkers who both glorified the Enlightenment and proclaimed that it came to an end in 1789—that it had nothing to do with democratic ideology. In his *Apologie de la Philosophie contre ceux qui l'accusent des maux de la Révolution* (Apology for Philosophy Against Those Who Accuse It of the Evils of the Revolution, 1796), he underscored the differences between *Philosophie* (Enlightenment philosophy) and the Revolution through a series of stark contrasts extending for several pages. "Philosophy taught that men deserved equal protection under the law, but not so they could annihilate all public order, all subordination, all inequality of wealth. . . . It sought to temper the authority of monarchical power, but it never taught that one could give a democratic government to a country with a diameter of two hundred leagues, populated with twenty-four million inhabitants."[12] And so on.

Much can be learned by considering Morellet's self-image as a liberal reformer before 1789 and by appreciating his critique of democracy afterward; but much can also be learned by identifying those aspects of his life and thought that do not fit neatly into the explicit framework of his own philosophy. In this context, his inability to control his penchant for defamation is more than a biographical curiosity. Paradoxically, the sociable man of letters was subject to fits of rage against those whom he repeatedly described in his memoirs as "the enemies of reason," that is, those who did not agree with him. He acknowledged that, as a student at the Sorbonne, "I was, and never ceased to be, violent in dispute. . . . Sometimes I would spit blood after an argument."[13] Imprisoned for libel, denounced by Diderot for treating his opponents too harshly in his writings, Morellet illustrates both the theory of sociability and its limits in practice. In his memoirs he acknowledged his contentious nature, but he tried to justify it by insisting on the righteousness of his ideas—thus giving further proof of his vindictiveness.

---

[12] Morellet, *Apologie de la Philosophie contre ceux qui l'accusent des maux de la Révolution*, reprinted in his *Mélanges de littérature et de philosophie* (Paris, 1818), 4:315–16.

[13] Morellet, *Mémoires*, 51.

I am aware that some people criticized me on account of my taste for literary wars; others, more unfairly, saw me as a slanderer. But I am not inclined to condemn myself on these grounds, for I believe, in fact, that among my accomplishments, I can include the justice that I meted out, in several confrontations, to certain enemies of reason.[14]

Although comments like this reveal a self-conscious personality trying to explain its emotional outbursts, they do not explain Morellet's failures. More importantly, they do not highlight the problem that riddled the identity of some men of letters in the late eighteenth century, a period in which the state became increasingly receptive to philosophical criticism of itself. The problem, in essence, was this: How could men of letters maintain the ideals and practices of sociability in a world in which philosophy was becoming increasingly political and politicians more philosophical? How could they be polite in the very act of competing against each other for the power to shape the state's policy?

Due to the strange combination of polite and competitive elements in his temperament, Morellet embodied a tension in Enlightenment thought between form and substance. This is the tension between "society" conceived as a thing in itself, a haven of egalitarian manners within a hierarchical regime (an ideal invented in the seventeenth century and upheld throughout the Enlightenment by *philosophes* such as Suard), and "society" conceived as a thing to be instituted and shaped by intellectuals and administrators (an ideal represented by the physiocrats and all those who envisioned progress not merely as the improvement of manners but as the implementation of rational legislation as well). One might also formulate it as a tension between *sociability*, in the sense of the rules that make exchange possible among individuals with different backgrounds and opinions, and *politics*, in the sense of the techniques used to shape opinion in order to transform the collectivity in a specific way.

Morellet tried to maintain commitments to both form and substance. Like Suard, he enjoyed *le monde* and appreciated the importance of reciprocity and moderation. But whereas Suard, the paragon of politeness in the late Enlightenment, was entirely a man of forms, Morellet was interested in shaping the content of state policy. The difference between them is evident in their use of the term "public opinion." Suard employed it to refer to "an agreement of opinions" that emerges in a "civilized" nation. As explained in the previous chapter, the term had an apolitical point for him. He used it to confer prestige upon sociability and to suggest that the unanimity of manners and belief that are essential for stability in any regime flowed, in the case of France, from exchange relations in "civil society" and not from the state. Morellet's conception of "public opinion" was different. It was not merely a

14 Ibid., 199.

reference point evoked to lend a spirit of autonomy to the proceedings of a salon or the Académie Française; it was real. It could pressure government and shape policy, though it was nothing without men of letters—who were also nothing without it. "Neither M. de Voltaire, nor M. d'Alembert, nor Rousseau, nor you," he wrote to the Italian jurist, Cesar Beccaria, in 1766, "nor any *philosophe* can produce an immediate effect on the mind of those who govern. We act upon public opinion [*opinion publique*] and public opinion will eventually subjugate fanatics and even tyrants."[15] Here the use of the plural verb in the phrase, "We act upon public opinion," implies that the *philosophes* propagandized in unison, and that they presented the same ideas to their audience. In actuality, the Enlightenment threatened to split apart on account of the struggle among the *philosophes* to gather support for mutually exclusive policies—a struggle in which Morellet was one of the most aggressive competitors.

The Rules of Criticism

Morellet's success as a *philosophe* began with an insult. After receiving a degree from the Sorbonne in 1752, he was unable to pursue the doctorate because of lack of funds to pay tuition. His father, a small paper merchant, could offer nothing to André, the oldest of his fourteen children. The thought of becoming a parish priest did not appeal to him, so he used the recommendation of a former teacher to became a tutor to the son of the marquis de la Galaizière, chancellor of the duchy of Lorraine. Morellet held this position until 1760 and was able to pursue other activities on the side. In 1756 he published his first brochure, *Petit écrit sur une matière intéressante* (Short Writing on an Interesting Subject), a defense of the Huguenots against religious persecution. Diderot, "delighted to see a priest rail against bigots,"[16] recruited him to write theological articles for the *Encyclopédie*. But Morellet did not win fame until his imprisonment for libel in 1760.

He was punished for a rude statement about the Princess of Robecq, Anne-Marie de Luxembourg, in his *Préface de la comédie des Philosophes* (Preface to the comedy *The Philosophes*, 1760). Morellet's real target was Robecq's protégé, the playwright Charles Palissot de Montenoy. Palissot's satirical drama, *Les Philosophes*, opened in the Comédie Française on May 2, 1760, and created a sensation with its corrosive caricatures of the encyclope-dists. The lawyer and diarist, Edmund Barbier, attended the opening perfor-mance and gave the following account in his diary.

> At the Comédie Française they have performed a play in three acts, in verse, entitled *Les Philosophes*, which is a criticism of the works and opinions of Di-

[15] Morellet to Beccaria, July (day unknown) 1766, *Lettres d'André Morellet*, 59.
[16] Morellet, *Mémoires*, 66.

derot, editor of the *Encyclopédie*, Duclos, historiographer of France, Jean-Jacques Rousseau of Geneva, Helvétius, and others. This play is by Monsieur Palissot, a man of letters of considerable wit and who writes very well. . . . The play is not considered a true dramatic production. It has no plot and no interest but is written very elegantly. At the same time, it is filled with a spitefulness that extends to particular personalities. Those on the stage are easily recognizable. The philosophers and savants are portrayed as rascals who seek to corrupt morals. . . . There was extreme excitement and competition [for seats] the day of the first performance. The tumult was unprecedented.[17]

The play exposed the absurd ideas of a pretentious salon hostess, Cydalise, and the parasitic band of *philosophes* who flatter yet despise her. Cydalise is a delirious admirer of the encyclopedists and tries to force her daughter, Rosalie, to marry Valère (Helvétius). Rosalie herself prefers another suitor, the virtuous but unphilosophic Damis. Valère, who feels nothing for Rosalie but is eager to acquire her family's wealth, justifies his greed by expounding the doctrine that all human action is rooted in self-interest. His friend Dortidius (Diderot) is a cosmopolitan and an advocate of the sentiment of "humanity" who feels no loyalty or affection for any particular person. The most vicious scene of the play represents the *philosophes* alone among themselves. Here, with no need to cover their base motives with humanitarian pronouncements, they reveal their petty interests and intricate plots. In other scenes, Palissot used light comedy to deflate the *philosophes*. Valère's servant, caught in the act of picking his master's pocket, defends himself by reiterating his master's theories of self-interest. In the last act, Damis's servant, Crispin, impersonates Rousseau in order to gain entry to the salon. He represents Rousseau's belief in the need to return to nature by walking on all fours with a piece of lettuce in his mouth, and at one point he comes close to taking off his clothes. In the end, he reveals his true identity, exposes the dishonesty of the *philosophes*, and induces Cydalise to support Damis.[18]

Morellet attended the second performance of the play. "I returned home indignant and wrote, in practically one sitting during a long part of the night, *La Préface de la comédie des Philosophes*."[19] The *Préface*, which appeared in print anonymously at the end of May, was written in the form of a satirical biblical vision. Palissot hears a voice urging him to write a play that will quell philosophy and revive the spirit of the Inquisition. When Palissot states that he has no talent for writing, the voice answers by telling him to plagiarize and

---

[17] Edmond Jean François Barbier, *Journal historique et anecdotique* (Paris, 1847), 4:346–47.

[18] Charles Palissot de Montenoy, *Les Philosophes, comédie en trois actes, en vers* (Paris, 1760). As a note at the end of the text indicates, this edition was printed just a few days after the first performance of the play. It undoubtedly conveys the theatrical production more accurately than later editions, which Palissot revised considerably.

[19] Morellet, *Mémoires*, 100.

to count on the help of ignorant critics and patrons. Morellet's fatal mistake was not only to allude to Robecq in this context but to mock her by drawing attention to her fragile health. "And there will appear a great lady, gravely ill, who, as her last consolation before dying, will hope to attend the first performance and say, 'Now, oh Lord, you may leave your servant in peace, for I have seen sweet revenge [taken against philosophy].'"[20]

Robecq had indeed attended the first performance, but she left early because of her illness. She died about three weeks later, though not before someone sent her a copy of Morellet's *Préface* "with compliments from the author." Morellet denied sending the copy and suggested that Palissot himself had done it.[21] The duc de Choiseul, the foreign minister and Robecq's lover, was incensed by the *Préface* and pressured Lamoignon de Malesherbes, the royal censor, to arrest the author. Malesherbes was sympathetic to the *philosophes* and was willing to allow virtually all intellectual viewpoints to be published, but he discouraged *ad hominem* invective. He, too, considered the passage about Robecq to be an unnecessary break in etiquette and ordered the head of the police to discover the identity of the author. The dramatic irony of the situation was that Morellet and Malesherbes were friends and had attended *Les Philosophes* together. The two had met through Turgot, who had been one of Morellet's fellow students at the Sorbonne. Morellet admitted his authorship to Malesherbes, and the latter had no choice but to issue a *lettre de cachet* for his imprisonment in the Bastille.[22]

Malesherbes used his influence to procure a short sentence and good treatment for Morellet.[23] In his *Mémoires*, Morellet took the opportunity to say "a small word" about the Bastille "for those of our contemporaries who never dwelled there." In order to undermine the image of the Bastille as a symbol of the alleged cruelty of the monarchy, he stealthily suppressed the fact that his treatment there was untypical. "Put in the Bastille by virtue of a royal order dictated by Monsieur de Choiseul who was then all-powerful and infuriated with me, I experienced none of the hardships with which the Old Regime is reproached." A library kept at the Bastille for the amusement of the prisoners had been at his disposal. He had had paper and ink. As for food, "They gave me a fairly good bottle of wine every day and bread of a good quality; for lunch, a soup, some beef, an entrée and dessert; for the evening, a roast and salad."[24]

During the easy six weeks that he spent in prison, Morellet fantasized

[20] Morellet, *Préface de la comédie des Philosophes, ou la vision de Charles Palissot* (Paris, 1760), 11–12. Morellet published a slightly altered version of this brochure in his *Mélanges de littérature*, 2:3–12.

[21] Hilde H. Freud, *Palissot and Les Philosophes* (Geneva, 1967), 152, argues that Morellet was right.

[22] Freud, 152–53.

[23] Ibid., 154.

[24] Morellet, *Mémoires*, 103, 104, 105.

about winning celebrity as a champion of the *philosophes*. "Persecuted, I might become more famous. My revenge for the men of letters and my martyrdom for philosophy would launch my reputation." When he was released, he found that the Bastille did in fact serve as "an excellent recommendation." Turgot and Diderot treated him more warmly than before, and he now had easy entry into the salons of Necker, Helvétius, and Holbach.[25] He had arrived.

Morellet's new status might be taken as evidence that the *philosophes* approved of his libelous style. In fact, they officially disapproved of personal attacks. They welcomed him into their midst only because he had shown unequivocally that he was on their side. They liked his substance but not his form, which did damage to the moral high ground they were then trying to take. Voltaire wrote to Madame d'Epinay, "The *Vision* has irritated me profoundly. It is the height of indecency and imprudence to have drawn the Princess of Robecq into the quarrel. It is outrageous to insult a dying woman. This will only stimulate opposition to the *philosophes*; it will make them look mad and wicked."[26] None of the *philosophes* whom Palissot satirized stooped to respond directly to his attack. When Palissot's publisher presented Rousseau with a copy of *Les Philosophes*, he refused to accept it because of its libelous tone, and he said nothing more.[27] (This restraint was consistent with Rousseau's general position until 1762, when his rising paranoia led him to denounce others arbitrarily as his personal enemies.)[28] Diderot explained his stance in a letter to Malesherbes:

> I have not seen the play *Les Philosophes*. I have not read it. . . . Instead of taking part in these outrageous insults, I will keep the promise I have made to myself and which I have so far kept—not to write a word of retaliation.[29]

Duclos, who was not impersonated in the play but whose works were vilified by other characters, remained completely silent, as did Helvétius.

Two authors, the abbé Coyer and Voltaire, provided the theory that lay behind this moral high ground. The abbé Coyer had already generated debate on the subject of commerce through his book *La Noblesse commerçante*. He now tried to stipulate some of the rules of intellectual contestation in his *Discours sur la satyre* (Discourse on Satire, 1760). "It is generally acknowledged that in the play *Les Philosophes*, particular persons are repre-

[25] Ibid., 106, 123.

[26] Voltaire to d'Epinay, 13 June 1760, *Voltaire's Correspondence*, ed. Theodore Besterman (Geneva, 1953–66), 42:111.

[27] Rousseau, *Les Confessions*, in *Oeuvres complètes* (Paris, 1959), 1:536–37; Freud, *Palissot and Les Philosophes*, 163.

[28] See the discussion of the Hume-Rousseau conflict in Chapter 5.

[29] Diderot to Malesherbes, 1 June 1760, *Correspondance*, ed. Georges Roth (Paris, 1955–70), 3:34. Diderot did take revenge on Palissot in a manuscript that he did not publish but that we know as *Le Neveu de Rameau*.

sented." This violated what Coyer called *honnêteté publique*—the decency to be observed in theatrical performances. "In the pictures which it [the theater] presents in order to correct our vices, it should portray only general characteristics; real individuals are excluded."[30]

Palissot had already published a self-defense, *Lettre de l'Auteur de la Comédie des Philosophes* (Letter from the Author of the comedy *The Philosophes*), in which he rebutted charges of libel by quoting the writings of Diderot and Helvétius on religious and political themes. The point was to show that these writers really were the enemies of "legitimate authority" and hence proper subjects for defamation.[31] Palissot also claimed that Molière, in *Les Femmes savantes* (1672), had poked fun at the salon of Madame de Rambouillet, thereby setting a precedent for portraying real men of letters in the theater.[32] Coyer answered that Molière deliberately kept his spectators guessing about whom, if anyone, the play was about. There was no consensus that it was about the Hôtel de Rambouillet, whereas in Palissot's play, "everything is clear, everything is transparent."[33] Coyer also argued that personal satire was a feeble way of responding to the intellectual views of an opponent. "If the *philosophes* or other writers declare war on wisdom, one should retaliate with reason. The jokes of the theater will never answer their arguments."[34]

Coyer's notion of *honnêteté publique*, with its emphasis on avoiding personal attacks and rude jokes, was an effort to apply the rules of conversational *politesse* to the space of the theater. The principles were clear enough, but they left some ambiguities concerning written discourse. At one point, Coyer seemed to say that the norms of *honnêteté publique* did not apply to written texts because the printed word was less "public" than the stage.

> Defamation in the theater is the most public, the greatest, and the most criminal of all. That which appears in *print* cannot be known to everyone because not everyone reads; but everyone has ears that can hear.[35]

This weak distinction was evidently formulated in order to lighten the culpability of authors like Morellet—authors of "small ephemeral attacks" such as those "which have prefaced the play *Les Philosophes*."[36] Coyer did not consider the problematic cases of malicious authors who published unprovoked personal attacks, or popular journalists whose readership could easily surpass the size of a theatrical audience.

[30] Gabriel François Coyer, *Discours sur la satyre contre les philosophes* (Athens, 1760).
[31] Palissot, *Lettre de l'Auteur de la Comédie des Philosophes, au public pour servir de préface à la pièce* (n.p., 1760), 16ff.
[32] Ibid., 11.
[33] Ibid., 12–13, 21.
[34] Ibid., 80.
[35] Ibid., 78 (Coyer's emphasis).
[36] Ibid., 78.

Voltaire's letters to Palissot dealt precisely with the issue that Coyer did not cover: Under what conditions are smear tactics permissible in writing? Voltaire had encouraged Palissot's literary efforts prior to *Les Philosophes*. Shortly after the production of *Les Philosophes*, Palissot wrote a letter to Voltaire in which he tried to establish himself as Voltaire's admirer and friend. He assured Voltaire that his play was not in any way intended as a critique of his ideas, which had no relation to those of the *philosophes*.[37] Voltaire responded to his former protégé by affirming that he was nothing if not a *philosophe*. He had popularized Newtonian science. He had criticized governments. He had contributed to the *Encyclopédie*, "the greatest monument ever raised in honor of the sciences." He had been one of the first to use the term *humanité*—a term Palissot derided. Voltaire then drew upon the law of reciprocity to define the grounds of acceptable personal satire. "It has always been permitted, by the laws of society [*les loix de la société*], to ridicule the people who have rendered us the same service." The *philosophes*, Voltaire stated, were "gentlemen." They were "the most well-bred people" (*les plus honnêtes gens du monde*). They had not insulted Palissot, so why should he insult them? Voltaire especially defended Diderot by emphasizing the persecution he had already experienced as editor of the *Encyclopédie*. Diderot's life of adversities, Voltaire argued, was reason enough not to attack him in writing.[38]

The correspondence between Palissot and Voltaire continued, with Palissot insisting that Voltaire was not truly a *philosophe* and Voltaire maintaining that he was. Eventually, Palissot was unable to argue with Voltaire about his own identity while simultaneously appealing to him for support. He was, in other words, unable to drive a wedge between the *philosophes* and their leader. As Palissot began to soften his position, Voltaire hardened his. He affirmed that Palissot had never read the works of the *philosophes*, that he had based his impressions on a pseudoanthology of their writings put together by a reactionary editor, Abraham Chaumeix. As evidence, he showed that the quotations from Diderot and others that appeared in Palissot's *Lettre de l'auteur de la comédie des Philosophes* were wildly inaccurate. He exhorted Palissot to publish an apology for his mistakes in all of the Parisian journals.[39] Palissot, in response, blamed his editor for the misquotations and insisted that he had indeed read the original works of the *philosophes*.[40] By this time, however, he was on the defensive. He sent a final letter to Voltaire stating that he wished to write no more about the whole affair, and concluded, "Let this little war end."[41]

---

[37] Palissot to Voltaire, 28 May 1760, *Voltaire's Correspondence*, 42:74–75.
[38] Voltaire to Palissot, 4 June 1760, Ibid., 42:89–93.
[39] Voltaire to Palissot, 23 June 1760, Ibid., 42:159–62.
[40] Palissot to Voltaire, 7 July 1760, Ibid., 42:210–12.
[41] Voltaire refers to this letter of 13 September from Palissot in his own last letter to Palissot,

Voltaire took no prisoners. He ended the conflict by publishing the entire correspondence with mordant footnotes that further discredited Palissot. "You are lying to the public," was the repeated refrain. As a commentary on Palissot's final statement in which he vowed not to discuss the matter further, Voltaire added, "You are right in putting down your pen, but you are guilty and worthy of chastisement for having taken it up first, and stupid for having belched so much deception that is easy to expose."[42]

It was a brilliant performance, merciless but eminently fair. Voltaire made his principles clear: one should not launch personal attacks against others except in direct response to an insult, and one should not arouse public hatred against those who had already been persecuted by the authorities. Within this scheme of values, Palissot's play looked like an unprovoked act of aggression. Moreover, Palissot had initiated an exchange with Voltaire and had tried to turn him against his friends. He thus invited a critical response from Voltaire, who could assail Palissot's moral and intellectual stature without violating his own principles of decency.

Or could he? The scene of Palissot's play in which Crispin had crawled on all fours would not have had a sensational effect, would not even have been intelligible, if Voltaire had not invented the image—the false image—of a ridiculously primitivistic Rousseau who wished humankind to return to the life of wild animals. This image stemmed from Voltaire's well-publicized letter of 1755 in which he thanked Rousseau for a copy of his "new book against the human race," the *Discourse on the Origins of Inequality*. "Never has anyone so brilliantly tried to convert us into beasts. One feels the urge to walk about on all fours when one reads your work. But as it has been more than sixty years since I've lost the habit, I regret that it would be impossible for me to regain it."[43] Was not Palissot simply trying to imitate Voltaire? Unprovoked by Rousseau, Voltaire had uttered the barb that made Palissot's wit possible. In a letter to Madame d'Epinay, moreover, Voltaire had stated that any caricature of Rousseau was entirely justified on account of his "bizarreness" and "affectation."[44] What, then, were the true rules of dispute carried out through the printed word? Was the law against unprovoked

---

24 September 1760, *Voltaire's Correspondence*, ed. Theodore Besterman, 43:177. Besterman notes that no copy of the Palissot letter can be found, but Palissot printed it in his own edition of the whole correspondence, *Lettres de Monsieur de Voltaire à M. Palissot avec les réponses, à l'occasion de la comédie des Philosophes* (Geneva, 1760), 67.

[42] Voltaire, *Recueil des facéties parisiennes pour les six premiers mois de l'an 1760* (Geneva, 1760), 122

[43] Voltaire to Rousseau, 30 August 1755, *Voltaire's Correspondence*, ed. Besterman, 27:230. Besterman adds in a note: "This letter was frequently copied and even more frequently printed." See also Arthur O. Lovejoy, "The Supposed Primitivism of Rousseau's *Discourse on Inequality*," in *Essays in the History of Ideas* (Baltimore, 1948), 14–37.

[44] Voltaire to d'Epinay, 25 April 1760, *Voltaire's Correspondence*, 41:232.

insults an absolute rule, an inviolable corollary of the "laws of society," or merely a rhetorical ploy used in those situations in which one appeared not to be the aggressor?

The entire affair—the play, Morellet's response, the actions of Malesherbes, Coyer's discourse, and the exchanges between Palissot and Voltaire—reveals several points of ambiguity in the idea of the literary public sphere around 1760. Though it is clear that the basis of disapprobation was tending to shift away from substantive and toward formal considerations, the definition of good form was unstable and inconsistently applied. Men of letters such as Coyer and Voltaire believed in a free market of ideas. When they advocated restrictions, they defined them not in terms of legal prohibitions but in terms of the civil forms for communicating one's ideas. Coyer and Voltaire scored many points against Palissot with their emphasis on gentlemanly conduct. But Coyer applied the principle of *honnêteté publique* only to the theater, the most "public" form of communication. And Voltaire, while extending the principle to the written word, did not follow it in practice. In writing about Rousseau, he had felt justified in ridiculing him and misrepresenting his ideas simply because he did not agree with them (and perhaps because Rousseau threatened his status as the preeminent writer of the age). This made Rousseau an exception to Voltaire's law of aggression, and it made Voltaire scarcely different from Palissot. Voltaire's duplicitous conduct suggests that the rules of civility in writing were not absolute. It also suggests that even though the members of the republic of letters advocated an open but civil exchange of ideas, a system of free debate devoid of slander, some of them were prepared to use slander, particularly in quarrels among themselves. Paradoxically, and as Morellet's subsequent conflicts would reveal, the *philosophes* were likely to reserve their most calumnious rhetoric for each other.

The Quest for Integration

After entering the salon milieu in 1760, Morellet adopted a more affable demeanor. His talent for composing light-hearted songs endeared him to his hosts.[45] He had an invitation for every day of the week, but his favorite resorts were the salons of the German baron d'Holbach and the bourgeois Madame Geoffrin. According to Morellet, Holbach's salon was the scene of "the most animated and instructive conversation that ever took place." The regular members included Diderot, Helvétius, Duclos, Raynal, Marmontel, and Suard. But the most distinguished participant was Holbach himself.

[45] Morellet gave samples of his songs in *Mémoires*, 125, 193–96, 220–24, 242–44.

The Baron was one of the best-informed men of his age. He knew several European languages, and was not ignorant of those of antiquity; and he had a large and excellent library, a valuable collection of drawings by the best masters, excellent paintings of which he was a fine judge, and a natural history cabinet. To these advantages he added a high degree of politeness and no less simplicity. He had supple manners [*un commerce facile*] and his good-heartedness was obvious at first sight. Small wonder that his society [*société*] was sought and valued as it was.[46]

According to Morellet, the discussions at Holbach's salon perfectly combined the spirit of free inquiry with the spirit of politeness—"plenty of discussion and never a quarrel; the simple manners that are suited to intelligent and educated men and that never degenerate into crudeness; gaiety without folly; and finally, so much charm in the society [*société*] that even though we arrived at two o'clock, which was then the custom, most of us were usually still there at seven or eight in the evening."[47] These descriptions come from the memoirs in which one of Morellet's concerns was to clear the *philosophes* of any responsibility for the Revolution. By pointing out the civility and the innocence of their gatherings, he wished to show that they were not radical conspirators, as many after the Revolution thought they were.[48]

Morellet spoke briefly about Madame Geoffrin in the section of his memoirs describing his activities in the 1760s.

> Shortly after my return [from the Bastille], I was presented to Madame Geoffrin by Trudaine de Montigny. I will not dwell here on this estimable women and the charms of her home because I have fulfilled this duty to her memory in the little work entitled *Portrait of Madame Geoffrin*, printed upon her death in 1777. There I tried to express the sentiments of gratitude which connected me to her and which continue to move me today.[49]

The "gratitude" Morellet felt was partly in response to Geoffrin's largesse. Shortly before her death she supplied him with a pension of 1275 livres per year.[50] Their relationship, however, was more than financial.

Morellet attended Geoffrin's salon religiously for over thirty years. The composition of the salon was similar to Holbach's, with the important difference that Geoffrin invited several artists and Mademoiselle de Lespinasse. Lespinasse, along with Geoffrin herself, added a feminine dimension that Holbach's salon lacked. Morellet also attended the smaller gather-

---

[46] Morellet, *Mémoires*, 129.

[47] Ibid., 130.

[48] Alan Kors has also used Holbach's salon as evidence for the moderate and urbane temper of the Enlightenment; see Kors, *D'Holbach's Coterie: An Enlightenment in Paris* (Princeton, 1975).

[49] Morellet, *Mémoires*, 96.

[50] Ibid., 216.

ings in the evening in which Geoffrin entertained men and women of the aristocracy and cultured bourgeoisie.[51] The sexually mixed composition of Geoffrin's gatherings holds one of the keys to Morellet's attachment: he was devoted to her because she was a woman who drew him into the company of women. Their relationship was a question of sociability in the strict sense established by Pufendorf, of mutual assistance among individuals with distinct identities yet overlapping needs—what Dena Goodman calls "the convergence of female and philosophic ambitions."[52]

Geoffrin belonged to a very select group of eighteenth-century women who sought to overcome the cultural disadvantages imposed on their sex by bringing the *philosophes* into their homes, the one area in which they had authority. Mademoiselle de Lespinasse, Madame Helvétius, Madame Necker, Madame du Deffand, Madame de Tencin, Madame de Boufflers, Madame d'Epinay, and the Marquise de Lambert were the other leading lights of this group. Denied access to the universities and the royal academies, unable to pursue legal and ecclesiastical careers that might bring them into contact with ideas and arguments—excluded, in short, from the public sphere—they created a forum of self-education in the domestic sphere. They did not invent the salon from scratch, for the tradition of the female-directed salon went back at least to the Hôtel de Rambouillet. Their innovation was to open their arms to men of letters regardless of their political and religious views. The women of the seventeenth-century salons had welcomed writers who wished to be independent of the rigid hierarchy of the court. The women of the eighteenth-century salon welcomed those who wished to be independent of all institutional constraints in the discussion of ideas. And in so doing, they created a space in which they themselves could learn.

In both centuries, the activity of organizing a salon involved considerable work and expense. Meals had to be provided for a dozen or more people on a regular basis. An effort had to be made to recruit talented and distinguished people. Gifts had to be distributed to the poorer artists and men of letters so they could maintain an appearance that would not embarrass them in the presence of wealthier guests. Above all, the salon organizer faced the challenge of sustaining vibrant exchange, goodwill, and decorum within the assembly. Although the theory of the art of conversation, from Méré to Holbach, portrayed sociability as a form of self-police, in practice the salon required the host or hostess to take final responsibility for producing a sociable experience.[53] The salon organizer had to personify *honnêteté* so as to be a constant reminder to the guests of the rules of politeness. It was also

[51] Ibid., 97.

[52] Dena Goodman, "Enlightenment Salons: The Convergence of Female and Philosophic Ambitions," *Eighteenth-Century Studies* 22, no. 3 (1989):329–50.

[53] Dena Goodman makes this point in "Governing the Republic of Letters: The Politics of Culture in the French Enlightenment," *History of European Ideas* 13 (1991):183–99.

necessary to maintain the spirit of dialogue by reprimanding the verbose and drawing out the taciturn. Silence was no less a threat than monologue. The host or hostess had to prepare questions and comments in advance to ensure the perpetual motion of conversation. Though costly and exacting, this role was worth playing for those who had no other theater for achieving distinction.

Geoffrin was attached to Morellet because, as one of the "regulars" of her salon, he helped to make her intellectual identity possible. But what connected Morellet to Geoffrin? Just as Geoffrin's feeling for Morellet cannot be understood apart from the obstacles that women faced in developing an intellectual life, so his feeling for her cannot be understood apart from the obstacles that men of letters faced in developing something more than an intellectual life. The *philosophes* aspired not only to understand the world but to make philosophy constitutive of human relations in the world. In order to inject philosophy into life, they had to be a part of it. This *quest for integration* ceaselessly generated a desire among men of letters to be affiliated with beings unlike themselves. While the *philosophes* needed each other to constitute an intellectual class, they needed people outside of the intellectual class to be *philosophes*. Just as a teacher cannot be a teacher without students, so a *philosophe* could not be a *philosophe*—an intellectual searching for influence—without contact with nonphilosophic beings. Since the *philosophes* were not welcome in educational institutions, they were obliged to find a living audience elsewhere.

Voltaire's scientific writings, designed to make physics intelligible to women; Rousseau's novels and theory of childrearing, directed toward female readers; the intimate correspondence of Diderot with Sophie Volland and of Condorcet with Mademoiselle de Lespinasse—all of these forms of communication with women stemmed from the quest for integration. Paradoxically, women were ideal readers, correspondents, and interlocutors on account of their intellectual limitations. They could understand *philosophie*, but because of their restricted formal education and the prejudice against their making a literary career, they could not be *philosophes*. Communication with a woman was meaningful because it could not be esoteric. The presence of a woman in a philosophic salon transformed the gathering from an intellectual club into an institution, a part of *le monde*, the world of real people that the *philosophes* wished to influence. This is what made Geoffrin's salon (and the smaller gatherings Morellet attended at her home) different from Holbach's. Her presence and that of Lespinasse were a guarantee that philosophy was not solipsistic. Holbach's salon was home to "the most animated and instructive conversation," but it was the Enlightenment closed in upon itself. Geoffrin's salon gave Morellet an opportunity to act as a representative of philosophy to a world outside of philosophy—a role he could not play when he was only with his peers.

In 1777, the year of Geoffrin's death, Morellet published a eulogy, "Portrait of Madame Geoffrin."[54] Though they have received scant attention from scholars, eulogies were an important form of literature in the eighteenth century.[55] No less vigorous in the Enlightenment than in the classical culture of the seventeenth century, the production of eulogies reflected a concern with that secular version of the afterlife known as posterity. Its purpose was both moral and magical: to instill virtue in the living through praise of the dead, and to bring the dead to life through the evocation of memory. Under the absolute monarchy, eulogies were composed in honor of public office-holders—kings, royal ministers, members of the Parlements, academicians—and they were generally read orally in a meeting of the decedent's professional associates. Morellet himself noted that eulogies were reserved for "public persons," but he maintained that Geoffrin's life had public significance because she had "all the social qualities" (*toutes les qualités sociales*) and because she had been the "charm of society" (*le charme de la société*) for fifty years.[56] For Morellet, the fact that Geoffrin's "society" never included more than a few dozen people at a time did not detract from her public importance, for her salon, with its egalitarian commerce between *gens de lettres* and *gens du monde*, was a model for the nation as a whole.[57]

Morellet also defended Geoffrin's spirit of independence. He noted that her critics were those who "made it a species of crime" for a women to seek knowledge. Morellet's friend, Antoine Thomas, also defended Geoffrin in a eulogy that Morellet later republished together with his own. Thomas, the recognized master of the genre in the 1770s and '80s, had been elected to the Académie Française on the basis of his eulogies. He even wrote a history of the eulogy as a sign of "civilization." In this *Essai sur les éloges*, he gave credit to the female sex for civilizing the French nation by encouraging "the sociable disposition" (*l'humeur sociable*) and stimulating the "taste and need for society" (*le goût et le besoin de la société*).[58] In his eulogy of Geoffrin, Thomas portrayed her as a model of both independence and sociability.

> One of the things that distinguished her the most was that she had her own character. . . . Women, who are enslaved by opinion, seem condemned to remain locked up in the narrow circle of conventions and usage. Unless they have

[54] Morellet, *Portrait de Madame Geoffrin* (Paris, 1777). Morellet later republished this, along with the eulogies by Thomas and d'Alembert, in *Eloges de Madame Geoffrin*, ed. André Morellet (Paris, 1812). Future citations of Morellet's eulogy are from this later edition.

[55] The only study of prerevolutionary eulogies appears to be Charles B. Paul, *Science and Immortality: The Eloges of the Paris Academy of Sciences, 1699–1791* (Berkeley, 1980).

[56] Morellet, *Portrait de Madame Geoffrin*, 3–4, 73.

[57] Ibid., 56–58.

[58] Antoine Thomas, *Essai sur les éloges*, in *Oeuvres* (Paris, 1773), 2:82. The *Essai* was first published in 1773. See also his *Essai sur le caractère, les moeurs et l'esprit des femmes dans les différents siècles*, in *Oeuvres*, vol. 4. Here he defended the right of women to be the subject of eulogies and praised women in general for polishing the manners of men (second pagination, 7–8, 47, 88–89, 110). On Thomas's career, see Etienne Micard, *Antoine-Léonard Thomas* (Paris, 1924).

a superior intellect, their souls, like their voices, are generally identical because they are not allowed to develop their own accent. Madame Geoffrin had a courageous spirit which followed its own ideas: she dared to be happy in her own way.[59]

Recalling how she treated the members of her salon with equality while artfully managing their idiosyncracies, Thomas likened her "to those wise legislators, who slightly bend the laws to fit manners."[60] By comparing Geoffrin to a legislator, Thomas made the same point Morellet had tried to make, that Geoffrin was a person of public significance. In doing so, he too presented the salon as a miniature model of a free regime. He noted that Geoffrin's salon had its moments of instability, but that it was always brought to rest under her guidance, for "she knew everything that moves and directs opinion." Like any free regime, the salon required an authority—not a sovereign authority to constrain but a mild authority to temper its movements. "It seems," Thomas added, "that this power cannot be better placed but in the hands of a woman."[61]

Morellet had launched his career with an insult, but now he was under the spell of a feminine and moderate culture. The influence of Geoffrin, the urbane spirit of the salons, the desire, which I have called the quest for integration, to be both a critical philosopher and a polite voice within a nonphilosophical public—all induced him to compose his polemics in a more polite style, at least for a while. The first book he published after his return from the Bastille was the *Manuel des inquisiteurs* (Manual for Inquisitors, 1762). The idea for the work stemmed from a trip to Rome that Morellet took in 1759 with his student, the young de la Galaizière. Finding that the museums did not appeal to his rational sensibility, he spent much of his time reading in the theological library of the abbé Canillac. Here he came across the *Directorium Inquisitorum* by Nicolau Eymeric (1320–99), the grand inquisitor under Innocent VI. In his memoirs, Morellet described the text as follows:

This work, as its title indicates, served as a guide to inquisitors in all Christendom before the invention of printing. It was first published at the beginning of the sixteenth century. The edition which I found was printed in 1575 in Rome, *in aedibus populi romani*, that is, in the Capitol. What a curious contrast to see this priestly, absurd, and barbarous legislation coming from the very place from which the conquerors of the globe had issued their commands, divided kingdoms, and legislated for so much of the world. The text filled me with horror.[62]

---

[59] Antoine Thomas, "A la Mémoire de Madame Geoffrin," in Morellet, ed., *Eloges de Madame Geoffrin*, 78. Thomas first published his eulogy in 1777.

[60] Ibid., 79, 82–83.

[61] Ibid., 88–89.

[62] Morellet, *Mémoires*, 79–80.

Morellet made a set of extracts "of everything that struck me as most revolting." In 1762 he arranged these extracts according to the procedure of inquisition, beginning with interrogation and ending with execution. "I refrained from adding any commentary because the text was sufficient to communicate what I would have expressed."[63]

This last remark is significant. Morellet had found a pungent way of criticizing institutions that did not run the danger of being slander. His translation of the extracts is indeed literal and without commentary. His preface is remarkably flat and nonjudgmental, pointing out only the difficulties of translation and the representative character of the book as an account of the procedures of the Inquisition. Readers were left to form their own impression and to note the affinities between the Inquisition and French criminal jurisprudence.[64] Malesherbes, who deplored the state of French criminal law, did not hesitate to give permission for publication.[65] D'Alembert sent a copy to Voltaire and added some words on Morellet's behalf.

> The editor is the same abbé Morellet, or *Morlet* [Pecker], or *Mords-les* [Bite 'Em] who eighteen months ago was subjected to the inquisition (not the great Spanish one but the little French one) for having stated in a vision that is better than Ezekiel's, that a vile women, whom he did not name, was truly sick. God did not delay in avenging his prophet, for before he stepped out of prison the vile woman was dead. This proves that she indeed was not well and that he had good cause to cast doubts on her health. . . . As we ought to encourage virtuous people, I ask you to send me a respectful message for this respectable priest. He deserves it on account of his zeal for the good cause and on account of his admiration for you.[66]

---

[63] Ibid., 80.

[64] As John H. Langbein has shown, judicial torture was becoming less frequent in the eighteenth century as the rules of evidence changed so as to make confession unnecessary for conviction. See his *Torture and the Law of Proof* (Chicago, 1976). Yet incidents of torture for religious crimes continued to occur, as the case of Françoise Jean Lefèvre, Chevalier de La Barre, shows. In 1766, Lefèvre, age nineteen, was accused of passing within twenty-five steps of a procession without removing his hat. He was also charged for singing impious songs and bowing before a copy of Voltaire's *Dictionnaire philosophique* in his own home. A court in Abbeville subjected him to the *question préparatoire* (torture to produce confession) and the *question préalable* (torture to produce information about accomplices). He was condemned to suffer the *amende honorable* (disgrace through public confession) and to have his tongue removed, his head cut off, and his body burned. The Parlement of Paris confirmed the decision on June 4, and the execution took place on July 1. See Marc Chassaigne, *Le Procès du Chevalier de La Barre* (Paris, 1920). Morellet informed Beccaria of this case in a letter of 17 July 1766, *Lettres d'André Morellet* (Oxford, 1991), 57–58.

[65] Morellet, *Mémoires*, 80.

[66] D'Alembert to Voltaire, 27 January 1762, in d'Alembert, *Oeuvres complètes* (Paris, 1822), 5:85–86.

Voltaire was happy to oblige. "My dear brother," he responded to d'Alembert, "embrace in my name the worthy brother who has produced this excellent work."[67] Voltaire, who had censured Morellet in 1760 for the comment about Robecq, was genuinely delighted by the *Manuel des inquisiteurs*. Even before he got the letter from d'Alembert, he expressed his enthusiasm. "The little book on the inquisition is a masterpiece."[68] "I am thrilled by the little book on the inquisition. Never has Bite 'Em been so biting" (*Jamais l'abbé Mords-les n'a mieux mordu*).[69]

The *Manuel des inquisiteurs* was the first in a series of forceful but civilized reform tracts that Morellet produced. In his *Mémoire sur la situation actuelle de la Compagnie des Indes* (Memoir on the Present Situation of the Indies Company, 1769), Morellet advocated the abolition of the trading monopoly, but without directly criticizing its directors.[70] Instead, he mounted an impressive statistical profile of the company's dismal performance. His rhetoric was again restrained as he invited "the public" to draw its own conclusions. "I believe I have done something useful in placing, for the first time, this question and the means of resolving it before the eyes of the public," he wrote in the *Avertissement* (Notice). "The documents will furnish to all persons interested in the subject the means of knowing the truth."[71]

Morellet culled his statistics from the archives of the company, opened to him by Maynon d'Invau, the Controller General who supported free trade.[72] Maynon d'Invau was intent on abolishing the company, so it would appear that its fate was determined from the start. Yet he was compelled to enlist a propagandist; for in the absence of a strong public case against the company, the directors and stockholders would protest vociferously and undermine confidence in the government. Morellet's *Mémoire* appeared in print on July 24, 1769. On July 30, Bachaumont observed, "Morellet's *Mémoire* is having a powerful effect and many of the people most connected to the Company, who until now desired its continuation, are intimidated by the assertions of this author and now ardently wish for its extinction."[73] On August 8, one of the company's syndics rose to its defense. It was Jacques Necker. At a meeting of the stockholders he refuted some of Morellet's

---

[67] Voltaire to d'Alembert, 10 February 1762, *Voltaire's Correspondence*, 48:89.

[68] Voltaire to Etienne Noel Damilaville, 26 January 1762, Ibid., 48:43.

[69] Voltaire to Nicolas-Claude Thierriot, 26 January 1762, Ibid., 48:50. See also Voltaire to Claude-Philippe Fyot de la Marche, 26 January 1762, Ibid., 48:45.

[70] The Compagnie des Indes was founded by John Law in 1719 when he merged the Compagnie d'Occident, Compagnie de la Chine, and Compagnie des Indes Orientales.

[71] Morellet, *Mémoire sur la situation actuelle de la Compagnie des Indes* (Paris, 1769), Avertissement.

[72] Jean Egret, *Necker, ministre de Louis XVI* (Paris, 1975), 18; Henry Weber, *La Compagnie des Indes, 1604–1875* (Paris, 1904), 593.

[73] Louis Petit de Bachaumont, *Mémoires secrets pour servir à l'histoire de la république des lettres* (London, 1780–89), entry for 30 July 1769, 4:279.

calculations and suggested that the company could be revivified with funds derived from a lottery.[74] A few weeks later Necker also published the *Réponse au Mémoire de M. l'abbé Morellet sur la Compagnie des Indes* (Response to the Memoir of M. the abbé Morellet on the Indies Company). Here he claimed that Morellet had underestimated the earnings of the Company by fifty percent and had ignored the pioneering role of the company in opening new markets in Canada, Louisiana, China, and India. He also argued that Morellet had mistakenly included as part of the company's debits the funds for ports, fortifications, roads, and churches. These projects were the responsibility of the government; public funds would have been laid out for them even if the Indies Company had not existed. Finally, Necker suggested that Morellet had exercised bad judgment in publicizing an account of the company's funds when he was not himself a member of the company, and when statistical information in itself could never yield conclusive arguments either for or against the company's existence.[75] (In retrospect, this argument against publicity is remarkably ironic. Necker rose to the office of director-general of finances in 1777, and with his *Comte rendu* of 1781, he became the first royal minister to publish the entire state budget.)

Necker's efforts were to no avail. On August 13, even before his *Réponse* appeared in print, Maynon d'Invau, with Morellet's *Mémoire* in hand, summarized the arguments against the company before the Conseil du Roi, which immediately issued an edict suspending the company's exclusive trading privileges. The issue was not entirely dead, however, because the Parlement of Paris still had the right to remonstrate. In addition, the edict did not liquidate the company but suspended its monopoly "until such time as His Majesty decides otherwise."[76] When Necker's *Réponse* appeared on August 28 and raised doubts about the wisdom of the policy, Morellet responded with *Examen de la réponse de M. N* au Mémoire de Monsieur l'Abbé Morellet sur la Compagnie des Indes* (Examination of the Response of M. N* to the Memoir of M. the abbé Morellet on the Indies Company). Besides addressing the accounting issues, he insisted on his right to present information to the public. In principle, he argued, everyone had an interest in knowing about the company's finances, for everyone could become a shareholder and anyone might have engaged in colonial commerce if the company had not existed. And the viability of the company, he insisted, could indeed be

[74] Bachaumont gave a detailed account of Necker's speech in his entry for August 9, in Ibid., 4:285–87; see also Weber, *La Compagnie des Indes*, 601–9.

[75] Jacques Necker, *Réponse au Mémoire de Monsieur l'abbé Morellet sur la Compagnie des Indes* (Paris, 1769).

[76] Weber, *La Compagnie des Indes*, 610, 612–13. The Parlement first defended the company, but ended by approving a version of the edict with minor changes. Without its privileges, the company terminated its commercial ventures and merely oversaw administrative functions, such as the issuing of passports to merchants. In April 1785, Calonne restored some of the Company's privileges.

adjudicated by "the public" on the basis of its economic performance. In fact, it was the duty of those who were not members of the company to scrutinize and publicize its doings so that the members of the company, who were biased in its favor, did not have overweening power as a pressure group.[77] Morellet was emphatic, but he couched his arguments in a tone that was respectful toward Necker. At both the beginning and the end of the text, he praised Necker's character and paid honor to his government service.

The antiliberal Bachaumont was not impressed. In his opinion, the work revealed "a man intent on negating everything opposed to him."[78] But Morellet's philosophic associates were satisfied with the politeness of his performance. Buffon congratulated him:

> Apart from the fact that you are undoubtedly right about the main issue, your form has also given you the upper hand: your tone, though firm, is very decent [*honnête*]. This work can only yield honor for you.[79]

Turgot concurred:

> I received, my dear abbé, your response to M. Necker. I thank you with all my heart; it has given me great pleasure. As a work in which you demonstrate the errors of your adversary, it is as moderate as it could be. I am sure that it will influence the public.[80]

The true sign that Morellet had maintained decorum was that he continued to see Necker regularly in his wife's salon.[81] Later, he would be forced to withdraw from the salon in the face of economic disagreement, but in this instance his zeal for reform did not push him beyond the border separating "debate" from "dispute."

The rhetoric that Morellet used in his books on the Inquisition and the Indies Company was documentary rather than declamatory. In each case, he allowed the opposition to incriminate itself through the record of its own activities. This method was exactly the one that Suard had used to condemn

---

[77] Morellet, *Examen de la réponse de M. N. au Mémoire de M. l'abbé Morellet sur la Compagnie des Indes*, especially 6, 12–15, 17.

[78] Bachaumont, *Mémoires secrets*, 30 September 1769, 4:314.

[79] Buffon to Morellet, 9 November 1769, cited by Morellet in *Mémoires*, 162. This particular letter cannot be found in any other source, but there is no reason to doubt its authenticity. The editors of Morellet's correspondence show that nearly all of the letters that he cited in his memoirs can be verified through the originals and are cited accurately. *Lettres d'André Morellet*, Appendix A.

[80] Turgot to Morellet, 3 October 1769, cited by Morellet in *Mémoires*, 162; also in *Oeuvres de Turgot et documents le concernant*, ed. Gustave Schelle (Paris, 1913–23), 3:109. See also Helvétius to Morellet, 8 October 1769, *Correspondance générale d'Helvétius*, ed. David W. Smith (Toronto, 1981), 640.

[81] Morellet, *Mémoires*, 149.

Rousseau in the conflict with Hume.[82] In each case, the writer played the role of a prosecutor exposing the "facts" of a case to a "public" acting as the jury. Morellet's tactics were similar in the two books on smallpox inoculation that he wrote with the Italian doctor Gatti in the 1760s.[83] Gatti had successfully inoculated many patients, including Helvétius and his family. The books promoted the legalization of inoculation by publicizing Gatti's techniques and results. Morellet's 1766 translation of Beccaria's *Dei delitti e delle pene* was less of a documentary work because of the philosophical nature of the original text. Yet the rhetorical strategy of the translator was essentially the same: to divulge something supposedly objective, in this case, the enlightened views of an eminent foreign jurist, so that the "public" could evaluate French laws and policies.[84]

Public Opinion and Civility

The civil tone that Morellet sustained in all of these works presupposed the existence of a "public" that not only had a right to be better informed but that would rationally consider the issues and reach a consensus about them. The documentary method went along with a concept of the public as a kind of collective mind, an entity that was persuaded above all by records, facts, experiments, and the clear ideas of theorists, rather than by sensational denunciations and passionate pleas. Although the substance of his tracts varied, Morellet's writings consistently appealed to this idealized public. Philosophers and historians have recently recognized that "public opinion," the imaginary target of the *philosophes'* ideas, was itself a central idea of the Enlightenment, the linchpin of a vision of political order that many *philosophes* presented as an alternative to traditional absolutist politics. As Jürgen Habermas sees it, the notion of "public opinion" took on its character in opposition to absolutist arguments about the inherently volitional nature of sovereignty. Absolutist thought emphasized that policy could emerge not

---

[82] See Chapter 5.

[83] Angelo Gatti and André Morellet, *Réflexions sur les préjugés qui s'opposent aux progrès et à la perfection de l'inoculation* (Brussels, 1764); *Nouvelles réflexions sur la pratique de l'inoculation* (Milan, 1767). Initially barred in 1763, the practice of inoculation was legalized in 1768. On Morellet's collaboration with Angelo Giuseppe Maria Gatti, see Dorothy Medlin, "Andre Morellet, Translator of Liberal Thought," *Studies on Voltaire and the Eighteenth Century* 174 (1978):192–93.

[84] The *Traité des délits et des peines* (Lausanne, 1766) was Morellet's most successful literary effort, though he did not benefit financially. It was reprinted seven times in six months. The Dutch, Greek, and Russian translations were based on the French edition. See Medlin, "André Morellet, Translator," 193–98. Morellet also translated Adam Smith's *Wealth of Nations*, but did not publish it because another French edition appeared just as he finished. The manuscript is preserved in the Bibliothèque de la Ville de Lyon.

from a multitude of beings but only from the commands of a ruler. The foundation of the community was the monarch's dominant *will*. Enlightenment authors, in contrast, presented *truth* as the basis of policy, and because truth did not have to be imposed upon the public but could emerge through its discussions, domination did not have to exist.

> Legislation was supposed to be the result not of a political will, but of rational agreement. . . . Public opinion was in principle opposed to arbitrariness and subject to the laws immanent in a public composed of critically debating private persons in such a way that the property of being the supreme will, superior to all laws, which is to say, sovereignty, could strictly speaking not be attributed to it at all. . . . The "domination" of the public, according to its own idea, was an order in which domination itself was dissolved: *veritas non auctoritas facit legem* [truth, not authority, makes the law].[85]

By focusing on the usage of the term "public opinion" in the last three decades of the Old Regime, Keith Baker has confirmed Habermas's theory of a shift away from royal will and toward collective reason as the imaginary basis of power. He has also underscored the paradox of an idea that imputed unity to a people but in reality unleashed protest and contestation. Public opinion was an imaginary supreme court to which individuals appealed when they could no longer get what they wanted within the traditional institutional circuit. The approval of "public opinion" was held to be a seal of truth upon an argument, even if it had been rejected by the monarch and his ministers. Individuals who had no constitutional standing expressed their criticism in books and pamphlets. Individuals who did have constitutional standing (such as members of the Parlements) went beyond their authority by spreading their views outside of the official space of remonstrance.[86]

Although many writers used the term, hardly any provided an elaborate theory of how "public opinion" took form or why it should be expected to embody truth rather than error. The notion had enormous value as a means of transferring the attributes of unity and reason, traditionally associated

[85] Jürgen Habermas, *The Structural Transformation of the Public Sphere: An Inquiry into a Category of Bourgeois Society* (Cambridge, 1989), 82–83.

[86] Keith Michael Baker, "Public Opinion as Political Invention," in *Inventing The French Revolution* (Cambridge, 1990), 167–202. See also Mona Ozouf, "L'Opinion publique," in Keith Michael Baker, ed., *The French Revolution and the Creation of Modern Political Culture*, vol. 1 (Oxford, 1987), 419–34; Benjamin Nathans, "Habermas's 'Public Sphere' in the Era of the French Revolution," *French Historical Studies* 16 (1990):620–44; Dena Goodman, "Public Sphere and Private Life: Towards a Synthesis of Current Historiographical Approaches to the Old Regime," *History and Theory* 31 (1992):1–20; Sarah Maza, "Le Tribunal de la nation: Les Mémoires judiciaires et l'opinion publique à la fin de l'ancien régime," *Annales: E.S.C.* 42 (1987):73–90; Daniel Gordon, "Philosophy, Sociology, and Gender in the Enlightenment Conception of Public Opinion," *French Historical Studies* 17 (1992):882–911; Anthony J. La Vopa, "Conceiving a Public: Ideas and Society in Eighteenth-Century Europe," *Journal of Modern History* 64 (1992):76–116.

with royal sovereignty, to a collective entity, the "public," thereby legitimating the propagandist's vocation. But in spite of its rhetorical value, the notion of public opinion was philosophically feeble. It went against the grain of the Western epistemological tradition from Plato to Descartes and Locke. In this tradition, "truth" was the product of a method that rigorous minds applied critically to their own experience and to the conventions and prejudices of the multitude. Although truth could be made public, so could falsehood, and there was nothing inherent in the dynamics of human interaction to ensure that people in general would prefer truth over lies.[87] Of course, if the "public" signified only the most learned elements of a regime, its alleged rationality would be more credible. But then it would be little more than a synonym for the class of men of letters and would lose its value for those authors who sought to integrate themselves into something beyond themselves—to legitimate their polemical activities by positing the existence of a rational audience. The notion of "public opinion" was a myth created by the *philosophes*, a myth that threatened to reveal itself as such if one tried to explain it in philosophical terms.

It is also worth bearing in mind that although the growth of the press and political discussion in the eighteenth century was evidence of the rise of a real public, this reality was intelligible to people only through a set of philosophical projections and rhetorical figures. Public opinion polls in France date from the middle of the twentieth century. In prerevolutionary France, there were no instruments for measuring what a large group of people actually thought about any particular issue. Opinions existed, but opinions are always divided, and there was no precise means of observing the distribution of opinion in the age in which the concept of public opinion was born. Public opinion was unknown and unknowable. Everything that anyone said about public opinion, particularly about its unity or rationality, tended to be either a lie or a fantasy.

Morellet stands out because he, and apparently he alone, extended his fanciful rhetoric concerning public opinion into something that came close to being a theory. While others simply invoked public opinion in the process of criticizing a policy, he discussed at length the process by which public opinion was allegedly formed.[88] In 1775 he published his *Réflexions sur les*

---

[87] Besides Habermas's *Structural Transformation*, I have found Peter A. Schouls, *The Imposition of Method* (Oxford, 1980), and Peter France, *Rhetoric and Truth in France: Descartes to Diderot* (Oxford, 1972), highly suggestive for the issues treated in this paragraph.

[88] The nineteenth-century sociologist Ferdinand Toennies observed that Morellet was one of the authors who "participated in what one may call the discovery of public opinion." Toennies, *On Sociology: Pure, Applied, and Empirical* (Chicago, 1971), 251. Most of the *philosophes* who idealized public opinion did so by means of passing phrases rather than lengthy discussion. Habermas, Baker, and Ozouf cite a wide range of French authors who used the term *"opinion publique."* Having consulted the texts that they cite, as well as several others, it appears to me that Morellet's account of the production of public opinion is the most developed in the French Enlightenment. This, of course, does not mean that he was a brilliant

avantages de la liberté d'écrire et d'imprimer sur les matières de l'administration
(Reflections on the Benefits of the Freedom of Writing and Publishing on
Administrative Matters). Morellet wrote the text in 1764 in response to the
law of silence of March 28 of the same year, but he was not able to publish it
until the ministry of Turgot, who was a great believer in freedom of the
press. The law of silence had reaffirmed the right of the Parlements to make
proposals directly to the king for fiscal reform, but it admonished "irresponsible persons who venture to make them public instead of submitting them
to the persons destined by their office to judge them." The declaration also
stated, "Writings which appear in public on these matters can only spread
alarms among the minds [of our subjects], . . . excite prejudices capable of
preventing the very good which we could effect . . . and bring about the
greatest injuries to the good of our estate and to that of our subjects."[89]
Intended to put a stop to the flood of pamphlets and circulated remonstrances that criticized royal taxes, the declaration expressed the absolutist
idea that grievances were to be channeled to the monarch alone, and that the
formation of an independent circuit of political communication would
breed licentiousness and disorder.

The royal declaration was based on a traditional conception of kingship in
which remonstrances were assumed to be particularistic—the self-interested
protests of one estate or its representatives. In this framework, it made sense
to insist that remonstrances be presented only to the king, because he
was responsible for weighing the interests of a specific corps against the
general welfare. Morellet appreciated that by 1764 the act of protest had
changed considerably: the remonstrances and other writings criticizing the
king's policies included not only particularistic grievances but universalistic
recommendations—a flood of general theories and concrete proposals
meant to benefit the entire nation. Morellet was thus able to turn the issue to
the following question: Is the monarch capable of governing without the
general intelligence of his subjects, and if not, what is the best mechanism
for activating and gathering this intelligence?

The personal wisdom of the king, Morellet affirmed, was not enough to
run the state well. He also felt that the system by which the ruler received
counsel did not enhance, but actually harmed, his capacity to make intelligent decisions. Morellet reviewed the method by which the king and his
ministers obtained advice through "manuscript memoirs" composed by
their subordinates in the bureaucracy. Here again, Morellet focused on an
aspect of the political system that had developed in previous decades and
that was against the traditional spirit of absolutism. From about 1680

---

thinker, but only that his writings provide an especially good opportunity to examine some of
the assumptions that informed the Enlightenment idealization of the public sphere.

[89] *Déclaration qui fait défense d'imprimer, débiter ou colporter aucuns écrits, ouvrages ou projet
concernant la réforme ou l'administration des finances*, in François André Isambert, ed., *Recueil
général des anciennes lois françaises*, (Paris, 1830), 22:400.

onward, the Conseil du Roi, the forum in which the king and his ministers had solicited the advice of distinguished magistrates in person, had been increasingly supplanted by a bureaucratic system. In this new system, the heads of administrative departments received proposals from subordinates via written reports and passed this information along to the king or the Controller General, who then made the final decisions without taking counsel. Long ago Tocqueville commented sarcastically upon this insipid system of communication, and more recently, Michel Antoine has suggested that the decline of a Conseil based on discussion and the rise of a bureaucracy under the Controller General were the most significant administrative transformations in prerevolutionary France.[90] In a harsh critique of this manuscript-based political culture, Morellet made three points: (1) The ministers received a vast number of poorly reasoned proposals because in the secrecy of private communication, the sponsors of these proposals had no fear of being ridiculed for their chimerical ideas. (2) Even assuming that the king or his ministers had enough sense to distinguish good advice from bad, they lacked the time needed to discover good ideas amidst the overwhelming quantity of reports submitted to them.

> Enter the offices of our ministers and you will see thousands of memoirs in which all imaginable projects relating to all parts of administration have been proposed. The majority of these projects are impractical and extravagant, but there are a certain number of good ones. Why have the latter remained useless? It is because instead of being disseminated in public, they have been addressed to the minister, and have not been read.[91]

(3) There were also enlightened individuals whose ideas went unnoticed simply because they were not inside the administration and had no means of conveying their ideas to the ministers.

In a general public constituted by a free press, Morellet saw a means of infusing vigor and rationality into the system of written communication. He believed that while people did not hesitate to make absurd suggestions in unpublicized memoranda, they always tried to appear reasonable when making public statements.

> They fear the examination of the public, always severe and just, much more than that of an official, however, enlightened he may be. When publication is required, they deliberate, they consult; but if it is only a matter of sending a

[90] Alexis de Tocqueville, *The Old Regime and the French Revolution* (New York, 1955), pt. 3, ch. 1; Michel Antoine, *Le Conseil du roi sous le règne de Louis XV* (Geneva, 1970), especially 329ff. See also Françoise Mosser, *Les Intendants des finances au XVIIIe siècle* (Geneva, 1978), 50–59.

[91] Morellet, *Réflexions sur les avantages de la liberté d'écrire et d'imprimer sur les matières de l'administration, écrites en 1764 à l'occasion de la déclaration du Roi de 28 mars* (London, 1775); reprinted in Morellet's *Mélanges de littérature*, 3:1–57 (from which I cite). The quotation is from p. 23; for the three points sketched in this paragraph, see 22–24.

manuscript memoir to a minister, can anyone hold back that crowd of bad writers and even worse reasoners when they no longer fear the public and ridicule?[92]

Printing thus engendered a sense of accountability. But Morellet also believed that it was necessary to revivify and deepen the oral dimension of counsel that had been lost.

"There is a source of instruction for the public and for the government . . . from which society [*société*] can draw the greatest advantage: I mean conversation." Conversation was a means of publicity, through which individuals learned about and evaluated written works. It was also a mechanism that created knowledge. "Conversation gives us a lively and alert attention that sometimes proves to be more useful than meditation itself. The latter is sometimes fatiguing. After we have concentrated for a long time on a subject and no longer grasp anything new, then conversation comes to the aid of the exhausted mind." According to Morellet, conversation compensated for the peculiarities of individual points of view and made people more objective:

> The manner in which another sees the object with which you are occupied, often being different from your own, makes you look at it under a new heading. The difficulties proposed to you make you know the weak point of your opinion, or, if you can resolve them, give it a new degree of solidity.[93]

The value of a free political press, Morellet said, was that it stimulated talk and directed the process, whereby knowledge emerged from conversation, toward important questions of administration and finance.

> The discussions of instructed persons then revolve around these important objects. One examines, one discusses, one defends; one sees enlightenment born from the shock of ideas and opinions.[94]

The result of political conversation would be conflict at first but consensus afterward. Indeed, generalized conversation, he believed, was the only way to achieve the stability of political principles without which a regime could not endure.

> Now, I say that to give them [political views] the stability they need, they must be embraced after discussion, and consecrated by public opinion. Only then will they take on a certain consistency, just as spirituous liqueurs acquire the power to resist time after having passed through that state called *fermentation*.[95]

[92] Ibid., 21.
[93] Ibid., 20–21.
[94] Ibid., 21.
[95] Ibid., 16 (Morellet's emphasis).

He also wrote that through the press and conversation, the public became a permanent depository of truth, and that it was never deceived. "When the public, instructed by writings and discussion, has adopted a truth, it becomes its faithful guardian. Opinion no longer changes because one cannot attack a truth that is well known except with sophistry, which cannot deceive a nation once it has been instructed in its true interests."[96]

The role Morellet ascribed to public opinion was essentially consultative. He called it "a source of instruction" for the rulers. Strictly speaking, then, the concept of public opinion was less democratic than Rousseau's concept of the general will, and for two reasons. First, it was clear that those who were illiterate or uncultivated in conversation could not be part of "public opinion," though Morellet did not explicitly exclude anyone. Second, public opinion arose in the private sphere and was *about* the policies of the sovereign state, whereas the general will arose from within the legislature, had immediate legal authority, and so *constituted* sovereignty. Yet Morellet did see public opinion as a power, though it was not technically sovereign. "All great operations in administration need to be aided by public opinion, or at least cannot succeed if public opinion is against them."[97]

Ideals of sociability clearly shaped Morellet's image of public opinion and helped to give it credibility in spite of its naïveté. His unabashed optimism concerning the private discussion of political affairs suggests that he was writing for an audience accustomed to reading about the advantages of communication in another context. This context was the courtesy literature, and in particular, the theory of the "art of conversation" (see Chapter 3 for a discussion of this literature). Morellet himself published two essays on polite conversation in 1778: "Essai sur la conversation" (Essay on Conversation) and "De l'Esprit de contradiction" (On the Spirit of Contradiction).[98] These essays reveal much about his theory of communication.

The "Essai sur la conversation" was a translation of Jonathan Swift's "Hints Towards an Essay on Conversation." Here, conversation was described as the noblest human faculty, the mark of distinction separating men from the beasts. It was also "the greatest, most abiding, most innocent, and at the same time most useful pleasure in life." To perfect this art, the essay pointed out, "although quite difficult, is nevertheless within the power of every man." The important thing was to avoid a small number of key faults: talking too much, especially about oneself; interrupting and trying

---

[96] Ibid., 16.

[97] Ibid., 26.

[98] The two articles were first published in the *Mercure de France*: "Essai sur la conversation," 5 November 1778, 5–22; "De l'Esprit de contradiction," began 15 August 1778, 138–52 and continued 25 August 1778, 258–77. In the bibliography of Morellet's works appended to the early editions of his *Mémoires*, the date of 1780 was mistakenly given for the two essays. Because the essays could not be located in that year, later bibliographers of Morellet's works dropped the references.

to resolve disagreements abruptly and authoritatively; attempting to be ceaselessly witty. The essay finished by evoking an ideal image of conversation from the past—the salons of France and England in the mid-seventeenth century, when "several women . . . used to have assemblies in their homes, where the most spiritual persons of both sexes would meet to pass the evening by discussing any subject born of the occasion."[99]

The second essay, "De L'Esprit de contradiction," was an original piece on the psychological origins of debate and politeness. The essay is in the style characteristic of the *Mercure de France*, filled with amusing paradoxes that convey serious insights on human nature and manners. Morellet perceived a natural love of liberty in the soul that created "a tendency for the individual to reject the ideas and sentiments that others want him to adopt . . . precisely because they try to infuse him with these ideas and sentiments." The penchant to contradict was "especially characteristic of the most civilized societies [*les sociétés les plus policées*]" because "in order to contradict, one must have a certain abundance of ideas and a facility of expression that are not found in less civilized nations [*les nations moins civilisées*]." Morellet developed this point by drawing on the universal history of sociability à la Suard:

> [In order to contradict] one must also have a vivacious and impatient spirit, a temperament unknown to nations in which the mind is less athletic and mobile. The peoples in which sociability [*sociabilité*] has yet to be perfected are slow and patient. . . . In nations in which society [*société*] is very active, the spirit of contradiction necessarily arises with the need to talk.[100]

Here "society" refers to the zone of communicative activity, a zone that is small or nonexistent in uncivilized regimes but which becomes bustling and broad in civilized ones. Paradoxically, according to Morellet, the rise of society stimulated the wish for interaction ("the need for talk"), which in turn bred contention as humans sought to affirm their freedom within the sociable relationship.

Paradoxically again, the spirit of contradiction in civilized nations engendered politeness. The habit of contradiction, Morellet observed, could lead to passionate obstinacy and violent fights. People sought conflict, but they also sought to moderate it in order to preserve it. In this context, Morellet presented *le monde* as the quintessential union of aggressive desire and accommodating manners.

---

[99] Morellet, "Essai sur la conversation," 7–8, 10–11, 13, 16–17, 18, 20. Swift's essay is in *Collected Prose Works* (Oxford, 1939–68), 4:87–95. Morellet's rendition is a loose translation, so I have translated his French into English instead of citing from the original essay.

[100] Morellet, "De l'Esprit de contradiction," 140, 148. Compare the last quotation with Suard's discussion of the differences between taciturn and communicative peoples; see Chapter 5.

Is it not contradiction which provides that inexhaustible fund of amusing conversations for so many people who get together in great towns and which consist almost entirely in doubting, modifying, or combatting what another advances? And the politeness of conversation, what is it but the continuous effort to conceal in oneself the spirit of contradiction and not to excite it in others?[101]

Morellet also mentioned Madame Geoffrin (who had recently died)—"a woman known for many virtues and for a great knowledge of men"—and praised her as a master of the rules of politeness.[102]

Morellet thus defined civility as a combination of egotism and politeness. Although he provided a justification for rules that were quite conventional in "the art of conversation," he removed one element, the concept of *douceur*, that figured so importantly in both the seventeenth-century courtesy literature and the Enlightenment philosophy of sociability.[103] That is, he did not portray politeness as the softening of character through commerce with others. He portrayed it as a veneer in the commerce of life, a disguising of one's ineradicable love of independence out of considerations of "enlightened self-interest."[104]

In a section of the essay dealing with the psychology of men of letters, Morellet rationalized his own polemical character. He stated that everyone had a duty to moderate the spirit of contradiction with polite forms, but men of letters were to be excused if they occasionally became immoderate.

Accustomed to exercising the faculties of their mind with more force and consistency, they suffer all the more impatiently any effort to get them to adopt sentiments which they have not discovered themselves. They do not like to be led by others because they generally walk alone.[105]

Morellet does not linger on this issue of exemption from the rules of politeness. But the implication was clear: men of letters were different from other people and deserved latitude in their conduct. He concluded with a glorious account of the spirit of contradiction as found in civilized nations. It "leads the human race insensibly to enlightenment and happiness through the gradual destruction of all error . . . it has given birth to discussion and the discovery of truths." He continued, "Even when truths are known, the spirit of contradiction serves to develop and prove them with good reasons; for the inventors and defenders of these truths, attacked by adversaries, must seek all means to sustain them."[106]

[101] Ibid., 140–41.
[102] Ibid., 141–42.
[103] On the concept of *douceur*, see Chapters 3 and 4.
[104] Morellet, "De l'Esprit de contradiction," 142. This conception of politeness has an important antecedent in Pierre Nicole's *Essais de morale* (Paris, 1679).
[105] Morellet, "De l'Esprit de contradiction, 264.
[106] Ibid., 273–74.

In depicting the conversational creation of knowledge, "De l'Esprit de contradiction" coheres with *Réflexions sur les avantages*. The two works, along with the "Essai sur la conversation," make up a philosophy of communication that accounts for many things: the motives for interaction, the progress of sociability in civilized nations, the psychological origins of politeness, the role of the salon as a model of good conversation, and the intellectual and political benefits of legally unrestricted expression. This philosophy perfectly suited the needs of Morellet's identity because it assigned meaning both to the passion for argument and the cultivation of urbanity. It thus conferred value on the two main activities of his life—writing critical tracts and conversing in the salons—and it merged these apparently heterogeneous activities into a single image of civilized existence. This philosophy struck a delicate balance between the legitimation of contention and the imposition of restraint. Morellet's reformist writings, such as the tracts on the Indies Company and the Inquisition, suggest that he was able to maintain an appropriate balance and thus maintain integrity within the terms of his own philosophy.

But what about his excuse for men of letters who occasionally become immoderate because they "walk alone"? Is this not a sign that Morellet himself had somewhere exceeded the limits, that he was guilty of having infringed the bounds of decency, and that he portrayed men of letters as a superior class of beings in order to absolve himself? His philosophy overall was a philosophy of integration. But his apology for the autonomous thinker who will not yield to anyone else was a vindication of the intellectual who alienates the public, or who feels alienated by it. This trace of the spirit of martrydom within a philosophy designed to foster sociability is a clue to the existence of another Morellet.

The Philosophy of Grain

In the last chapter of his memoirs, Morellet described an encounter he had with Napoleon near the end of 1803.[107]

> Ah yes, he [Napoleon] exclaimed, you are the abbé Morellet. You are a physiocrat,[108] are you not?—I told him that there were different kinds of physiocrats; that I was not among the pure ones; that I brought certain modifications to their doctrines.

[107] Morellet recounted this episode at the very end of his *Mémoires*, 451–54. The occasion of the meeting was a reception for some members of the newly created Institut de France.

[108] The French term used here was *économiste*. In the eighteenth century and very early nineteenth century, this term designated a particular school of economic thought, physiocracy. It did not mean "economist" in the sense of any practitioner of political economy.

Bonaparte began to question Morellet about his economic ideas.

> You also desire, he said to me, free trade in grain?—Yes, Citizen Consul, I believe that in the long run, complete and unlimited freedom is the best, indeed the only, means to prevent or control price variations and to establish the mean price that is most favorable for all classes of inhabitants in a large country.

Bonaparte immediately remarked that cities sometimes fell short of grain and had to be provisioned by the government, to which Morellet answered curtly, "Citizen Consul, the exception does not contradict the rule." "You also do not want customs duties?" Bonaparte asked. "No, Citizen Consul," replied Morellet, " and when they are necessary, we should not make them exorbitant because they then become an incentive to black-market trade that is more powerful than any prohibition." Morellet developed his point in detail by explaining that the loss of customs revenue under a system of free trade was outweighed by the benefits to consumers, who could buy the goods at a lower price. The French Minister of Interior, Jean-Antoine Chaptal, was present at the meeting and stated that the customs taxes had brought a substantial thirty-five million in revenue in the past year. Morellet again had an answer: "I pointed out the expenses that went along with this revenue, the multitude of employees required, and the inconveniences of the customs border. . . . But the First Consul, always taking the offensive and never responding to my reasons, moved on to other objections that . . . "

Here the memoirs come to an abrupt end. Unfinished, they leave us with an image of Morellet in the midst of an economic dispute. Frustrated by his failure to be persuasive, he attributed this failure to the obstinacy of his interlocutor. This image is an appropriate symbol of one aspect of Morellet's career—his interest in pure economic theory and his blindness to the unsociable implications of his overweening confidence in free-market logic.

Under the monarchy, Morellet's belief in free trade was absolute, more absolute than the above dialogue suggests, for his remark, "the exception does not contradict the rule," at least acknowledges that there were exceptions. Although he preferred not to be called a physiocrat, his views on economic policy were in fact those of the physiocrats. He supported the abolition of all restrictions on the production and sale of grain and the establishment of a single tax on the net income of land—the two key planks of the physiocratic reform movement. More importantly, his vision of the economic domain, like that of the physiocrats, had a distinctively philosophical—one could even say ontological—flavor.

What was physiocratic philosophy? François Quesnay, the leader of the school, drew many of his particular insights from earlier economic writers, such as Pierre de Boisguilbert, Richard Cantillon, and J.-C.-M. Vincent de Gournay. But Quesnay was the first to attempt to analyze the free-market economy as a whole, and to depict the process of production, circulation, and consumption of the entire national product.[109] Moreover, Quesnay and his immediate disciples, such as P.-P. Mercier de la Rivière, Guillaume Le Trosne, Nicholas Baudeau, and Pierre-Samuel Dupont de Nemours, were the first group of economists to be conscious of themselves as a school. Their sense that they were promoting not only new policies but a new intellectual discipline added to their confidence and quest for rigor. "The first discovery of a science is the discovery of itself," Joseph Schumpeter observed in *The History of Economic Analysis*.[110] Physiocracy transformed inherited economic proposals into strenuous theory by means of technical terminology: "movable property" and "landed property," "fixed capital" and "circulating capital," "use value" and "sales value," "fundamental price" and "good price," "net income" and "net product." The physiocrats were also the first band of economists who were alive to the importance of propaganda—the first to launch their own journal, the *Ephémérides du citoyen* (1765–76), and the first to issue textbooks of their ideas.[111]

One of these textbooks, Dupont de Nemours's *De l'Origine et des progrès d'une science nouvelle* (On the Origin and Progress of a New Science, 1768), conveys very well the novelty of physiocracy as a political philosophy. At the outset, Dupont rejected Montesquieu's belief "that the policies of government must vary according to the form of the constitution." According to Dupont, Montesquieu failed to realize that all governments have the same foundation, economic stability, as well as the same goal, economic prosperity. "Men have not united by chance into civil societies [*sociétés civiles*]," he wrote. Physical needs brought people together. The universality of these needs dictated that a single set of political principles was valid for all states.[112] "There is thus a natural, essential, and general order which encompasses the constitutive and fundamental laws of all societies [*sociétés*]; an

---

[109] There is a large secondary literature on the physiocrats. I have found especially useful Catherine Larrère, *L'Invention de l'économie au XVIIIe siècle* (Paris, 1992); Elizabeth Fox-Genovese, *The Origins of Physiocracy* (Ithaca, 1976); Louis Dumont, *From Mandeville to Marx: The Genesis and Triumph of Economic Ideology* (Chicago, 1977); and Joseph Schumpeter, *The History of Economic Analysis* (Oxford, 1954), 223–49.

[110] Schumpeter, *History of Economic Analysis*, 242.

[111] "The impressions a reader gets as he wades through the volumes of the *Ephémérides* . . . will of course vary from one reader to another. Personally, I have been greatly struck by a certain similarity they display to the scientific journals of late nineteenth-century Marxist orthodoxy, especially the *Neue Zeit*: the same fervor of conviction, similar controversial talent, quite the same inability to take any other but the orthodox view of anything, comparable capacity for bitter resentment, and equal absence of self-criticism." Schumpeter, *History of Economic Analysis*, 227.

[112] Pierre-Samuel Dupont de Nemours, *De l'Origine et des progrès d'une science nouvelle* (London, 1768), 6–7.

order from which societies cannot depart without being less societies [*un ordre duquel les sociétés ne peuvent s'écarter sans être moins sociétés*]."[113]

The physiocratic belief that society had its own needs and rules that were prior to the constitution of sovereign power was similar to the emphasis on the autonomy of society in Méré, Scudéry, Bellegarde, Holbach, and Suard. But there was an important difference between the physiocrats and these authors. The latter saw society as "natural" in the sense of spontaneous. They believed that society issued from the pursuit of communication— whether the communication in question was conversation or commerce. But when the physiocrats described society as a "natural order" rather than a "positive order," they meant that society was a kind of Platonic model to be instituted by a theoretically informed state, not a structure of interaction that generated itself apart from the state. Missing in the physiocrats' notion of civil society was the notion of an immanent civilizing process by which individuals spontaneously formed a group and adopted enlightened patterns of interaction within it.

The physiocrats wished to create favorable conditions for the development of large-scale capitalist agriculture. The French rural situation, with its small-scale peasant holdings and sharecroppers, was inimical to their vision of the proper economic order. So was the traditional belief in a "subsistence pact" according to which the king, in return for the obedience of his subjects, provided cheap food through close regulation of the production and sale of agricultural products.[114] Since existing practices could be eradicated only through a new legislative program that would reorganize property relations and violate the corporate spirit of French jurisprudence, the physiocrats were actually calling for a good deal of governmental interference. Absolute power was an essential tool of reform for them. As Dupont wrote:

> In order for this authority to fulfill the important ministry which is conferred
> upon it, it must be sovereign; it must be armed with a force superior to all the

---

[113] Ibid., 7. Quesnay himself had insisted that constitutional forms were irrelevant to the definition of the natural order: "Some societies [*sociétés*] are governed by a monarchical authority, others by an aristocratic authority, and others by a democratic authority, etc. But these different forms of authority do not determine the essence of the natural law of men united in societies [*sociétés*]." François Quesnay, "Observations sur le droit naturel des hommes réunis en société" (first published in September 1765 in the *Journal de l'Agriculture, du commerce, et des finances*), reprinted in Eugene Daire, ed., *Physiocrates* (Paris, 1846), 51–52. Vincent de Gournay made the same point; see Larrère, *L'Invention de l'économie*, 149. Clearly, the whole modern natural-law tradition tended to make the "natural order" prior to constitutional forms. But only the physiocrats emphasized the inconsequential character of constitutional forms.

[114] On the "subsistence pact" and other aspects of the state's traditional role in the provisioning of bread, see Steven L. Kaplan, *Bread, Politics and Political Economy in the Reign of Louis XV* (The Hague, 1976), vol. 1, especially chapters 1–2.

obstacles that it could encounter. It must also be unique. The idea of many authorities in the same state is nothing but a complete absurdity.[115]

Physiocracy thus inscribed the absolutist conception of sovereign power within its own cult of the "natural order" as an entity ontologically prior to the constitution. The physiocrats saw the monarch as absolute, but they believed that he should devote his power to the "sacred ministry" of promulgating "the essential laws of the social order [*l'ordre social*]."[116]

The physiocrats saw no need for constitutional limits upon the sovereign. Institutions like the Parlements, in their view, only impeded the process of coercive liberalization. The monarch was to rule as a "despot"—a term they tried to strip of its pejorative connotations.[117] The only check on the king's authority was to be an economic one. Individuals were to be taxed as a function of their contribution to the net product. The king's revenue would then be limited to a certain percentage of the net product. His own interest would compel him to stimulate the prosperity of the whole community. Political conflict would disappear. "By this device, all species of contestation will forever be banished between the depositories of authority and the subjects; for once the ratio of the tax [to net product] is established and known, mere arithmetic will exercise the sovereign power to decide the share of each individual in the net product of the territory."[118]

Grimm said that Morellet was "not in the bosom of the physiocratic church but at the entrance."[119] His major point of disagreement with Quesnay was over the question of the "sterility" of industry. Quesnay believed that agriculture was the only mode of productivity that created new material substance beyond that which existed beforehand, an augmentation that did not take place in industry because industrial production simply imparted new form to received substances. Morellet did not share this view. He also found distasteful the manner in which the physiocrats used the term "despotism" to glorify unlimited state power.[120] But he did see the absolutist state as an instrument of progress, and he believed in the irrefutable logic of economic science with a passion that was characteristic of the physiocrats. In his *Fragment d'une lettre sur la police des grains* (Fragment of a Letter on the Administration of Grain, 1764), he stated that the principles of free

---

[115] Dupont de Nemours, *De l'Origine*, 29.

[116] Ibid., 30–31; see also 75–76.

[117] Ibid., 78–80 (including footnote).

[118] Ibid., 60.

[119] Friedrich Melchior von Grimm, *Correspondance littéraire, philosophique et critique par Grimm, Diderot, Raynal, Meister, et al.* (Paris, 1877–82), 9:82. Similarly, a twentieth-century scholar called Morellet an "auxiliary" of the physiocratic school; see Proteau, *Etude sur Morellet*.

[120] Morellet, "Sur le Despotisme légal et contre M. de la Rivière," a manuscript written in 1767, edited by Eugenio di Rienzo, in *Individualismo, Assolutismo, Democrazia*, ed. Vittorio Dini and Domenico Taranto (Naples, 1992), 321–44.

trade had been "demonstrated with such proof in so many writings . . . that I dare to say that no one could deny them except through lack of concentration, through simple-mindedness, or self-interest."[121] Morellet observed that some opponents of free trade in grain had pointed to the examples of Naples and Sicily, where famine arose after the abolition of export restrictions. Morellet first answered that the famine was due to the government's continued interference in the domestic market. But above all he denied the value of consulting history and case studies. In economic science, according to Morellet, "facts" were less important than "principles." He believed that the economist and legislator should not derive their principles by considering the ambiguous effects of half-measures: "It is a question of discovering not what has been done but what ought to be done. There is a machine to be constructed, and in order to succeed, one must act in accordance with the nature of things."[122]

It may seem odd that Morellet, who was fashioning an identity in the salons, made the grain trade his field of expertise. Indeed, in the seventeenth century, the issue of how best to supply common peasants with bread was considered an unworthy subject for a writer cultivating recognition in *le monde*. But as Voltaire observed in a famous remark, this changed in the middle of the eighteenth century.

> Around 1750, the nation, tired of verse, of tragedies, of comedies, of operas, of novels, of fantastical stories, of even more fantastical moral reflections, and of theological disputes about grace and convulsions, began to philosophize on grain.[123]

The growing interest in liberal economics stemmed not only from the original theories and astonishing language of the physiocrats but from the formation of a powerful "liberty lobby" consisting of elements within the provincial estates, agricultural improvement organizations, the growing economic press, and a large number of landowners, merchants, and above all, state officials.[124] The physiocrats and other supporters of free trade held appointments in the royal government and were well positioned to turn theory into policy. Jacques-Claude-Marie Vincent de Gournay, who coined the phrase, "*laissez-faire, laissez-passer*," was *conseiller au grand conseil* and *intendant du commerce* from 1749 to 1758. Daniel-Charles Trudaine and his son Jean-Charles-Philibert Trudaine de Montigny were *intendants des finances* (1734–69 and 1754–77, respectively). Both were profoundly influenced by free-market theory. Etienne-François Choiseul, who believed in

---

[121] Morellet, *Fragment d'une lettre sur la police des grains* (Brussels, 1764), 3.

[122] Ibid., 28–29.

[123] Voltaire, "Blé," in *Dictionnaire philosophique* (part of the 1770 supplement, "Questions sur l'Encyclopédie"), in *Oeuvres de Voltaire* (Paris, 1829), 27:389.

[124] Kaplan, *Politics, Bread, and Political Economy*, 1:121–22.

the liberalization of the foreign grain trade, was *secrétaire d'Etat de la marine* (1761–66), *secrétaire d'Etat de la guerre* (1761–70), and *secrétaire d'Etat des affaires étrangères* (1766–70). A series of economic liberals held the highest financial office in the French government—the position of *contrôleur général des finances*: Henry-Léonard-Jean-Baptiste Bertin (1759–63), who employed the physiocrats as advisers and liberalized the domestic grain trade in May 1763; Clément-Charles-François de Laverdy (1763–68), who succeeded Bertin and liberalized the foreign grain trade through the edict of July 1764 (which Dupont helped to write); Etienne Maynon d'Invau (1768–69), who succeeded Laverdy and maintained the liberal policy until December 1769, when he was dismissed and replaced by the antiliberal Joseph-Marie Terray; and Turgot (often listed among the immediate disciples of Quesnay), who reimplemented free trade in the years 1774–76.[125] Quesnay himself was the court physician to Madame de Pompadour, the mistress of Louis XV, who was herself a supporter of the free-trade party. This is only a sample of a large contingent of technocrats who believed in the need to impregnate the state's policies with economic science.[126]

As his letters repeatedly reveal, Morellet tried over the course of many years to obtain a post in the finance administration. He failed to do so, but his ties to the bureaucracy were still close. In the 1760s and 1770s he received periodic grants from the Bureau of Commerce to compose a multivolume dictionary of commerce. He managed to complete only the prospectus. In his memoirs, he explained this failure by noting that he had been distracted by the many other tasks that the government had assigned to him. Maynon d'Invau asked him to write against the Indies Company. Choiseul and Trudaine de Montigny enlisted him to refute Ferdinando Galiani's, *Dialogues sur le commerce des blés* (Dialogues on the Grain Trade, 1769). And Turgot frequently consulted him during his term as Controller General.[127]

Observing these connections, Robert Darnton has seen Morellet as an intellectual mercenary, eager to support whoever was in power in return for money.[128] This image of Morellet is consistent with Darnton's conception of a whole post-*Encyclopédie* generation of writers who lost interest in criticism and pandered to the establishment.[129] But it does not take into account

[125] I mention only the administrative positions that these figures held at the height of their career. For more information, see Michel Antoine, *Le Gouvernement et l'administration sous Louis XV: Dictionnaire biographique* (Paris, 1978).

[126] Though not specifically concerned with the economic views of royal officials, Keith Baker has analyzed "the impregnation of government with knowledge" and the "movement from bureaucracy toward technocracy" in "Science and Politics at the End of the Old Regime," in Baker, *Inventing the French Revolution*, 153–66.

[127] Morellet, *Mémoires*, 169–70.

[128] Robert Darnton, "Une Carrière littéraire exemplaire," in *Gens de lettres, gens du livre* (Paris, 1991), 47–68.

[129] See Chapter 4 for a fuller discussion of Darnton's view of the "High Enlightenment."

that many members of the royal administration in the second half of the eighteenth century were themselves theoretically inclined. As Jean-Claude Perrot has written, men of letters and men of state shared the belief that "every practical activity ought to be reinserted into a system of scientific discourse that can bring it a higher degree of coherence and efficiency."[130] Governmental patronage became a source of support for intellectuals whose untraditional ideas bolstered the untraditional plans of bureaucrats. Morellet was thus assisting a group of administrators who shared his liberal economic views. He hoped to be rewarded financially, but above all he was pursuing the quest for integration in one of the areas of the real world that was receptive to his ideas. The institution of the state had the same existential significance for him as the salons. But this is not to say that his service to the administration was wholly unproblematic, for as Morellet's conflict with Galiani shows, the effort to establish an identity within these two spheres, the salons and the state, could create a clash of loyalties.

When Choiseul and Trudaine de Montigny urged Morellet in 1770 to defend the government's liberal grain policy against Ferdinando Galiani's *Dialogues sur le commerce des blés*, they were offering Morellet a challenge that suited his polemical temperament. The popularity of Galiani's work, Morellet stated in his memoirs, "goaded me on and I dreamt of the glory to be gained by beating the odds and making a strong response."[131] This explanation of his own motives rings with truth, unlike the description that he gave of his opponent. Galiani, he stated in the memoirs, was not sincerely interested in economics and wrote about grain policy only to "spite" Choiseul and the *philosophes*.[132] No description could be more false.

Far from being an adversary of the *philosophes*, Galiani was their favorite foreign visitor. He had arrived in Paris in 1759 as a secretary to the embassy of Naples, and his star immediately rose in the salons, thanks to his unparalleled gift for philosophical humor.[133] When another Italian, Pietro Verri, toured the salons in 1767, he found Galiani everywhere. "He is all the rage in Paris and much sought-after. . . . Wherever he is, everyone keeps quiet and lets him shine."[134] Diminutive and plump, and with a hundred wisecracks at hand, Galiani endeared himself as a clown among intellectuals. Diderot was one of the first to become enchanted. "In came abbé Galiani," he wrote to Sophie Volland in 1760, and with him "gaiety, imagination,

---

[130] Jean-Claude Perrot, *Une Histoire intellectuelle de l'économie politique, XVIIe–XVIIIe siècles* (Paris, 1992), 106.

[131] Morellet, *Mémoires*, 172.

[132] Ibid., 170.

[133] Benedetta Craveri has given a lively description of Galiani's personality in "Conqueror of Paris," *New York Review of Books* 39 (December 17, 1992):63–68.

[134] Pietro Verri to Alessandro Verri, 25 January 1767, in Pietro Verri, *Viaggio a Parigi e a Londra (1766–1767): Carteggio di Pietro Verri*, ed. G. Gaspari (Milan, 1980), 249–50.

wit, madness, and everything that makes one forget the hardships of life."[135] But, as Marmontel observed, underneath Galiani's jovial exterior was a "melancholy soul."[136] A current of nihilism pushed his galley of jokes forward and added irony to everything he said. Morellet himself gave an account of an episode in Holbach's salon in which Galiani asked to have a moment to respond to Diderot's religious skepticism. Galiani developed the argument from design, a classic proof for the existence of God; but by likening God to a crooked owner of a gambling establishment, he turned the whole demonstration into a blasphemous joke.

The abbé squatted in an armchair with his legs crossed, as was his manner. Since it was hot, he held his wig in his hand, and, gesticulating with the other, he began more or less as follows:

"Let us suppose, Messieurs, that the man among you who is most convinced that the universe is the work of chance was gambling with three dice—I will not say in a house of ill repute but in the best home in Paris—when his opponent rolled sixes once, twice, three times, four times, and so on constantly.

"During the competition, which would be brief, my friend Diderot loses his money in the process and says without hesitation and without a moment of doubt, 'The dice are loaded, I'm being swindled.'

"Ah, *philosophe*! how so? Because ten or twelve throws of the dice have rolled from the box in such a way as to make you lose six francs, you are confident that this is the result of a deft move, a fake combination, a well-woven scam. But in seeing in this universe such a vast number of combinations which are thousands upon thousands of times more difficult, complicated, continuous, useful, etc., you do not suspect that nature's dice are also loaded and that there is a great rascal up there who makes a sport of cheating you."[137]

As an economic writer, Galiani was considerably more original than Morellet acknowledged. At age twenty-three, he had written a brilliant treatise, *Della Moneta* (On Money, 1751), in which he articulated, among other things, the principle of what subsequently became known as marginal utility.[138] In the *Dialogues sur le commerce des blés*, he poked large holes in physiocratic theory and underscored the practical need for state grain depots and controls on exports. Galiani supported protectionist policies by means of economic reasoning, but his economic reasoning was not deduc-

---

[135] Diderot to Sophie Volland, 25 November 1760, in Denis Diderot, *Correspondance*, ed. Georges Roth (Paris, 1955–70), 3:268.

[136] Jean François Marmontel, *Mémoires* (Clermont-Ferrand, 1972), 1:166.

[137] Morellet, *Mémoires*, 132.

[138] Henry William Spiegel, *The Growth of Economic Thought* (Durham, 1991), 203, calls this work a "precocious effort, which is without parallel in the early history of economics." Schumpeter, *The History of Economic Analysis*, 300–302, also discusses the work as a remarkable anticipation of modern economic concepts.

tive like that of the physiocrats because he emphasized the geographical and political conditions that shape economic behavior.

> Let us establish principles drawn from the very nature of things. What is man? What is the relationship between bread and man? Let us then apply these principles to time, place, and circumstances. With which kingdom are we concerned? How is it situated? What are the mores, the opinions, the opportunities to pursue, the risks to avoid? Let us then decide.[139]

Galiani classified the European countries into five categories: small commercial nations, medium-sized commercial nations, medium-sized agricultural nations, large agricultural nations, and large agricultural and commercial nations. He argued that the different types of nations had to pursue different policies in order to obtain an adequate supply of bread for their populations. He also distinguished nations according to the geographical location of their most fertile province. A nation in which most of the grain was produced in its geographical center could liberalize the foreign grain market because merchants would have to transport the grain through the provinces before sending it out of the country. They would naturally sell to buyers at hand in the provinces before incurring the costs of further export. But in a nation in which the fertile land was located in a coastal province, export restrictions were essential. Without them, merchants would sell abroad, ignoring much of the domestic demand on account of the higher costs of transporting grain by land to the interior.[140]

Although he did not challenge the general concept of supply and demand, Galiani stressed the need for government stockpiles by underscoring the factors that disrupted equilibrium.

> Nothing is more true than that the prices of grain, if unregulated, will be in equilibrium. Nothing is more true than that unregulated commerce will distribute grain everywhere where there are consumers and money. Nothing is more true in theory. . . . But in practice, you must take into account the period of time required for posting letters to send the news of the local grain shortage to the country where grain can be had. Another period of time elapses before the grain arrives. And if this period of time is two weeks, and there are provisions only for one week, the town goes a week without bread. And that insect called man does not need more than a week to die of hunger.[141]

Galiani also believed that grain policy was a matter of *raison d'état* (his phrase)—something the physiocrats never considered. Grain, he reminded his readers, was necessary to provision an army. A nation had to prohibit the

---

[139] Ferdinando Galiani, *Dialogues sur le commerce des blés* (Paris, 1984), 27. This edition by the publisher Fayard is based on the first edition (London, 1770).

[140] Ibid., 20.

[141] Ibid., 211.

sale of grain to an enemy power. And in order to protect itself against the possibility of an embargo, a state had to stockpile grain.[142]

Galiani's economic arguments took on great charm in the context of his witty style. Even some of his stiffest economic opponents acknowledged the beauty of his work. "Such a book," Turgot wrote to Morellet, "written with so much elegance, lightness of tone, propriety, and originality of expression, and by a foreigner, is perhaps a unique phenomenon. The work is most amusing and unfortunately it will be very difficult to respond to it."[143] Mixing his observations on economic policy with philosophical reflections on human nature, and turning the whole into a series of dinner conversations among a "Marquis," a "Chevalier," and other noble characters, Galiani sought to give pleasure to *le monde* at least as much as he sought to influence government policy. While opposing the dogmatism of the physiocrats, he offered no dogma of his own, but only a good-humored sense of moderation. "You are the only intelligent man of my acquaintance who does not promote freedom of exportation," says the Marquis to the Chevalier. "I do not promote anything at all," answers the Chevalier, who represents Galiani's views. "The only kind of exportation that disturbs me is that of common sense."[144] The skeptical Chevalier emphasizes the plasticity of human nature and the impossibility of constructing a universal social science.

> All the problems of political economy stem from the effort to improve human life. But there is no good which is not connected to some bad. . . . Add to this first difficulty the fact that there is no fixed and constant quantity to insert into the formulation of the problem. Man! Man himself is an indeterminate quantity. He is (if I may employ the expression) a ductile substance, a wire shaped by habit. He can be bent and formed in any way without being destroyed. Through habit, his energies, nature, and inner being assume a shape that would seem impossible. And what is most extraordinary, as soon as his features are set, he finds that they are utterly natural, that they have existed since the beginning of time and could not have been otherwise.[145]

Galliani believed that those who advocated all-encompassing theories were dangerous, especially when they did so out of moral zeal. "Virtue, the desire to do good, is a passion like all the others." Virtue is even more violent than other passions, for "when goodness inspires us, no feeling of guilt checks our conduct."[146] Like Machiavelli, Galiani argued that the truly responsible person had to cultivate qualities that appeared opposed to each other. "He

---

[142] Ibid., 33–34, 37.

[143] Turgot to Morellet, 19 January 1770, *Oeuvres de Turgot*, 3:408; also cited by Morellet in *Mémoires*, 171.

[144] Galiani, *Dialogues*, 18.

[145] Ibid., 204.

[146] Ibid., 206.

must ardently pursue the good, as the virtuous man does, but he must have a coolness or indifference [regarding his means], like evil people. He must exercise his will and yet discuss in tranquillity."[147]

To discuss in tranquillity is precisely what Morellet was not able to do in response to Galiani. Obsessed with defending the free-market policies that had been in effect since the edicts of 1763–64, he did not appreciate the need to respond delicately to a compatriot of the salons. Galiani had finished his book shortly before being recalled to Naples in May 1769. He left the manuscript with Diderot, who made some stylistic revisions with further help from Grimm and Madame d'Epinay.[148] The work thus had the approval of three members of the republic of letters even before it was published. Sartine, the Paris Lieutenant of Police, who understood the practical difficulties of an unregulated market, also wanted to see the text published but believed that Maynon d'Invau, the more liberal Controller General, would use his influence to block its distribution. When Maynon d'Invau was replaced by the antiliberal Terray on December 21, 1769, Sartine felt reassured, and the work went into press at the end of December. "It was necessary to dismiss a Controller General . . . and bring about the transformation of the state before my little book could appear," Galiani noted.[149] Morellet wrote his *Réfutation de l'ouvrage qui a pour titre Dialogues sur le commerce des blés* (Refutation of the Work Entitled Dialogues on the Grain Trade) during the first three months of 1770, a period of economic and political crisis in which peasants rioted in favor of price controls and many local authorities refused to apply the liberalization edicts. Terray ultimately revoked the edicts in December 1770, but when Morellet was composing his book, the future of the liberal edicts appeared to hang in the balance.

Galiani and Morellet fell out even before the *Réfutation* appeared in print. In February, the rumor reached Galiani in Naples that Morellet had worn all the skin off his little finger by furiously rubbing his hand against the table in the course of writing his refutation.[150] By late March, Morellet had finished, and Galiani, who was sensitive to criticism and misunderstanding of his work, had his worst fears confirmed by Diderot, who had read the unpublished manuscript. In April, Galiani wrote a letter to Morellet that was answered on May 1. Galiani's letter is not extant, but from Morellet's response it is clear that Galiani asked Morellet to explain why he was so intent on refuting his *Dialogues* and ruining their friendship. In a long and angry answer, Morellet stated:

[147] Ibid., 206–7.

[148] Philip Koch, "Les Véritables 'Dialogues' de Galiani," *Atti del convegno italo-francese di Roma, 25–27 May 1972* (Rome, 1975), 185–97.

[149] Galiani to Madame d'Epinay, 20 January 1770, in Ferdinando Galiani, *Correspondance* (Paris, 1881), 1:52–53.

[150] Madame d'Epinay to Galiani, 3 February, 1770, in Galiani, *Correspondance*, 1:66.

I do not understand why you find it so extraordinary that I have undertaken to refute you. . . . I simply wish to defend a cause which I believe to be that of truth and public utility. . . . I would prefer to have disputes only with my enemies but I am somewhat like that merchant who was accused of overcharging his friends and who responded, "I would like to profit from my enemies alone but they never come into my shop." It is you who have come into mine. I was living in peace with M. Necker and you. I was not the aggressor against either of you. But both of you *have* attacked liberty.[151]

Morellet criticized Galiani for using the frivolous dialogue form to write about economics and for suggesting that grain policy was an endlessly complex subject. "I believe that the question is too important to be treated with the gaiety and indifference that you ask for. I am convinced that the question is *terminable* and that the principles for resolving it are evident."[152] Morellet then stated that Galiani's ideas supported tyranny all over the world. He also quoted a passage from Galiani's earlier treatise on money and claimed it contradicted the dialogues on grain. He insisted that he had not misinterpreted Galiani at all. "You are very set against liberty, at least you want to place restrictions and limits on it. I am ready for combat to the death on behalf of unlimited freedom. We understand each other very well."[153]

Galiani expressed his dismay in a clever letter of May 26. He informed Morellet that he had received a letter from an impostor, someone who claimed to be Morellet, but whose "tone and style" were clearly not his. "What can I tell you about this unbelievable letter from the pseudo-Morellet? He proclaims his creed and draws honor and glory from it. . . . He fancies himself the Don Quixote of liberty. . . . Then he finds me in contradiction with myself, then he tells me I am set against liberty, then he proposes a combat to the death."[154] Galiani bemoaned the fact that he had not heard from his friend, the real Morellet, for so long. "While waiting for your book to be published, write to me from time to time. Remember that you were my first acquaintance in Paris. You are to me (and I cannot think about it without tears) *primogenitus mortuorum*, the oldest of my lost friends. To you I owe my introduction to Madame Geoffrin, d'Alembert, and so many others."[155]

Galiani's effort to remind Morellet of their common bonds in the republic of letters did not induce Morellet to tone down his *Réfutation*. Nor did Turgot's remarks about the difficulties of refuting a great writer like Galiani. Morellet organized his work mechanically by quoting passages page by

[151] Morellet to Galiani, 1 May 1770, *Lettres d'André Morellet*, 1:126 (Morellet's emphasis).
[152] Ibid., 128 (Morellet's emphasis).
[153] Ibid., 1:131.
[154] Galiani to Morellet, 26 May 1770, in Galiani, *Correspondance*, 1:152–53.
[155] Ibid., 1:159.

page from Galiani's text and criticizing them one by one. When he could not effectively respond to Galiani's arguments about the practical need for regulations, he argued that grain was a form of private property belonging to the producers, wholesalers, and retailers. Since the right of private property was absolute, it took priority over the subsistence needs of any particular group.[156] As for Galiani himself, Morellet stated in his Notice that he had tried to distinguish between the author and his book and wished only to criticize the latter. Yet he admitted that some "excessively lively" expressions might have escaped from his pen.[157] This was an understatement, for the first chapter of the book paints Galiani as a flatterer of despots and a panderer to the opinions of ignorant people.[158] And throughout the work, Morellet shows disdain for Galiani and his ideas.

Morellet's work was printed in May 1770, but Sartine and Terray had virtually all of the copies confiscated and held in the Bastille. Morellet was able to recover them only when his friend Turgot became Controller General in August 1774.[159] The work was sold in December of the same year. As a refutation of another work that was then four years old, it did not attract much attention.[160] Morellet was lucky that his book did not come out in 1770. At that time, just a year after Galiani's return to Naples, the vivid memory of the Italian's brilliant book and amiable personality would have been enough to turn many of the *philosophes* against Morellet. Even as it was, he did not go unreproached, for a small group of people had seen either the original manuscript or the few unconfiscated copies. Turgot thought that Morellet had made an untasteful mistake in trying to refute Galiani page by page. He told the duchesse d'Enville that he was glad the work had been confiscated.[161] It is doubtful, however, that he said this openly, because we

---

[156] Morellet, *Réfutation de l'ouvrage qui a pour titre dialogues sur le commerce des blés* (London, 1770), 98, 100, 271, 273–74.

[157] Ibid., Avertissement.

[158] Ibid., 3–4, 6.

[159] The following provide information about the publishing history of the *Réfutation*: Morellet to Turgot, 19 May 1770, in Morellet, *Lettres d'André Morellet*, 1:139; Morellet, *Mémoires*, 173; Paul Varnière, Introduction to Diderot's *Apologie de l'abbé Galiani*, in Diderot, *Oeuvres politiques* (Paris, 1963), 63–64; the "Nouvel Avertissement, Novembre 1774," inserted in Morellet's *Réfutation* after the table of contents; and Bachaumont, *Mémoires secrets*, 7:252 (20 December 1774).

[160] Grimm wrote, "This refutation is making so little noise that it is hard to understand today why the administration denied the author the pleasure of publishing it for so long." *Correspondance littéraire, philosophique et critique*, 1 December 1774, 10:514. According to Madame d'Epinay, "Except for the author's friends, no one is reading or talking about it." Madame d'Epinay to Galiani, 5 December 1774, in Louise-Florence-Pétronville de Lalive d'Epinay, *Gli ultimi anni della Signora d'Epinay: Lettere inedite all'abate Galiani*, ed. Fausto Nicolini (Bari, 1933), 130.

[161] Turgot to the duchesse d'Enville, 17 September 1770, in Turgot, *Lettres de Turgot à la duchesse d'Enville, 1764–74 et 1777–80*, ed. Joseph Ruwet (Louvain, 1976), 56.

find Morellet, in his letters from this period, approaching Turgot as a confidant and complaining about the "vexations" and "unpleasantness" he was experiencing in his relations with his friends.[162] He did not provide details, but there is no doubt that it was Diderot who was at the center of his troubles.

Diderot was the first person to read the *Réfutation*. When Sartine wished to obstruct its publication, his first tactic had been to appoint Diderot as official censor of the work. In his censor's report of March 10, 1770, Diderot assailed what he saw as the improper form and intellectual shallowness of the *Réfutation*. "He slanders and pretends not to understand [Galiani] in several places and he does not in fact understand him in others." Morellet's "tone" was not "*honnête*." According to Diderot, Morellet would have done better to send his economic objections to Galiani in a letter instead of writing a boring book that no one would want to read. Galiani was "a man of genius who understands the world, men, and the human heart. . . . This refutation will do much harm to the abbé Morellet, who should expect indulgence neither from the public nor from his friends."[163]

Diderot believed too strongly in freedom of the press to recommend that the work be banned. But he showed his critical report to Madame d'Epinay, who sent a copy to Galiani (it was this that prompted Galiani's April letter to Morellet). Galiani, in turn, complained about Morellet to Suard and Holbach.[164] Morellet knew that critical judgments about his character were circulating behind his back—these were the "vexations" that he described to Turgot. As 1770 became 1771, Diderot continued to act as Galiani's chivalrous defender. In November, he conceived the idea of writing a thorough refutation of Morellet's *Réfutation*. In January, he completed a manuscript book, *Apologie de l'abbé Galiani*, but never published it. It was found in 1913 with the disclosure of Diderot's private papers.[165]

The work resembles Voltaire's denunciation of Palissot: it is severe and personal but makes the other out to be the aggressor. "What kind of man is this abbé Morellet who is Galiani's friend yet writes against Galiani?"[166] "He is the most impertinent man I know; he is violent and scatter-brained."[167] Diderot gave Morellet a taste of his own medicine by quoting and refuting him page by page. He pointed out Morellet's "insupportable

---

[162] Morellet to Turgot, 19 May and 28 June 1770, in Morellet, *Lettres d'André Morellet*, 1: 139, 142.

[163] Diderot, "Sur la Réfutation des Dialogues de Galiani sur les Grains," *Oeuvres* (Paris, 1818), 1:745–46.

[164] See Paul Vernière's editorial notes in Diderot, *Oeuvres politiques*, 64.

[165] Herbert Dieckmann, *Inventaire du Fonds Vandeul et inédits de Diderot* (Geneva, 1951), xxxvii, 62–63. The text is published in Diderot, *Oeuvres politiques*, ed. Paul Vernière, 69–124.

[166] Diderot, *Apologie de l'abbé Galiani*, 69.

[167] Ibid., 71.

arrogance" and "vile rage."[168] Morellet had violated the principle of reciprocity, the very foundation of human relations. "You love dispute," Diderot wrote, addressing himself directly to Morellet, "while he loves conversation. . . . You want to laugh but you do not want others to laugh back."[169] Citing a passage in which Morellet had rebuked Galiani for being "impolite" toward the physiocrats, Diderot added: "It is really amusing that the abbé Morellet urges Galiani to treat the physiocrats—whom Galiani does not know and to whom he owes nothing—with politeness; while he, the abbé Morellet, treats the abbé Galiani, his friend, in the most insulting manner and denounces him publicly in the most odious colors, touching indiscriminately on both his person and his opinions."[170]

Diderot accused Morellet of being a lackey of the government. "The abbé Morellet is nothing. He is no philosopher, no gentleman, no citizen, no friend. He is the puppet of the grandees and does whatever pleases them."[171] Although this accusation was unfair, it reflected Diderot's view that one could not be an independent man of letters and a servant of the government at the same time. He did not believe that the quest for integration could go through the state. Diderot also targeted a contradiction in Morellet's thought that was evident when Morellet poured scorn on Galiani for pandering to the opinion of ignorant people who favored government controls. "May I ask you with regards to common opinions why you devalue so strongly the notions of the people? Isn't the people's instinctive knowledge of what is beneficial the foundation of your sermons on liberty?"[172] This was a shrewd remark and pointed to the tension between the sociable and technocratic elements in Morellet's thought: he idealized discussion and public opinion in defending freedom of the press, but he belittled the dialogue form and popular opinion when defending economic freedom.

Though he did not argue in a technical manner, Diderot adroitly opposed complete freedom of trade. He considered it "feeble and defective" to invoke the absolute principle of private property when some people were starving. Private property was subordinate to considerations of "public welfare" and "general utility." How else could one justify taxation, or the right of the government to build a road through a man's estate?[173] "Property rights are sacred between private persons. . . . This is not so as concerns the relation of these rights to society [société]."[174] Quoting a passage in

---

[168] Ibid., 88, 108.
[169] Ibid., 74–75.
[170] Ibid., 123–24.
[171] Ibid., 113.
[172] Ibid., 75–76.
[173] Ibid., 85.
[174] Ibid., 99.

which Morellet had stated that the property rights of landowners and merchants outweighed the subsistence needs of the majority,[175] Diderot commented: "This principle is the principle of a tartar, a cannibal, and not of a civilized man [*homme policé*]. Isn't the sentiment of humanity more sacred than property rights?"[176] Diderot's critique of Morellet's economic principles thus dovetailed with his critique of Morellet's character. In both cases, he showed that Morellet was unsociable—uncivilized in relation to his friends and in relation to his fellow countrymen.

Diderot revised and polished the draft of the *Apologie de l'abbé Galiani* four times.[177] That was a sign that he intended to publish the work. One can assume that he ultimately decided not publish it only because Morellet's own *Réfutation* was not published in 1770 as planned. But although the work remained in manuscript form, Diderot undoubtedly showed it to others. Grimm's review of Morellet's *Réfutation* in the *Correspondance littéraire* of July 1770 reiterated many of the points that Diderot made in the *Apologie de l'abbé Galiani*.[178] The hostile reaction to Morellet's *Réfutation* shows that debates about economic policy came close to ruining relations among the very writers who liked to see themselves as part of a sociable republic of letters. Morellet was most responsible for the strains. For him, there was simply more at stake in saving the credibility of free-market policies than in saving the tone of civilized communication. Influencing legislation was more important to him than maintaining the bonds of sociability. His hard treatment of Galiani inevitably rankled not only Galiani but Galiani's friends. The *philosophes* generally expressed their criticism of each other in letters that they circulated among themselves but kept from their collective enemies. That is why Diderot and Grimm were angry with Morellet: he had criticized Galiani in a book designed to shape public opinion. Grimm made the point that Diderot had made in his report to Sartine—that it would have been more "polite" if Morellet had outlined his criticism in a letter to Galiani and given the Italian a chance to respond before writing the *Réfutation*.[179] Diderot and Grimm severely rebuked Morellet, but there were limits to their anger. The fact that Diderot did not

---

[175] The passage reads, "Although only two million men are involved in the production of grain and eighteen million eat it, this is not a good reason to decide that the superfluous grain belonging to the two million cultivators should be regulated against their wishes; for this grain which is superfluous for [the cultivators], in spite of the fact that it is a necessity for their fellow citizens, is their property." Cited by Diderot, *Apologie*, 117, from Morellet, *Réfutation*, 274.

[176] Diderot, Apologie, 118.

[177] See Dieckmann, *Inventaire du Fonds Vendeul*, 62–63; see also Vernière's remarks in Diderot's *Oeuvres politiques*, 65–67.

[178] Grimm, *Correspondance littéraire*, 1 July 1770, 9:82–84. Grimm especially criticized Morellet for failing to sustain the politeness that was appropriate in "discussion among *honnêtes gens.*"

[179] Grimm, *Correspondance littéraire*, 9:82–83.

publish his *Apologie* suggests that he was less interested in harming Morellet than in maintaining the economy of politeness. The conflict between Morellet and Galiani's friends did not degenerate into a civil war. Morellet was made to feel uncomfortable for a time, but there were no purges in the republic of letters. He continued to attend the various salons, where he encountered Diderot regularly. Like Morellet's next polemical battle, his conflict with Necker, the incident took on an episodic quality.

In 1775, Necker published *Sur la Législation et du commerce des grains* (On the Legislation and Trade of Grain, 1775), a critique of economic liberalism that reiterated many of Galiani's arguments. Turgot was Controller General at the time and was trying to liberalize the domestic grain market. Morellet responded to Necker with *Analyse de l'ouvrage intitulé De la Législation et du commerce des blés* (Analysis of the Work Entitled On the Legislation and Trade of Grain, 1775). The work began with the suggestion that Necker was more interested in gaining power than discovering the truth about the grain trade.[180] But in spite of this insult and the condescending tone of the work as a whole, Morellet maintained friendly ties with the Neckers. He withdrew from the salon after the appearance of Necker's book, but he explained to his English friend, Lord Shelburne, that this was primarily a matter of loyalty to Turgot and involved no rancor on his part.[181] He continued to correspond warmly with Madame Necker when he did not attend the salon. In June 1777, a year after Turgot's fall from power, Necker became Director General of Finances. (He performed the duties of Controller General but was not given the title because he was a Protestant.) In October of that year, the Neckers attended the marriage of Morellet's niece to Jean-François Marmontel. In December, Madame Necker invited Morellet back into the salon. He politely refused, saying that others would view him as a hypocrite and careerist if he renewed his regular contact with Necker during the height of Necker's power.[182] The following year, Necker gave Morellet's brother a position in the royal domains.[183] After Necker's fall from power in May 1781, Morellet finally rejoined the salon.[184] As with Diderot, so with Necker: economic policy debates revealed a seam in Enlightenment sociability, but they did not tear it apart.

[180] Morellet, *Analyse de l'ouvrage intitulé De la Législation et du commerce des grains* (Paris, 1775), 5.

[181] Morellet to Lord Shelburne, 12 April 1776, in Morellet, *Lettres d'André Morellet*, 1:337. A previous letter to Shelburne, 25 November 1774, shows that Morellet was attending the salon during Turgot's ministry prior to the appearance of Necker's book. He thus withdrew only when Necker publicly expressed opposition to Turgot's policies.

[182] Morellet to Madame Necker, 28 December 1777, Ibid., 1:372–73.

[183] Morellet, *Lettres d'André Morellet*, 1:332, editors' note 9. See also Morellet to Lord Shelburne, 17 July 1778, 1:385–86.

[184] Morellet, *Mémoires*, 149.

Revolution and the New Liberalism

The 1780s were years of peace and pleasure for Morellet. He continued to write articles on free trade for the *Mercure de France* and worked on his interminable dictionary of commerce. He held concerts at his home and attended several salons, where he became particularly friendly with Benjamin Franklin.[185] When Turgot died in 1778, Morellet lost his connection with a truly powerful statesman whose ideas he shared, but Lord Shelburne soon made up for the loss. Morellet's friendship with the Englishman dated back to Shelburne's visit to Paris in 1771. The two were introduced by Trudaine de Montigny and maintained a rich correspondence that spanned thirty-four years until Shelburne's death. In July 1782, Shelburne became the prime minister. The following year, in the midst of the negotiations over the Treaty of Paris, he informed leading figures in the French Foreign Ministry that it was Morellet who had convinced him of the importance of free trade. Shelburne requested that they convey to the king his wish that Morellet receive a substantial pension, and it was promptly done.[186] "I ow'd [*sic*] it to you," Shelburne wrote. "Your conversation and information had essentially contributed to liberalize my ideas on these subjects."[187] Shelburne's letter, which Morellet circulated among his friends, conferred great prestige upon him. Whether or not Morellet had truly been responsible for influencing Shelburne's political outlook is debatable. But at the time, he and other men of letters seized upon any evidence suggesting that they had successfully integrated philosophy into political affairs. The marquis de Chastellux cited the letter when he delivered the oration officially welcoming Morellet into the Académie Française in 1785.[188] He also praised Morellet for influencing "public opinion" on economic matters.[189] This was the high point of Morellet's career. As he said in his memoirs, his membership in the Académie helped to make the 1780s a period that "flowed deliciously for me."[190]

As the Estates General prepared to convene, Morellet was enthusiastic about the prospects of reform. In a pamphlet written in the winter of 1788, he supported the idea of doubling the number of the representatives of the third estate. "Public opinion," he claimed, was in favor of a "national assem-

---

[185] Ibid., 241–60.

[186] Shelburne to Morellet, 23 March 1783, cited in *Lettres d'André Morellet*, 1:484, editors' note 1; see also Morellet, *Mémoires*, 228–30.

[187] Shelburne to Morellet, 23 March 1783, in Morellet, *Lettres d'André Morellet*, 484 (the letter is provided in editors' note 1); also cited in French by Morellet in *Mémoires*, 228–29.

[188] François-Jean Chastellux, *Réponse de M. le Marquis de Chastellux au discours de M. l'Abbé Morellet*, in Morellet, *Mélanges de littérature*, 1:47.

[189] Ibid., 42, 47.

[190] Morellet, *Mémoires*, 225.

bly," a representative body that recognized no distinctions of order within itself and that was willing to abolish any privileges necessary to solve the national debt.[191] With its emphasis on the priority of public utility over privilege, Morellet's rhetoric in this pamphlet seems radical. He was not, however, interested in promoting the abolition of everything that made the three estates distinct. He only wished to do away with the tax exemptions making it impossible to resolve the state's financial crisis. After the Estates General convened, transformed itself into the National Assembly, and proceeded to dismantle the corporate structure of the Old Regime on the night of August 4, 1789, Morellet began to turn against the Revolution. From this time onward, his writings illustrate the evolution of an Enlightenment intellectual concerned with placing limits on absolute monarchy into a postrevolutionary intellectual obsessed with the defects of democratic sovereignty.

It is worth remembering that most of the *philosophes* died before 1789. One can only speculate about how they would have responded to the events of the Revolution. Others, such as Condorcet, died during the Terror and did not have a chance to revamp their conceptions of civilization and progress in the light of the violence perpetrated in the name of democracy. Morellet thus provides one of the few opportunities to study the structure of philosophic conversion after 1789.

In the session of the night of August 4, members of the National Assembly rose to denounce the privileges of the nobility, clergy, provinces, and municipal corporations. The decrees of August 11 endorsed these declarations by formally annihilating "the feudal regime." All *cens* payments, seigneurial courts, tithes, tax exemptions, and privileges of particular geographic regions were abolished. The Assembly decided on August 13 that all dues formerly paid to the clergy would be redeemed not at their "equivalent" value but at an "appropriate" value to be established by the revolutionary government. This policy directly concerned Morellet because he had himself acquired a benefice with dues in 1788. Before his death in 1781, Turgot had arranged for Morellet to take over a benefice in the village of Thimert upon the death of its occupant. This sinecure included a house, gardens, and "all the seigneurial rights of hunting, *cens*, honorific rents, etc."[192]

Morellet quickly composed a pamphlet, *Réflexions du lendemain* (Reflections of the Day After), designed to show that the Assembly had become intoxicated by its passion for vital change and had made a grave mistake in

---

[191] Morellet, *Observations sur le projet de former une Assemblée nationale sur le modèle des Etats-Généraux de 1614* (n.p., n.d.), 1, 2. In his *Mémoires* (274–75), Morellet indicates that he wrote the pamphlet in the winter of 1788.

[192] Morellet, *Mémoires*, 270–71.

its decrees.[193] He took the principle of redemption at an "appropriate" value to mean that members of the clergy would be stripped arbitrarily of their benefices and reduced to the lowest possible standard of living. The purpose of a national assembly, he argued, was to protect the rights of the subjects, not to take them away. The Assembly was unjustly depriving the clergy of its property rights by eliminating its dues. Morellet knew that members of the Assembly had argued that all dues were the initial property of the "nation." The "nation," so the argument went, had granted the dues and could take them away at will. Morellet argued that the nation could not take away the dues, at least not without full compensation, because "far from being able to take a thing back because one gave it away, it is precisely because one gave it away that one cannot take it back."[194] The nation, he reasoned, was bound by its previous acts, and no new law could have a retroactive effect.[195]

Morellet devoted several pages of the pamphlet to explaining why the Assembly had failed to "deliberate maturely" on August 4 and 11. First of all, the Assembly's fear of peasant uprisings against seigneurial authority had led it to take action too quickly against the old system. Secondly, the Assembly had spent too much time in general meetings and not enough in small committees where the issues could have been formulated with precision. Thirdly, the "interior order" (*police intérieure*) of the Assembly was defective and allowed the passions of the moment to rule. Morellet claimed that the Assembly should have followed the examples of the English House of Commons and American state legislatures, which required a substantial period of debate to precede the ratification of a bill. The Assembly had also ordered that no speech could exceed five minutes. This rule, according to Morellet, precluded intelligent analysis of even the simplest questions and unleashed "bizarre, unexpected, and badly reasoned movements."[196]

Morellet's critique of the forms of the Assembly shows that he had not yet abandoned the concept of the public sphere that had inspired so much of

---

[193] Morellet, *Réflexions du lendemain, sur les arrêtés pris dans l'Assemblée Nationale, relativement aux biens ecclésiastiques, le 11 août 1789* (n.p., n.d.). References in the pamphlet to events indicate that Morellet wrote the pamphlet in the last week of August. It was published in September.

[194] Ibid., 15. Morellet's conception of the *cens* and clerical dues as the "property" of the recipient is a remarkable simplification bearing no relation to French law and seigneurial customs in the prerevolutionary period. In a system in which land was generally not "owned" but "held" in exchange for dues and services, it was impossible for jurists to construe the land in terms of absolute property rights. To construe the dues within such a system of land tenure as private property would have been even more absurd. See James Q. Whitman, "'Les seigneurs descendent au rang de simples créanciers': Droit romain, droit féodal et révolution," *Droits, Revue Française de Théorie Juridique* 17 (1993):19–32.

[195] Morellet, *Réflexions du lendemain*, 25–26.

[196] Ibid., 81–82.

his reformist writing before the Revolution. Continuing to believe that discussion produced truth, he interpreted the untruthful declarations of the Assembly in a circular manner as a sign that "there was no real discussion."[197] The Assembly had not instituted the "essential conditions" of rational speech, and so the speech that emanated from it was bound to be irrational.[198] His critique of the Assembly was thus procedural and did not bring into question the very viability of popular government. In effect, he had transferred his prerevolutionary ideal of publicity into the revolutionary situation; for under the Old Regime he had accepted royal sovereignty but had tried to supplement it with a public sphere grounded in a free press and enlightened discussion. He now accepted the sovereignty of the Assembly, but he also wished to impose a set of ideal speech conditions on its deliberations.

Morellet's greatest mistake in these early days of the Revolution was to fail to grasp that the revolutionary leaders had promulgated an absolute rupture in time. In abolishing the "feudal system," the Assembly had not merely aimed to eliminate certain abuses inherited from the past; it sought to nullify the past as a whole and to give meaningful history only one horizon, that extending into the future.[199] The character of revolutionary authority was inherently creative, rather than preservative, because the revolutionaries believed that they were regenerating a world in a state of total corruption. From August of 1789 onward, the liberal argument that a law should not have a retroactive effect carried no weight, for revolutionary culture was founded on the aspiration to dissolve the whole relationship between the individual and the state that had existed under the *ancien régime*. The idea that the state could not violate a right that it had previously granted was meaningless now, because it implied a continuity of trust between the absolutist government and the revolutionary government. This notion of a continuing trust was incompatible with the very idea of revolution.

At the end of *Réflexions du lendemain*, Morellet naively affirmed that most "reasonable and educated" people opposed the decrees of August 11. He observed that because such people "shape public opinion in the long run," the Assembly would eventually revoke its decrees.[200] But this energetic faith in the public sphere dissolved in the wake of ensuing events. In November, the Assembly decreed the confiscation of all ecclesiastical property. In June

[197] Ibid., 84.

[198] Ibid., 97.

[199] On the radical temporal aspects of early revolutionary ideology, see François Furet, "Ancien Régime," and Mona Ozouf, "Regeneration," in François Furet and Mona Ozouf, eds., *A Critical Dictionary of the French Revolution* (Cambridge, Mass., 1989), 604–15 and 781–91, respectively. See also Lynn Hunt, "The 'National Assembly'," in Keith Michael Baker, ed., *The French Revolution and the Creation of Modern Political Culture*, vol. 1, 403–18.

[200] Morellet, *Réflexions du lendemain*, 97.

of 1790, Morellet witnessed with anger the auction of his home in Thimert. He had just repaired it with the intention of retiring there, but he had never been able to enjoy it.[201] In the following months, all of his state pensions were terminated, although the National Assembly granted him a small pension in compensation for his losses. He continued to live in Paris, confident that his achievements as a reformer in the prerevolutionary period could vindicate him against any personal attacks. In 1791 and 1792 he busied himself defending the Académie Française against Sébastien Chamfort, who denounced the Académie and called for its abolition..[202] Marmontel, who had been the Permanent Secretary of the Académie since d'Alembert's death in 1783, fled to Normandy just before the uprising of August 10, 1792, which led to the abolition of the monarchy and the formation of a republic. Morellet became the Acting Secretary of the Académie in the new republic. In August 1793, the assembly, now called the National Convention, abolished the Académie. A special decree also ordered that all signs of royalty and corporate distinction were to be removed from the Louvre, where the Académie met. Morellet stored the portraits of the academicians in a locked room in the palace. The charter of the Académie and the minutes of its meetings from 1673 to 1793 he took home.[203]

During the Reign of Terror of 1793–94, when all priests and aristocrats were suspected of being counterrevolutionaries, Morellet lived alone in the faubourg Saint-Honoré, where he found himself surrounded by the daily ceremonies of execution.

> I could not go onto the Champs-Elysées in the afternoon without hearing the cries of a wild people applauding the falling of heads. If I went out along the street of my faubourg in the direction of the city, I saw the same people running en masse to the Place de la Révolution to feast its eyes on the spectacle. And sometimes I encountered, without being able to avoid them, the fatal carts [carrying the victims].[204]

In the summer of 1793, the beginning of the Reign of Terror, when "they executed few prisoners in a single day, and there were intervals in between," Morellet continued to feel safe.[205] The Convention had decreed that no one could collect a state pension without obtaining a certificate of patriotism

[201] Morellet, *Mémoires*, 300.

[202] Morellet's principal publication in this struggle was *De l'Académie Française, ou réponse à l'écrit de M. de Chamfort, qui a pour titre, Des Académies* (Paris, 1791), reprinted in Morellet's *Mélanges*, 1:116–227.

[203] Charles Nisard published a set of documents concerning the abolition of the Académie and Morellet's efforts to save its papers in "Portefeuille d'un Académician du XVIIIe siècle: Suppression des académies," *Revue Contemporaine*, 26 (1856):225–52. See also Morellet, *Mémoires*, 336ff.

[204] Morellet, *Mémoires*, 374.

[205] Ibid., 372.

(*certificat de civisme*). Morellet presented himself as a candidate for a certificate to the Commune, the revolutionary government of Paris, in July. "As a man of letters constantly occupied with useful works, and a zealous defender of all types of liberty compatible with public order in a good government, I was then unconcerned about the success of my application, of which I soon understood the danger."[206] Morellet encountered several delays, and by the time his case was heard, the Law of Suspects of September 17 was in effect. This raised the stakes of his application enormously, for under Article 3 of the law, those who sought and failed to obtain a certificate were to be arrested as enemies of the Revolution.[207]

Because Morellet was a priest and had been a member of the Académie Française, the President of the Commune appointed three citizens to examine him separately. In his memoirs, Morellet described in detail the "bizarre adventure" that followed.[208] On September 18, he met with the first examiner, a hairdresser named Vialard. Morellet took along a large sack containing the works he had composed before the Revolution. When he began to explain his views on free trade and freedom of the press before 1789, Vialard cut him off. "What you are showing me has nothing to do with the matter at hand. You must demonstrate your patriotism [*civisme*] during the days of August 10 and May 31, and none of this proves anything. Really, we know very well that some men of letters had some fairly decent sentiments hitherto and long ago; but none of them has shown himself of late, and all academicians are enemies of the republic."[209] Morellet now grasped the temporal rupture that made the Revolution so radical: no matter how enlightened he thought he had been before the Revolution, his interrogator considered his intellectual contributions to be a part of the *ancien régime*. What counted was the timing of his activity, not its content. Vialard made it clear that one could be a patriot only after the Revolution. The litmus test was where one had been and what one had done on the days of the great popular uprisings. For Vialard, those were August 10, 1792, when a mob attacked the Tuileries and forced the National Assembly to suspend the king's powers, and May 31, 1793, when an insurrectionary crowd of extremists forced the Convention to arrest the moderate Girondin deputies.

Morellet's second examiner, a former priest named Bernard, also responded to Morellet's disquisition on his prerevolutionary writings with

---

[206] Ibid., 340–41.

[207] "The Law of Suspects" can be found most conveniently in Keith Michael Baker, ed., *The Old Regime and the French Revolution* (Chicago, 1987), 353–54; and in John Hall Stewart, ed., *A Documentary Survey of the French Revolution* (New York, 1951), 477–79.

[208] Morellet. *Mémoires*, 339–65. Robert Darnton has also described this episode in Darnton, *Gens de lettres, gens du livre*, 146–49

[209] Morellet, *Mémoires*, 349.

"that terrible argument that I had not demonstrated my patriotism on August 10, September 2 [the prison massacres in Paris, 1792], and May 31; upon which it will be observed that he was more demanding of proofs of patriotism than his colleague Vialard, who had not mentioned September 2."[210] The third examiner was Pâris, a professor of languages and literature. Morellet assumed that he had found a friend when Pâris praised his writings and did not ask him if he had fought with the people in the revolutionary *journées*. But when Morellet expressed his horror for the arbitrary executions that had begun to escalate, Pâris became afraid that the conversation would make himself suspect, and he offered Morellet no support. Seeing that even men of learning spoke the language of "political expediency and fear," Morellet believed that he was doomed.

In the end, he was saved by the Commune's decision, on September 21, to consider more closely everyone who had already received a certificate.[211] The Commune refused to deal with new applicants until the old ones had been reviewed. This meant that Morellet could not collect his pension, but it also meant that he did not have to be judged.

After this episode, Morellet feared for his life. He rarely left his home. He slept badly every night, "believing that I saw or heard a man who wanted to arrest or assassinate me."[212] On July 15, 1794, less than two weeks before Robespierre's downfall, a woman whom Morellet had employed to wash his clothes denounced him in the revolutionary committee of his neighborhood. That evening, the committee ordered him to appear immediately. Morellet reported at ten o'clock at night and found that the committee consisted of a group of artisans, most of whom he had never seen before. The interrogation began.

> "What is your name? — André Morellet. — How old are you? — Sixty-seven years. — Where are you from? — From Lyons." One of these men corrected me: "From Commune-Affranchie." I repeated, "from Commune-Affranchie." They had just changed this unfortunate town's name, after cutting the throats of five or six thousand people and reducing it to rubble.[213]

The committee then questioned Morellet about his profession. He emphasized that he had never been a practicing clergyman. He was a man of letters who had supported freedom under the Old Regime. The next question was, "What were you doing in 1789?" Morellet answered that he attended meetings of the Académie Française and wrote pamphlets in defense of freedom.

[210] Ibid., 253–54.

[211] Ibid., 358.

[212] Ibid., 378.

[213] Ibid., 382. Lyons was the site of resistance against the National Convention in the summer and autumn of 1793. Massive executions and destruction of property took place after the forces of the Convention captured the city on October 9.

"Where were you August 10?" Morellet stated that he was visiting friends outside of Paris and had returned the next day. "I saw that this answer did not displease them, and that they gave me some credit for returning to Paris on August 11, when everyone else was trying to get out." A few more questions followed and "then my interrogation became more strange."

> "Why," they asked me, "were you gay before August 10, and why have you been sad since?"

This question probably reflected the suspicions of Morellet's former washer-woman. She had denounced him because he was not happy!

> "Citizens," I answered, "I do not think I have been either gay or sad." "I have," I added, trying to appear as grave as I could, "I have a serious character, as befits a man of my age."[214]

Morellet adroitly evaded several more questions and managed to emphasize his old age. After a short deliberation, the committee declared that he was not a counterrevolutionary.

Through this episode and the previous one in the Commune, Morellet encountered a form of communication that he had not envisioned before. Under the absolute monarchy, he had criticized the government for relying too much on bureaucratic memoranda. He had called for open discussion, believing that a civilized public sphere, resembling a vast salon, would emerge. Revolutionary political culture, however, was grounded in the substantive ideal of *civisme*, not the formal ideal of *civilité*. Virtuous deeds, not polite manners, were important. Direct action meant more than words, or more precisely, language became a mode of direct action in a way it had not been in the Enlightenment. In the system of denunciations and interrogations of the Revolution, language became a means of imposing a public identity on others so as to justify their annihilation. Even in his slander of Robecq and Galiani, Morellet had not wielded a weapon for directly inflicting harm on someone else's person. Moreover, Morellet's polemical excess was checked, first by the government that sent him to the Bastille, then by Diderot and Grimm who rebuked him for violating the norms of sociability. In the Revolution, in contrast, even false denunciations were not deemed irresponsible, for violent language, whether it was true language or not, was a means of proving one's own patriotism. Jean-Paul Marat, the Revolution's great theorist of denunciation, repeatedly declared in his journals that it was the duty of every citizen to publicly denounce the enemies of the Revolution. He affirmed that those who denounced others falsely were not guilty of a crime so long as their accusations stemmed from virtuous intentions. In his journal, *L'Ami du peuple*, Marat wrote:

---

[214] Ibid., 383–84.

Every corroborated denunciation will be a title of public esteem. A false denunciation that is made out of love of the *patrie* will not make its author liable for punishment, for man is not infallible and an error does not make him a criminal.

In an article in another journal, *Le Junius français*, he declared: "If your denunciations are true, the esteem of your compatriots will be your reward. If your denunciations are not true, you will pass as a visionary."[215]

The democratic revolution thus generated an attitude toward communication that was the opposite of the one Morellet had articulated in *Réflexions sur les avantages de la liberté d'écrire et d'imprimer* and *De L'Esprit de contradiction*. He had imagined that the vigorous exercise of discourse, moderated by a voluntarily adopted set of good manners, would lead to the collective creation of sound administrative principles. But in the Revolution, the truth of the ideal of equality, the value of the popular insurrections of the previous months, was always already established. The purpose of speech was not to create truth but to prove to others that one identified with it, or that others did not. With the truth defined in advance, politeness could be nothing but a superfluous ornament to language, and language itself could only be a tool of didacticism and denunciation.

These formulations, of course, are mine, not Morellet's. Yet they are filtered through Morellet's prerevolutionary ideals and postrevolutionary experience, and they help to explain how his thought developed after 1789. Morellet's ideas on freedom of the press and public opinion went through a number of contortions after *Réflexions du lendemain*, the pamphlet of 1789 in which he offered the hope that "public opinion" would overturn the decrees of August 11. He never repudiated the ideal of publicity entirely, but he ceased to view it as the motor of progress. At the beginning of 1790, Morellet believed that some radical journalists, by slandering the nobles and urban officials of the provinces of Limousin and Angoumis, were inciting popular acts of violence in the region. In a pamphlet in which he defended the large property owners, he wrote:

One should always seize the quickest and most efficacious means of publishing and spreading the truth, denouncing oppression, and avenging innocence; but it must be a proven truth, a demonstrated oppression, a recognized innocence.[216]

---

[215] These quotations come, respectively, from Marat's journals, *L'Ami du peuple*, no. 37, 13 November 1789, and *Le Junius français*, no. 12, 23 June 1790. See Jean-Paul Marat, *Oeuvres politiques* (Brussels, 1989), 1:296–97 and 2:941. See also "Système de dénonciation ou de surveillance, 1789–1793," in Alfred Bougeart, *Marat, l'ami du peuple* (Paris, 1865), 255–78. The theory and practice of denunciation was also discussed by Jacques Guilhaumou in his paper, "Fragments d'un discours de dénonciation (1789–1794)," at the conference "The Terror in the French Revolution," Stanford University, December 10–13, 1992.

[216] Morellet, *Mémoire des députés de la ville de Tulle, relatif aux troubles du bas-Limousin* (Paris, 1790), reprinted among the *pièces justificatives* appended to the 1822 edition of Morellet's

This assertion is reasonable in itself, but it contradicts his previous conception of publicity. Now he was saying that one should publicize only established truths, whereas before the Revolution he had argued that publicity
itself was the space in which true propositions became established through
unlimited debate. He had argued that the defenders of truth would sharpen
their formulations in response to their adversaries—the more vigorous the
debate, the more the truth would stand out in relief. Now he was aware that
falsehoods could have an immediate effect on a situation and could stimulate violence even before the defenders of truth had a chance to respond.
Morellet was particularly concerned about the potency of popular journalism. He distinguished the book, an instrument of enlightenment, from the
periodical press, a pernicious instrument for arousing the rabble:

> A calumny disseminated in an ordinary book can only spread slowly. . . . One
> has some time to foresee its effects or to defend against them; and by repudiat-
> ing it in a printed work, one can combat it with an equal weapon. But how can
> one defend oneself against a calumnious charge received in a single morning by
> ten thousand people, and transmitted in the day to twenty or forty thousand
> others? Is there any means of undeceiving men who are eager to believe bad
> news, whose ears are always open to calumny, and who are bored by any
> suggestion of a response, defense, or apology?[217]

Morellet urged the nation to find "some remedy" to the abuse of freedom of
the press, but he did not say what that remedy was.

He did not again address the issue of freedom of communication until
1796, when Marie-Joseph Chénier proposed to the Convention that it
impose strict limits on all aspects of cultural life. Chénier was an artist-
politician who believed that intellectuals should serve nothing but the republican state. He had launched his career in 1789 with *Charles IX*, a play
vilifying the monarch and clergy. He had been on the commission that
issued the revolutionary calendar in October 1793. And he had been one of
the principal organizers of the Festival of the Supreme Being of June 8,
1794, which celebrated the Revolution's new civil religion, its cult of itself.
As a member of the Committee of General Security after the fall of Robespierre, Chénier delivered a series of reports to the National Convention
between April 10 and May 13, 1795, on the need to impose severe measures
against "that vast conspiracy extending from one end of the republic to the
other." Chénier's speeches show that paranoia and draconian measures to
"save" the republic did not die with Robespierre. The imaginary conspiracy

---

Mémoires sur le dix-huitième siècle et sur la Révolution (Paris, 1822), 2:383 (not appended in the
1988 edition of the *Mémoires* that I have cited throughout this chapter). Morellet composed
this pamphlet upon the request of a some deputies from the provinces of Tulle and Limousin;
see Morellet, *Mémoires* (1988 edition), 305–6.
    217 Morellet, *Mémoire des députés*, 384.

that Chénier denounced was an unlikely combination of royalists and supporters of Robespierre who were undermining the Revolution through "unpatriotic writings [*écrits inciviques*] the sole aim of which is the defamation of the representatives of the people."[218] Chénier's proposed decrees, which the Convention immediately ratified, included two articles that elicited a response from Morellet. Article 4 ordered the arrest of all writers who criticized the Convention. Article 7 ordered the Committee on Public Instruction "to direct the schools, the theaters, and generally all the arts and sciences toward the exclusive goal of the National Convention: that of consolidating the Republic."[219]

The day after Chénier proposed these edicts, Morellet wrote a pamphlet, *Pensées libres sur la liberté de la presse* (Free Thoughts on Freedom of the Press). He argued that "public reports" given in the Convention, by virtue of the fact that they pertained to "public affairs," were appropriate subjects for criticism in the press. As for Article 7, he asked, "Will anatomists be forced to discover some essential difference between the brain of an aristocrat and the brain of a republican? Will doctors only cure patients who have certificates of patriotism?" Morellet drew a line between culture and politics:

> We must observe that every science and art has a goal that is particular to it and that has only a remote and accidental relation to government. . . . The fine arts can, it is true, be partly directed in some circumstances toward a political end; but since they also share an immediate and primary goal, imitation, and since the moral goal toward which they tend is absolutely distinct from that purely political goal toward which Chénier wants them to be directed, it is patently ridiculous to want them to be directed *exclusively* in that way.[220]

Morellet's pamphlet had no effect but to arouse the scorn of Chénier, who ridiculed him in a speech the following year by referring to him as a member of the class of "old slaves," "pensioned abbés," and "men formerly subsidized by tyranny."[221]

When Morellet had originally formulated his doctrine of freedom of the press, he had never envisaged that the written word would have to compete against the spoken. He had imagined a "public" whose discussions revolved around the ideas of authors, just as conversation unfolded in a salon. But the

[218] Marie-Joseph Chénier, *Rapport sur le désarmament des pré-thermidoristes*, 10 April, 1795, in Chénier, *Oeuvres de M.-J. Chénier* (Paris, 1826), 5:213–14.

[219] Chénier, *Rapport sur la situation de la République*, 1 May 1795, in Chénier, *Oeuvres*, 5:231–32. For the discussion and ratification of the decrees in the Convention, see *Réimpression de l'ancien Moniteur* (Paris, 1854), 24:360–61.

[220] Morellet, *Pensées libres sur la liberté de la presse* (1795), reprinted among *pièces justificatives* in Morellet's *Mémoires* (1822 edition, see note 216), 494, 495–96 (Morellet's emphasis).

[221] Chénier, *"Discours en faveur d'une loi prohibitive de la presse,"* 17 March 1796, in *Oeuvres*, 5:337–38.

dramatic oratorical proceedings of the revolutionary assemblies had scripts of their own, scripts that liberal men of letters had not written. The issue of freedom of the press was becoming ever more complex for Morellet. He had started with the position that complete liberty was the surest guarantee of political rationality. In 1789, he saw that his own writings in defense of property failed to slow down the dismantling of the old order—free discussion did not yield enlightenment. In 1790, he saw that radical journalists could take advantage of a free press to incite hatred and violence—free discussion was abused by fraudulent manipulators. In the Terror, he saw that democrats could stifle the press in the name of liberty, and after the fall of Robespierre, he saw that the fear of a resurgence of terror made the revolutionaries even more eager than Robespierre had been to control all forms of discourse.

In his memoirs, Morellet acknowledged that under the absolute monarchy he had possessed excessive confidence in the inherent benefits of open communication and that the French people had not been mature enough in 1789 to engage in "slow and deliberate discussion." He now admitted that even truth should be kept secret sometimes. "A great truth, no matter how incontestable, no matter how useful, can be such that it must not be spoken to a certain people, in a certain moment, without any preparation." But Morellet also tried to explain that neither he nor the other *philosophes* were responsible for the abuse of freedom in the Revolution. They had never believed that "it is permitted to say everything all at once, suddenly, and in any way possible."[222] What exactly did they believe? Morellet did not say. Though he would not admit it, the *philosophes* had been more concerned with breaking down the barriers to full publicity than theorizing about the necessary restrictions on free communication. They had seen defamation as a threat to sociability, and as Diderot's response to Morellet's *Réfutation* shows, they had personally taken measures to counteract it. But because they had not imagined that slander could engender violence on a large scale, they had not considered it a serious legal issue. Morellet himself had advocated complete freedom and had not discussed the need for limits at all. It was disingenuous of him to suggest otherwise. Most importantly, even with the advantages of hindsight, he was unable to formulate with any precision the proper limits on freedom of communication. His discussion of the issue in the memoirs is lengthy but vague. He decries "horrible excess,"[223] yet offers no formulation of the middle ground between too much freedom and too little.

As his confidence in the public sphere dissolved into confusion, Morellet invested his faith entirely in the concept of private property. The concept

---

[222] Morellet, *Mémoires* (1988 edition), 139–41.
[223] Ibid., 141.

was not new to him, but it took on a new status. Before the Revolution, he had invoked the "sacred" right of property as one of several reasons to support free trade. After the Revolution, property became the linchpin of his philosophy. Disenchanted with sociability, the interaction between man and man, Morellet redefined the individual in terms of ownership, the interaction between man and things. Whereas before he had grounded the public sphere in the human faculty of communication, he now declared that "political rights" stemmed from property alone. The Revolution was doomed from the start, he affirmed in his memoirs, because the abbé Sieyès and other writers had convinced the public that humans were mere "numerical units," interchangeable with each other. This view, Morellet pointed out, was the basis of democracy and entailed government by the will of the majority instead of government by property owners. Morellet himself had taken the numerical view of humanity in 1788, when he advocated voting by head rather than by order. Yet in his memoirs he declared, "the right to constitute and reform government belongs exclusively to proprietors . . . and these principles have always been mine."[224]

Morellet developed his new theory of proprietary politics in the *Traité de la propriété de l'homme sur les choses* (Treatise on Man's Ownership of Things), a projected magnum opus that he started in 1790 and never completed.[225] Here he attempted to systematize Locke's idea that men had acquired property through their labor before the formation of government. In numerous passages resembling the following, he insisted that man's relationship to things was "anterior" to society.

> Now, anterior to the formation of regular societies [*sociétés régulières*], in which property is transmitted in various ways, such as succession, donation, sale, etc., a relation was established between each individual and the natural objects to which he applied his labor and on which he exercised his faculties. . . . When he gathered the fruit, when he killed the animal, from this was manifestly born between the man and the object satisfying his needs a relation that did not exist between other men and the same objects.[226]

This exclusive possession, according to Morellet, was the foundation of an individual's property right, a right that could not be taken away by the government, for "sovereignty is given to the sovereign with conditions, and property to the proprietor, without conditions." Democracy was an enemy of property because "it naturally tends to move toward equality through the spoliation of property owners."[227] What is most striking about this text in

---

[224] Ibid., 276, 290–91.
[225] The text is now available in André Morellet, *Traité de la propriété e il carteggio con Bentham e Dumont*, ed. Eugenio Di Rienzo and Lea Campos Boralevi (Florence, 1990), 3–97.
[226] Ibid., 20–21.
[227] Ibid., 5.

relation to Morellet's previous philosophy is that society, which formerly represented a site of growing rationality through exchange, now represented a threat to reason. "We have heard much in books about the liberty of social man [*l'homme social*] and not enough about property."[228] Under the absolute monarchy, he had embedded justice in civil society; he now sought to extricate it.

> In considering with some attention the numerous and sustained violations against property throughout the whole civilized world [*le monde civilisé*], I have drawn the conclusion that they are the fatal result of a profound misunderstanding of the true origins and principles of private property.[229]

. . . . .

> I have demonstrated that the right of property was a direct consequence of man's use of his personal powers and faculties, of which the free use is anterior to any relation with his fellows; from which it obviously follows that his right to things belongs to him independently of these relations in society [*société*] with other men.[230]

It is important to add that terms such as "social," "civilized," and "society" do not have exactly the same meaning here as they had for Morellet and other philosophers of sociability before 1789. "Society" had meant exchange in the private sphere. Even "public opinion" emanated from the exercise of reason by *private* persons. The revolutionaries had a more political conception of the individual, hence a more political conception of "society." For them, as for Rousseau, "society," or "civil society," was a synonym for "state" or "polity," the entity brought into being by a contract among citizens. The revolutionaries argued that the formation of "society" was prior to the creation of laws instituting private property. "Society" was thus anterior to property and could place limits upon it to suit its need.[231]

In defending property, Morellet was repudiating the Revolution's statist concept of society, not his own concept of society as the site of private sociability. But as property became his key idea, the language of sociability

---

[228] Ibid., 10.

[229] Ibid., 5.

[230] Ibid., 25.

[231] Although the French Revolution is sometimes seen as a "bourgeois" effort to sanctify private property, the principle of private property was subordinate to the principle of economic and political equality to most of the revolutionaries, even in the years 1789–91 that allegedly constituted the Revolution's liberal phase. See Marcel Gauchet, *La Révolution des droits de l'homme* (Paris, 1989), especially 211–16, and Eugenio di Rienzo's introduction to Morellet's *Traité de la propriété*, especially xxxv–li. Morellet himself quoted several revealing passages from the revolutionaries' speeches that show how the revolutionaries considered property to be a conditional concession made to the individual by "society" (see especially 7–8).

disappeared, for that language was simply not well suited to protect property against a democratic government. Although it was a *nonrevolutionary* language that idealized civility rather than citizenship, polite exchange rather than political activism, it was not an effective *antirevolutionary* language. It was designed primarily to idealize the private liberty that absolutist sovereignty allowed, not to criticize the public liberty that democratic sovereignty abused. The ideal of sociability, in other words, did not provide the tools Morellet needed to criticize a hyperpoliticized people. In the *Traité de la propriété*, Morellet adopted the more political conception of "society" popularized by the revolutionaries, but only to criticize it, to establish that something was "anterior" to democracy. *Sociabilité*, then, got lost in the rhetorical shuffle through which he adopted a new idiom to counteract the idiom of popular sovereignty.

In this new era in which bourgeois liberalism squared off against democratic statism, there was no philosophical space for the ideal of politeness broadly conceived; in the struggle between *propriété* and *souveraineté*, there was no ideological room for *le commerce du monde*. This is not to say that conversation, manners, and their institutional model, the salon, dropped out of French life, but only that they lost their universal significance. Under the Napoleonic regime, Morellet himself, once again in favor and enjoying an Indian summer as a member of the Institut de France and the Corps Législatif, tried to revivify the spirit of sociability in his own home. "The salons of the abbé Morellet," wrote Lémontey in 1822, "were perhaps the last example of those meetings, so splendid in the previous century, where the distinction of ranks gave way to the pleasure of company and enlightenment, where good taste was the sole law, and *le bon esprit* the only authority."[232] But the nineteenth-century salon could only be a feeble imitation of its predecessor. Revolutionary violence ruined the myth that politeness was modernity's essence and that France was the most sociable nation in the world. After the Revolution, a salon could still entertain its guests, but they could not entertain *it* as the imaginary center of a "civilized society." Though Morellet's was not the last philosophic salon, the institution did decline in the first half of the nineteenth century.[233] At the same time, intellectuals living in a chronically unstable regime no longer found it meaningful to see themselves as urbane *gens du monde*. A new age of recurrent revolution produced a more violent, incisive, and profound literature than the generation of Morellet and Suard. The ideal of sociability endured only in the topography of memory. It ceased to be a living philosophy and became a heritage, an idealized site of nostalgia for conservatives and liberals in moments when they grew tired of ideological conflict and sought refuge

---

[232] Editor's note in Morellet, *Mémoires* (1822 edition), 2:268.

[233] Maurice Agulhon, *Le Cercle dans la France bourgeoise, 1810–1848: Etude d'une mutation de sociabilité* (Paris, 1977).

in a world in which politics was not primary. Morellet's memoirs are one example. There are many others, such as Pierre Roederer's *Histoire de la société polie* (History of Polite Society, 1835), Victor Cousin's *La Société française au XVIIe siècle* (French Society in the Seventeenth Century, 1858), and Charles-Augustin Sainte-Beuve's *Causeries du lundi* (Monday Chats, a weekly column, 1849–61). "Happy time!" Sainte-Beuve exclaimed. "When life as a whole revolved around *sociabilité*; when everything was arranged for the sweetest commerce of the mind and the best conversation."[234] In the nineteenth century, French intellectuals continued to adore the women of the salons, the "art of conversation," and the *philosophes*, but only to avoid present reality. The Age of Sociability was not forgotten—but it was over.

---

[234] Charles-Augustin Sainte-Beuve, "Lettres de Mademoiselle de Lespinasse," in *Causeries du lundi*, 3d ed. (Paris, 1862), 2:125. For discussion of other authors' nostalgia for prerevolutionary sociability, see Marc Fumaroli, "La Conversation," in Pierre Nora, ed., *Les Lieux de mémoire*, vol. 3, pt. 2, *Les Frances, Traditions* (Paris, 1992), 678–743.

CONCLUSION

ACCORDING TO DURKHEIM, a community "is not made up merely of the mass of individuals who compose it, the ground which they occupy, the things which they use, and the movements which they perform, but above all is the idea which it forms of itself."[1] As a warning against a materialist approach to history, this observation has the merit of emphasizing that identity stems not from the motions of behavior but from the categories of self-definition. Its weakness, however, is to imply that these categories are generally stable and uniform within a community. Since the Reformation, Western history has experienced not only constant cultural change but also constant fragmentation of the collective consciousness. That is, not only particular images of community but the very possibility of a shared image of collective life became problematic through the rise of criticism and the validation of diversity in the early-modern period. We have long passed the hope of revivifying a common creed, and the only question that remains is this: In spite of our differences, is dialogue possible?

As an ideal that was designed from the start to constitute areas of mutual accommodation among diverse individuals, sociability emerged in the early-modern period as one of the few possible ways of imagining a stable system of exchange among liberated subjects. In Chapter 1, I presented a series of ideal types to highlight the meaning of sociability as a bond among equal individuals—a system of coordination for people who had stepped outside of the hierarchy of estates in search of less ontologically grounded forms of interaction; in search of roles not dictated by the great chain of being. In Chapters 2 and 3, I examined the rules of sociability as found in courtesy literature and the ways in which these rules functioned as the imaginary basis of an idealized space called *société*. The territory of *société* became a refuge that allowed authors to avoid a series of stark choices. These were the choices between the absolutist idea of sovereignty and the democratic idea of freedom, between the model of selfish Economic Man and the model of the selfless hero, between nationalist chauvinism and Catholic universalism. Like all ideas that manage to become widespread and to infiltrate a variety of genres of speculation, the idea of sociability was a single alternative to many different dilemmas.

Chapters 4 and 5 dealt with the processes through which the idea of

[1] Emile Durkheim, *The Elementary Forms of the Religious Life* (New York, 1965), 470.

sociability was integrated into schemes of universal history and visions of a growing rationality in the public sphere. When authors portrayed sociability not only as a set of polite and moral rules but also as a fact, a general feature of France as a "modern" country, a peculiar utopianism took root. The norms of civil conversation became the historical trend of "civilization." And on the basis of this presumed trend toward peace, reciprocity, and rationality, the political was theoretically subsumed by the sociable. The culmination of this reductionism was the idea of "public opinion," for "public opinion" signified the belief that individuals, merely by cultivating themselves through urbane communication, could establish order and good policy. The discretionary decisions of the monarch were supposed to give way to the consensual outcomes of debate, stimulated by men of letters and moderated by the nation's own penchant for politeness.

To those advocates of the sociable spirit who survived into the revolutionary years, it became clear that violent conflict was not just a characteristic of life in the "barbarous" Middle Ages but was also an inherent part of modern democracy. In a sense, the instability and terrors that ensued after 1789 vindicated the philosophy of sociability by showing that a rival philosophy, republicanism, was full of dangers when put into practice. But the explosion of republican energy in 1789 was itself inexplicable within the "progress-of-society" scheme of universal history invented by the Scots and taken over by liberal advocates of sociability in France. To Morellet, the Revolution also showed that polite men of letters, practicing the urbane modes of argumentation typical of the late Enlightenment, could not influence "public opinion" in a climate of denunciation and populist hatred of all elites.

What inspirational value the ideal of sociability retains today can only be a matter of opinion. The distinguished historian of French classicism, Marc Fumaroli, has eloquently described the ideal of sociable communication as a great heritage to be cherished and cultivated.[2] Richard Sennet and Jürgen Habermas have partly formulated their criticisms of Western capitalism by comparing it to the polite ideals of the eighteenth century.[3] It strikes me, however, that the spirit of sociability is at odds with modern culture in a variety of ways that militate against any effort to revive it on the scale envisioned in prerevolutionary Europe. Society, in other words, is dead.

First, as the Revolution showed, there is a competitive spirit in democracies, a voracious pursuit of power, and a degeneration of language that render absurd the Enlightenment belief that free communication is enough

---

[2] Marc Fumaroli, "La Conversation," in Pierre Nora, ed., *Les Lieux de mémoire*, pt. 3, vol. 2, *Les France: Traditions* (Paris, 1992), 678–743. See especially the conclusions on 739.

[3] Richard Sennet, *The Fall of Public Man: On the Social Psychology of Capitalism* (New York, 1978); Jürgen Habermas, *The Structural Transformation of the Public Sphere: An Inquiry into a Category of Bourgeois Society* (Cambridge, 1989).

to constitute and temper authority. It is more important to devise legal and institutional checks against power than to sustain the illusion that power can be eliminated by transferring the functions of the state to the idealized workings of an imaginary public. Second, the proliferation of nondialogical forms of communication, such as television, concerts, and films, inevitably leads to the parceling of consciousness and creates a taste for intense and novel stimulation via the media, rather than a taste for urbane discussion of the kind that sustained the salons of the Enlightenment. Moreover, the sheer volume of cultural goods being produced has a similar effect of fracturing the ideal of a learned public into scholarly communities of individuals who are not learned but merely knowledgeable about specific things and isolated from the nonscholarly masses.

One could argue that without Enlightenment norms we would never be able to think critically about these trends. Yesterday's ideals cannot be today's ideals, but they can be today's ideal types by means of which we attain a perspective on our own environment. It is true that the juxtaposition of past ideals and present realities is one of the most effective ways of stimulating acute insights into our surroundings. But the capacity of an ideal to suggest an interesting critique of the world is not a sufficient reason to try to reform the world in accordance with the ideal (as opposed to maintaining the world, which does after all already include the ideal within it, albeit only as a form of critical reflection).

A great problem inevitably emerges when one tries to deploy the history of philosophy in order to formulate a practical critique of the world. This problem is the overabundance of critical vantage points that historical understanding inevitably affords whenever it is not subordinated to political ends. Habermas's book, *The Structural Transformation of the Public Sphere*, is philosophically the most rich account of Western ideals of communication and their relationship to the concepts of privacy and publicity. But even this work has one shortcoming that is perhaps typical of works that evoke the past in order to criticize the present situation: its meaning is contingent on the idea of universal history. The two key features of universal history are the organization of all "significant" cultures into a continuous story, and the characterization of each culture or phase of history in terms of an essential unity or spirit of the age. In *The Structural Transformation*, each period—antiquity, the Middle Ages, absolutism, modernity—seems to embody only one ideal of the relationship between private and public life. Habermas streamlines history in this way so as to be able to formally ground his critical theory in something other than his own preferences, namely, modernity's self-idealization, which, he suggests, first emerged in the Enlightenment. The Enlightenment, for Habermas, thus represents the normative content of present-day culture. It is the "immanent" standard against which its actual performances can be compared.

But the Enlightenment was not a single philosophy. As this study suggests, ideals of sociability took on their meaning not as the expression of the unified aspirations of the age but in competition with other ideologies. We must also not forget about the formation of rival philosophies after the Enlightenment. The Romantics, for example, underscored the limitations of sociability as a mode of being. From them we may learn that some truths are not to be had through exchange but come only through solitary introspection and from an imagination liberated from existing communicative standards.

Once we recognize the presence of distinct modes of thought in the Enlightenment and beyond, it is hard to see why any one of them should be taken as a standard for the present. If history were like a single person, then we might be able to measure its institutions by its concurrent normative declarations, just as we compare a person's deeds to his or her avowed convictions. But history is a horde. Even the canonical thinkers of the past three centuries are a multitude of warring gods. To invoke an eighteenth-century philosophy in order to decry a current institution can only be an act of poetic comparison, not an objective evaluation. We who are intrigued by the ideas of bygone ages will always live poetically to some degree, but we are obliged to respect those who are not so intrigued, or who are intrigued in a different way. This civility is the one sure truth.

SELECT BIBLIOGRAPHY

MANUSCRIPTS

The Papers of William Robertson. National Library of Scotland, mss. 3942:73–273; 3943:258–59; 3944:34–41.

Letters between Amélie Suard and Marie-Jean-Antoine-Nicolas, marquis de Condorcet. Bibliothèque Nationale, ms. (Nouvelles Acquisitions françaises) 23639:1–223.

Letters of Jean-Baptiste Suard to various persons. Bibliothèque Nationale, mss. (Nouvelles Acquisitions françaises) 10844:1–70; 16814:253–62.

PRINTED SOURCES

Alemand, Louis-Augustin. *Nouvelles observations, ou guerre civile des français sur la langue*. Paris: J. B. Langlois, 1688.

Alembert, Jean d'. *Eloges lus dans les séances publiques de l'Académie Française*, 6 vols. Paris: Panckoucke, 1779.

———. *Oeuvres complètes*, 5 vols. Paris: A. Belin, 1822.

———. *Oeuvres et correspondances inédites*, ed. Charles Henry. Paris: Didier, 1887.

Anonymous. *Conduite pour se taire et pour parler, principalement en matière de religion*. Paris: Simon Bénard, 1696.

Anonymous. *L'Homme sociable et lettres philosophiques sur la jeunesse*. London and Paris: J. B. Dessain, 1772.

Anonymous. *Manuel de l'homme du monde*. Paris: Guillyn, 1761.

Anonymous. *Séjour de Paris c'est à dire instructions fidèles pour les voiageurs de condition, comment ils se doivent conduire, s'ils veulent faire un bon usage de leurs temps et argent . . .* Leiden: Chez Jean Van Abcoude, 1727.

Anonymous. *Tablettes de l'homme du monde*. Paris: Chez Auguste le Catholique, 1715.

Archives Parlementaires de 1787 à 1860, 95 vols., ed J. Mavidal and E. Laurent. Paris: Librairie administrative de Paul Dupont, 1862–1919.

Argens, Jean-Baptiste d'. *Lettres juives*, 6 vols. The Hague: P. Paupie, 1738.

Aulnoy, Marie-Catherine le Jumel de Barneville, baronne d'. *Relation du voyage d'Espagne*. Paris: Plon, 1874.

Bachaumont, Louis Petit de. *Mémoires secrets pour servir à l'histoire de la république des lettres*. London: John Adamson, 1780–89.

Bacon, Francis. *Works*, 14 vols. London: Longman, 1861–79.

Badinter, Elisabeth. *Correspondance inédite de Condorcet et Madame Suard, 1771–1791*. Paris: Fayard, 1988.

Balzac, Jean-Louis Guez de. *Les Oeuvres de Monsieur de Balzac*. Paris: T. Jolly, 1665.

Barbier, Edmond Jean François, 4 vols. *Journal historique et anecdotique* Paris: Renouard, 1847–56.

Pierre Bayle, *Nouvelles de la république des lettres* in *Oeuvres diverses*, 5 vols. Hildesheim: Golms, 1964.

Beccaria, Cesar. *Traité des délits et des peines*, trans. André Morellet. Lausanne: n.p., 1766.

Bellegarde, Jean-Baptiste Morvan de. *The Letters of Monsieur l'Abbé de Bellegarde to a Lady of the Court of France on Some Curious and Useful Subjects*. London: Strahan, 1705.

———. *Lettres curieuses de littérature et de morale*. The Hague: Adrian Moetjens, 1702.

———. *Livres moraux de l'Ancien Testament*. Paris: Jean & Michel Guignard, 1701.

———. *Modèles de conversation pour les personnes polies*. Amsterdam: H. Schelte, 1709.

———. *La Morale des ecclésiastiques et des clérics*. Paris: Arnoul Seneaze, 1691.

———. *Pensées édifiantes et Chrétiennes pour tous les jours du mois*. Paris: Jean Barbon, 1715.

———. *Réflexions sur ce qui peut plaire ou déplaire dans le commerce du monde*. Paris: Seneuze, 1690.

———. *Réflexions sur la politesse des moeurs*. Paris: Jean Guignard, 1698.

———. *Réflexions sur l'élégance et la politesse du style*. Paris: A. Pralard, 1695.

———. *Réflexions sur le ridicule et sur les moyens de l'éviter*. Paris: Jean Guignard, 1696.

———. *Sentiments que doit avoir un homme-de-bien sur les vérités de la religion*. Paris: Jean & Michel Guignard, 1704.

———. *Suite de réflexions sur ce qui peut plaire ou déplaire dans le commerce du monde*. Amsterdam: Chez les Héritiers d'Antoine Schelle, 1699.

Bodin, Jean. *The Six Books of the Commonwealth*, ed. M. J. Tooley. New York: Macmillan, 1955.

Bond, Donald F., ed. *The Spectator*, 5 vols. Oxford: Clarendon Press, 1965.

———. *The Tatler*, 3 vols. Oxford: Clarendon Press, 1987.

Bonno, Gabriel, ed. *Correspondance littéraire de Suard avec le Margrave de Bayreuth*. Berkeley: University of California Press, 1934.

———. *Lettres inédites de Suard à Wilkes*. Berkeley: University of California Press, 1932.

Bossuet, Jacques-Bénigne. *Politique tirée des propres paroles de l'Ecriture Sainte*. Geneva: Librairie Droz, 1967.

Bouhours, Dominique. *Remarques nouvelles sur la langue française*. Paris: Mabre-Cramoisy, 1675.

Brosses, P. de. *Grand dictionnaire français-latin*. Lyon: C. Largot, 1625.

Buffier, Claude. *Traité de la société civile et du moyen de se rendre heureux, en contribuant au bonheur des personnes avec qui l'on vit*. Paris: Chez Marc Bordelet, 1726.

Callières, François de. *De la Science du monde et des connaissances utiles à la conduite de la vie*. Paris: Etienne Ganeau, 1717.

———. *Des Mots à la mode et des nouvelles façons de parler*. Paris: Claude Barbin, 1696.

Castiglione, Baldassare. *The Book of the Courtier*. New York: Anchor Books, 1959.

Chalesme [first name unknown]. *L'Homme de qualité, ou les moyens de vivre en homme de bien, et en homme du monde*. Paris: A. Pralard, 1671.

Chateaubriand, François René. *Mémoires d'outre-tombe*, 4 vols., ed. Maurice Levaillant. Paris: Gallimard, 1949.

Chaudon, Louis. *Dictionnaire anti-philosophique*. Avignon: Seguin, 1767.

Chénier, Marie-Jospeh. *Oeuvres de M.-J. Chénier*, 5 vols. Paris: Guillaume, 1826.

Choix de discours de réception à l'Académie française, vol. 2. Paris: Demonville, 1808.

Claville, Claude-François-Nicolas Le Maître de. *Traité du vrai mérite*. Paris: Saugran, 1736.

Correspondance administrative sous Louis XV, ed. G. Depping. Paris: 1851.

Cotgrave, Randle. *Dictionarie of the French and English Tongues* London: A. Islip, 1611.

Courtin, Antoine de. *Nouveau traité de la civilité qui se pratique en France parmi les honnêtes gens*. Paris: H. Josset, 1672.

_____. *Traité de la paresse*. Paris: H. Josset, 1677.

Coyer, Gabriel-François. *Discours sur la satyre contre les philosophes*. Athens: Chez le librairie anti-philosophe, 1760.

_____. *La Noblesse commerçante*. London and Paris: Duchesne, 1756.

Crane, Thomas F., ed. *La Société française au dix-septième siècle*. New York: G. P. Putnams Sons, 1907.

Daire, Eugene, ed. *Physiocrates: Quesnay, Dupont de Nemours, Mercier de la Rivière* . . . Paris: Guillaumin, 1846.

Delamare, Nicolas. *Traité de la police*, 3 vols. Amsterdam: Aux Dépens de la Compagnie, 1729.

Delille, Jacques. *La Conversation*. Paris: Michaud, 1812.

Dictionnaire de l'Académie Française. Paris: Coignard, 1694.

Dictionnaire de l'Académie Française. Paris: Chez les Librairies Associés, 1765.

Dictionnaire de l'Académie Française. Paris: J. J. Smits, 1799.

Dictionnaire universelle français et latin, vulgairement appelé Dictionnaire de Trevoux. Paris: Compagnie des Libraires Associés, 1704.

Dictionnaire universelle français et latin, vulgairement appelé Dictionnaire de Trevoux. Paris: Compagnie des Libraires Associés, 1771.

Diderot, Denis. *Correspondance*, 16 vols., ed. Georges Roth. Paris: Editions de Minuit, 1955–70.

_____. *Lettres à Sophie Volland*, 3 vols., ed. André Babelon. Paris: Gallimard, 1930.

_____. *Oeuvres*, 6 vols. Paris: A. Belin, 1818.

_____. *Oeuvres complètes*. Paris: Garnier, 1875.

_____. *Oeuvres complètes*, 15 vols., ed. Roger Lewinter. Paris: Editions Chronologiques, 1969.

_____. *Oeuvres politiques*, ed. Paul Vernière. Paris: Garnier, 1963.

Dieckmann, Herbert. *Inventaire du Fonds Vandeul et inédits de Diderot*. Geneva: Droz, 1951.

Dinouart, Jospeh Antoine Toussaint. *L'Art de se taire*, ed. Jean-Jacques Courtine and Claudine Haroche. Paris: Jérome Millon, 1987.

Doumic, René, ed. "Lettres d'un philosophe et d'une femme sensible, Condorcet et Mme. Suard." *Revue des Deux Mondes* 5 (1911):302–25, 835–60; 1 (1912):57–81.

Druhen, Maxine, ed. "Mlle de Lespinasse et Suard, correspondence inédite." *Académie des Sciences, Belles-Lettres et Arts de Besançon, Procès-Verbaux et Mémoires* 1927, 1–23.

Duclos, Charles Pineau. *Considérations sur les moeurs*. Paris: n.p., 1751.

Dupont de Nemours, Pierre-Samuel. *De l'Origine et des progrès d'une science nouvelle.* London: Desaint, 1768.

Encyclopédie, ou dictionnaire raisonné des sciences, des arts, et des métiers, par une société de gens de lettres, 17 vols. Paris: Briasson and Neûchatel: Samuel Faulche, 1751–65.

Epinay, Louise-Florence-Pétronville de Lalive d'. *Gli ultimi anni della Signora d'Epinay: Lettere inedite all'abate Galiani,* ed. Fausto Nicolini. Bari: G. Laterza, 1933.

Estienne, Henri. *Deux dialogues du nouveau langage français italianizé,* 2 vols. Paris: Liseux, 1883.

Estienne, Robert. *Dictionnaire français-latin.* Paris: Imprimerie de Robert Estienne, 1539.

Eymeric, Nicolas. *Le Manuel des inquisiteurs,* trans. André Morellet. Lisbon: n.p., 1762.

Faret, Nicolas. *L'Honnête homme, ou l'art de plaire à la cour,* ed. Maurice Magendie. Paris: Presses Universitaires de France, 1925.

Féraud, Jean-François. *Dictionnaire critique de la langue française.* Marseille: J. Mossy, 1787.

Ferguson, Adam. *An Essay on the History of Civil Society,* ed. Duncan Forbes. Edinburgh: Edinburgh University Press, 1966.

Franklin, Julian H., ed. *Constitutionalism and Resistance in the Sixteenth Century; Three Treatises by Hotman, Beza, and Mornay.* New York: Pegasus, 1969.

Furetière, Antoine. *Dictionnaire universel, contenant généralement tous les mots français.* The Hague: A. and R. Leers, 1690.

Galiani, Ferdinando. *Correspondance,* 2 vols. Paris: Calmann-Lévy, 1881.

———. *Dialogues sur le commerce des blés.* Paris: Fayard, 1984.

Gatti, Angelo, and André Morellet. *Nouvelles réflexions sur la pratique de l'inoculation.* Milan: J. Galeazzi, 1767.

———. *Réflexions sur les préjugés qui s'opposent aux progrès et à la perfection de l'inoculation.* Brussels: Musier, 1764.

Gazette littéraire de l'Europe, 8 vols. Paris, 1764–66.

Grimm, Friedrich Melchior von. *Correspondence littéraire, philosophique, et critique par Grimm, Diderot, Raynal, Meister, etc.,* 16 vols. Paris: Garnier, 1877–82.

Grotius, Hugo. *The Right of War and Peace.* London: W. Innys, 1738.

Guizot, François. *Trois générations.* Paris: Michel Lévy, 1863.

Helvétius. *Correspondance générale d'Helvétius,* 3 vols., ed. David W. Smith. Toronto: Voltaire Foundation, 1981.

Hobbes, Thomas. *De Homine.* London: Typis T. C., 1658.

———. *Leviathan,* ed. C. B. Macpherson. Harmondsworth: Penguin, 1968.

———. *Man and Citizen,* trans. Charles T. Wood. Gloucester: P. Smith, 1978.

Holbach, Paul-Henri-Thiry, baron d'. *La Morale universelle,* 3 vols. Amsterdam, n.p., 1776.

———. *La Politique naturelle, ou discours sur les vrais principes de gouvernement.* London: n.p., 1773.

———. *Système de la nature, ou des loix du monde physique et du monde moral.* London: n.p., 1770.

————. *Système social ou principes naturels de la morale et de la politique avec un examen de l'influence du gouvernement sur les moeurs.* London: n.p., 1773.

Hume, David. *A Concise and Genuine Account of the Dispute Between Mr. Hume and Mr. Rousseau,* ed. Jean-Baptiste Suard. London: T. Becket and P. D. de Hond, 1766.

————. *David Hume's Enquiries Concerning Human Understanding and Concerning the Principles of Morals,* ed. L. A. Selb-Bigge. Oxford: Clarendon Press, 1975.

————. *Dialogues Concerning Natural Religion,* ed. Norman Kemp Smith. Indianapolis: Bobbs-Merril, 1947.

————. *Essays, Moral, Political, and Literary.* Indianapolis: Liberty Classics, 1987.

————. *Exposé succinct de la contestation qui s'est élevée entre M. Hume et M. Rousseau avec les pièces justificatives,* ed. Jean-Baptiste Suard. London: n.p., 1766.

————. *The Letters of David Hume,* 2 vols, ed. J.Y.T. Grieg. Oxford: Clarendon Press, 1932.

————. *A Treatise of Human Nature,* ed. L. A. Selby-Bigge and P. H. Nidditch. Oxford: Clarendon Press, 1978.

————. *La Vie de David Hume, écrite par lui-même,* trans. Jean-Baptiste Suard. London: n.p., 1766.

Isambert, François André, ed. *Recueil général des anciennes lois françaises,* 29 vols. Paris: Berlin-Leprieur, 1821–33.

Johnson, Samuel. *A Dictionary of the English Language.* London: Strahan, 1755.

Journal des Gens du Monde, 4 vols. Paris, 1782–85.

Journal Etranger, 91 vols. Paris, 1754–62.

Kant, Immanuel. *Anthropology from a Pragmatic Point of View.* Carbondale: Southern Illinois University Press, 1978.

La Bruyère, Jean de. *Les Caractères.* Geneva: Cercle du Bibliophile, 1970.

Locke, John. *An Essay Concerning Human Understanding,* 2 vols., ed. Alexander Campbell Fraser. New York: Dover, 1959.

Loyseau, Charles. *Traité des ordres et simples dignités.* Paris: Balthazard, 1613.

Macpherson, James. *Fragments of Ancient Poetry, Collected in the Highlands of Scotland and Translated from the Galic or Erse Language.* Edinburgh: G. Hamilton and J. Balfour, 1760.

Marat, Jean-Paul. *Oeuvres politiques,* 2 vols. Brussels: Pôle Nord, 1989.

Mercier, Louis-Sebastien. *Tableau de Paris.* Amsterdam: n.p., 1782.

Mercure de France, 134 vols (1724–91). Geneva: Slatkine Reprints, 1968–74.

Méré, Antoine Gombaud, Chevalier de. *De l'Esprit.* Paris: D. Thierry and C. Barbin, 1677.

————. "Divers propos du Chevalier de Méré en 1674–1675." *Revue d'histoire littéraire de la France, publiée par la Société d'Histoire littéraire de la France* 19 (1922):76–98, 214–24; 30 (1923):78–89, 380–83, 520–29; 31 (1924):490–96; 32 (1925):68–78, 432–56, 596–601.

————. *Lettres de Monsieur le Chevalier de Méré.* Paris: Au Palais, par la Compagnie des Libraires, 1689.

————. *Oeuvres complètes du Chevalier de Méré,* 3 vols, ed. Charles H. Boudhours. Paris: Editions Fernand Roches, 1930.

Millar, John. *Observations Concerning the Distinction of Ranks in Society.* London: J. Murray, 1773.

Mirabeau, Victor Riquetti, marquis de. *L'Ami des hommes*, 3 vols. Avignon, n.p., 1756. *L'Ami des hommes* appeared in at least two different formats bearing the date 1756 and the city as Avignon. I have used the 17 cm. version in 3 vols. (vols. 121294–97 in the Kress Collection, Harvard University).

Moncrif, François de. *Essais sur la nécessité et sur les moyens de plaire*. Paris: Prault fils, 1738.

Monet, Philibert. *Inventaire des deux langues française et latine*. Lyon: Obert, 1636.

Montaigne, Michel de. *The Complete Essays of Montaigne*, trans. Donald M. Frame. Stanford: Stanford University Press, 1965.

Montchrétien, Antoine de. *Traité de l'oeconomie politique*, ed. Th. Funck-Brentano. Paris: Plon, 1889.

Montesquieu, Charles-Louis de Secondat, baron de. *Lettres persanes*. Paris: F. Roches, 1929.

————. *Oeuvres complètes*, 2 vols., ed. Roger Caillois. Paris: Gallimard, 1951.

————. *Oeuvres complètes*, ed. D. Oster. Paris: Seuil, 1964.

Morellet, André. *Analyse de l'ouvrage intitulé De la Législation et du commerce des grains*. Paris: Pissot, 1775.

————. *Examen de la réponse de M. N* ... sur la Compagnie des Indes*. Paris: Dessaint, 1769.

————. *Fragment d'une lettre sur la police des grains*. Paris: Musier, 1764.

————. *Lettres d'André Morellet (vol. 1) 1759–1785*, ed. Dorothy Medlin, Jean-Claude David, and Paul Leclerc. Oxford: Voltaire Foundation, 1991.

————. *Lettres de l'abbé Morellet à Lord Shelburne*. Paris: Librairie Plon, 1898.

————. *Mélanges de littérature et de philosophie*, 4 vols. Paris: Lepetit, 1818.

————. *Mémoire sur la situation actuelle de la Compagnie des Indes*. Paris: Dessaint, 1769.

————. *Mémoires sur le XVIIIe siècle et sur la révolution*, 2 vols. Paris: Ladvocat, 1822.

————. *Mémoires sur le dix-huitième siècle et sur la révolution*, ed. Jean-Pierre Guicciardi. Paris: Mercure de France, 1988.

————. *Observations sur le projet de former une Assemblée nationale sur le modèle des Etats-Généraux de 1614*. n.p., n.d.

————. *Préface de la comédie des Philosophes, ou la vision de Charles Palissot*. Paris: Chez l'auteur de la comédie, 1760.

————. *Prospectus d'un nouveau Dictionnaire de commerce*, with a preface by Jean-Claude Perrot. Munich: Krauss Reprint, 1980.

————. *Réflexions du lendemain, sur les arrêtés pris dans l'Assemblée Nationale, relativement aux biens ecclésiastiques, le 11 août 1789*. n.p., n.d.

————. *Réflexions sur les avantages de la liberté d'écrire et d'imprimer sur les matières de l'administration, écrites en 1764 à l'occasion de la déclaration du Roi du 28 mars* ... London: Chez les Frères Etienne, 1775.

————. *Réfutation de l'ouvrage qui a pour titre Dialogues sur le commerce des blés*. London: n.p., 1770.

————. *Traité de la propriété e il carteggio con Bentham e Dumont*, ed. Eugenio Di Rienzo and Lea Campos Boralevi. Florence: Cèntro Editoriale Toscano, 1990.

Morellet, André, ed. *Eloges de Madame Geoffrin*. Paris: H. Nicolle, 1812.

Mosser, Françoise. *Les Intendants des finances au XVIIIe siècle*. Geneva: Droz, 1978.

Necker, Jacques. *Réponse au Mémoire de Monsieur l'abbé Morellet sur la Compagnie des Indes*. Paris: Imprimerie royale, 1769.

_____. *Sur la Législation et du commerce des grains*. Paris: Pìssot, 1775.

Nicole, Pierre. *Essais de morale*. Paris: Guillaume, Desprez, 1679.

Nicole, Pierre, and Blaise Pascal. *Traité de l'éducation d'un prince*. Paris: C. Savreux, 1670.

Nisard, Charles. "Portefeuille d'un académicien du XVIIIe siècle: Exclusion de Delille et Suard de l'Académie Française en 1772." *Revue Contemporaine* 25 (1856):622–49.

_____. "Portefeuille d'un académician du XVIIIe siècle: Histoire littéraire." *Revue Contemporaine* 25 (1856):3–32.

_____. "Portefeuille d'un Académician du XVIIIe siècle: Suppression des académies." *Revue Contemporaine* 26 (1856):225–52.

Palissot de Montenoy, Charles. *Lettre de l'Auteur de la comédie des Philosophes, au public pour servir de préface à la pièce*. n.p.: n.p., 1760.

_____. *Lettres de Monsieur de Voltaire à M. Palissot avec les réponses, à l'occasion de la comédie des Philosophes*. Geneva: n.p., 1760.

_____. *Les Philosophes, comédie en trois actes, en vers*. Paris: Duchesne, 1760.

Pluquet, François Adrien. *De la Sociabilité*. Paris: Barrois, 1767.

Pufendorf, Samuel. *Le Droit de la nature et des gens*, 5th ed., trans. Jean Barbeyrac. Amsterdam: Briasson, 1734.

_____. *De Officio Hominis et civis*, 2 vols., Latin text and English translation by Frank Gardner Moore. New York: Oxford University Press, 1927.

Ramsay, André-Michel, Chevalier de. *Essai philosophique sur le gouvernement civil . . . selon les principes de feu M. Francois de Salignac de la Mothe-Fénelon*, in *Oeuvres de Fénelon*, vol. 3. Paris: Didot Frères, 1843.

Raynal, Guillaume-Thomas-François. *Histoire philosophique et politique des établissements et du commerce des européens dans les deux Indes*. Paris: Lacombe, 1778.

Recueil de diverses pièces, servant de supplément à l'Histoire philosophique et politique des établissements et du commerce des européens dans les deux Indes par Guillaume-Thomas Raynal. Geneva: J.-L. Pellet, 1783.

Refuge, Eustache de. *Traité de la cour*. n.p.: n.p., 1616.

Réimpression de l'ancien Moniteur de la Révolution française, 30 vols. Paris: Plon, 1854–63.

Revue Française, 16 vols. Paris, 1828–30.

Richelet, Pierre. *Dictionnaire français*. Paris: Widerhold, 1680.

Robertson, William. *The History of America*. London: n.p., 1777.

_____. *L'Histoire de l'Amerique*, 2 vols., trans. Jean-Baptiste Suard. Paris: Panckoucke, 1778.

_____. *The History of America*. New York: Harper, 1839.

_____. *L'Histoire du règne de l'Empereur Charles-Quint, précedé d'un Tableau du progrès de la société en Europe, depuis la destruction de l'Empire Romain jusqu'au commencement du seizième siècle*, 6 vols., trans. Jean-Baptiste Suard. Amsterdam and Paris: Saillant et Noyer, 1771.

_____. *The History of the Reign of the Emperor Charles V*, 3 vols. Boston: Phillips, Sampson, and Co., 1857.

Rousseau, Jean-Jacques. *Du Contrat social*. Paris: Garnier-Flammarion, 1966.

————. *Oeuvres complètes*, 3 vols., ed. B Gagnebin and M. Raymond. Paris: Gallimard, 1959–64.

Smollett, Tobias. *The Expedition of Humphrey Clinker*, ed. L. M. Knapp. Oxford: Oxford University Press, 1966.

Saint-Pierre, Jacques-Henri Bernardin de. *Etudes de la nature*. Paris: Deterville, 1804.

————. *Harmonies de la nature*, in *Oeuvres posthumes*, vol. 3. Paris: Lefèvre, 1840.

Scudéry, Madeleine de. *Choix de conversations de Mlle. de Scudéry*, ed. Phillip J. Wolfe. Ravenna: Longo Editore, 1977.

————. *Conversations nouvelles sur divers sujets*, 2 vols. Paris: Barbin, 1684.

————. *Conversations sur divers sujets*, 2 vols. Paris: Barbin, 1680.

————. *Entretiens de morale*, 2 vols. Paris: Anisson, 1692.

————. *La Morale du monde, ou conversations*. Paris: Guillain, 1686.

————. *Nouvelles conversations de morale*, 2 vols. Paris: Mabre-Cramoisy, 1688.

Seyssel, Claude de. *The Monarchy of France*, trans. Donald R. Kelley and Michael Sherman, ed. J. H. Hexter. New Haven: Yale University Press, 1981.

Spanheim, Ezéchiel. *Relation de la cour de France en 1690*. Mayenne: Mercure de France, 1973.

Staël-Holstein, Anne-Louise-Germaine Necker, baronne de. *Considérations sur les principaux événements de la Révolution française*. Paris: Charpentier, 1845.

Suard, Amélie. *Essais de mémoires sur M. Suard*. Paris: Firmin-Didot, 1881.

Suard, Jean-Baptiste. *Discours prononcés dans l'Académie française, le jeudi 4 août à la réception de M. Suard*. Paris: Demonville, 1774.

————. *Discours prononcés dans l'Académie française le . . . 15 juin, 1784 . . . à la réception de M. Montesquiou*. Paris: Demonville, 1784.

————. *Mélanges de littérature*, 4 vols. Paris: Dentu, 1803.

————. "Notice sur la personne et les écrits du duc de la Rochefoucauld," in *Maximes et réflexions morale du duc de la Rochefoucauld*. Paris: Imprimerie de Monsieur, 1782.

Supplément aux Journaux des Sçavans et de Trevoux ou Lettres critiques sur les divers ouvrages périodiques de France. Amsterdam: 1758.

Swift, Jonathan. *Collected Prose Works*, 14 vols. Oxford: Blackwell, 1939–68.

Thomas, Antoine. *Oeuvres*, 4 vols. Paris: Moutard, 1773.

Trublet, Nicolas. *Essais sur divers sujets de littérature et de morale*. Paris: Briasson, 1735.

Turgot, Anne-Robert-Jacques. *Lettres de Turgot à la duchesse d'Enville, 1764–74 et 1777–80*, ed. Joseph Ruwet. Louvain: Bibliothèque de l'Université, 1976.

————. *Oeuvres de Turgot et documents le concernant*, 5 vols, ed. Gustave Schelle. Paris: F. Alcan, 1913–23.

Pietro Verri. *Viaggio a Parigi e a Londra (1766–1767): Carteggio di Pietro Verri*, ed. G. Gaspari. Milan: Adelphi, 1980.

Viau, Théophile de. *Oeuvres poétiques*, 2 vols. Geneva: Droz, 1951.

Voiture, Vincent. *Lettres*, vol. 1 of *Les Oeuvres*. Paris: A. Courbe, 1654.

Voltaire, François-Marie Arouet de. *Dictionnaire philosophique*. Paris: Garnier, 1954.

————. *Oeuvres de Voltaire*, 72 vols. Paris: Firmin Didot, 1829–40.

————. *Recueil des facéties parisiennes pour les six premiers mois de l'an 1760*. Geneva: Morellet, 1760.

———. *Voltaire's Correspondence*, 107 vols., ed. Theodore Besterman. Geneva: Institut de Musée Voltaire, 1953–66.

———. *Zaïre*. Paris: Ernest Leroux, 1889.

SECONDARY SOURCES

Aarsleff, Hans. *From Locke to Saussure, Essays on the Study of Language and Intellectual History*. Minneapolis: University of Minnesota Press, 1982.

Agulhon, Maurice. *Le Cercle dans la France bourgeoise, 1810–1848: Etude d'une mutation de sociabilité*. Paris: Armand Colin, 1977.

———. *Pénitents et francs-maçons de l'ancienne Provence: Essai sur la sociabilité méridionale*. Paris: Fayard, 1984.

———. *La Sociabilité méridionale: Confréries et associations en Provence*. Aix-en-Provence: Pensée Universitaire, 1966.

Althusser, Louis. *Lenin and Philosophy and Other Essays*. London: New Left Books, 1971.

Antoine, Michel. *Le Conseil du roi sous le règne de Louis XV*. Geneva: Droz, 1970.

———. *Le Gouvernement et l'administration sous Louis XV: Dictionnaire biographique*. Paris: Editions du Centre National de la Recherche Scientifique, 1978.

Antoine, Michel, et al. *Origines et histoire des cabinets des ministres en France*. Geneva: Droz, 1975.

Apostolides, Jean-Marie. *Le roi machine: Spectacle et politique au temps de Louis XIV*. Paris: Minuit, 1981.

Arendt, Hannah. *The Human Condition*. New York: Doubleday, 1958.

Ariès, Phillipe, and Georges Duby, eds. *Histoire de la vie privée: De la Renaissance aux lumières*. Paris: Seuil, 1986.

Aronson, Nicole. *Mademoiselle de Scudéry ou le voyage au pays du tendre*. Paris: Fayard, 1986.

Auerbach, Erich. "La Cour et la Ville," in *Scenes from the Drama of European Literature*. Manchester: University of Manchester Press, 1984.

Baker, Keith Michael. "Enlightenment and the Institution of Society: Notes for a Conceptual History," in W.F.B. Melching and W.R.E. Velema, eds. *Main Trends in Cultural History*. Amsterdam and Atlanta: Rodopi, forthcoming.

———. Baker, Keith Michael. "Enlightenment and Revolution in France: Old Problems, Renewed Approaches." *Journal of Modern History* 53 (1981): 281–303.

———. *Inventing the French Revolution*. Cambridge: Cambridge University Press, 1990.

Baker, Keith Michael, ed. *The French Revolution and the Creation of Modern Political Culture*, vol. 1: *The Political Culture of the Old Regime*. Oxford: Pergamon Press, 1987.

———. *University of Chicago Readings in Western Civilization*, vol. 7: *The Old Regime and the French Revolution*. Chicago: University of Chicago Press. 1987.

Barbier, A.-E. *Dictionnaire des ouvrages anonymes*, 4 vols. Paris: G. Maisonneve & Larose, 1964.

Barling, Thomas. "La Guerre des brochures autour des Philosophes de Pallisot," in *Modèles et moyens de réflexion politique au XVIIIe siècle*. Villeneuve-d'Ascq: Université de Lille III, 1973.

Bergson, Henri. *Mélanges*, ed. André Robinet. Paris: Presses Universitaires de France, 1972.

Berlin, Isaiah. *The Crooked Timber of Humanity, Chapters in the History of Ideas*. New York: Vintage Books, 1992.

Bertaut, Jules. *La Vie littéraire au XVIIIe siècle*. Paris: Jules Tallandier, 1954.

Besselink, Leonard "The Impious Hypothesis Revisited," *Grotiana*, n.s., 9 (1988):3–63.

Biographie universelle, 45 vols. Paris: Delegrave, 1811.

Boislisle, A. de. "Nicolas Delamare et le *Traité de la police*. *Bulletin de la Société de l'histoire de Paris et de l'Ile de France*, vol. 3, 1876.

Blair, Ann M. "Restaging Jean Bodin: The 'Universae Naturae Theatrum' (1596) in Its Cultural Context." Ph.D. diss., Princeton University, 1990.

Bluche, François, and Jean-François Solnon. *La Véritable hiérarchie sociale de l'ancienne France: Le tarif de la première capitation (1695)*. Geneva: Droz, 1983.

Bongie, Laurence. "Hume en France au XVIIIe siècle." Ph.D. diss., University of Paris, 1952.

Bosher, John. *French Finances, 1770–1795: From Business to Bureaucracy*. Cambridge: Cambridge University Press, 1970.

Bougeart, Alfred. *Marat, l'ami du peuple*. Paris: Librairie Internationale, 1865.

Bourdieu, Pierre. *Distinction, A Social Critique of the Judgement of Taste*. Cambridge, Mass.: Harvard University Press, 1984.

Bredvold, Louis. "The Contributions of John Wilkes to the *Gazette Littéraire de l'Europe*." *University of Michigan Contributions in Modern Philology* 15 (1950):1–36.

Brockliss, L.W.B. *French Higher Education in the Seventeenth and Eighteenth Centuries: A Cultural History*. Oxford: Clarendon Press, 1987.

Brunner, Otto, Werner Conze, and Reinhart Koselleck. *Geschichtliche Grundbegriffe. Historisches Lexicon zur Politische-sozialen Sprache in Deutschland*, 26 vols. (to date). Stuttgart: E. Klett, 1972–.

Brunot, Ferdinand. *Histoire de la langue française des origines à 1900*, 13 vols. Paris: A. Colin, 1905–79.

Buisson, Henry. *La Police: Son histoire*. Vichy: Wallon, 1950.

Burke, Peter, ed. *A New Kind of History: From the Writings of Lucien Febvre*. New York: Harper and Row, 1973.

Cassirer, Ernst. *The Philosophy of the Enlightenment*. Princeton: Princeton University Press, 1979.

Castan, Yves. *Honnêteté et relations sociales en Languedoc (1715–1780)*. Paris: Plon, 1974.

Chartier, Roger. *Cultural History, Between Practices and Representations*. Ithaca: Cornell University Press, 1988.

———. *Lecture et lecteurs dans la France d'Ancien Régime*. Paris: Seuil, 1987.

Chartier, Roger, ed. *A History of Private Life*, vol. 3: *The Passions of the Renaissance*. Cambridge, Mass.: Harvard University Press, 1989.

Chartier, Roger, and Henri-Jean Martin, eds. *Histoire de l'édition française*, vol 2. Paris: Promodis, 1984.

Chassaigne, Marc. *Le Procès du Chevalier de La Barre*. Paris: J. Gabalda, 1920.

Clark, Henry C. "Passions, Interests, and Moderate Virtues: La Rochefoucauld and the Origins of Enlightenment Liberalism." *Annals of Scholarship* 7 (1990):33–50.

Clive, John, and Bernard Bailyn. "England's Cultural Provinces: Scotland and America." *William and Mary Quarterly* 11 (1954):200–213.

Cochin, Augustin. *La Révolution et la libre-pensée*. Paris: Copernic, 1979.

_____. *Les Sociétés de pensées et la démocratie moderne*. Paris: Copernic, 1978.

Cohen, Jean L., and Andrew Arato. *Civil Society and Political Theory*. Cambridge, Mass.: MIT Press, 1992.

Cousin, Victor. *La Société française au XVIIe siècle d'après le Grand Cyrus de Mademoiselle de Scudéry*. Paris: Didier, 1905.

Craveri, Benedetta. "Conqueror of Paris." *New York Review of Books* 39 (December 17, 1992):63–68.

Curtius, Ernst Robert. *Die Französische Kultur*. Berlin: Deutsch Verlags-Anstalt, 1930.

Cushing, Max P. "Baron D'Holbach." Ph.D. diss., Columbia University, 1914.

Darnton, Robert. *Gens de lettres, gens du livre*. Paris: Odile Jacob, 1991.

_____. *The Kiss of Lamourette: Reflections on Cultural History*. New York: Norton, 1990.

_____. *The Literary Underground of the Old Regime*. Cambridge, Mass.: Harvard University Press, 1982.

Davis, James Herbert, Jr. *Fénelon*. Boston: Twayne Publishers, 1979.

Delafarge, Daniel. *L'Affaire de l'abbé Morellet en 1760*. Paris: Hachette,1912.

Dens, Jean-Pierre. "L'Art des agréments: le Chevalier de Méré et la sensibilité mondaine." Ph.D. diss., Columbia University, 1971.

_____. "L'Honnête Homme et l'esthétique du paraître." *Papers on French Seventeenth Century Literature* 6 (1976–77):69–82.

Derathé, Robert. *Jean-Jacques Rousseau et la science politique de son temps*. Paris: Presses Universitaires de France, 1950.

Dickey, Laurence. "Historicizing the Adam Smith Problem: Conceptual, Historiographical, and Textual Issues." *Journal of Modern History* 58 (1986):579–609.

Dieckman, Herbert. *Le Philosophe: Texts and Interpretation*. Washington University Studies, St. Louis, 1948.

Dini, Vittorio, and Domenico Tarano, eds. *Individualismo, Assolutismo, Democrazia*. Naples: Edizioni Scientifiche Italiane, 1992.

Doncieux, Georges. *Un Jésuite homme de lettres au dix-septième siècle: Le Père Bouhours*. Paris: Hachette, 1886.

Downing, Brian M. *The Military Revolution and Political Change*. Princeton: Princeton University Press, 1992.

Doyle, William. *The Origins of the French Revolution*. Oxford: Oxford University Press, 1980.

Dumont, Louis. *From Mandeville to Marx: The Genesis and Triumph of Economic Ideology*. Chicago: University of Chicago Press, 1977.

Duby, Georges. *The Three Orders: Feudal Society Imagined*. Chicago: University of Chicago Press, 1980.

Durkheim, Emile. *The Elementary Forms of the Religious Life*. New York: Free Press, 1965.

Egret, Jean. *Necker, ministre de Louis XVI*. Paris: H. Champion, 1975.

Eisenstein, Elizabeth L. *Grub Street Abroad: Aspects of the French Cosmopolitan Press from the Age of Louis XIV to the French Revolution*. Oxford: Clarendon Press, 1992.

Elias, Norbert. *The Court Society*. Oxford: Blackwell, 1983.

———. *The History of Manners*, vol. 1 of *The Civilizing Process*. New York: Pantheon, 1978.

Evans, R.J.W. "The Wechel Presses: Humanism and Calvinism in Central Europe, 1572–1627." *Past and Present*, supplement 2 (1975):1–53.

Fabre, Antonin. *Lexique de la langue de Chapelain*. Paris: Leon Techener, 1889.

Febvre, Lucien. *A New Kind of History*, ed. Peter Burke. New York: Harper and Row, 1973.

Fitzsimmons, Michael P. "Privilege and Polity in France, 1786–1791." *American Historical Review* 92 (1987):269–95.

Fox-Genovese, Elizabeth. *The Origins of Physiocracy*. Ithaca: Cornell University Press, 1976.

France, Peter. *Politeness and Its Discontents: Problems in French Classical Culture* Cambridge: Cambridge University Press, 1992.

——— *Rhetoric and Truth in France: Descartes to Diderot*. Oxford: Clarendon Press, 1972.

France, Peter, and Anthony Strugwell, eds. *Diderot: Les Dernières années, 1770–84*. Edinburgh: Edinburgh University Press, 1985.

François, Etienne, ed. *Sociabilité et société bourgeoise en France, en Allemagne, et en Suisse*. Paris: Editions Recherches sur les civilisations, 1986.

Franklin, Alfred. *La Civilité, l'étiquette, la mode, le bon ton, du XIIIe au XIX siècle*, vol. 1. Paris: Emile-Paul, 1908.

———. *La Vie Privée d'autrefois*, vol. 13: *Le Café, le thé, et le chocolat*. Paris: Plon, 1893.

Freud, Hilde H. *Palissot and Les Philosophes*. Geneva: Droz, 1967.

Fumaroli, Marc. *L'Age de l'éloquence. Rhétorique et "res literaria" de la Renaissance au seuil de l'époque classique*. Geneva: Droz, 1980.

Furet, François. *Interpreting the French Revolution*. Cambridge: Cambridge University Press, 1981.

Furet, François, and Mona Ozouf, eds. *A Critical Dictionary of the French Revolution*. Cambridge, Mass.: Belknap Press, 1989.

Ganochaud, Collette. *L'Opinion publique chez Jean-Jacques Rousseau*. Paris: H. Champion, 1980.

Garat, Dominique-Joseph. *Mémoires historiques sur la vie de M. Suard*, 2 vols. Paris: A. Belin, 1820.

Gauchet, Marcel. *Le Désenchantement du monde, une histoire politique de la religion*. Paris: Gallimard, 1985.

———. *La Révolution des droits de l'homme*. Paris: Gallimard, 1989.

Gierke, Otto. *Natural Law and the Theory of Society*. Boston: Beacon Press, 1957.

Goffman, Erving. *Encounters*. Indianapolis: Bobbs-Merrill, 1961.

Goldsmith, Elizabeth C. *Exclusive Conversations: The Art of Interaction in Seventeenth-Century France*. Philadelphia: University of Pennsylvania Press, 1988.

Goodman, Dena. "Enlightenment Salons: The Convergence of Female and Philosophical Ambitions." *Eighteenth-Century Studies* 22 (1989):329–50.

———. "Governing The Republic Of Letters: The Politics Of Culture in the French Enlightenment." *History of European Ideas*, 13 (1991):183–99.

———. "The Hume-Rousseau Affair: From Private *Querelle* to Public *Procès*." *Eighteenth Century Studies* 25 (Winter, 1991–92):171–202.

———. "Public Sphere and Private Life: Towards a Synthesis of Current Historiographical Approaches to the Old Regime." *History and Theory* 31 (1992):1–20.

———. "Seriousness of Purpose: Salonières, Philosophes, and the Shaping of the Eighteenth-Century Salon." *Proceedings of the Annual Meeting of the Western Society for French History* 15 (1988):111–18.

Gordon, Daniel. "Philosophy, Sociology, and Gender in the Enlightenment Conception of Public Opinion." *French Historical Studies* 17 (1992):881–911.

Goré, Jeanne-Lydie. *L'Itinéraire de Fénelon: Humanisme et spiritualité*. Grenoble: Allier, 1957.

Gourcuff, Olivier de. "Un Moraliste Breton: L'Abbé de Bellegarde." *Revue de Bretagne* 2 (December 1887):447–56; 3 (January 1888):46–54; 3 (February 1888):132–45.

Grande encyclopédie, 31 vols. Paris: Société Anonyme de la Grande Encyclopédie, 1886.

Haakonssen, Knud. *The Science of a Legislator: The Natural Jurisprudence of David Hume and Adam Smith*. Cambridge: Cambridge University Press, 1981.

Habermas, Jürgen. *The Structural Transformation of the Public Sphere: An Inquiry into a Category of Bourgeois Society*. Cambridge, Mass.: MIT Press, 1989.

Halévi, Ran. *Les Loges maçonniques dans la France d'Ancien Régime: Aux Origines de la sociabilité démocratique*. Paris: A. Colin, 1984.

Hazard, Paul. *The European Mind, 1680–1715*. Middlesex: Penguin, 1964.

Henderson, G. D. *Chevalier Ramsay*. London: Thomas Nelson, 1951.

Hexter, J. H. *The Vision of Politics on the Eve of the Reformation*. New York: Basic Books, 1969.

Hintze, Otto. "The Commissary and His Significance in General Administrative History," in *The Historical Essays of Otto Hintze*, ed. Felix Gilbert. Oxford: Oxford University Press, 1975, 267–301.

Hirschman, Albert O. *The Passions and the Interests: Political Arguments for Capitalism Before Its Triumph*. Princeton: Princeton University Press, 1977.

Hobsbawm, Eric, and Terence Ranger, eds. *The Invention of Tradition*. Cambridge: Cambridge University Press, 1983.

Hocart, Arthur. *Kings and Councilors*. Chicago: University of Chicago Press, 1970.

Hont, Istvan, and Michael Ignatieff, eds. *Wealth and Virtue: The Shaping of Political Economy in the Scottish Enlightenment*. Cambridge: Cambridge University Press, 1983.

Huguet, Edmond. *Dictionnaire de la langue française du seizième siècle*, 7 vols. Paris: E. Champion, 1925–73.

Hunter, Alfred C. *J.B.A. Suard, un introducteur de la littérature anglaise en France*. Paris: E. Champion, 1925.

———. *Lexique de la langue de Jean Chapelain*. Geneva: Droz, 1967.

Jacob, Margaret C. *Living the Enlightenment: Free Masonry and Politics in Eighteenth-Century Europe*. New York: Oxford University Press, 1991.

Jaeger, C. Stephen. *The Origins of Courtliness: Civilizing Trends and the Formation of Courtly Ideals, 939–1210*. Philadelphia: University of Pennsylvania Press, 1985.

Jehasse, Jean. *Guez de Balzac et le génie romain*. Saint-Etienne: Publications de l'Université de Saint-Etienne, 1977.

Kaplan, Steven L. *Bread, Politics and Political Economy in the Reign of Louis XV*, 2 vols. The Hague: Martinus Nijhoff, 1976.

Kelley, Donald R. *The Beginning of Ideology: Consciousness and Society in the French Renaissance*. Cambridge: Cambridge University Press, 1983.

Klein, Lawrence Eliot. "Politeness in Seventeenth-Century England and France." *Cahiers du dix-septième* 4 (1990):97–100.

———. 'The Rise of 'Politeness' in England, 1660–1715." Ph.D. diss., Johns Hopkins University, 1983.

Koch, Philip. "Les Veritables 'Dialogues' de Galiani." *Atti del convegno italo-francese di Roma, 25–27 May 1972* (Rome 1975):185–97.

Kors, Alan. *D'Holbach's Coterie: An Enlightenment in Paris*. Princeton: Princeton University Press, 1975.

Krieger, Leonard. *The Politics of Discretion: Pufendorf and the Acceptance of Natural Law*. Chicago: University of Chicago Press, 1965.

Langbein, John H. *Torture and the Law of Proof*. Chicago: University of Chicago Press, 1976.

Larousse, Pierre, ed. *Grand dictionnaire universelle*. Paris: Administration du Grand dictionnaire, 1866.

Larrère, Catherine. *L'Invention de l'économie au XVIIIe siècle* Paris: Presses Universitaires de France, 1992.

Lathuillère, Roger. *La Preciosité: Étude historique et linguistique*. Geneva: Droz, 1966.

La Vopa. Anthony J. "Conceiving a Public: Ideas and Society in Eighteenth-Century Europe." *Journal of Modern History* 64 (1992):76–116.

Lebrun, François, Marc Venard, and Jean Quéniart. *Histoire générale de l'enseignement et de l'éducation en France*, 4 vols. Paris: Nouvelle Libraire de France, 1981.

Lévy-Bruhl, Henri. "La Noblesse de France et le commerce à la fin de l'Ancien Régime." *Revue d'Histoire Moderne* 8 (1933):209–35.

Lewis, David K. *Convention, A Philosophical Study*. Oxford: Basil Blackwell, 1986.

Livingston, Donald W. *Hume's Philosophy of Common Life*. Chicago: University of Chicago Press, 1984.

Loft, Leonore. "*Le Journal du Licée de Londres*: A Study in the Pre-Revolutionary French Press." *European History Quarterly* 23 (1993):7–36.

Lougee, Carolyn C. *Le Paradis des Femmes: Women, Salons, and Social Stratification in Seventeenth-Century France*. Princeton: Princeton University Press, 1976.

Lough, John. *An Introduction to Seventeenth-Century France*. London: Longmans, Green, 1954.

Lovejoy, Arthur O. *Essays in the History of Ideas*. Baltimore: Johns Hopkins University Press, 1948.

———. *The Great Chain of Being*. Cambridge, Mass.: Harvard University Press, 1936.

Lynn, John A. "The Growth of the French Army during the Seventeenth Century." *Armed Forces and Society* 6 (1980):568–85.

Mackrell, J.Q.C. *The Attack on "Feudalism" in Eighteenth-Century France*. London: Routledge and Kegan Paul, 1973.

Magendie, Maurice. *La Politesse mondaine et les théories de l'honnêteté en France au XVIIe siècle, de 1600 à 1660,* 2 vols. Paris: Félix Alcan, 1933.

Mann, Thomas. *Reflections of a Nonpolitical Man,* trans. Walter D. Morris. New York: F. Ungar, 1983.

Mannheim, Karl. *Essays on the Sociology of Knowledge.* New York: Oxford University Press, 1956.

Marion, Marcel. *Dictionnaire des instititutions de la France, XVIIe–XVIIIe siècles.* Paris: Picard, 1984.

Marmontel, Jean François. *Mémoires,* ed. John Renwick. Clermont-Ferrand: G. de Bussac, 1972.

Matoré, Georges. *La Méthode en lexicologie.* Paris: Dider, 1953.

Mauzi, Robert. *L'Idée du bonheur au XVIIIe siécle.* Paris: Armand Colin, 1960.

Maza, Sarah. "Le Tribunal de la nation: Les Mémoires judiciaires et l'opinion publique à la fin de l'ancien régime." *Annales: E.S.C.* 42 (1987):73–90;

Mazure, Auguste. *Les Idées de l'abbe Morellet.* Paris: Société du Recueil Sirey, 1910.

Meaux, Antoine de. *Augustin Cochin et la genèse de la révolution.* Paris: Librairie Plon, 1928.

Medlin, Dorothy. "André Morellet and the Idea of Progress." *Studies on Voltaire and the Eighteenth Century* 189 (1980):239–46.

———. "André Morellet, Translator of Liberal Thought." *Studies on Voltaire and the Eighteenth Century* 174 (1978):189–202.

Meek, Ronald L. *Social Science and the Ignoble Savage.* Cambridge: Cambridge University Press, 1976.

Meek, Ronald L., ed. *Turgot on Progress, Sociology and Economics.* Cambridge: Cambridge University Press, 1973.

Mennell, Stephen. *Norbert Elias: Civilization and the Human Self-Image.* Oxford: Blackwell, 1989.

Micard, Etienne. *Antoine-Léonard Thomas.* Paris: Honoré Champion, 1924.

Moine, Marie-Christine. *Les Fêtes à la cour du roi soleil, 1653–1715.* Paris: Fernand Lanore, 1984.

Mongredien, Georges. *La Vie de société au XVIIe et XVIIIe siècles.* Paris: Hachette, 1950.

Moriarty, Michael. *Taste and Ideology in Seventeenth-Century France.* Cambridge: Cambridge University Press, 1988.

Mornet, Daniel. *Histoire de la clarté française, ses origines, son évolution, sa valeur.* Paris: Payot, 1920.

———. *Les Origines intellectuelles de la Révolution française.* Paris: A. Colin, 1933.

Mousnier, Roland. *Les Hiérarchies sociales de 1450 à nos jours.* Paris: Presses Universitaires de France, 1969.

———. *L'Homme rouge ou la vie du Cardinal de Richelieu (1585–1642).* Paris: R. Laffont, 1992.

———. *The Institutions of France Under the Absolute Monarchy, 1598–1789,* vol. 1: *Society and the State.* Chicago: University of Chicago Press, 1979; vol. 2: *The Organs of State and Society.* Chicago: University of Chicago Press, 1980.

Mousnier, Roland, ed. *Richelieu et la culture.* Paris: Editions du Centre National de la Recherche Scientifique, 1987.

Mousnier, Roland, and Hartung, Fritz. "Quelques problèmes concernant la monarchie absolue." *Relazioni del X Congresso Internazionale di Scienze Storiche* 4:1–55, Florence, 1955.

Mullan, John. *Sentiment and Sociability: The Language of Feeling in the Eighteenth Century.* Oxford: Oxford University Press, 1988.

Nathans, Benjamin. "Habermas's 'Public Sphere' in the Era of the French Revolution." *French Historical Studies* 16 (1990):620–44.

Naville, Pierre. *D'Holbach et la philosophie scientifique au XVIII siècle.* Paris: Gallimard, 1967.

Nora, Pierre, ed. *Les Lieux de mémoire*, vol. 3, pt. 2: *Les Frances: Traditions.* Paris: Gallimard, 1992.

Nourrisson, Paul. *Histoire de la liberté d'association en France depuis 1789.* Paris: Librairie Recueil Sirey, 1920.

Oestreich, Gerhard. *Neostoicism and the Early Modern State.* Cambridge: Cambridge University Press, 1982.

Olivier-Martin, François. *Histoire du droit français des origines à la Révolution.* Paris: Domat Montchrestien, 1948.

Pagden, Anthony. *The Fall of Natural Man: The American Indian and the Origins of Comparative Ethnology.* Cambridge: Cambridge University Press: 1982.

Pagden, Anthony, ed. *The Languages of Political Theory in Early-Modern Europe.* Cambridge: Cambridge University Press, 1987.

Palmer, William G. "Exploring the Diffusion of Enlightened Ideas in Prerevolutionary France." *Eighteenth Century: Theory and Interpretation* 26 (1985):63–72.

Paul, Charles B. *Science and Immortality: The Eloges of the Paris Academy of Sciences, 1699–1791.* Berkeley: University of California Press, 1980.

Pellison, Maurice. *Les Hommes de lettres au XVIIIe siècle.* Paris: Armand Colin, 1911.

Perrot, Jean-Claude. *Une Histoire intellectuelle de l'économie politique, XVIIe–XVIIIe siècles.* Paris: Editions de l'Ecole des Hautes Etudes en Sciences Sociales, 1992.

Picard, Roger. *Les Salons littéraires et la société française, 1610–1789.* New York: Brentano's, 1943.

Pocock, J.G.A. *The Machiavellian Moment: Florentine Political Thought and the Atlantic Republican Tradition.* Princeton: Princeton University Press, 1975.

Polanyi, Karl. *The Great Transformation: The Political and Economic Origins of Our Time.* Boston: Beacon Press, 1957.

Porter, Roy, and Mikulas Teich, eds. *The Enlightenment in National Context.* Cambridge: Cambridge University Press, 1981.

Proteau, Pierre. "Etude sur Morellet considéré comme auxiliaire de l'école physiocratique." Ph.D. diss., Université de Poitiers, 1910.

Quine, Willard v. O. "Semantic Ascent," in *The Linguistic Turn, Essays on Philosophical Method*, ed. Richard Rorty. Chicago: University of Chicago Press, 1992.

Raeff, Marc. "The Well-Ordered Police State and the Development of Modernity in Seventeenth- and Eighteenth-Century Europe: An Attempt at a Comparative Approach." *American Historical Review* 80 (1975):1221–43.

Rahe, Paul A. *Republics Ancient and Modern: Classical Republicanism and the American Revolution.* Chapel Hill: University of North Carolina Press, 1992.

Ranum, Orest. "Courtesy, Absolutism, and the French State." *Journal of Modern History* 52 (1980):426–51.

Reichardt, Rolf, and Eberhard Schmitt. *Handbuch politisch-sozialer Grundbegriffe in Frankreich, 1680–1820*, 10 vols. (to date). Munich: Oldenbourg, 1985–.

Richter, Melvin. "*Begriffsgeschichte* and the History of Ideas." *Journal of the History of Ideas* 29 (1987):247–63.

———. "Conceptual History (*Begriffsgeschichte*) and Political Theory." *Political Theory* 14 (1986):604–37.

———. "Montesquieu, the Politics of Language, and the Language of Politics." *History of Political Thought* 10 (1989):77–88.

———. "Reconstructing the History of Political Languages: Pocock, Skinner, and the *Geschichtliche Grundbegriffe*." *History and Theory* 29 (1990):38–70.

Ricken, Ulrich. "Réflexions du XVIIIe siècle sur 'l'abus des mots.'" *Mots* 4 (1982):29–45.

Roche, Daniel. *Le Siècle des lumières en province*, 2 vols. Paris: Mouton, 1978.

———. *Les Républicains des lettres: Gens de culture et lumières au XVIIIe siècle*. Paris: Fayard, 1988.

Roederer, P. L. *Mémoire pour servir à l'histoire de la société polie en France*. Paris: Imprimeurs de l'Institut de France, 1835.

Sainte-Beuve, Charles-Augustin. *Causeries du lundi*, 15 vols., 3d ed. Paris: Garnier, 1852–62.

Saint-Germain, Jacques. *La Vie quotidienne en France à la fin du Grand Siècle*. Paris: Hachette, 1965.

Salmon, J.H.M. "Storm Over the Noblesse." *Journal of Modern History* 53 (1981):242–57.

Schmitt, Charles B., et al., eds. *The Cambridge History of Renaissance Philosophy*. Cambridge: Cambridge University Press, 1988.

Schouls, Peter A. *The Imposition of Method*. Oxford: Clarendon Press, 1980.

Schumpeter, Joseph. *The History of Economic Analysis*. Oxford: Oxford University Press, 1954.

Segur, Pierre de. *Le Royaume de la rue Saint-Honoré*. Paris: Calmann Levy, 1897.

Sennet, Richard. *The Fall of Public Man: On the Social Psychology of Capitalism*. New York: Vintage, 1978.

Sewell, William H., Jr. "Etat, Corps and Ordre: Some Notes on the Social Vocabulary of the French Old Regime," in *Sozialgeschichte Heute, Festschrift für Hans Rosenberg zum 70. Geburtstag*, ed. Hans-Ulrich Wehler. Göttingen: Vandenhoek and Ruprecht, 1974, 49–68.

———. "Ideologies and Social Revolutions: Reflections on the French Case." *Journal of Modern History* 57 (1985):57–85.

Shapiro, Gary. "The Man of Letters and the Author of Nature: Hume on Philosophical Discourse." *The Eighteenth Century, Theory and Interpretation* (1985):115–38.

Sher, Richard B. *Church and University in the Scottish Enlightenment: The Moderate Literati of Edinburgh*. Princeton: Princeton University Press, 1985.

Simmel, Georg. *The Sociology of Georg Simmel*, ed. Kurt H. Wolff. Glencoe, Ill.: Free Press, 1950.

Singer, Brian C. J. *Society, Theory, and the French Revolution: Studies in the Revolutionary Imaginary*. London: Macmillan, 1986.

T. C. Smout. *A History of the Scottish People*. London: Fontan/Collins, 1969.

Soboul, Albert. *La Civilisation et la Révolution française*, vol. 1. Paris: Arthaud, 1970.

Spiegel. Henry William. *The Growth of Economic Thought*. Durham: Duke University Press, 1991.

Stanton, Domna C. *The Aristocrat as Art: A Study of the Honnête Homme and the Dandy in Seventeenth- and Nineteenth-Century French Literature*. New York: Columbia University Press, 1980.

Starobinski, Jean. *Blessings in Disguise*. Cambridge, Mass.: Harvard University Press, 1993.

Strosetzski, Christoph. *Rhétorique de la conversation*. Paris: Biblio 17, 1984.

Tocqueville, Alexis de. *The Old Regime and the French Revolution*. New York: Doubleday, 1955.

Toennies, Ferdinand. *On Sociology: Pure, Applied, and Empirical*. Chicago: University of Chicago Press, 1971.

Trésor de la langue française: Dictionnaire de la langue du XIXe et du XXe siècles (1789–1960), 15 vols. (to date). Paris: Editions du Centre National de la Recherche Scientifique, 1977–.

Tuck, Richard. "Grotius, Carneades, and Hobbes." *Grotiana*, n.s., 4 (1983):43–62.

———. *Natural Rights Theories, Their Origin and Development* Cambridge: Cambridge University Press, 1979.

Tully, James, ed. *Meaning and Context: Quentin Skinner and His Critics*. Oxford: Polity Press, 1988.

Van Tieghem, Philippe. *Ossian en France*, 2 vols. Paris: F. Rieder, 1917.

Venturi, Franco. *Jeunesse de Diderot, 1713–1753*. Paris: Albert Skira, 1939.

Vickers, Brian, ed. *Arbeit, Musse, Meditation*, ed. Brian Vickers. Zurich: Verlag der Fachvereine, 1985.

Viguerie, Jean de. *L'Institution des enfants, l'éducation en France 16e–18e siècles*. Paris: Calmann-Lévy, 1978.

Walters, Gordon B. *The Significance of Diderot's Essai sur le mérite et la vertu*. University of North Carolina Studies in Romance Languages and Literatures No. 112, Chapel Hill, 1971.

Wartburg, Walther von. *Französisches Etymologisches Wörterbuch*, 27 vols. (to date) Bonn: Schroeder, 1922–.

Weber, Henry. *La Compagnie des Indes, 1604–1875*. Paris: Librairie Nouvelle de Droit et de Jurisprudence, 1904.

Weber, Max. *From Max Weber: Essays in Sociology*, ed. H. H. Gerth and C. Wright Mills. New York: Oxford University Press, 1946.

———. *The Protestant Ethic and the Spirit of Capitalism*. London and New York: Charles Scribner's, 1976.

Weil, Georges-Denis. *Le Droit d'association et le droit de réunir*. Paris: Félix Alcan, 1893.

Wells, Charlotte Catherine. "The Language of Citizenship in Early Modern France: Implications of the *droit d'aubaine*." Ph.D. diss., Indiana University, 1992.

Whitman, James Q. "'Les seigneurs descendent au rang de simples créanciers': Droit romain, droit féodal et révolution." *Droits, Revue Française de Théorie Juridique* 17 (1993):19–32.

Wickwar, W. H. *Baron D'Holbach*. London: George Allen, 1935.

Williams, Alan. *The Police of Paris*. Baton Rouge: Louisiana State University Press, 1979.

Williams, Raymond. *Keywords: A Vocabulary of Culture and Society*. New York: Oxford University Press, 1976.

Youssef, Zobeidah. *Polémique et littérature chez Guez de Balzac*. Paris: A.-G. Nizet, 1972.

Zuber, Roger. *Les "Belles Infidèles" et la formation du goût classique*. Paris: Armand Colin, 1968.

INDEX

Aarsleff, Hans, 45
absolutism, 5, 11, 14–15, 18, 23, 24, 27,
  29, 33, 34, 119, 128, 136; and linguistic
  reform, 46; and sociability, 34–37, 54–
  61, 166–69, 173–74; and speech, 40–
  42
Académie française, 46–48, 51, 74, 137–
  40, 143–45, 150–51, 156, 160, 182,
  193, 226, 230, 231, 232
Addison, Joseph, 28
Alembert, Jean le Rond d', 6, 48, 52, 74,
  77, 83, 163, 195, 220
Alemand, Louis Augustin, 46
Althusser, Louis, 49
Antoine, Michel, 203
Arendt, Hannah, 71
Aristotle (and Aristotelianism), 19, 21, 40–
  41, 133
Arnaud, François, 146

Bachaumont, Louis Petit de, 196, 198
Baker, Keith Michael, 35n., 200, 214n.
Balzac, Jean-Louis Guez de, 74, 112–15,
  127
Barbeyrac, Jean, 62, 64
Bayle, Pierre, 118
Beccaria, Cesar, 182, 199
Bellegarde, Jean-Baptiste Morvan de, 95–
  100, 104, 115, 116, 118, 122–26, 139,
  211
Bien, David, 41
Blair, Hugh, 145–46, 149, 150, 173
Bodin, Jean, 14–15, 17
Bossuet, Jacqies-Bénigne, 40, 56–57, 60,
  61, 62
Bouhours, Dominique, 87, 95
Bourdieu, Pierre, 91–92
Buffier, Claude, 79–81, 83
bureaucracy, 17, 100, 136, 203
Burke, Edmund, 176

Callières, François de, 100, 105–7, 129
Cassirer, Ernst, 6, 77
Castan, Yves, 38
Castiglione, Baldassare, 119, 122
chain of being. *See* great chain of being

Chamfort, Sébastien, 230
Chartier, Roger, 92
Chénier, Marie-Joseph, 235–36
Christianity, 5, 80, 82, 84, 122–26. *See also*
  religion
citizenship, 3, 22
civil society, 79, 80, 144, 181, 210–11,
  239. *See also* civilization; commerce; public sphere
civility, 86–88, 92–94, 104, 126, 143,
  174, 189, 207, 233. *See also* conversation,
  art of; manners; politeness
civilization, concept of, 4, 19, 89–92, 133,
  135, 137, 148–49, 151–53, 155–59,
  163, 164, 168, 171–73, 175, 176, 206–
  8
Clark, Henry C., 71n.
Cochin, Augustin, 30–33, 34, 38, 111
commerce, 36–37, 125, 131–33, 134–35,
  136, 155–57, 159, 167–68, 207. *See also*
  trade, freedom of
constitution, 23
convention, 38, 45, 62, 87, 201
conversation, art of, 41–42, 68, 79, 115–
  18, 127–28, 241; Balzac on, 112–15;
  Bellegarde on, 95–100, 122–26; Callières on, 105–7; Holbach on, 67–69;
  Hume on, 165–69; Méré on, 100–105;
  Montesquieu on, 130–31; Morellet on,
  204–8; Scudéry on, 107–11
court, 4, 68, 87–91, 93, 94, 98, 99, 101,
  104, 106, 108, 118, 119, 118–22, 124,
  139, 145
courtesy books, 39, 67, 86–128. *See also*,
  conversation, art of
Courtin, Antoine de, 86–88, 93, 106, 122
Cousin, Victor, 107
Coyer, Gabriel-François, 36–37, 185–87,
  189
Curtius, Ernst Robert, 91

Darnton, Robert, 4, 137–39, 214
Delamare, Nicolas, 9–11, 18, 20–23, 34,
  58–59, 60, 61, 62
democracy, 6, 33, 111, 180, 238, 240, 242.
  See also republicanism

DATE DUE

NOV 2 1 1998			
GAYLORD			PRINTED IN U.S.A.